Foundations of Anglican Evangelicalism in Victoria

Australian College of Theology Monograph Series

SERIES EDITOR GRAEME R. CHATFIELD

The ACT Monograph Series, generously supported by the Board of Directors of the Australian College of Theology, provides a forum for publishing quality research theses and studies by its graduates and affiliated college staff in the broad fields of Biblical Studies, Christian Thought and History, and Practical Theology with Wipf and Stock Publishers of Eugene, Oregon. The ACT selects the best of its doctoral and research masters theses as well as monographs that offer the academic community, scholars, church leaders and the wider community uniquely Australian and New Zealand perspectives on significant research topics and topics of current debate. The ACT also provides opportunity for contributors beyond its graduates and affiliated college staff to publish monographs which support the mission and values of the ACT.

Rev Dr Graeme Chatfield
Series Editor and Associate Dean

Foundations of Anglican Evangelicalism in Victoria

Four Elements for Continuity, 1847–1937

WEI-HAN KUAN

WIPF & STOCK · Eugene, Oregon

FOUNDATIONS OF ANGLICAN EVANGELICALISM IN VICTORIA
Four Elements for Continuity, 1847–1937

Australian College of Theology Monograph Series

Copyright © 2019 Wei-Han Kuan. All rights reserved. Except for brief quotations in critical publications or reviews, no part of this book may be reproduced in any manner without prior written permission from the publisher. Write: Permissions, Wipf and Stock Publishers, 199 W. 8th Ave., Suite 3, Eugene, OR 97401.

Wipf & Stock
An Imprint of Wipf and Stock Publishers
199 W. 8th Ave., Suite 3
Eugene, OR 97401

www.wipfandstock.com

PAPERBACK ISBN: 978-1-5326-8216-2
HARDCOVER ISBN: 978-1-5326-8217-9
EBOOK ISBN: 978-1-5326-8218-6

Manufactured in the U.S.A.

To dear Valerie,
Alexandra, Samuel, and Josephine

Contents

List of Illustrations | viii
2017 Preface | ix
Acknowledgements | xiii
List of Abbreviations | xv

Introduction | 1
1. Literature Review | 14
2. Defining Evangelicalism | 34
3. Charles Perry: The Evangelical Founding Bishop of Melbourne | 45
4. Evangelical Energy, 1847–1875 | 78
5. Mission at Home and Abroad, 1876–1900 | 117
6. Entrusted with the Gospel, 1901–1937 | 162

Conclusion | 249
Epilogue | 257

Appendix I: Charles Perry's Letter to the Clergy with Regard to the Use of Music in Services | 263
Appendix II: Interview Question Guide and Checklist | 266
Appendix III: Interviews and Conversations | 269
Bibliography | 271

Illustrations

Four vital contributors to growing evangelicalism in a diocese | 2

Inscription from Charles Perry to H. B. Macartney | 72

Image from the Eighth Annual Report of the BFBS Auxiliary of Australia Felix | 94

St. Mary's Caulfield Advertisement for the G. C. Grubb Mission | 141

"What is Christianity" pew sheet notice for St. Matthew's Prahran | 178

"Good News for Everybody" Advertisement, 1922 | 184

Percentage of Clergy in ADOM by College | 230

CMS League of Youth Membership Card | 236

Four vital contributors to growing evangelicalism in a diocese | 250

2019 Preface

Questions

WHAT FACTORS MAKE FOR long-term evangelical continuity in a denominational context?—long-term meaning over the span of a century or more. Why and how have some denominations maintained or even grown their evangelical flavour while others have lost it? What do past strategies for evangelism, leadership selection, partnership in Gospel ministry, and engagement with wider society and the world have to teach us about the longevity and intergenerational persistence of evangelical faith and culture?

These were the driving questions behind this study. These questions remain important ones as churches seek to maintain their witness in the face of growing secularism in the Minority World, and as they experience rapid expansion in many parts of the Majority World. Will churches have an ongoing evangelical witness in either context beyond this present century?

Evangelicals have long prized the work of evangelism, alongside a focus on the authority and reliability of the Scriptures expressed in their preaching and Bible study activity. Contemporary evangelical movements are busying themselves in church-planting—making communities that express these priorities, sometimes eschewing their mainline denominational connections.

However, one lesson from the growth of Methodism is that successful movements inevitably institutionalize and get organised into a larger entity over time. Either that or they die and are consigned to the dustbin of history. If successful in securing a future then how is that wider institutional existence assured, maintained or built on over the long-term? Do theological movements such as evangelicalism have an inevitably limited shelf-life within denominations, needing to be born again in other settings? Or can particular strategies and factors make for long-term continuity?

Personally Anglican context

The context of this study is my personal one. For I remember being completely astounded when I was first told that the Diocese of Melbourne was originally the most vigorously evangelical of all the Australian Anglican dioceses. This piece of information was passed on to me some time in the 1990s when, to my historically naïve mind, nothing could seem further from the truth.

The Anglican Diocese of Melbourne of the time was so obviously mixed in theological variety. In the 1990s the majority of parishes were Anglo-Catholic in ritual and probably liberal in theological flavour. Evangelicals, it seemed to me, were a minority either concentrated in a few flagship parishes such as St Jude's Carlton, St Hilary's Kew and St Mark's Emerald—the domain of the three Peters—Peter Adam, Peter Corney and Peter Crawford—or huddled in outposts such as St Paul's Glen Waverley, where I lived; or St Matthias' North Richmond, which I attended.

In 1997, a reading of the brief, broad brush-stroke official sesquicentenary history of the Diocese, confirmed what had been planted in my mind—that Melbourne had indeed been founded with a vigorously evangelical bishop at its helm. There was no denying the facts of the historical record: that in 1847, an evangelical Englishman, Charles Perry, was selected as the founding bishop of Melbourne. But that official history, and later still, the great majority of histories and narratives presented to me from within the Diocese, whether in print or in conversation, communicated a particular implied metanarrative; a narrative that attempted to minimise the impact and legitimacy of evangelicalism in the Diocese Melbourne.

And here it is: that Melbourne, founded evangelical, eventually grew up, left its harsh conservative, wowser-ish foundations—no drink, no smokes, no dancing, no music—and became more cultured and intellectually mature, reaching the full flowering of Anglican identity, that is liberal Catholicism. Evangelicalism was, and is, good for the fundamental certainties required in infancy and youth—but as surely as a seed turns into a tree, true grown-up Anglican maturity looks like liberal Catholicism.

According to this metanarrative this dynamic is true of the Diocese of Melbourne's evangelical past and also true of the individual Melbourne Anglican's personal spiritual experience: and so I was fed story after story of an Anglican life starting in an evangelical parish or youth group, but eventually graduating, maturing into a liberal Catholic faith. A version of this same metanarrative has been and is currently at play in the worldwide Anglican Communion. There are those who believe that the evangelical fervour of much of the Global South will eventually settle down or mature into a more liberal comprehensive Catholicism.

It seemed to me that such a powerful and persistent metanarrative should not go unchallenged. Why is it that evangelicalism has persisted and even thrived in some quarters within the Diocese? Why hasn't it just rolled over and died out as a movement? The prevailing metanarrative described above implies that it should have, and it should have long ago. But it hasn't! Quite the opposite in fact. Why? How?

If Melbourne had indeed been an evangelical powerhouse in Australian Anglicanism, then how did it change over the course of time to become the broad and comprehensive Diocese that I knew in the 1990s? And what were the elements of the Diocese of Sydney's story that charted an opposite course from less uniformly evangelical to more? Put bluntly, what might history teach us about the factors that make for long-term evangelical continuity in a large institutional setting such as an Anglican diocese? That became the heuristic question at the heart of this study. I trust that these findings will have applicability beyond Anglicanism and will be of wider interest to those who ponder the long-term future of their faith tradition.

This study is a start

I am grateful that, a number of years after completion, this research is now about to become more easily accessible. Changes for clarity and to update information have been made. The literature review section has been added to but without an attempt to be a comprehensive update for changes in the field since 2010. This preface and an epilogue have been added, but this book is otherwise almost identical to the examined thesis.

In writing this preface, I am reminded that the process of research and writing was hard labour indeed. It began with a passionate interest in the history of evangelicals in the Anglican Diocese of Melbourne and a burning desire to find out as much as I could about the people and the movement. A great deal of preceding work had been done by giants in the field of evangelical history in Australia: their names are in the acknowledgments or bibliography or turn up as contributors to the ADEB.

After some initial reading I came to a relatively early realisation that not much had been written describing evangelicalism as a whole, and especially no overall explanation had been offered for its development as a significant movement within the Diocese and State. Many significant individuals, societies, and churches had been accounted for, but no wider account had been given. There is still much more to be uncovered, understood and written for the benefit of present and future generations. I hope that many others will take up the challenge and privilege. Stories untold are stories forgotten.

Yet here is a start. I suspect that much of the value and delight of this volume is to be found in details not previously published or well known to a wider audience. The strength of evangelicalism and evangelical conviction in much of Victoria's history is consistently impressive. In places the evidence for particular assertions will be weak or tentative or mistaken. Many opportunities for correction, future research and more precise analysis will be obvious. Yet here is a start that I am honoured to commend to you. I trust that some of my conclusions will prove profitable to those interested in understanding the reasons behind the long-term persistence and success of evangelical movements in denominational settings.

ἀληθεύοντες δὲ ἐν ἀγάπῃ αὐξήσωμεν εἰς αὐτὸν τὰ πάντα.

Revd Dr Wei-Han Kuan
Church Missionary Society—Victoria

Acknowledgements

THIS RESEARCH WAS MADE possible by the generosity, kindness and support of many, and apologies are offered in advance to any whom I have inadvertently omitted from the list below.

Great thanks are due to my research supervisor Canon Dr. Peter Adam and co-supervisor the Reverend Prof. Ian Breward.

Generous prayerful and practical support was received from Beng Teik, May Ling and Su-Hsien Kuan, Dr. Peter Wong, and Dr. Karen Chia. Research grants were received from The Leon and Mildred Morris Foundation and the Australian College of Theology.

Interviewees and conversation partners were invariably generous with their comments and time. A full list of these is included at the end of the thesis. Generous assistance was received at the Diocese of Melbourne and CMS Victoria Archives from archivists Leonie Duncan and Janine Stewart. Leonie Cable gave access to the national treasure that is the Cable, Cable & Pollard Index of Australian Clergy. Access was granted to the St. Paul's Cathedral Chapter archive, the Mollison Library, the Stonnington City Council archive collection, the archives of the Anglican Evangelical Trust of Victoria, the archives of the Evangelical Fellowship in the Anglican Communion (Victoria), and the archives of St. Columb's Hawthorn. Material was received from Dr. Brian Dickey; the Reverend Richard Trist; Tim Gibson, Diocese of Gippsland; the Reverend Dr. Charles Sherlock, Diocese of Bendigo; the Reverend Michael Flynn, St. Columb's Hawthorn; the Reverends Jonathan Gunthorpe and Tracy Lauersen, St. Matthew's Prahran; the Reverend Dr. Mark Durie, St. Mary's Caulfield; the Reverend Jason Hobba, Berwick Anglican Church; the Reverend Neil Bach, St. Mark's Forest Hill and Secretary of the Anglican Evangelical Trust of Victoria; Kathleen Malone (Griffiths family papers); Prof Michael Pain (Bishop Pain papers); and Alma Ryrie Jones, All Saints' Northcote.

Thank you also to these sons and daughters of encouragement: the Reverend Tim Anderson, Dr. Brian Dickey, Dr. Audrey Grant, Dr. Geoff Treloar, Archbishop Dr. Peter Jensen, the Reverend Simon Koefoed, the Reverend Rod McArdle, Ruth Millard, Nicole Harvey, the Reverend Dr. Darrell Paproth, Dr. Ian Welch, the Reverend Dr. Lindsay Wilson; the learning and working community of Ridley College; and the community of St. Alfred's Anglican Church Blackburn North.

Abbreviations

ADB	Australian Dictionary of Biography
ADEB	Australian Dictionary of Evangelical Biography
BCP	Book of Common Prayer (1662)
BFBS	British and Foreign Bible Society
CEZMS	Church of England Zenana Mission Society
CIM	China Inland Mission
CMA	Church Missionary Association
CMS	Church Missionary Society
COEM	Church of England Messenger
CPAS	Church Pastoral Aid Society
CSSM	Children's Special Service Mission
DEB	Dictionary of Evangelical Biography
DNB	Dictionary of National Biography
EFAC	Evangelical Fellowship in the Anglican Communion
ESV	Evangelisation Society of Victoria
LJS	London Jew's Society or The London Society for Promoting Christianity amongst the Jews

LMS	London Missionary Society
LOY	Church Missionary Society League of Youth
MAHA	The Missionary at Home and Abroad
MSJSJ	Mission of St. James and St. John
SPCK	Society for Promoting Christian Knowledge
SPG	Society for the Propagation of the Gospel
SU	Scripture Union
TCD	Trinity College Dublin
VC	Victorian Churchman
YPU	Young People's Scripture Union

Introduction

The things that you have heard me say in the presence of many witnesses, entrust to faithful others who will also be qualified to teach others.

2 TIMOTHY 2:2

Thesis

THIS STUDY REPRESENTS THE first attempt at a comprehensive description of Melbourne Anglican evangelicalism for the broad period chosen. The literature review shows that no previous attempt has been undertaken, although various other studies of evangelicalism and of Anglicanism have been conducted. In particular, this study argues that evangelicalism in Melbourne Anglicanism has been dependent on the presence of four vital contributors in support of the movement. These are:

1. vibrant and vital evangelical parishes;
2. vibrant and vital evangelical societies focused on mission and evangelism;
3. a robustly evangelical Anglican theological college; and
4. a diocesan bishop willing to promote and support evangelicals and their causes.

Although there are important relationships between all four of the contributors, the particular connection between the four, which is of significance for this thesis, can be illustrated by the circular flow of the four arrows in the following graphic:[1]

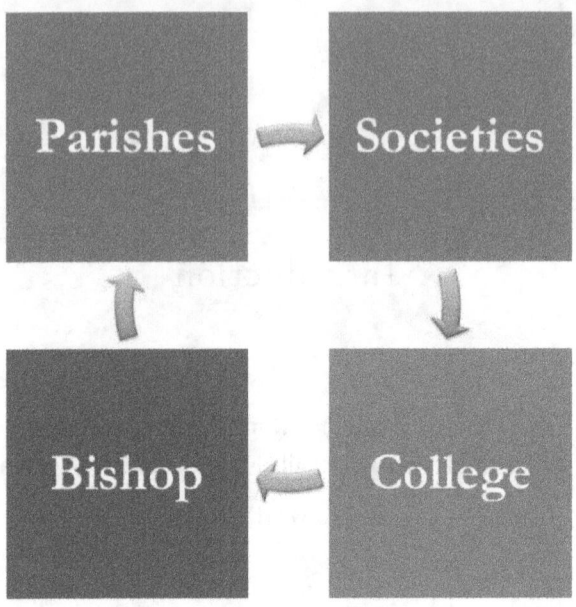

Four Vital Contributors to Growing Evangelicalism in a Diocese

The elements of this graphic will now be explained in more depth.

Parishes

During the period of the study, parishes were the basic unit of organization of a diocese, the context in which most regular week-to-week ministry occurred and in which powerful evangelical ministers based the bulk of their preaching, teaching, and evangelistic ministries. Parishes also provided ministry to all age groups and all comers—by definition, they existed to serve any and all within their geographical location.

Vibrant and vital evangelical parishes occurred where capable ministers were able to model evangelism, win converts, and build lively—and

---

1. The other relationships between the various contributors is a subject area ripe for further investigation and analysis. The literature review shows that much of the writing to date has tended to focus on persons, parishes, or societies with only incidental interest in the interactions between them. The contributions of parishes and laity have been particularly poorly served.

often large—congregations with ministry to the full range of age groups. Critically, these were Anglican contexts in which young people were converted, inspired, and directed towards active ministry. They were the breeding grounds for future Anglican evangelical leadership.

In the general absence of large endowments and philanthropic largesse, parishes had to raise their own finances in order to survive, build property, and grow.[2] Parishes thus relied on a vital partnership between leading laity and the local vicar to fund ministry and building programs. The absence of endowment funding meant that parishes were also a significant source of support—financial and spiritual—for other evangelical interests: namely societies and an evangelical theological college.

Throughout the period of this study, most parishes were single clergy operations. In active parishes, the laity held a significant role in superintending Sunday Schools and running all manner of groups for boys, girls, men, and women. So parishes were also a sphere of vital evangelical activity. From the local parish, able leaders might be identified and nurtured, with some feeling led to offer for the ordained ministry. Active laypeople could test their vocations in the sphere of parish work. From the parishes, many of the most energized evangelicals found a context for their activities in the evangelical societies.

Societies

Evangelical societies were, from their founding, a significant outlet for lay leadership energy. While the diocese remained largely uniformly low-church and clergy-driven, there was little creative ministry in the parishes, especially of an evangelistic kind, with Sunday Schools and groups for children and younger people being a notable exception. Hence, parishes tended to funnel the most capable and enthusiastic evangelical laity through to membership and service in the societies. Some evangelical clergy also found it easier to focus on creative and evangelistic society work rather than the regular ministry of the parish.

Such societies rapidly developed into the main context in which new and youthful leaders were trained and raised up for evangelistically-focused ministry. Participation in ministry from an early age, in a lay capacity, and

---

2. Unlike the Church of England in England, colonial dioceses did not have long-established sources of property or trust income. Endowments were relatively small, and significant colonial government support ceased within a few decades of foundation. Hence colonial churches were relatively more dependent on the fundraising capacity and commitment of local laity.

with encouraging results from evangelism, proved to be a significant formative experience for many laypeople. Evangelicals' enthusiasm and commitment to evangelism and world mission was awakened through the societies. Societies also provided vital leadership experience—unfettered by diocesan controls or interference. This sort of practical, hands-on ministry and leadership experience led to some considering ordained or missionary service. Such men and women then went on to further training in a theological or missionary Bible college.

College

The theological college acted as a kind of finishing school for evangelical talent, receiving those who felt powerfully led by God to offer for ordained ministry or missionary service. For most evangelicals, the prior experience of ministry in the parish or society setting tended to have a more significant formative effect on their theological perspectives and ministry methods than their college experience. However, the college where they received theological training also had a powerful impact, especially on their intellectual formation.

The attitude of the college principal appears to have had a significant impact on student formation. During the period of this study, staff numbers at colleges—whether of Moore College in Sydney or Ridley College in Melbourne—remained low, with the principal typically the only full-time staff member, with the bulk of the teaching responsibilities. The ethos of the college—its sense of priorities in ministry, focus on overseas missionary work, and attitude towards the diocese and ecclesial matters—also proved influential on students.

Bishop

From college, those entering ordained ministry were dependent on the presence of a diocesan bishop willing to ordain and license them to particular parishes or ministries. The bishop's endorsement was also crucial to advancement in the ranks of diocesan affairs, effectively promoting or stifling evangelicalism's impact on the diocese as a whole. In periods when the diocesan bishop did not actively encourage evangelical ministry, opportunities for such ministry elsewhere—like with CMS in East Africa, or outside Anglican structures—were increasingly viable alternatives for younger and future evangelical leaders. The same influence extended to coadjutor or assistant bishops and archdeacons, but on a lesser scale. At various times, the power and influence of other personalities overshadowed the diocesan bishop's leadership, but the system of licensing clergy meant that the diocesan bishop wielded critical influence over the long-term character of the parishes and hence the diocese. A bishop's active encouragement or discouragement of evangelical appointments altered the character of a vacant parish radically. This in turn altered the kind of culture and ministry offered by the parish to its locality.

The circular flow shown by the four arrows in the graphic above represent the flow-on effect of the relationships described. It will be argued that a bishop's active discouragement of evangelical leaders led, over time, to decreased vitality of evangelicalism within the diocese. It will also be argued that a shift in theological emphasis in the training college, away from a robust adherence to the penal substitutionary theory of the atonement, led to decreased fervor for and effectiveness in evangelism. This in turn led to future weakness in the movement, in particular in its ability to inspire a next generation of leaders. The circular flow described reflects the main interest of this thesis: the theme of evangelical continuity, and what made this continuity possible in the period and context chosen. Other important relationships between the vital contributors are not discussed at length and are subjects for potential further research.

Overview

Evangelicalism has been an integral part of Melbourne Anglicanism from its very foundation. This study of the history of evangelicalism within the diocese thus contributes to an understanding of Melbourne Anglican identity more generally. Because of the rise of evangelicalism as a major social and political force today, this is a subject of increasing relevance. This overview outlines the broad claims of this study.

Evangelicalism is a movement of conservative Protestant Christianity with roots in the sixteenth century European Protestant Reformation, the English Puritan movement of the late sixteenth and seventeenth centuries, the European Pietist movements of the seventeenth and eighteenth centuries, and the English Evangelical Revival and North American Great Awakening of the eighteenth century.[3] In this study, the terms "evangelical" and "evangelicals" will be used to refer to those groups and individuals who identify with evangelicalism, the movement.[4]

---

3. Piggin, *Evangelical Christianity in Australia*, vii.

4. The term "evangelical" is sometimes also used to refer to the denominations that emerged out of the sixteenth century Protestant Reformation, all of which referred to

Melbourne Anglican evangelicalism was highly influenced, in particular, by the English Evangelical Revival of the late eighteenth century. The energy and vision of that movement was exported to Australia through the first Anglican chaplains and many leading laypeople.

Melbourne's emergence as a "city" was tied to the issuing of Royal Letters Patent appointing a first bishop, the evangelical Charles Perry. Prior to this, Melbourne was designated a "village." Perry stood in a direct line of continuity with some of the Revival's leading lights, such as Charles Simeon of Cambridge. He established their brand of socially progressive, conversion-focused evangelicalism in the Diocese of Melbourne, which was then geographically identical with the state of Victoria. There were political implications to evangelicalism's early presence in the colonies, too, as "many of the most prestigious families of Melbourne shared [this] crusading spirit and evangelical Anglican faith."[5] They were hence active not just in the church, but also in the judicial and political spheres and in the founding of schools, hospitals, and other social institutions.

However, the rise of biblical criticism and the Tractarian movement posed a serious challenge to Perry's brand of evangelicalism. The economic prosperity and population growth that came with the discovery of gold made Melbourne a chief city of the Empire: industrialized, urbane, sophisticated, and self-made. These developments matched poorly with key aspects of evangelicalism, such as its insistence on the fundamental and innate sinfulness of humanity, the eternal destiny of the individual soul, the necessity of conversion to Christ, sacrificial care for the poor and underprivileged, and prophetic denunciation of sins: social and personal.[6]

In the public and wider church sphere, the evangelistic and social reform impulse of evangelicalism, driven by theological commitments and a sense of divine imperative, began to lose ground, in the latter half of the nineteenth century, to theological and social liberalism and increasing secularism. Evangelicalism itself became heavily influenced by the Keswick holiness and missions movement, turning its metaphysical attention inwards towards individuals and its pragmatic attention outwards towards the spheres of rural and international missions. Yet evangelicalism remained a persistent, even powerful, force in the life of the diocese as whole—both in the city and through what was later the state of Victoria.

---

themselves as "evangelical" or "gospel-proclaiming."

5. Russell, *A Wish of Distinction*, 20.

6. Cf. Hilton, *The Age of Atonement*. Hilton argues for the congruence between moderate evangelical theological ideas and contemporary nineteenth-century social views.

One of the interests of this study is the changing character of Melbourne Anglican evangelicalism during the ninety years from 1847 to 1937. David Bebbington has produced a widely accepted definition of evangelicalism as a movement bounded by four key attributes: conversionism, crucicentrism, biblicism, and activism. This quadripartite definition is discussed and examined in the light of the Melbourne historical experience, in order to define the scope and limits of evangelicalism in Melbourne Anglicanism.[7] Critiques of Bebbington from theologians and historians are also engaged with briefly. Of course, evangelicalism is not static; markers of identity, boundary markers, and actual core commitments changed over time. For most of the period 1847–1937, parish worship in the diocese was predominantly low-church in ritual and strictly Book of Common Prayer in liturgical form. There were a few notable exceptions of "innovation" and "Romish practices," but otherwise clergy were attired in cassock and surplice and black preaching scarf. There were no colored stoles or candles on the table, and only tables, never altars. This predominantly low-church tradition did not change till the episcopate of Frank Woods, who in the late 1960s was the first to wear a cope and miter in the cathedral.[8]

However, although the Diocese of Melbourne remained broadly low-church until the mid-twentieth century, it had long before surrendered its "mainly evangelical" identity. Bebbington's four markers of evangelical identity had faded from prominence in the language of the official records of the diocese. Evangelicalism became more and more restricted to particular parishes and societies—especially the Church Missionary Society.

This study is also interested in the reasons for evangelicals' persistence and growth in the diocese despite the lack of consistent episcopal support. After Perry, both subsequent nineteenth-century bishops of Melbourne, James Moorhouse and Field Flowers Goe, were increasingly based in the city and were either personally more inclined towards a broad church that included varieties of theological and liturgical traditions, or simply allowed this to develop during their episcopates. By the early twentieth century, evangelicalism had moved from a position of power and dominance in the diocese into a minority position—one that was, at times, actively oppressed.

At the turn of the century, conflict between Bishop (later Archbishop) Henry Lowther Clarke and evangelical Anglicans led to the founding of

---

7. Bebbington, *Evangelicalism in Modern Britain*.

8. Interviews with Peter Adam, 12 November 2009; Peter Corney, 30 May 2007 and 24 November 2009; and John Moroney, 4 June 2007 and 4 March 2008. James Grant related the incident in a conversation, saying that he protested in the vestry when Archbishop Frank Woods first put on the cope and miter on the basis that it had never been done in St. Paul's before.

subsequently significant institutions such as Ridley College, the Church of England of Victoria Evangelical Trust, the Melbourne Bible Institute, and the Upwey Convention. The same group of evangelical Anglicans—clerical and lay—were behind these bodies, partnering interdenominationally in the case of the latter two institutions. They were heavily influenced by the strategies employed by an earlier generation of English evangelicals, including Perry, who had learnt that concentration of power in the hands of bishops, no matter how friendly to the evangelical cause, was no guarantee of the continuity of evangelical ministry. Ironically, it was Clarke's persecution of Clifford Harris Nash, the leading evangelical cleric in early twentieth century Melbourne, that opened the way for Nash to take on a wider interdenominational evangelical leadership role upon his resignation from Anglican ministry.

Within Anglican evangelicalism, those unwilling to relax their commitment to the denomination—"churchmen," as they styled themselves—focused their energies on Ridley College, the Church Missionary Association (CMA), and Church Missionary Society (CMS), and the Mission of St. James and St. John (MSJSJ). It was a highly activist faith with sparse intellectual resources. The devastating impact of World War I and the following economic depression further weakened evangelicalism's capacity for robust engagement in the academic sphere, partially paving the way for Ridley's movement down a more liberal theological path. In this environment, it was the evangelistic activism of the missionary societies that preserved evangelical continuity within the diocese itself.

This study seeks to show that evangelicalism is essentially a movement characterized by vital piety that has persisted and been strongest when it has focused its energy on the *evangel*, the good news of the gospel of Jesus Christ, and especially on the necessity of personal conversion to a life of serving the gracious Savior and Lord, Jesus Christ. For evangelicals, that salvation is won by Christ through the cross. Evangelicals have adhered to the biblical understanding of the cross as an act of atonement for sin and rebellion against God, and hence for them the death of the perfect Christ in the place of the sinner is an act of penal substitution. Jesus died that the sinner may not have to. Jesus' resurrection from the dead was the firstfruits of the promise of the same resurrection and eternal life to every repentant sinner. The structure and content of this philosophy is authoritatively informed by the Scriptures of the Christian canon. While awaiting the hope of heaven, the demands of the life of service are not vague or diffuse, but sharply focused on particular works that the individual is led or "called" to do by God. These elements of

INTRODUCTION

evangelicalism—conversionism, crucicentrism, biblicism, and activism—are those recognized by Bebbington.[9]

Evangelical Identity

This study shows that through the period in question, evangelical identity in Melbourne Anglicanism has correlated with Bebbington's four factors. Perry's founding work and ministry philosophy meant that the elements of biblicism, crucicentrism, conversionism, and activism were firmly laid down in the diocese. Evangelicalism was able to be strengthened in the foundation period because Perry kept such a firm handle on clergy selection, training, and licensing. In this he was ably assisted by Dean Macartney, who shared his evangelical views.

The rise of the Keswick movement, with its concern for world mission, was critical in cementing these evangelical priorities in Melbourne. Without the authority of the Scriptures, there could be no certainty about the necessity for conversion or the efficacy of the cross of Christ to achieve forgiveness and salvation. Further, there would be no impetus for the kind of evangelical energy and activism seen in the work to extend parishes and the work of the evangelical societies.

For Melbourne evangelical history, it was the commitment to conversionism and world mission that has been the most determinative and significant of Bebbington's four factors. Identification with the missionary cause and activism in relation to the missionary societies has been the key marker of evangelical identity in Melbourne. The CMA and CMS were the most important and vital of Melbourne evangelical networks in the period of this study.

Contents

Chapter 1 contains a review of the literature relating to this study. In chapter 2, an overview of the sometimes-heated discussion over the precise definition of evangelical identity is provided, focusing on the leading contribution of historian David Bebbington and indicating that his working definition of evangelicalism is appropriate for this particular study.

Chapter 3 focuses on the diocese's founding bishop, Charles Perry, who dominated the foundation period, 1847 to 1875. Perry's significance was

---

9. These four elements have become known as the Bebbington quadrilateral definition of evangelicalism. See Bebbington, *Evangelicalism in Modern Britain*.

extremely long lasting and influential. For this reason, his ministry track record and priorities prior to appointment, the context and circumstances of his appointment, and his early priorities in episcopal ministry are examined in detail. The chapter corrects the prevailing narrative of the circumstances of Perry's appointment, arguing that the process exemplified the tensions between high churchmen and evangelicals in the period. It also demonstrates that Perry's early priorities and strategies in ministry were determinative for laying a solid evangelical foundation in Melbourne and, indeed, throughout what would later be known as the state of Victoria. It therefore indicates that an appreciation of his evangelicalism and leadership activity is critical to understanding the foundation ethos of the diocese.

Chapter 4 examines the diocese in that foundation period. It demonstrates that early leading parishes were established by evangelical activism on the part of both laity and clergy. It also shows that much evangelical energy was also expended through the founding of social institutions and especially evangelical societies, in particular the British and Foreign Bible Society auxiliary and various missionary societies. These reflected the strength of evangelicals' biblicism and missionary concern. The chapter also focuses on the vital contribution of Perry's administrative and theological leadership, particularly in the areas of clergy selection, training, and management. It argues that the prevailing narrative, which is that the roots of the Diocese of Melbourne's present diverse liturgical and theological character can be located in the episcopate of James Moorhouse, is incorrect. It demonstrates rather that the seeds of future diversity are to be found in Perry's care for and defense of clergy licensed to his diocese, and in his tolerance of liturgical diversity within the bounds of his views of theological orthodoxy as expressed by canonical legality.

Chapter 5 examines the period 1876 to 1900. It argues that the vital contribution of an evangelical bishop evaporated after Perry's departure. Neither the broad churchman James Moorhouse (from 1876 to 1886) nor the evangelical but weak leader Field Flowers Goe (from 1887 to 1901) provided the kind of theological and administrative leadership required for evangelicalism to continue to grow in strength and meet the challenges of the changing social context. The chapter argues that in this period evangelical energy was focused more sharply in the work of local parishes and, increasingly, in evangelical societies such as the Church Missionary Society and the Scripture Union. The chapter shows that the importance of local parish work and the influence of the societies increased in this period. The chapter also notes that the missing contribution of a firmly evangelical theological college continued to be a significant impediment to the movement.

Chapter 6 examines the period 1901 to 1937. Henry Lowther Clarke's episcopate from 1901 to 1920 and his treatment of Melbourne's leading evangelical of the day, Clifford Harris Nash, dominated evangelicals' responses to the diocese in this period. The chapter argues that the sustained absence of the vital contribution of a supportive diocesan bishop, and Clarke's perceived persecution of evangelicals, led to a further concentration of evangelical focus and energy in the local parishes and in missionary societies. Clarke's antipathy was the catalyst for the founding of Ridley College, which had the active and energetic support of the bishops of Bendigo and Gippsland. John Langley and Arthur Pain were firmly evangelical, and able and strategic leaders. This chapter shows that they were appointed because of the Perry heritage of a strong culture of evangelicalism in the new dioceses of the province of Victoria. The chapter argues that evangelical leaders followed Perry's lead in recognizing the need for a constitutionally evangelical training college to secure supply of future evangelical clergy for their dioceses and for the province of Victoria more generally.

The chapter also argues that the vitality of Melbourne evangelicalism moved, in the early part of the twentieth century, away from the bishop and parishes towards societies and Ridley College. It demonstrates that the CMS emerged as the key institution for evangelical continuity and vitality. The founding of its League of Youth (LOY) in 1930 was especially important, as this later developed into perhaps the most significant organization within Australian Anglican evangelicalism of the mid-twentieth century. However, chapter 6 also argues that the LOY's focus on overseas mission meant that the most able young leaders of that generation were deployed outside Australia—especially in Africa. Hence the many reflex benefits of missionary concern and enthusiasm also came with the loss of leadership talent and ability from the Melbourne church. It was in 1937 that the man who would become Australia's greatest missionary bishop, Alfred Stanway, first sailed for Kaloleni in Kenya.[10] It was also in 1937 that the appointment of the pious and devout Donald Baker as principal of Ridley marked a turning point that would lead to a renewed, determined, and intellectually-fertile evangelicalism in Melbourne. Baker arrested the liberal trend and set in place a firm focus on the necessity of personal conversion and devotion to God. He had experienced such a moment of personal conversion himself as an adult. Baker was followed by Stuart Barton Babbage's charismatic and intellectual engagement with society and culture. It was Babbage who recognized the need for an intellectually robust but also evangelistically focused interaction with society. Babbage inspired and nurtured men like Leon Morris, David Williams, and Frank Andersen, and developed a strong evangelical academy at Ridley, but that history is beyond the scope of this particular study.[11]

10. See upcoming biography of Alfred Stanway by Audrey Grant, unpublished as of 2019.

11. See Bach, *Leon Morris: One Man's Fight For Love and Truth*.

Methods and Assumptions

This research study has been primarily interested in uncovering and documenting sources and patterns of evangelical history for the Anglican Diocese of Melbourne. The structure revolves around the four vital contributors outlined in the introduction above. The main argument is that the presence of at least two of the four vital contributors in every period examined has been critical to evangelical continuity and persistence in the Diocese of Melbourne. The corollary argument is that the lack of the presence of all four vital contributors in any period of the diocese's history has meant that a more uniformly evangelical character has not been created throughout the diocese. The signs of, and reasons for, evangelical continuity and persistence are the main interests of this research; other important questions and issues therefore receive less emphasis.

The period selected for this study covers ninety years, from the founding of the Diocese of Melbourne in 1847 to 1937. Ending the study in 1937 means that the complex changes occurring because of and after World War II are not dealt with. The year 1937 also represents a distinct watershed in the history of evangelicalism in the Diocese of Melbourne, for in that year the trend towards liberal evangelicalism at Ridley College was definitely arrested with Eustace Wade's retirement and the appointment of Donald Baker as his successor. It was also in the year 1937 that Alfred Stanway left Australia to begin his remarkable missionary work in East Africa. It will be argued that Stanway exemplified the loss of evangelical talent and "brain drain" from Australia that had such a negative impact on the health of Anglican evangelicalism locally through the middle part of the twentieth century.

This study's primary interest is in vital evangelical activity of the kind that points to reasons for its continued persistence and growth. Hence, the interest in institutional activity such as Assemblies and Synods and in the actions of bishops and archbishops prevalent in other historical studies are not a feature, except where they intersect with the factors contributing to evangelical persistence and growth. So for example, it will be noted that although Archbishops Harrington Clare Lees (from 1921 to 1929) and Frederick Waldegrave Head (from 1929 to 1941) were recognizably evangelicals, they are hardly discussed because, in my judgment, they barely affected the movement as a whole.

Throughout the course of this study, unprecedented access was given to the Ridley College archives, which the researcher helped to catalogue and organize. Access to the CMS archival collection was also generously granted. Primary source documents relating to historically evangelical parishes and institutions such as the Church of England in Victoria Evangelical Trust and the Anglican Evangelical Fellowship of Victoria (later the Evangelical Fellowship in the Anglican Communion—Victoria) were also accessed. Newspapers and periodicals such as the *Church of England Messenger* (which for a period was known as the *Church Record*), the *Argus*, the *Victorian Churchman*, and *The Missionary at Home and Abroad* were perused. Together these form the main documentary sources for this study.

Additionally, ethics clearance was granted for the conduct of interviews, and a full list of interview subjects is listed in the acknowledgments. The interviews were wide ranging and often directed by the subjects' recollections and emphases. The guide or template of interview questions is included in Appendix III.

As this study revolves around the question of evangelical identity, chapter 1 contains discussion of the current debates concerning the definition of evangelicalism. For the Diocese of Melbourne, the impact of the founding bishop Charles Perry is adjudged so significant and lasting that chapter 2 is squarely focused on his evangelicalism, appointment, and ministry priorities. It overlaps with chapter 3, which is the first of three chronological chapters organized around the four vital contributors central to the thesis. These chapters supersede the existing biographies of Charles Perry in three ways.[12] First, they focus more intently on the way his evangelicalism affected his ministry priorities and leadership over the diocese. Second, they document and discuss new and important information about his appointment that corrects the prevailing narrative of how Melbourne obtained an evangelical founding bishop. Third, they describe the significant impact of Perry's evangelicalism on the subsequent history of the diocese.

In chapters 3, 4, and 5, which cover the time period 1847 to 1937, each of the four vital contributors is discussed in a sequence determined by the narrative flow of events. In chapter 3, parishes are discussed first, and the lay connection leads to a discussion of societies, then the role of the bishop, and finally and briefly the college is described *in absentia* by reference to Perry's strategy for clergy training. However, a different sequence of the four vital contributors is followed in chapters 4 and 5, according to the narrative structure employed in each.

---

12. Two monograph-length biographies of Charles Perry exist: Goodman, *Right Reverend Charles Perry: First Bishop of Melbourne*; Robin, *Charles Perry, Bishop of Melbourne*.

I

Literature Review

Primary Sources

THE MELBOURNE DIOCESAN NEWSPAPER started by Perry remains an invaluable primary source for historical research. *The Church of England Messenger*, known briefly as the *Church Record*, subsequently as *See*, and more latterly as *The Melbourne Anglican*, records episcopal messages, clergy moves, newsworthy items, and letters to the editor.

In addition, evangelicals had their own periodical from 1890 to 1913, *The Victorian Churchman*, edited by one of their clerical leaders, Alfred Charles Kellaway.[1] The mood of the paper is at times strident in its advocacy of the evangelical faith over and against the Roman and liberal tendencies of the rest of the diocese. Again, it provides useful information on personalities, events, and ideas.

From 1873 to 1898, H. B. Macartney Jr., the son of Melbourne's first dean, single-handedly edited *The Missionary at Home and Abroad*, a periodical containing missionary news, prayer points, and calls-to-arms. It is testament to his perseverance and passion for missions and the evangelical priority on conversion. It recorded letters from missionaries abroad, news of state-wide missions run by Melbourne clergy and leading laity, and lists of financial subscribers, personal and parochial. Up to very recently, CMS Victoria archives held a nearly complete set—now part of a large CMS Victoria collection lodged in the State Library of Victoria.

The official Diocesan archives contain such material as the early bishops' letter books. Unfortunately, most of these are almost completely illegible due to spreading of the ink on paper. The collection of Diocesan Year

---

1. See ADEB entry.

Books, with parochial and clerical information, is probably the best indicator of the size and distribution of evangelicals in the diocese over time.

Two significant early memoirs are accessible. Charles Perry's wife Frances Perry, herself a notable figure in early Melbourne history, kept a journal, now held by the Royal Victorian Historical Society. Towards the end of his life, between 1889 and 1890, Dean Hussey Burgh Macartney wrote a memoir in two volumes "for his children." It was rediscovered in the vault of the law firm Mallesons in 1984, and is now held in the Diocesan archive.[2]

Parish historical records are in varied states of preservation and collation. All Saints' Northcote, St. Matthew's Prahran, St. Columb's Hawthorn and St. Mary's Caulfield have especially accessible and useful archives. Other parishes like St. Jude's Carlton and St. Michael's North Carlton have records lodged in the State Library of Victoria and the University of Melbourne's Baillieu Library respectively. Where possible, interviews with leading evangelical and diocesan personalities have been conducted, including of descendants of the persons discussed in this study.

Anglican studies[3]

Bruce Kaye, General Secretary of the Anglican Church of Australia for the decade 1994 to 2004, is a leading proponent of national Anglican studies. His *A Church Without Walls: Being Anglican in Australia* (2005)[4] and *Reinventing Anglicanism* (2003)[5] provide a theological commentary on the development of Anglicanism in Australia and suggests some future directions for study. The latter book emerges out of the major study he edited *Anglicanism in Australia: A History* (2002).[6] This in turn was the result of the General Synod Anglican History Seminar, which Kaye convened. It is the leading commentary on the development of Australian Anglicanism and the church's contribution to Australian life. The book has two parts: narrative history and thematic discussion. It is exhaustively indexed and there is discussion of evangelicalism and evangelicals in most of the

---

2. A cover letter dated 20 September 1984 from Mallesons' partner Gerald Ryan surmises that the memoirs may have been lodged there by an early partner of the firm, William Stawell, the son of Sir William Stawell, who had been converted under Charles Perry's preaching at St. James' Melbourne.

3. A comprehensive review of scholarship up to 2001 may be found in Carey et al., "Australian Religion Review, 1980–2000, Part 2."

4. Kaye, *A Church without Walls*.

5. Kaye, *Reinventing Anglicanism*.

6. Kaye, *Anglicanism in Australia*.

chapters, making this the most useful single volume secondary source currently available. A number of contributors are themselves major scholars of Australian Anglican history and feature in the paragraphs below. However, it is national in focus, and although particular events, persons, and issues are discussed, there is no sustained or specific analysis of evangelicalism in Melbourne.

Similarly, a recent volume from the prolific Tom Frame, *Anglicans in Australia*, majors on an overview of national Anglicanism and its historical antecedents rather than on evangelicalism or Melbourne in particular.[7] A very recent volume from Frame deals with the challenge of Anglican unity, reflecting on the tensions between evangelicals and others.[8]

Diocesan Histories

Tasmania

The historic dioceses of Australia are Sydney (the seat of the Diocese of Australia, 1835–1847) and Tasmania (1842). The oldest remaining diocese in Australia is served by *The Anglican Church in Tasmania: a Diocesan History to Mark the Sesquicentenary, 1992* by Geoffrey Stephens.[9] This replaces the earlier *History of the Church of England in Tasmania* by W. R. Barrett (1942).[10] Stephens's quarto-sized publication is interspersed throughout with annotated photographs of historic church buildings and monuments; this seems to have been a major focus of the work. This focus on historic buildings is also reflected in Dorothy Henslowe's *Our Heritage of Anglican Churches in Tasmania*.[11] It is clear that by "church" she means buildings and not people. Stephens's book contains some history of people, ideas and events, but it is brief and interesting rather than carefully researched and closely argued. Stephens argues that the "Erastian and latitudinarian" character of the diocese was settled by the first cleric, the naval and convict chaplain Robert Knopwood, who held the first service there in 1804. The sole impression Stephens gives of the early evangelicals such as William Bedford, Philip Palmer, and Henry Phipps Fry is that they were argumentative, inept, and prone to conflict with each other and with Bishop Nixon. There is no

---

7. Frame, *Anglicans in Australia*.
8. Frame, *A House Divided?* See review by Rhys Bezzant in *Essentials*, Autumn (2001) 13.
9. Stephens, *Anglican Church in Tasmania*.
10. Barrett, *Church of England in Tasmania*.
11. Henslowe, *Our Heritage*.

analysis of subsequent theological development or of the interests or activities of evangelicals in the diocese.

Sydney

The recent publication of Marcia Cameron's *Phenomenal Sydney: Anglicans in a Time of Change, 1945–2013* has provided an important update to histories of that diocese.[12] The standard diocesan history covering the period from foundation forwards is still Kenneth Cable and Stephen Judd's *Sydney Anglicans* (1987).[13] Given the strength of evangelicalism in Sydney, it contains a good deal of analysis of the history of evangelicalism within that diocese, with due attention to socioeconomic and political context. It also examines some of the conflict and tension between evangelicals and other parties and within evangelicalism itself. The early twentieth-century triumph of conservative evangelicalism over liberal evangelicalism is outlined, and the role of key clergy is focused on. In common with other diocesan histories, there is no comprehensive analysis of ministry at a parish level, although there is a useful appendix of all licensed clergy who have served in the Diocese of Sydney. Key events, personalities, agencies, and parishes are noted, including the role of Moore College and its theologians. Interestingly, there is some reflection on the relationship between Melbourne and Sydney evangelicals, movements of clergy between the dioceses, and the early training of Melbourne ordinands at Moore in the Perry period and the eventual cessation of the practice. It is, in the final analysis, a history of a diocese rather than a history of evangelicalism.[14] *Sydney Anglicans* supersedes *A Century of the English Church in New South Wales* by E. C. Rowland (1948).[15]

Adelaide

The short-lived Diocese of Australia was divided into Sydney, Newcastle, Adelaide, and Melbourne in 1847. David Hilliard authored "a brief historical survey" of the Diocese of Adelaide, *Godliness and Good Order: A History of the Anglican Church in South Australia* (1986),[16] for the occasion of that

12. Cameron, *Phenomenal Sydney*.
13. Judd and Cable, *Sydney Anglicans*.
14. An archbishop of Sydney has commented that *Sydney Anglicans* is not evangelical history at all as God is missing from the narrative (conversation with author, 26 October 2007).
15. Rowland, *A Century of the English Church in New South Wales*.
16. Hilliard, *Godliness and Good Order*.

diocese's 150th anniversary. Hilliard's main focus is on the church as a social force, responding to changing social and political realities around it. As such, he is less interested in the internal politics and theological differences within the diocese. This is not to say that he is unaware of these issues, as his other writing amply demonstrates.[17] With regard to evangelicals, Hilliard notes that the first colonial chaplain, Charles Beaumont Howard, was an evangelical—as was Governor Gawler. There is acknowledgement of the presence of evangelical persons and parishes and their response to liturgical innovation in the late nineteenth century,[18] but the length of the book precludes further in-depth analysis or argument. Holy Trinity North Terrace is consistently mentioned as an evangelical center, and twice mentioned as the largest congregation in the diocese. Brian Dickey has authored that parish's history, *Holy Trinity Adelaide, 1836–1988*.[19] Hilliard himself has authored a number of articles on Anglicanism in Australia and in Melbourne in particular, often with a focus on the contribution of Anglo-Catholicism.[20]

Newcastle

The noted Professor of Anthropology at the University of Sydney, commissary to the bishop, and former priest of the Diocese of Newcastle, A. P. Elkin, compiled on Bishop Batty's invitation a 900-page history, *The Diocese of Newcastle: a History* (1955) to mark its centenary in 1947.[21] Paul Robertson calls it "an enormous achievement considering his other responsibilities,"[22] but is mainly a huge collection of data without much interpretation or argument. Robertson is correct in observing that Elkin's churchmanship means that he is usually critical or patronizing of evangelicals. Elkin also ignores at least two significant conflicts between Tyrrell and evangelicals in Newcastle.

Paul Robertson's *Proclaiming Unsearchable Riches* (1996) is a compelling history of minority evangelical Anglicans in Newcastle from 1788–1900.[23] Robertson notes three modes of operation of minority groups

---

17. Spooner, *Golden See*.
18. Hilliard, *Godliness and Good Order*, 63–7.
19. Dickey, *Holy Trinity Adelaide*. See especially 55–8, 148–53 and 168.
20. Hilliard, *Godliness and Good Order*; "The Anglo-Catholic Tradition in Australian Anglicanism"; "The Anglican Schism at Port Lincoln"; "Intellectual Life in the Diocese of Melbourne"; "Anglo-Catholicism and the Religious Ecology of Melbourne"; "The Ties That Used to Bind"; "Dioceses, Tribes and Factions."
21. Elkin, *Diocese of Newcastle*.
22. Robertson, *Proclaiming "Unsearchable Riches,"* 12.
23. Robertson, *Proclaiming "Unsearchable Riches,"* 12.

within larger structures: seeking to dominate the majority, cooperation with the majority, and being subversive within the majority structure. He argues that, for the particular period and diocese he writes about, the cooperative mode was the norm—and further, that this should provide a model for evangelical influence more generally.

Robertson's great strength is in his critical engagement with both primary and secondary sources, leading to his reassessment of held "myths" in his final chapter. His framework of the three modes enables him to identify both strengths and weaknesses in evangelical action and engagement. However, he tends to oversimplify the labels "evangelical" and "High Church"; and there is little discussion of the possible varieties of evangelicalism or Anglo-Catholicism within the period of interest. Also, the social impact of evangelicalism is only of secondary importance to Robertson.

Melbourne

Turning to Melbourne, the Rev H. W. Nunn authored the *A Short History of the Church of England in Victoria: 1847–1947*.[24] It serves as a brief chronicle of the first century of the life of the diocese, to which it was hoped, by Archbishop Joseph Booth in his foreword, a larger work might be added. That work has yet to materialize. Nunn's view of theological development in Anglicanism is unequivocal. Reflecting on the Anglo-Catholic bishop of London's leadership in forming the Colonial Bishoprics Fund, Nunn writes, "The Evangelical revival was enriched and fulfilled by the Oxford Movement, and this in its turn prepared the way for more general and enthusiastic attention to the needs of the Church overseas."[25] Nunn engages in hagiography of the bishops and archbishops, and arguably of the diocese itself. He is silent on conflicts involving evangelicals, and on the reasons for the founding of Ridley College to provide an evangelical alternative for clergy training in the early part of the twentieth century when theological and party-political dispute was increasing in intensity.

Brian Porter edited a useful volume for Melbourne's sesquicentenary in 1997: *Melbourne Anglicans*.[26] The contributors span the range of theological traditions, but write on discrete subjects in each chapter, so there is no succinct or comprehensive overview of the development of evangelicalism. The general overview history of the diocese, provided by James Grant, focuses on the leadership of the bishops (and later, archbishops) of Mel-

24. Nunn, *Short History*.
25. Nunn, *Short History*.
26. Porter, *Melbourne Anglicans*.

bourne. Grant was at that time dean, assistant bishop, and archivist of the diocese. He has had a long-term interest in, and is deservedly acknowledged as an authority on, the history of the diocese. Perhaps more than any other writer, it is Grant who has established the metanarrative of diocesan history in relation to party politics. This narrative is detectable in Nunn and may be summarized along the following lines:

Melbourne's first bishop was an unreasonably stern evangelical: "Perry's reputation as a narrow-minded bigot in matters of churchmanship was established early in his episcopate."[27] From this narrow evangelical beginning, Melbourne gained a more enlightened culture through the broad-church leadership of the second bishop, who encouraged theological diversity: "Moorhouse is usually accorded the accolade as the greatest of Melbourne's bishops. Nowhere was this more apparent than in his encouragement of a true catholicity within the diocese."[28] By the time of the third, and again evangelical, bishop, Goe, this diversity was set in place: "[Goe] maintained what Moorhouse had established, namely, the character of Melbourne as a tolerant diocese."[29]

This interpretation of Melbourne's history is largely unchallenged and indeed expanded upon in two other volumes, both edited by Colin Holden, that were also published around the diocese's sesquicentenary: *People of the Past?*[30] which focuses on the interaction between Melbourne Anglicanism and Melbourne culture and *Anglo-Catholicism in Melbourne*.[31] Apart from incidental commentary, neither volume examines the place of evangelicalism in the history of Melbourne Anglicanism. Instead, the overriding tone and message is summarized by Holden himself in his paper, "*Melbourne Anglicanism: A Distinctive Culture?*"[32] in which he suggests that the entire Melbourne Diocese, evangelical and otherwise, "offers a tolerance of diversity" and lower degree of "combativeness" not found, by contrast, in Sydney.[33] This extends, historically, to the conflict over vestments, ordination of women, and the nature of public debates.

The Anglo-Catholic narrative is an argument for a civil, tolerant, and broad church that is marked by absence of party conflict. However, this narrative tends to focus on events and currents on a diocesan level, ignoring

27. Grant, "Overview," 7.
28. Grant, "Overview," 9.
29. Grant, "Overview," 11.
30. Holden, *People of the Past?*
31. Holden, *Anglo-Catholicism in Melbourne*.
32. Holden, "Melbourne Anglicanism."
33. Holden, "Melbourne Anglicanism," paragraphs 5 and 6.

developments on the ground—the sphere of greatest activity and success for evangelical laity and parishes—and inter-parish and inter-denominational networks. It is also disinterested in the key cause of heated conflict and party politics within the church: real theological differences.

The original Diocese of Melbourne encompassed the state of Victoria but—in common with the original Dioceses of Sydney, Newcastle, and Adelaide—it was too large to administer and was progressively divided as new dioceses were created.[34] A number of histories of these provincial dioceses have been written.

Ballarat

John Spooner's *The Golden See* is a history of the Diocese of Ballarat from 1875 to 1975.[35] Ballarat was the first of the provincial dioceses to be separated from Melbourne. Although his is a mainly narrative account focusing on successive episcopacies and attempts to build a cathedral, Spooner does engage with issues of churchmanship. He does not shy away from accounts of the political tussles that took place, particularly over the first, and then successive, episcopal appointments. The history begins with the Perry period, when Ballarat was still a part of Melbourne, and the first half of the book contains observations about the gradual movement away from Perry's evangelicalism, which he attempted to stamp on Ballarat, towards the Anglo-Catholicism of the twentieth century.

Spooner writes from an unabashedly Anglo-Catholic perspective and is clearly grateful for the movement away from Perry's mode of evangelicalism.[36] In the afterword he writes in the third person voice bemoaning the death of the dream of reunion with Rome.[37] He pays scant attention to the major parochial ministry contribution of significant evangelicals such as Peter Teulon Beamish and Francis Thomas Cusack Russell, focusing almost exclusively on their contribution to episcopal politics. There is next to nothing on ministry efforts and achievements at the local parish level, no matter what the churchmanship. He also pays scant attention to the fact that with Perry in charge before the foundation of the Diocese of Ballarat, most of the ministry leadership supplied would have been at least nominally evangelical in character. Spooner's analysis of the movement away from evangelicalism

---

34. For a useful flowchart and diagram of the geography, creation and amalgamation of Australian Anglican Dioceses, see *Australian Anglican Directory 2007*, 4–7.
35. Spooner, *Golden See*.
36. Spooner, *Golden See*, 146.
37. Spooner, *Golden See*, 243.

towards Anglo-Catholicism lacks depth, and the reasons for this movement deserve to be revisited.

Bendigo

In 1902 both the Diocese of Bendigo and the Diocese of Gippsland were carved out of Melbourne. Keith Cole has written a large number of histories, mainly missionary and CMS, but also of the diocese he retired to: *A history of the Diocese of Bendigo, 1902–1976: an Anglican diocese in rural Victoria*.[38] It was updated in a second volume covering 1977–2002.[39] A third volume, *A History of the Diocese of St. Arnaud, 1926–1976*,[40] completes Cole's trilogy of the history of the present day Bendigo diocese. In common with his numerous other works, the trilogy contains much detailed information but little by way of analysis. His diocesan history centers on bishops, senior clergy, significant laity, diocesan affairs, and—reflecting his CMS connection—an obsession with obituaries. There is practically no analysis of even the bishops' churchmanship, theological movements, social impact, or political controversy.

Gippsland

The centenary chronicle of the Diocese of Gippsland, edited by Ted Gibson, was published in 2002: *Great Faithfulness—a Centenary Publication of the Diocese of Gippsland 1902–2002*.[41] The publication collects information from a good number of local sleuths who write up the stories of local parishes and Gippsland personalities (lay and clerical, men and women). A brief history of the development of the diocese and the life and ministry of each of the bishops is also provided. The information is broad in scope, but shallow in detail and any analysis is completely absent.

More interesting is *Light and Life: a History of the Anglican Church in Gippsland, 1845–1977* compiled by Ivan Maddern, with substantial portions written by Frank Lowe.[42] This supplements rather than supersedes *The Church of Our Fathers* (1947),[43] a history of the Diocese of Gippsland by

---

38. Cole, *Diocese of Bendigo, 1902–1976*.
39. Cole, *Diocese of Bendigo, 1977–2002*.
40. Cole, *Diocese of St. Arnaud, 1926–1976*.
41. Gibson, *Great Faithfulness*.
42. Maddern, *Light and Life*.
43. Clark, *Church of Our Fathers*.

Albert E. Clark, added to in the jubilee year of the diocese by Clark with the publication of a separate *Supplement to the Church of Our Fathers* (1952).[44] These histories are, again, typical in their episcopal focus and absence of interest in churchmanship and wider issues. They function mainly as chronicles, helpfully provide detailed parochial histories, and include lists of clergy for each parish, clergy ordained in the diocese, deaconesses, registrars, chancellors, and advocates.

Wangaratta

Colin Holden's history of the Diocese of Wangaratta, *Church in a Landscape*,[45] is, in contrast, a well-researched and argued academic history. Until recently, there has been little attention paid to the impact of geography on Australian history. Church of England historiography has been influenced by a long tradition in England, but physical proximity and ease of communication between persons, bishop and clergy, and central diocesan power and outlying parishes is very different in England to what it is in Victoria. The impact of geography on history is only recently coming under scrutiny in Australia, and *Church in a Landscape* is rightly praised for leading the way in this.[46]

Holden acknowledges Perry's evangelical influence over the entire province, but notes that there was a "sprinkling of high churchmen in the north east, most obviously among the clergy."[47] Holden gives attention to overt evangelicals like Harry Braddock, "the energetic rector of Broadford ... a committed evangelical Anglican."[48] His argument is that it was the tolerant moderate Anglo-Catholic group that paved the way for the development of the diocese's culture—not the overtly aggressive Puseyites. However, Holden does not track the history of evangelical parishes like Broadford or analyze how they or their laity fared after men like Braddock moved on.

Other Australian Dioceses

Other diocesan histories are almost invariably chronicles of bishops and buildings, either large and exhaustive, like the relatively recent centenary history of the Anglican Church in West Australia, *West Anglican Way*

---

44. Clark, *Supplement*.
45. Holden, *Church in a Landscape*.
46. Sherlock, "Review."
47. Holden, *Church in a Landscape*, 41.
48. Holden, *Church in a Landscape*, 41.

(1989) by A. E. Williams,[49] or more brief, such as Ted Doncaster's *Spinifex Saints: The Diocese of North West Australia 1910–1985* (1985).[50] Many are old and brief, for example, Ransome T. Wyatt's *The History of the Diocese of Goulburn* (1937),[51] and similarly the histories of the Riverina[52] and North Queensland.[53]

A notable exception is the last bishop of Carpentaria Anthony Hall-Matthews' almost autobiographical account of the demise of the diocese, *A Remarkable Faith Venture*—a monograph that emerged out of his doctoral dissertation on the same.[54]

Melbourne Parish Histories

There are certainly too many local parish histories to list, with many published privately, in small circulation, and difficult to find. Trinity College's status as the official diocesan college means that several have found their way to that college library's collection, or more specifically into the collection of the Diocese's Mollison Library, which is housed at Trinity. Many are the love labors of amateur historians with a long connection to a parish, for example, Jim Patterson's *A Pioneer Church: A History of Sorts of Holy Trinity Upwey* (2004),[55] and Henry Speagle's *A Light in the Hills: A History of St. Michael and All Angels Mount Dandenong* (1990).[56] At least one is the early work of a future professional historian: Peter Sherlock's history of his then parish, St. Augustine's Moreland.[57] For the most part they are brief chronicles of events and records of fixtures and gifts.

There are other more substantial histories researched by professional historians with a connection to particular parish. In the present-day Diocese of Melbourne these are almost exclusively written from the liberal Catholic or Anglo-Catholic perspective. They include Colin Holden's history of St. Peter's Eastern Hill (1846–1990), *From Tories at Prayer to Socialists at Mass* (1996);[58] a series of lectures by Holden on a significant Anglo-Catholic vicar

49. Williams, *West Anglican Way*.
50. Doncaster, *Spinifex Saints*.
51. Wyatt, *Diocese of Goulburn*.
52. Clyde, *In a Strange Land*.
53. Rowland, *Tropics for Christ*.
54. Hall-Matthews, *Remarkable*.
55. Patterson, *Pioneer Church*.
56. Speagle, *Light in the Hills*.
57. Sherlock, *One Foundation*.
58. Holden, *Tories at Prayer*.

of that parish, *"Awful Happenings on the Hill": E. S. Hughes and Melbourne Anglo-Catholicism before the War* (1992);[59] a history of St. Stephen's Richmond by Morna Sturrock, *Fruitful Mother*;[60] and Paul Nicholls's *Highs and Lows: The Anglican Parish of Christ Church Brunswick*.[61] The only substantial history of an evangelical parish is Graham and Margaret Bride's history of St. Matthew's Prahran, *Proclaiming the Gospel*.[62] Few other current leading evangelical parishes in Melbourne have even the most basic published histories; St. Hilary's Kew,[63] Holy Trinity Doncaster,[64] and All Saint's Greensborough[65] are exceptions rather than the rule.

Then of course there are small souvenir booklets published at significant anniversaries such as *Christ Church Geelong Centenary* (1943)[66] and *Christ Church Marysville: Seventieth Anniversary Souvenir* (1982).[67] These tend to contain interesting anecdotal material rather than exhaustive analyzed information. Interestingly, the three historic parishes of Victoria in existence at Perry's arrival in 1847 have each published histories, indicating the value ascribed to their particular historical status. There is Christ Church Geelong's centenary booklet and the history of St. Peter's Eastern Hill, both mentioned above, and *The Story of St. Stephens, Portland* by Noel F. Learmonth (1956).[68]

Keith Cole's many volumes include several parish histories from the present Diocese of Bendigo, which was part of the original Diocese of Melbourne until 1902. These include histories of Christ Church Echuca (1865–1990),[69] Holy Trinity Taradale,[70] and Holy Trinity,[71] All Saints',[72] and

---

59. Holden, "Awful Happenings."
60. Sturrock, *Fruitful Mother*.
61. Nicholls, *Highs and Lows*.
62. Bride and Bride, *Proclaiming the gospel*.
63. McCullaugh and Rodda, *St. Hilary's*. This supersedes an earlier history by William Lloyd, the then vicar, and Arthur Mace: Lloyd and Mace, *St. Hilary's, Kew, 1889–1970*.
64. Uebergang and Plumb, *Holy Trinity Doncaster*.
65. All Saints' Anglican Church, *Green and Growing*.
66. *Christ Church, Geelong*.
67. *Christ Church Marysville*.
68. Learmonth, *St. Stephens*.
69. Cole, *Christ Church, Echuca*.
70. Cole, *Church on the Hill*.
71. Cole, *Holy Trinity, Bendigo*.
72. Cole, *All Saints' Church, Bendigo*.

St. Paul's Cathedral, all of Bendigo.[73] They form part of the large bookshelf of testimony to Cole's productivity as a historian.

Parish histories such as Cole's tend to chronicle people, property, and events rather than make a sustained argument of any sort. Most parish histories fall into this category. The best researched of them contain helpful information about churchmanship, connection to diocesan figures, local issues, and ministry priorities.

Biographies

Two early biographies of the first two bishops, Perry and Moorhouse, are a major source of early diocesan history. George Goodman was Perry's examining chaplain, archdeacon of Geelong, and vicar of Christ Church. Goodman's biography, *The Church in Victoria during the Episcopate of the Right Revd Charles Perry*,[74] was researched and written by Goodman in Perry's lifetime, its publication financed in part by Perry, and printed just after Perry's death in 1892. It remains an invaluable source of information and correspondence relating to the period, although it lacks modern footnotes, citations, and an index. Written by a firsthand observer, within Perry's lifetime, and with his endorsement, the book is laced throughout with excerpts from Frances Perry's journals and letters and Charles Perry's letters and addresses. For these reasons, it may properly be regarded as a primary source of historical data. Goodman also writes as a loyal follower of Perry, but the book is by no means a plain hagiography, as he includes many instances of conflict and tension between Perry and others.[75]

Similarly, Edith Rickards's 1920 biography of James Moorhouse provides much contemporary data for study.[76] Again, however, her sources are not cited or footnoted, and there is no index. Rickards's work is more hagiographical than Goodman's and she places undue prominence on the then "new" information about Moorhouse's mystical experience in early life and the impact it had on his ministry.

Both early sources have been supplemented by more recent and academic biographies focusing on the bishops' terms in Melbourne. These are Arthur de Quetteville Robin's 1967 biography of Perry, *Charles Perry, Bishop of Melbourne*,[77] and Morna Sturrock's 2005 biography of Moorhouse, *Bishop*

73. Cole and Bendigo Anglican Diocesan Historical Society, *St. Paul's Cathedral*.
74. Goodman, *Church in Victoria*.
75. Parson's "Church in Victoria" also contains helpful information.
76. Rickards, *Bishop Moorhouse*.
77. Robin, *Charles Perry*; Piggin, *Spirit, Word and World*.

of Magnetic Power: James Moorhouse in Melbourne.[78] These more recent volumes also make good use of diocesan archival material like the bishops' letter books, *The Church of England Messenger*, and the bishops' lectures, sermons, and synod addresses. Importantly, they are referenced adequately so that further study is facilitated. Although not the main focus of either biographer, both Perry's evangelicalism and Moorhouse's broad churchmanship are commented upon.

The only subsequent diocesan of Melbourne to have received scholarly attention is Frank Woods.[79] Brian Porter's thesis and resultant biography of Woods both contain useful information sourced from the extensive archive of the archbishop's personal papers. Porter describes Woods's departure from his family's evangelical heritage towards a broader liberal position during his formation for ministry at Cambridge. That vision came to dominate his ministry and leadership of the diocese, but Porter does not delve into any significant interaction between the archbishop and evangelicals in his diocese.

The Second Sydney Smith Memorial lecture, "Four Archbishops of Melbourne,"[80] by John McKie, bishop of Geelong from 1946 to 1960, contains useful anecdotal information and observations by someone who knew the archbishops personally. In similar vein, monographs on Joseph Booth[81] and David Penman[82] have also been written by clergymen who served under them. As such, they tend to be hagiographical and sympathetic, as is the memoir of the first bishop of Gippsland, *In The Master's Service for 52 Years in Australia: Arthur Wellesley Pain (1841–1920): A Biographical Memoir* by his grandson Arthur Franklyn Pain (1981).[83] A brief attempt at critical historical research is James Grant's short lecture on Field Flowers Goe,[84] but overall, the main impression of existing serious biographical scholarship on Melbourne diocesans is that it is almost nonexistent except for the more recent volumes on Perry and Moorhouse.

This mirrors the scene in Australian Anglican and evangelical studies generally. There are few first-rate biographical studies and a plethora of hagiographical memoirs. Three recent examples of the former are Marcia Cameron's biography of David Broughton Knox,[85] John Poynter's of

78. Sturrock, *Bishop of Magnetic Power*.
79. Porter, *Frank Woods*; Porter, "Frank Woods."
80. McKie, "Four Archbishops."
81. Robin, *Making Many Rich*.
82. Nichols, *David Penman*.
83. Pain, *In the Master's Service*.
84. Grant, "Field Flowers Goe."
85. Cameron, *An Enigmatic Life*.

Alexander Leeper,[86] and Robert Withycombe's of Bishop Henry Montgomery of Tasmania.[87] An older example is G. P. Shaw's biography of Bishop W. G. Broughton.[88] Two significant monographs for evangelicalism in Melbourne are Darrell Paproth's biography of C. H. Nash, a giant figure in Melbourne evangelicalism for most of the twentieth century, *Failure is Not Final*,[89] and Lance Shilton's autobiography, *Speaking Out: A Life in Urban Ministry*.[90]

Memoirs abound, but special mention must be made of Marcus Loane who, over many years, has published several titles that are perhaps best described as devotional biographies of evangelical heroes.[91] These serve to record a great number of helpful names, places, and facts for subsequent research—not least because they preserve the names of key evangelicals and yield clues to their potential associates. Loane also draws attention to the significance of succession and training of clergy for evangelicalism, not least through his earliest titles *Oxford and the Evangelical Succession* and *Cambridge and the Evangelical Succession*.[92]

Other Relevant Australian Studies

Evangelicalism has historically given rise to volunteer organizations focused especially on mission and evangelism. These have lent it a degree of strength and stability, especially when diocesan or parochial support has been wanting. As such, the histories of the Church Missionary Society (CMS), the Australian Fellowship of Evangelical Students (AFES), Crusaders, Scripture Union, the Bible Society, Ridley College, and the Melbourne Bible Institute—subsequently the Bible College of Victoria and, from 2011, the Melbourne School of Theology—are intimately linked to the history of evangelicalism.

---

86. Poynter, *Doubts and Certainties*.
87. Withycombe, *Montgomery of Tasmania*.
88. Shaw, *Patriarch and Patriot*.
89. Paproth, *Failure Is Not Final*.
90. Shilton, *Speaking Out*.
91. Loane, *Masters*; *Cambridge and the Evangelical Succession*; *Oxford and the Evangelical Succession*; *Sons of the Covenant*; *Three Faithful Servants*; *John Charles Ryle*; *Mark These Men*; *Centenary History of Moore*; *Archbishop Mowll*; *No Other Name*; *Hewn from the Rock*.
92. Loane, *Cambridge and the Evangelical Succession*; *Oxford and the Evangelical Succession*.

Lawrence Langley Nash, the cleric son of C. H. Nash, penned the jubilee history of Ridley College, *Forward Flows the Time*.[93] It helpfully records many of the details of the genesis of the college, paying particular attention to council minutes and early correspondence with Archbishop Lowther Clarke. However, it is less strong on the impact of Ridley graduates in the province and on the shifting definition of its evangelical self-identity.

The Reverend H. R. Holmes's *The Story of the C. M. A.* (1913) is a basic chronicle of the Victorian Church Missionary Association from 1892 to 1913 when it was superseded by CMS Victoria.[94] Keith Cole has written several useful histories of CMS Australia and Victoria as organizations, a history of the Roper River Mission, and biographical histories of missionaries.[95] In common with Cole's other work, these are mainly chronicles of people and events. A group with great influence over the course of Anglican evangelicalism in the twentieth century is the CMS League of Youth (LOY). The League's history is well served primarily by the two volumes *The Torch* and *Bearers of the Torch*; a history of LOY and a subsequent book of testimonies of its members.[96] They read as a "who's who" of twentieth-century Anglican evangelicalism in Australia. Although slim, both volumes are an invaluable source for this study. Other references to the LOY are to be found in autobiographies and biographies such as those of Lance Shilton and C. H. Nash.[97]

Cole has also penned *Commissioned to Care*, a history of the Mission of St. James and St. John, published in its golden jubilee (1969).[98] The Mission was planted out of the historic city parishes of St. James' Old Cathedral (West Melbourne) and the now closed St. John's Latrobe Street, both evangelical strongholds of yesteryear. *Commissioned to Care* gives us an insight into a much-neglected aspect of more recent evangelical history: its social concern and action.

John and Moira Prince's *Out of the Tower* is a history of the Australian Fellowship of Evangelical Students (AFES), which notes several significant Anglican and Melbourne Anglican connections with student work.[99] Histories of the Student Christian Movement (SCM) such as Robin Boyd's *The*

---

93. Nash, *Forward Flows the Time*.

94. Holmes, *Story of the CMA*.

95. Cole, *Sharing in Mission*; Cole, *History of the Church Missionary Society of Australia*; Cole, *Roper River Mission, 1908–1969*; Cole and CMS Australia, Victorian Branch, *Servants for Jesus' Sake*; Cole and Pethybridge, *Pethy, Lee and Mary*; Cole and St. Hilary's, *Letters from China 1893–1895*.

96. Cutler, *Torch*; *Bearers of the Torch*.

97. Shilton, *Speaking Out*; Paproth, *Failure Is Not Final*.

98. Cole, *Commissioned to Care*.

99. Prince and Prince, *Out of the Tower*.

Witness of the SCM also provide useful commentary on the divergences between evangelical students and the pre-existing SCM.[100]

Early mission to the indigenous peoples of Australia is an area of recent increasing interest in university history departments. John Harris's books, *We Wish We'd Done More: Ninety Years of CMS and Aboriginal Issues in North Australia*, and more especially *One Blood*, have become standard reference points in the study of missionary encounter with the indigenous peoples of Australia.[101] Many missionary efforts were undertaken by evangelical Anglicans, and these histories give us an insight into evangelical attitudes to mission, culture, and class.

Studies of Evangelicalism

Early histories of evangelicalism tended to focus either on the lives of famous preachers, for example H. J. Hughes's 1892 *Life of Howell Harris*,[102] or on records of conversion narratives, such as Jonathan Edwards's "A Narrative of Surprising Conversions."[103] Of course, a great deal of primary source material from the pens of Edwards and the Wesleys and subsequent leaders is widely available. General works on the history of the movement as a whole did not appear till the early twentieth century. Examples of these include G. R. Balleine's 1908 *A History of the Evangelical Party in the Church of England*,[104] which was widely read and went to a fifth edition in 1951, G. W. Russell's 1915 *A Short History of the Evangelical Movement*,[105] and L. E. Binns's 1928 *The Evangelical Movement in the English Church*.[106]

Momentum in studies of evangelical history only really started taking off in the late twentieth century following the publication of David Bebbington's *Evangelicalism in Modern Britain* in 1989.[107] Several other smaller studies had preceded this work but Bebbington's study was perhaps the first serious full-length examination of evangelical history.[108] At the same time in Canada, George Rawlyk published *The Canada Fire: Radical Evangelicalism*

---

100. Boyd, *Witness*.
101. Harris, *We Wish We'd Done More*; *One Blood*.
102. Hughes, *Howell Harris*.
103. Edwards, *Select Works Vol. 1*.
104. Balleine, *Evangelical Party*.
105. Russell, *Evangelical Movement*.
106. Binns, *Evangelical*.
107. Bebbington, *Evangelicalism*.
108. An earlier excellent study with a narrower focus was Hilton, *Age of Atonement*.

in British North America.[109] In the USA, Mark Noll, who had cofounded with Nathan O. Hatch the Institute for Study of American Evangelicals in 1982,[110] published *Princeton and the Republic,* his study of the relationship between American religion, science, and society.[111] Between them, Bebbington, Noll, and Rawlyk edited two major historical surveys of English-speaking evangelicalism, *Amazing Grace* and *Evangelicalism.*[112] The former volume was heavily focused on the UK and North America, but included a contribution from Stuart Piggin on Australian evangelicalism.

These works signaled the start of a relatively rich period of evangelical historiography. The focus has largely been on North America and the United Kingdom. In the United States, the interest has been fuelled in part by the prominence of evangelicals in that country's political life. Together, Bebbington and Noll have edited a five-volume series, *A History of Evangelicalism: People, Movements and Ideas in the English-Speaking World.*[113] These five volumes represent UK, USA, and Australian scholarship that attempts to trace the global expansion and impact of evangelicalism in the English-speaking world. Additionally, a rich body of monographs has been published in the series edited by Bebbington entitled *Studies in Evangelical History and Thought.*[114]

Bebbington's thesis about the origins of evangelicalism in the eighteenth-century revival and Age of Enlightenment has been recently challenged by various scholars in the edited volume *The Emergence of Evangelicalism,*[115] which seeks to link evangelicalism's origins to the earlier Protestant Reformation. This is an important volume that illustrates well the point that arguments about historical origins are invariably complex and multilayered.

Australian evangelical historiography has been served by a small but growing group of scholars. Mention has already been made of biographical studies above. In 1987 the Evangelical History Association (EHA) was established. Among its founding members were Stuart Piggin, Mark Hutchinson,

109. Rawlyk, *Canada Fire.*

110. The ISAE operated from 1982 to 2014; https://www.wheaton.edu/academics/academic-centers/isae. Last accessed 31 October 2018.

111. Noll, *Princeton.*

112. Rawlyk and Noll, *Amazing Grace*; Noll et al., *Evangelicalism.*

113. Noll, *Rise of Evangelicalism*; Wolffe, *Expansion of Evangelicalism*; Bebbington, *Dominance of Evangelicalism*; Stanley, *Global Diffusion of Evangelicalism*; Treloar, *Disruption of Evangelicalism.*

114. Two recent examples are the dissertations of Meldrum, *Conscience and Compromise,* and Harris, *Evangelicals and Education.*

115. Haykin and Stewart, *Emergence of Evangelicalism.*

and Brian Dickey, each of whom has made significant contributions to the field.[116] The EHA launched its own journal, *LUCAS*, and undertook the compilation and publication of *The Australian Dictionary of Evangelical Biography* (1994).[117] The ADEB remains the most important single-volume resource of Australian evangelical biography, containing much data not documented or preserved elsewhere.

Piggin in particular has focused sharply on Australian evangelicalism in *Evangelical Christianity in Australia: Spirit, Word and World*, republished in a second edition as *Spirit of a Nation*.[118] There he argues that the evangelical synthesis of Spirit, word, and world concern is the tripartite distinctive that evangelicalism's mission prospers or fails by. He identifies its mission as twofold: 1) to preserve society by reforming it according to the word; and 2) to bring members to faith in Christ through the proclamation of the gospel.[119] His analysis is broad in scope and not particular to Melbourne or to Anglicanism, although his membership in, knowledge of, and concern for the Anglican Church is evident.

Piggin also played a leading role in the formation of the Centre for the Study of Australian Christianity (CSAC), which has published several volumes of note for evangelical studies, including several mentioned above.[120]

Australian evangelicals have also maintained a sustained interest in the history of revivals. Piggin and Hutchinson edited a well-researched volume investigating the topic.[121] Robert Evans's *Early Evangelical Revivals in Australia* is more focused on Wesleyan Methodism, but still an extremely useful and helpfully referenced survey.[122]

The Leon Morris Library at Ridley College, Melbourne, inaugurated its Charles Perry collection in 2009 and aims to continue increasing its significant collection of local and wider evangelical studies.[123] In partnership with

116. For example, Dickey, *Holy Trinity Adelaide, 1836–1988*; Hutchinson and Piggin, *Reviving Australia*.

117. Dickey, *ADEB*.

118. Piggin, *Spirit of a Nation*.

119. Piggin, *Spirit of a Nation*, 222.

120. Paproth, *Failure Is Not Final*, and Shilton, *Speaking Out*. Also published by CSAC are Hutchinson and Campion, eds., *Re-Visioning Australian Colonial Christianity*; Robertson, "Unsearchable Riches."

121. Hutchinson and Piggin, *Reviving Australia*. See also Piggin's contribution on the history of revivals in Australia in Hutchinson and Campion, eds., *Re-Visioning Australian Colonial Christianity*.

122. Evans, *Early Evangelical Revivals*. See also Evans' 2010 Charles Perry lecture, "Evangelicalism in Australia in 1910."

123. See https://www.ridley.edu.au/library/special-collections/ for information on the Charles Perry collection. Last accessed 31 October 2018.

St. James' Old Cathedral, Ridley relaunched the Charles Perry lecture series in 2009, with David Bebbington speaking on the CMS Islington conference.[124] The biennial Perry lectures alternate with another biennial series at Ridley sponsored by the Evangelical History Association, so that in each year there is a lecture either on evangelicalism or by an evangelical scholar.

---

124. Bebbington, "Essence of Evangelicalism."

2

Defining Evangelicalism

*I want to remind you of the gospel I preached to you . . .
that Christ died for our sins according to the Scriptures,
that he was buried,
that he was raised on the third day according to the Scriptures,
and that he appeared to Peter and then to the Twelve.*

1 CORINTHIANS 15:1–5

Evangelicalism is, first and foremost, a movement of women and men within the Christian church who share a common creed and vocation. It is a movement that has both theological and historical aspects that are inextricably interlinked. Although many contemporary historians trace the roots of evangelicalism back to early eighteenth-century revivals or further back to the sixteenth-century Reformation, it may be useful to look briefly even further back to the origins of Christianity itself; more particularly to its sources in the Scriptures.

Etymology, the Early Church, and the Reformation

The noun "evangelicalism" derives from a group of related words in the Greek New Testament.

First, the noun *euangelion*, the "evangel" or gospel (derived from the Middle English "godspell," god-story or a story about God)[1] or good news. William Tyndale, the English Reformer and Bible translator, wrote that it denotes, "good, mery, glad and ioyfull tydinge, that maketh a mannes hert glad, and maketh hym synge, daunce, and leepe for ioye."[2] The noun appears seventy-six times in the Greek New Testament in the majority of the canonical books and is used by all the writers except James, Jude, and the writer to the Hebrews. The leading technical lexicon of New Testament Greek defines it as "God's good news to humans proclaimed."[3] The content of the good news is highlighted in the second and related word.

Second, the verb *euangelizo*, "to evangelize." The verbal aspect of the noun is highlighted in the fifty-four occurrences of the verb the Greek New Testament. The highest concentration of the verb is found, unsurprisingly, in the Acts of the Apostles. There the rapid and dramatic spread of the gospel through the known world, from Jerusalem to Judea, Samaria, and then to the uttermost limits of civilization, is recounted as historical record and exemplary exhortation to the early church to fulfill Christ's Great Commission.[4]

This second word is used in the overwhelming majority of cases to refer to the activity of proclaiming the gospel, the particular content of the message of divine salvation centered on the death and resurrection of Jesus Christ, summarized by the apostle Paul in 1 Corinthians 15:1–4:

> Now I would remind you, brothers and sisters, of the good news that I proclaimed to you, which you in turn received, in which also you stand, through which also you are being saved, if you hold firmly to the message that I proclaimed to you—unless you have come to believe in vain. For I handed on to you as of first importance what I in turn had received: that Christ died for our sins in accordance with the scriptures, and that he was buried, and that he was raised on the third day in accordance with the scriptures . . .

Several features of the gospel may be noted from this passage. The gospel is proclaimed by Paul, received by the Corinthian Christians, and is held firmly by them till the anticipated salvation in the end. The gospel is Christ's death for sins, his burial and his resurrection. The gospel is unoriginal—it was received by Paul, contained in the Scriptures, and proclaimed by Paul

---

1. Elwell, *Evangelical Dictionary of Theology*, 379.
2. *Prologue to the NT*, cited in Elwell, *Evangelical Dictionary of Theology*, 472.
3. Danker and Bauer, *Greek-English Lexicon*.
4. Matthew 29:18–20.

to others. Elsewhere Paul calls down condemnation on himself if he should preach a variant gospel.[5] The gospel is personally appropriated—it is Christ's death "for our sins," which Paul has received himself,[6] and which the Corinthians have received themselves.[7] Also featured in the passage is the activity of evangelism, which Paul engaged in with the Corinthians.

Third, a second noun, *evangelistes* or "evangelist." This occurs only three times, referring to Philip and Timothy in particular, and to God's gift of evangelists to the church in general.[8] In the case of Philip, one of the seven original deacons, the industry, activity, and spiritual empowerment of the evangelist is indicated in the Acts 8 narrative of his proclamation to the Ethiopian eunuch, his miraculous transport to Azotus, and his preaching throughout the whole region until he returned to Caesarea. Paul encourages Timothy to do the work of an evangelist, using language that implies it is hard labor, and he identifies such evangelists as one of the gifts to the church. This tripartite etymology is instructive, for the words indicate something of the creed, activity, and vocation of evangelicalism.

Although evangelism as an activity and evangelist as a vocation were established in the first generation of Christians, the movement was known as The Way, or pejoratively as "atheists," because they did not worship the pantheon of Greco-Roman gods. No evidence has yet been uncovered of the use of the term "evangelical" to describe the Christian movement or any part of it until the sixteenth-century Reformation.[9] It occurred by way of the adjective "evangelical" being applied to the group of reformers centered first around Martin Luther and Wittenberg, and then more generally in Germany and Switzerland. Indeed, it was Luther's career as "the evangelical doctor"—in particular his focus on the gospel and his use of the term *evangelische* in his characteristically robust rhetoric of protest against the prevailing practices of the Western church—that gave the movement its initial burst of energy and life. "Gospel" occurs just four times in Luther's Ninety-Five Theses, nailed to the door in 1517. The occurrences are at theses fifty-five, sixty-two, sixty-five, and seventy-eight. However, the primacy of the good news of God's gracious salvation in Christ, above and beyond the authority or glory of either Pope or Church itself, is clearly the main object of his protest. Thesis sixty-two states:

5. Galatians 1:8, 1:11–12.
6. Galatians 2:20—incidentally the only place in the New Testament where the gospel is referred to in an individual context.
7. 1 Corinthians 1:4–9.
8. Acts 21:8, 2 Timothy 4:5 and Ephesians 4:11.
9. Noll notes various uses of the adjective "evangelical" in Middle English in Noll, *Rise of Evangelicalism*, 14.

The true treasure of the Church is the Most Holy Gospel of the glory and the grace of God.[10]

By 1531, Sir Thomas More was able to refer to advocates of the Reformation as "Evaungelicalles . . . who cease not to pursue and punishe their bretherne."[11] What began in the language of protest had turned into the name of a recognizable group. Further, it had gained sufficient currency to be used pejoratively. The sectarian nature of the label has stuck: in 1945 the entire Protestant church in Germany was known as part of the "Evangelical Church in Germany," as opposed to Catholic.[12] Large sections of the Lutheran church still wear the label *evangelische*,[13] although more for historical reasons than present-day theological or spiritual ones.

The Early Eighteenth Century

Leading contemporary historians of evangelicalism regard the revivals of the early eighteenth century as the beginnings of modern evangelicalism.[14] By this period, many of the perceived gains of the Reformation were obscured or confused by the political, theological, and bloody battles fought since 1517. Reformation was followed by Counter-Reformation, the Thirty Years' War by the Peace of Westphalia, and the Cromwellian Protectorate by Restoration. An uneasy peace settled over the Western world just at a time when maritime advances were accelerating the processes of colonialism across the globe. Technological advances were leading towards the Industrial Revolution and an increased preoccupation with economic gains. Just at this moment, a revival and reform movement as momentous as that begun by Luther's Ninety-Five Theses broke out.

Historians of evangelicalism look in particular to the careers of George Whitefield, John and Charles Wesley, and Jonathan Edwards. Each of these owed a debt to the Reformers, perhaps the most direct and famous being John Wesley's debt to Martin Luther, as Wesley felt his "heart strangely warmed" while hearing the preface to Luther's *Commentary on the Epistle to the Romans* read out at a meeting. Of that moment in Aldersgate Street, he later wrote:

10. See http://www.projectwittenberg.org/pub/resources/text/wittenberg/luther/web/ninetyfive.html. Last accessed 31 October 2018.

11. Balleine, *Evangelical Party*, 40. Cited but not sourced at footnote 1.

12. Hart, *Dictionary of Historical Theology*, 197.

13. Phillips and Okholm, *Family of Faith*, 166.

14. See, e.g., Bebbington, *Evangelicalism*; Noll, *Rise of Evangelicalism*; Rawlyk and Noll, *Amazing Grace*; Piggin, *Spirit of a Nation*.

> I felt I did trust in Christ, Christ alone for salvation: And an assurance was given me, that he had taken away *my* sins, even *mine*, and saved *me* from the law of sin and death.[15]

An essential element of evangelicalism is described here: a personal faith and assurance, a vital piety, appropriated personally and inwardly at the moment of conversion. The protest this time was directed not at outward institutional structures and practices but inwards towards the heart of the person in need of spiritual transformation.

John Wesley, his brother Charles, and Whitefield had all been members of the so-called "Holy Club" at Oxford. There they had sought to grasp the true meaning of the gospel and express their piety and commitment to God in lives of holiness, discipline, and endeavor. Wesley's every attempt to secure personal holiness and assurance of saving faith for himself failed—no attempt more spectacularly than his failed expedition to North America where he was challenged by the joyful and vital faith of Moravian missionaries. He was following a similar failed path of seeking assurance of faith through good works as that trod by the Augustinian monk Luther two centuries beforehand.

However, in the same week in May 1738 both Wesley brothers received assurance of faith and salvation as they finally grasped the Reformation doctrine of justification by faith—Christ dying for their sins as the simple and complete guarantee of salvation distinctly, apart from works. Whitefield had received this assurance some two years previously, at about the same time as the Great Awakening was occurring in Northampton, Massachusetts, where Edwards was presiding minister and preacher.

Personal revival, for Whitefield and John Wesley in particular, led to personal evangelism and effort. They began a furious spurt of proclamation or preaching of the gospel on both sides of the Atlantic. Wesley is especially noted for his industry and indefatigability.

Again, two common features may be discerned: a yearning for assurance of saving faith, and conversion to a fuller apprehension of Christ's saving death "for our sins" (in Paul's words) or for "my sins" (in Wesley's) and assurance of the same. The content of evangelical faith started with that apprehension, internalization, and assurance of salvation. In evangelical perception, the gospel is quintessentially unoriginal. Wesley's conversion was to a faith experience based on what Luther had found in Romans two centuries before, which in turn looked to what Paul had written fifteen centuries before. The content of the evangelical faith is circumscribed by the Scriptures. The gospel activates its adherents to the work of proclaiming

---

15. *Journal*, May 24, 1738. As cited in González, *Story of Christianity*, vol. 2, 212.

the gospel itself, to the work of evangelism and proclamation to those outside and inside the visible church, and also to the application of the self to honest vocational labor.

Current Scholarly Definition

In the past few decades, Bebbington's quadripartite description has become the standard working definition of evangelicalism for historians. Derek Tidball describes it as the consensus view among historians.[16] Mark Noll views it as one of the most effective summaries of the convictions and attitudes of evangelicals[17]—so effective and dominant, in fact, that it is being used as the working definition in a major five-volume history of evangelicalism edited by Noll and Bebbington themselves.[18] Numerous other studies of evangelical history in the series *Studies in Evangelical History and Thought*, published by the evangelical Paternoster label, have shown their debt to Bebbington's definition.[19] Khim Harris, in a relatively recent scholarly study, cites him with approval, saying of Bebbington's quadrilateral: "It is a definition that has now become a standard reference point for researchers in the field."[20]

The four elements are, in the order that Bebbington presents them:[21]

1. conversionism,
2. activism,
3. biblicism, and
4. crucicentrism.

Conversionism reflects the gospel's call to repent from sin and turn to Christ and be saved. It speaks to the absolute necessity of a changed life, a life converted from the priorities and habits of the world to the priorities and rule of Christ. Bebbington writes that conversion "marked the boundary between a Christian and a pagan."[22] In perhaps the most famous of Jonathan Edwards's sermons, *Sinners in the Hands of an Angry God*, for example, the delights of

---

16. Tidball, *Who Are the Evangelicals?* 14.
17. Noll, *Rise of Evangelicalism*, 16.
18. Noll, *Rise of Evangelicalism*, 19.
19. Harris, *Evangelicals and Education*.
20. Harris, *Evangelicals and Education*, 28.
21. Bebbington, *Evangelicalism*, chapter 1.
22. Bebbington, *Evangelicalism*, 5.

heaven and the terrors of hell were clearly delineated in the preaching of the gospel and the call to conversion made on that basis.

Once converted, the evangelical Christian comes under the rule of Christ and in particular his Great Commission to go make disciples. This issues in an *activism* expressed mainly in evangelism—activity seeking the conversion of others. Hence, the Evangelical Revival saw great numbers of converts, by converts winning converts, following the principle of compound multiplication. However, activism was not confined to the evangelistic arena alone, although this was a chief preoccupation. Bebbington notes the busy schedule of preaching, services, lectures, Bible classes, united bands (small groups for prayer and Bible study), work among the poor, parochial visitations, and writing.[23] The Clapham Sect's and Nonconformist's political campaigns are also examples of such activism.

Bebbington uses the word *biblicism*, a usage that Donald Carson calls "ugly,"[24] to express John Wesley's dictum "Let me be *homo unius libri* (a man of one book)."[25] For evangelicals, the Bible is the source of all spiritual truth and the focus of spiritual devotion, hence the amount of energy poured into personal and corporate Bible study and the attention paid to preaching the Scriptures. The Reformation principle of the perspicuity of Scripture is emphasized so that ordinary laypeople are encouraged and enjoined to attend to the Scriptures daily for their spiritual nourishment. There is evidence that this led to the abandonment of academic study of the scriptural texts and sources in favor of the activism described above.[26]

The final element of *crucicentrism* describes the centrality of the cross of Christ, and especially the doctrine of the atonement. For evangelicals, the necessity of conversion is linked to the unique efficacy of the atoning sacrifice of Christ on the cross.[27] In particular, it is the doctrine of the substitutionary nature of the atonement that is cherished by evangelicals. This is not to say that other christological themes are unimportant—for example, the incarnation—but that it is the glorious salvific efficacy of the cross that comes to the fore. Further, for evangelicals, the cross has been a central rallying point, even amid strong disagreement on other points of theology.

Despite the wide acclamation and common usage of the Bebbington's quadripartite definition, it is not without its critics. Carson views Bebbington's discussion of the four categories as having much that is commendable

23. Bebbington, *Evangelicalism*, 11–12.
24. Carson, *Gagging of God*, 450.
25. Bebbington, *Evangelicalism*, 12.
26. Bebbington, *Evangelicalism*, 12.
27. Bebbington, *Evangelicalism*, 145–51.

but identifies two main potential abuses of the labels.[28] First, the focus on just four areas may imply that evangelicals are agnostic on other key aspects of theology, such as the Trinity. According to Carson, the reality is that evangelicals have tended to be highly loyal to the historic creeds of the church. Second, the four labels are, in Carson's view, insufficiently specific so that they can obscure the precise reasons for theological conflict between evangelicals and others. Many groups can and do claim "biblicism" or "crucicentrism," but have variant ideas about what it means to be Bible believing or cross-focused. Hence, Carson cites with approval David Wells's analysis of the modern evangelical shift away from doctrine and theology as the locus of self-identification while, rather problematically, retaining the label "evangelical."[29]

The issue that Carson highlights, although he does not describe it in these precise terms, is that of the tension between descriptive history and prescriptive theology. Historians tend to understand their craft as that of unearthing, describing, and giving order to the facts as revealed by the sources of history, however varying in reliability those sources might be. Theologians, meanwhile, tend to busy themselves grappling with the intersection between contemporary culture and the transcendent divine, described by Stanley Grenz and Roger Olsen as the tension between the immanence and transcendence of God.[30] However, the distinction is not as simple as a merely professional one, as the gap between conservative and progressive evangelical theologians, exemplified by Carson and Grenz, illustrates.[31] The distinction has become one between those who look to Scripture as the only "text" or source revealing the divine mind and action, and those who consider that Scripture is the first or primary text, but that divine action in the world today, however discerned, is a second text.

Additionally, there is the chief difficulty that both historians and theologians—and journalists and pundits also, for that matter—utilize the words "evangelical" and "evangelicalism"—but they do so with differing definitions and purposes in mind. At the risk of oversimplification, but for the sake of clarity, it may be said that historians are focused on trying to describe

---

28. Carson, *Gagging of God*, 449–51.

29. Carson, *Gagging of God*, 451. Wells, "On Being Evangelical: Some Theological Differences and Similarities," in Noll et al., *Evangelicalism*, 390–410.

30. Grenz and Olson, *20th-Century Theology*.

31. Grenz and Olson (self-identified evangelicals) are criticised by Carson and others for drifting away from traditional evangelical views of the doctrine of Scripture and revelation. See Erickson et al., *Reclaiming the Center*. The volume is a response to Grenz, *Renewing the Centre*.

something that has *already been* accurately, but theologians are usually trying to precisely prescribe their idea of what something *is* or *ought to be*.

Second, there is a further exacerbation of the problem because eventually both historians and theologians, or their followers, turn into philosophers who draw conclusions from their sources and apply them to the present. It is in that programmatic application that conflict can erupt, as it did in the heated debate in Sydney evangelicalism between the lay historian Stuart Piggin and the clerics Robert Doyle and Phillip Jensen.[32] Their disagreement stemmed, in part, from a differing understanding what evangelicalism is: a fixed theological stance informed by the intellectual norms of the Reformation, or a living movement in history with its currents of thought and action?

A similar tension is seen in a recent and important critical response to the Bebbington thesis of evangelicalism's roots in the Enlightenment.[33] Among other things, the authors in the edited volume *The Emergence of Evangelicalism* assert that the Reformation's influence on evangelicals is not to be underestimated. This simply illustrates that all history is by nature contextual; the matter of historical origins and roots is complex and to be approached with due care, diligence, and nuance. It also highlights that phenomenological observations of historical fact also include observations about theological positions, or historical theology.

Diversity and Variation

There has always been a degree of diversity within the evangelical camp. For example, in the eighteenth-century revivals there was considerable divergence between the Arminian Wesleyans and Calvinists such as Whitefield. However, that difference did not—for the most part—preclude a large measure of cooperation and warm fellowship between the Wesleys and Whitefield and their supporters. What they held in common far outweighed their differences in theology. The *evangel* at the core of their system of belief held practical priority over other theological tenets. However, this prioritizing of the gospel mission over theological difference has not subsequently always been a feature of evangelical practice, most notably when evangelicals achieve ascendancy or a majority position in their context.

We should also not underestimate the fact that what it means to be identified as an evangelical has varied significantly over time. For example,

---

32. See the description and analysis of this debate in Treloar, "History as a Vocation," 21–22.

33. Haykin and Stewart, *Emergence of Evangelicalism*.

early twentieth-century Australian Anglican evangelicalism was defined by the strict use of the Prayer Book service, northward position at the Lord's table, and the cassock, surplice, and black preaching scarf. Theologically, a vigorously premillennial understanding of eschatology was standard evangelical doctrine—for example, the landed property of the training college of CMS Australia, St. Andrew's Hall, is ceded by its early twentieth-century trust deed to the chief rabbi of London, England, upon the Lord's return.[34] By contrast, contemporary Anglo-Catholic Anglicans used innovative services outside of the Prayer Book, took the eastward position, and wore chasubles. They were much more ambivalent over matters eschatological. Strict observation of these outward practices and eschatological views came to define which camp a cleric stood in within the diocese. These were the defining issues for that generation.

However, by the end of the twentieth century the situation had become almost reversed, with evangelicals eschewing Prayer Book services for informal innovative ones, taking a west-facing position, and almost abandoning clerical robes altogether. Similarly, amillennial eschatology became increasingly common within evangelical ranks. The defining theological issues for evangelicals at the end of the century were different again.

This diversity and variation in practice indicates that evangelicalism is a living and active movement of people and ideas. Evangelicalism may be defined at a personal, institutional, political, grassroots, and universal level—to name but a range of options.

Concluding Comment

In this work the Bebbington quadrilateral will be assumed as the basic working definition, subject to modification and comment where necessary. It is a historian's definition that serves to describe evangelicalism as a coherent social and religious phenomenon. It is a live tradition currently experiencing renewed attention, not least in the United States where it has significant prominence in political affairs.

However, it is also true to assert with Carson that evangelicalism has always had strong theological commitments, especially with respect to the centrality of the crucifixion, the necessity of conversion to Christ, active confession and profession of Christ's lordship in life, and the hope of Christ's return as Savior and Judge. These commitments emerge directly from the

---

34. Conveyance and Deed of Trust between John Griffiths and The Church of England Evangelical Trust of Victoria, registered with Registrar-General of Victoria on 26 June 1910, paragraph 11.

gospel message. For evangelicals, this message is communicated through the Scriptures and applied in each individual's life on an ongoing basis. This active and vital personal piety lies at the core of the evangelical's self-identity, with effects rippling out all around, even to the shaping of events in world history such as the abolition of the African slave trade and the global Make Poverty History campaign. It was with such global ambitions for the gospel that the Diocese of Melbourne was founded in 1847.

3

Charles Perry: The Evangelical Founding Bishop of Melbourne

> We are therefore Christ's ambassadors,
> as though God were making his appeal through us.
> We implore you on Christ's behalf: Be ye reconciled to God.
>
> 2 CORINTHIANS 5:20

Introduction

THE FOCUS OF THIS study is the development of evangelicalism within the present-day Anglican Diocese of Melbourne. Evangelicals had been present in the colony before the appointment of a bishop, but so were other traditions within the Anglican denomination. Significantly, none of the early clergy—visiting or permanent—were identifiably evangelical, although they were almost certainly all low churchmen.[1] It was with the appointment and arrival of the evangelical Charles Perry in 1847 that evangelicalism in Melbourne received focused and energetic leadership not just from the bishop down, but also at a grassroots level from his team of clergy and

---

1. They were certainly all low church. For example, Adam Thomson, the second permanent clergyman appointed to Melbourne following John Grylls was also the first chaplain of the first Lodge of Australia Felix. See Shaw, *Port Phillip District*, 218. Shaw rightly notes that the Masonic lodges were centers for middle-class male fellowship and public ceremonies but also fuelled sectarianism against Catholics and stood firmly against anything that was not distinctly low-church Protestant.

lay leaders. Perry brought with him his brand of decided and principled evangelicalism, with ministry methods worked through over a decade of ministry in Cambridge that had included evangelism, church- and school-planting. He also brought a small team of clergy to double the clerical resources of the colony and left behind in England a trio of commissaries to vet potential clergy for the diocese: all three were personal friends and firmly evangelical peers in ministry.

The challenge of ministry in the foundation period of the diocese was immense, and this chapter describes the historical context for the period and examines the context and process of Perry's appointment. This chapter argues that the process of appointing Melbourne's first bishop exemplifies the heightened tensions within Anglicanism as a result of theological differences between evangelicals and high churchmen in England—and especially their differing views of what mission work in the colonies looked like. In the case of Melbourne, an evangelical was appointed, and this set the course for Melbourne to be established as Australia's first—and for a time, only—evangelical diocese. This chapter also demonstrates that the brand of evangelical leadership Perry brought to Melbourne, his methods and priorities in episcopal leadership, and the foundational ministries of the first clergy of the diocese, were determinative in shaping the diocese's evangelical culture for future generations.

Social Context

On 20 June 1837, the death of William IV led to the accession of his daughter to the British throne. Alexandrina Victoria would reign until the start of the next century as Queen Victoria, overseeing a period of tremendous industrial, military, colonial, social, and religious growth and development. Despite the demoralizing loss of its North American colonies, the expansion of British naval power and colonial ambition had continued unabated especially within a rich and massive triangle in the East: stretching from India across to China and south to New Zealand. Where a declaration of absolute ownership based on a fiction such as *terra nullius* was not possible, colonial powers simply established trading posts at key points along vital sea routes such as the Straits of Malacca that quickly developed into points of control and colonial power. From these dominions, substantial wealth arising from raw materials for primary production and trade accrued to Britain, just as the might of her Industrial Revolution was reaching its peak.

However, the earlier part of the century had been a time of revolution and conflict—in part fueled by the lure of so much uncovered and apparent wealth. The British-American War of 1812 to 1815 was followed the next year by the Battle of Waterloo, which ended Napoleon's decade long reign as self-styled Emperor terrorizing most of Europe. The frontier parts of North America, from Texas to the Californian coast and below into Central and South America, were all regions of upheaval as, one-by-one, regional groups asserted their independence, often violently, in the face of the pressure of the colonial ambitions of others. The River Plate, Chile, Peru, Bolivia, and Central America all declared independence from Spain and Portugal by 1825. Texas declared itself a republic in 1836.

The year before, in South Africa, the Great Trek or mass migrations of mainly Dutch settlers away from places of British colonial oversight had begun. The Trek was fundamental to the formation of Boer identity and another example of a response to colonial pressure in this period. These migrants eventually formed the independent settlements of Natal, Northern Cape, and the aptly named Orange Free State. Irish emigration also accelerated in this period—especially in the wake of the Great Potato Famine of 1847. Large numbers went to North America, but many also came to Australia, bringing their wit, gifts of speech and literature, and sectarian fervor.

Movement towards the founding of Australian colonies had been begun in 1786 when the Pitt administration announced its intention to establish a penal settlement at Botany Bay. The First Fleet sailed the following year, arriving in 1788. On board was Richard Johnson, the chaplain appointed by Royal Warrant after lobbying by evangelicals led by William Wilberforce and Henry Thornton. To the south, Van Diemen's Land was similarly colonized by the British in 1803, again as a penal colony.[2] The convict history of both stands in contrast to the free settler origins of Port Philip and Adelaide, which were colonized by the British in 1834 and 1836 respectively.[3] Entrepreneurial free settlers and the availability of land and opportunities made the colonies increasingly attractive to those seeking economic advancement. These came from across the British Isles and brought their religious affinities with them: Scottish Presbyterians, Irish Catholics and Protestants, and English Anglicans.

Pressure in Australia to establish greater autonomy of colonial governance reflected many of the themes affecting the colonial mood of this period. Many white colonists in Australia mirrored their contemporaries in North America and South Africa in asserting a desire for greater independence and

---

2. Robson, *History of Tasmania,* volumes 1 and 2.

3. Shaw, *Port Phillip District.* Whitelock and Baker, *Adelaide: A Sense of Difference*—previously published as *Adelaide from Colony to Jubilee.*

autonomy, the substantial difference being that in Australia the grand majority maintained fidelity to the Crown along the way.

Both British and Dutch East India Companies controlled not just lucrative trade and commerce but were also highly influential on social and religious life in the colonies. They brought social institutions such as churches, schools, public houses ("pubs"), and cricket clubs. Colonies, especially those under direct Crown control such as Upper Canada and New South Wales, often experienced the wholesale transposition of British forms of government, bureaucracy, and social ordering. The Westminster system of bicameral representative parliaments was generally established, along with a strict separation of powers between executive, legislative, and judicial arms of government. Such structures were displayed in form, even if it was obvious to contemporaries that the substance was a thing yet to come. Hence, by convention, it was not until the issue of Royal Letters Patent in 1847, declaring Melbourne a Diocese of the Church of England, that the former District of Port Philip was able to be known as the city of Melbourne within the province of Victoria. It was a tiny backwater settlement, not yet made rich by the discovery of gold, yet one in whose naming, the Queen of the era and her Prime Minister, Lord Melbourne, were indelibly marked.

The Christian church was itself in the midst of the greatest expansionary surge in its history. National churches rode the wave of colonialism to establish far-flung outposts like the Dutch *Engelsche Kerk* in Batavia, today All Saints' Jakarta.[4] Evangelical missions to unreached people groups were especially energetic. This was the age of their great mission agencies and heroic missionaries to whole continents, like William Carey of India (1793), Robert Morrison of China (1807), and David Livingstone of Africa (1841). The interdenominational London Missionary Society (LMS) had been founded in 1795, the Church of England Church Missionary Society following suit four years later in the same year that Sierra Leone was founded for emancipated African slaves. Kelvin Crombie observes that the founding of the London Society for Promoting Christianity amongst the Jews, or the London Jews Society (LJS) in 1809, reflected both the evangelicals' enthusiasm for the founding of independent societies in pursuit of their chosen causes, and their premillennial eschatology centered on the place of the nation of Israel.[5] One of its first supporters was the celebrated emancipator of slaves, the evangelical William Wilberforce. The LJS later agitated successfully for Jerusalem's first Protestant bishopric in 1841 and subsequent

---

4. Lake, *Changes and Chances*, xviii.

5. See Crombie, *Jewish Bishop in Jerusalem*, for an account of the LJS and an overview of Palestine context.

restoration of the nation-state of Israel, contributing to the complex geopolitical and sociocultural history of Palestine.

British evangelicals in the early nineteenth century were energetically involved in social reform work at home and evangelistic missions work abroad. However, in terms of the affairs of the national church, they were still in the minority and outside the main corridors of power. There were only three decidedly evangelical bishops in the Church of England just prior to the publication of Tract I in 1833. Evangelicals were not to be confused with the main rivals of the Tractarians, the Low Church party.[6] The Oxford Movement, especially through John Henry Newman and his Tract XC, sought to redefine the identity of the Church of England as essentially Catholic rather than Protestant. In the intra-ecclesial conflict that followed, evangelicals often found themselves swept up with the Low Church party, with whom they had more natural liturgical affinity.

However, the projects of both Low and High Church parties were equally inimical to evangelical spirituality and ministry. Neither was interested in the brand of biblical, personal, evangelistic, and socially energetic spirituality emphasized by evangelicals. Externally, there was some basis for the perceived threat of resurgent Catholic theological error. Newman defected to Rome, returned to England, and was later made a cardinal. From the papal chair came the Dogma of the Immaculate Conception of Mary in 1854, followed by the publication of the *Syllabus of Errors* in 1864, and the Dogma of Papal Infallibility in 1870.

Conflicts and tensions at home and elsewhere were invariably exported to the colonies as well. Even where there were decidedly evangelical bishops like Frederic Barker in Sydney or Charles Perry in Melbourne, who were determined to steer a united course for their fledgling dioceses, the flow of ideas and people from Britain meant that the same issues and challenges quickly arose wherever they settled. However, the positive activities of many evangelical societies were also exported and found keen support in the colonies—especially among the faithful *nouveau riche*. Auxiliaries of the BFBS and CMS were quickly established around the globe. Colonial evangelicals' interest in the work in China and India and Africa ran high. The priority and privilege of evangelism, pastoral care, planting new and needed churches, and establishing business, educational, and social institutions, gave more than adequate vent to evangelical activism.

---

6. Balleine, *Evangelical Party*, 165–67. See his extended footnote on the definition of the Low Church party.

Australian, Church of England and Evangelical Context

The District of Port Philip and the Diocese of Melbourne

The diocese that Perry came to was much larger than the present Diocese of Melbourne. In 1847 it encompassed the whole of the present state of Victoria. Its boundaries were identical to the limits of the District of Port Phillip, which remained under the control of the Governor of New South Wales. Separation of the District and its birth as a colony in its own right occurred in 1851, when it was renamed Victoria.

Perry realized from the outset that the geographical size of the diocese presented a huge challenge to pastoral ministry. The documentary record has many examples of him pleading for finances and qualified clergy to do the work of ministry in Melbourne.[7] Perry was not ashamed to beg, both in Melbourne among the leading citizens and back in England among his friends and supporters.

Increased wealth from the gold rush and the rapid increase in population meant that Perry was finally able to successfully divide the diocese and create the new Diocese of Ballarat in 1875 with its own financial foundation. This came at a cost to Melbourne's endowment, but Perry realized that it better served the evangelistic and pastoral mission of the church to have geographically smaller, more easily managed dioceses. Perry was unable to continue with his plans for further subdivision, but in 1902 the task was completed—largely by the evangelical Archdeacon Hindley—with the creation of the dioceses of Bendigo, Wangaratta, and Gippsland, and the present-day boundaries of the Diocese of Melbourne were set. Separate accounts have been given of the history of the Diocese of St. Arnaud, which was subdivided out of Ballarat in 1926 but absorbed into Bendigo in 1978.[8]

Early Evangelicals in Australia and Melbourne, 1788–1834

Any account of evangelicalism in Australian Anglicanism must begin with the arrival of the earliest colonial chaplains. Brian Fletcher notes that with one exception, the early chaplains were all products of the eighteenth-century evangelical revival, "united by a strong sense of mission and an inner strength that made them determined to succeed."[9]

---

7. Goodman, *Church in Victoria*.

8. Cole, *Diocese of St. Arnaud, 1926–1976*; *Diocese of Bendigo, 1902–1976: Anglican Diocese in Rural Victoria*; Spooner, *Golden See*.

9. Brian Fletcher, "Anglican Ascendancy 1788–1835."

The chaplains were "exported" to the colonies as a result of the expansion of the English colonial empire. This expansion spread English social, economic, and military affairs, and also its state religion. The process began the Church of England's transformation from an Established national church into today's international Anglican Communion. However, at the beginning of that process, it was very much the Church of England that was transported to Australia along with the first convicts. The English state organized and paid for chaplains to accompany their nationals to penal settlements as part of the scheme of rehabilitation.

However, colonial postings were not highly sought after. Conditions were harsh and life was difficult without the comforts of home. For clergymen, it was tempting to stay home and seek patronage to a better living or some other form of ecclesiastical preferment. It was in this context that members of the evangelical Eclectic Society met to discuss religious and moral issues of the day and to strategize for social action. Spurred by government proposals to establish a penal colony in Australia, the meeting of 13 November 1786 asked, "What is the best method of planting and promulgating the Gospel in Botany Bay?" Public activity to abolish the slave trade led to similar questions being asked of the West Indies and Africa at subsequent meetings.[10] It was the evangelical party of the Church of England, which included the reformer William Wilberforce and other members of the Eclectic and Elland Societies, who used their influence and finances to encourage evangelicals like Richard Johnson and Samuel Marsden towards difficult colonial postings.[11]

These early chaplains' priorities were in line with the sponsoring Societies' aim of "planting and promulgating the Gospel": to provide pastoral care to the settlement, to rehabilitate the convicts—or if that were to prove impossible, then at least their children[12]—and to convert the natives. Both Johnson and Marsden took an Aboriginal child into their families in an attempt to win friendship and understand the culture. Marsden, in particular, was an early activist and supporter of Aboriginal missions and to this end

10. Cole, *A History of the Church Missionary Society of Australia*.

11. Johnson was sponsored by the Eclectics and Marsden by the Elland Society. See Judd and Cable, *Sydney Anglicans*. Both Societies were networks of evangelicals. The Eclectic Society was founded by Reverend John Newton in 1783 to discuss moral, religious and social issues of the day, while the Elland Society was founded by Reverend Henry Venn (the older) to assist evangelicals in university and theological training.

12. Marsden wrote to the bishop of London, "The future Hopes of this Colony depends upon the rising generation—Little can be expected from the Convicts who are grown old in vice, but much may be done for their Children under proper Instruction." 11 March 1821, Bonwick Transcripts, Box 51, 776, Mitchell Library, Sydney. Cited at Fletcher, "The Anglican Ascendancy, 1788–1835," 12–13.

founded the Australian Auxiliary of the Church Missionary Society[13]—itself the product of an Eclectic Society discussion.

By the time of Port Philip's first permanent European settlement in 1834, the early evangelical chaplains of Sydney had been succeeded by other Anglican clergy—most notably William Broughton, the second archdeacon of Australia and, subsequently, the first and only bishop of Australia. Broughton was not a Tractarian, but was sympathetic to their cause, promoting high churchmen and refusing to countenance dissent from low-church evangelicals. Broughton appointed the first Anglican clergy to Port Philip, and there is no evidence that any of these appointments were evangelicals.

However, this is not to say that evangelicalism was totally absent in the fledgling colony. Joseph Orton, a Wesleyan evangelist, was active in Port Philip between 1836 and 1842 promoting work among the Aboriginal peoples and founding "Buntingdale," a missions station along the Barwon River outside Geelong near modern-day Birregurra. He was the resident preacher in Melbourne between 1840 and 1842.

Also in October 1836, Captain William Lonsdale arrived to take charge of the new settlement as police magistrate, commandant, and justice of the peace. It has yet to be comprehensively ascertained if he identified with the evangelicals, but he was certainly a devout and dutiful Christian who welcomed the arrival of the missionary George Langhorne in 1839 as someone who would advance the work among the Aboriginal peoples, perform the offices of religion, and establish a school.[14]

In 1839, Lonsdale's future friend and close partner in the work in the settlement, Charles La Trobe arrived as Superintendent.[15] The La Trobe family were leaders among the Moravian Brethren and heavily involved in the English evangelicals' anti-slavery campaign. Charles's father and elder brother had been successive heads of the Moravian church missionary society.[16] Upon arrival La Trobe received an address of welcome at the newly founded Melbourne Club from 236 settlers. Shaw notes that this response reflected his background:[17]

> I pray to God to whom I look for strength and power, that I may be enabled through His grace to know my duty and do it

---

13. Cole, *History of Church Missionary Society of Australia*, 7. Marsden formed the Auxiliary in 1825 primarily to advance the work of the CMS among Aboriginal Australians.

14. Shaw, *Port Phillip District*, 67–69. See also ADB entry.

15. See also the published PhD thesis by Drury, *La Trobe*.

16. Shaw, *Port Phillip District*, 172.

17. Shaw, *Port Phillip District*, 172.

diligently, temperately and fearlessly . . . It is not by individual aggrandizement, by the possession of numerous herds or by costly acres that the people shall secure for the country enduring prosperity and happiness, but by the acquisition and maintenance of sound religious and moral institutions, without which no country can become truly great.

La Trobe's evangelicalism was especially focused on the social activism and vital spirituality that characterized the Clapham Sect, whose influence in England extended to Perry's appointment of the first bishop of the Diocese of Melbourne. There does not seem to be any evidence that La Trobe or any other Melbourne evangelicals were directly involved. The circumstances surrounding Perry's appointment are worth considering in detail, for they throw light on the intensity of the competition between church parties in England, their differing attitudes towards episcopal office, and most importantly on the background to Perry's own attitudes towards his subsequent ministry in Melbourne.

The Appointment of Charles Perry, Bishop of Melbourne, 1847

By 1846, the growth and development in Port Philip had rendered the penal chaplaincy system obsolete. Emancipation of convicts, the adulthood of their children, and the arrival of free settlers had all changed the nature of society there. Port Philip was much less a penal colony than Sydney or Van Diemen's Land. It was a place of economic opportunity and trade and industry. There was an increased demand for colonial clergy and increased complexity in the activities of the church. Education and building of schools, for example, was an increasing priority for its citizens. Unsurprisingly, demand grew for the colony to have greater independence from Sydney and to be constituted as its own diocese with its own bishop. The fact that settlements achieved "city" status in concurrence with their establishment as a diocese established by Royal Letters Patent was also not insignificant.

Current Theories and Narratives

The view, presently unchallenged, put forward by James Grant in the official history of the diocese, is that Melbourne got an evangelical, unlike Newcastle and Adelaide, because of "the vociferous nonconformist minority headed by the Congregationalist, Fawkner, and the Free Presbyterian,

William Kerr."[18] Additional factors were the large number of Irish among influential Anglican laity and the need to balance the churchmanship of the colonial bishops. However, there is no evidence that local factors played any such part in the selection process, which was almost exclusively handled in London.[19]

It was notoriously difficult to find able and willing bishops for colonial sees. Bishop Frederic Barker, for example, was at least the eighth person approached to take the job of bishop of Sydney.[20] The fact is that colonial bishoprics were not lavishly endowed, involved separation from the comforts and social prestige of home, and meant pioneering hard work in difficult contexts. And for all that, there was no guarantee of a safe translation to a home see in England. Further, men with the appropriate "superior qualifications" necessary were often already committed to jobs that they were "unwilling to quit" before they "arrived at the age of being promoted to Episcopal office." Such was the assessment of the aged and experienced archbishop of Canterbury, William Howley.[21] Then, as now, it was difficult to get ministers to serve in challenging cross-cultural, foreign contexts.

F. T. Whitington has led the way in proposing that the names of at least two other clergymen came up before Perry's for Melbourne, neither of whom could in any way be described as evangelical.[22] The first was Canon Robert Allwood, vicar of St. James' Sydney. According to Whitington, in response to a letter from Canterbury, Broughton suggested only one name for Melbourne: "his valued helper in training candidates for ordination."[23] Allwood was one of the younger clergy in Sydney, and not averse to taking on the new liturgical innovations of the times. He was principal of St. James' College, which had definite Tractarian inclinations, leading to a later charge from

---

18. Grant, "Overview," 3. In his chapter on the Diocese of Melbourne in Porter et al., *Colonial Tractarians*, 66, Grant calls Perry's appointment "reasonably predictable" for the same reasons outlined above.

19. Paul Robertson's work on the appointment of the first bishop of Newcastle has been determinative in working out the sequence of events and political manoeuvring around the appointments of the first bishops of Newcastle, Cape Town, Adelaide, and Melbourne in 1846–1847. Only Robertson, and preceding him George Shaw, have worked closely with the original papers of the third Earl Grey held in Durham. The Grey Papers do not reveal any evidence of local Melbourne factors affecting Perry's appointment. See Robertson, *"Unsearchable Riches"*; Shaw, *Patriarch and Patriot*.

20. Cable, "Good Government," 68–69.

21. Howley to Grey, 12 March 1847, Grey Papers.

22. Whitington, *William Grant Broughton*. He is followed by Robin, *Charles Perry*. Goodman, *Church in Victoria*, 35, asserts that "several clergymen" declined the offer of Melbourne before Perry—but there is no documentary evidence of this.

23. Whitington, *William Grant Broughton*, 164.

two Irish evangelical deacons against the college of "Tractarian teaching and harbouring crypto-Romanism."[24] Broughton was intent on making a bishop out of Allwood, and for his part he was successful. Allwood was confirmed for Newcastle, and the Royal Letters Patent had been directed to be prepared when news of his own withdrawal reached London.[25]

The next name to come up was that of Bishop Francis Russell Nixon of Tasmania, an avowed Tractarian credited with establishing Tractarian theology and practice in Tasmania.[26] Prior to relocating to Van Diemen's Land from England, he had authored a huge volume entitled *Lectures, Historical, Doctrinal and Practical, on the Catechism of the Church of England*, which clearly identifies his Tractarian stance. Whitington cites a private letter from Broughton to his friend Edward Coleridge, in which he hints that a strong conflict between the bishop and the Governor of Tasmania might be a good reason for Nixon being transferred to Melbourne, but there is no firmer evidence that Nixon ever entered into consideration for Melbourne.[27]

What is clear is that power over the appointment of bishops to colonial sees was in the hands of the Crown, with the authority delegated to the Secretary of State for the Colonies. A change of government in 1846 meant

24. Cable, "The Diocese of Newcastle and Sydney." Cable notes that in Sydney it was the younger clergy who moved with the new innovations, whereas the older clergy such as Archdeacon William Cowper held a firm evangelical line. Broughton, in his view, neither promoted the move towards Tractarianism nor defended evangelical orthodoxy but grew increasingly uncomfortable as secessions to Rome mounted: one of the most significant being that of his protégé Robert Sconce. The two Irish evangelical deacons were Russell and Beamish, who were exiled to Melbourne, priested by Perry and went on to have illustrious ministry careers in Victoria. See below.

25. Allwood was evidently unconvinced that he should take up episcopal duties but allowed his patron Broughton to forward his name to London. The reasons for the delay in formalising his appointment to Newcastle were probably twofold: there were complications with regard to the precise legalities of episcopal government in the colonies, which Howley writes at length about to Grey; and Howley himself probably already knew that Allwood's final agreement to his appointment was not forthcoming. Word might have already been out because Grey nominates two names for Melbourne and Newcastle in December, which would be strange if Allwood was all but confirmed in June for Newcastle, as asserted by Howley. See Howley to Grey, 21 December 1846, Grey Papers; Howley to Grey, 23 December 1846, Grey Papers. Howley's final word on Allwood to Grey was that Allwood had "taken alarm at the responsibility attached to a Bishopric, and has declined the office." Whitington is incorrect in saying that Allwood declined Melbourne for health reasons; he had been appointed to Newcastle or Maitland.

26. Porter et al., *Colonial Tractarians*. See chapter 3 on the Diocese of Tasmania by Geoffrey Stephens.

27. Whitington, *William Grant Broughton*. Again followed by Robin, *Charles Perry*. Nixon's name does not appear anywhere in correspondence between Howley and Grey with regard to Melbourne.

a new colonial secretary, Henry George Grey, Viscount Howick and later the third Earl Grey. An expert on Grey's policies in the Australian colonies, John Ward, describes him as a forceful and impatient political pragmatist.[28] Significantly, Grey was a supporter of the evangelical cause: he had resigned an earlier post when Cabinet refused to support his push for the immediate abolition of slavery in the Empire, preferring instead a gradual process. Whether he himself held evangelical convictions of faith is more difficult to ascertain from the documentary record. However, the strength of his advocacy of evangelical candidates in the face of stiff opposition from powerful senior episcopal clerics in the archbishop of Canterbury and bishop of London, and the absence of any reasons for personal animosity towards them, makes this seem at least a strong possibility.

Prior to June 1846 the Colonial Secretary, by convention, acted without question on the advice of the archbishop of Canterbury in matters of appointment of colonial bishops. There is evidence that the archbishop in turn was assisted in finding names by the Secretary of the Society for the Propagation of the Gospel (SPG), Ernest Hawkins. Hawkins was also Honorary Secretary of the Colonial Bishoprics Committee and writes that in that capacity he was "asked to propose for the Archbishop's consideration names of such clergymen as I may consider well qualified for the new Colonial sees."[29] However, Grey was determined to promote evangelicals where he could.

The Grey Papers

The papers of Earl Grey were deposited in the University of Durham Archives by the family progressively from the mid-twentieth century. Prior to this they have remained in private hands and unexamined by historians. They include the correspondence between William Howley, archbishop of Canterbury, and Grey on the matter of the appointment of the four colonial bishops in 1847.

In September 1846, Howley wrote to Grey recommending the vicar of Broomfield, Henry Eley, for Melbourne. He asserted that Eley was a "entirely free from the extravagant notions which have led some the clergy into opposite extremes," meaning that he was neither strongly Tractarian nor evangelical.[30]

---

28. See ADB entry: "Grey, Henry George [Third Earl Grey] (1802–1894)."

29. Hawkins to R. Gray, 30 June 1847, in Gray, *Life of Robert Gray*, vol. 1, 100, cited in Robertson, *"Unsearchable Riches."*

30. Howley to Grey, 7 September 1846, Grey Papers.

This qualification was foremost in the minds of the main players in the process, who all mention this as a necessary trait. Reference to the idea appears no less than eight times in the correspondence, including an explicit statement by Grey to Howley of his understanding that it was their shared opinion that the adoption of "the opinions of an extreme party in the Church" would be a "disqualification for a Colonial Bishop."[31]

Grey, however, asserted his independence, made his own investigations, and wrote back to Howley within a week saying that he had found that Eley was unfit for the harshness of colonial duty. In a further and unexpected stroke of proactivity, he recommended a Mr. Hamilton for Melbourne.[32]

There was still no response from Howley in December, when Grey's wife Maria dined with the vicar of Battersea, Robert John Eden—chaplain to the Queen and soon to be bishop of Sodor and Man, and later Lord Auckland. Eden wrote to Grey a few days later mentioning that Maria had told him that he was "still anxious to find a bishop for Melbourne" and that she had "rather encouraged me to assist you in the search." Although not an evangelical himself, Eden proved to be Grey's main agent in gathering information about potential candidates. The letter reveals that he had already consulted his neighbor Henry Sykes Thornton, a London banker connected to the evangelical Thorntons of Clapham, the neighboring parish to Battersea. Thornton was friends with Henry Venn, the Secretary of the CMS, son of John, and grandson of Henry—leading evangelicals and chief Claphamites. Eden wrote to Grey with three names that Thornton, probably through his connection with Venn, had given him: Davis, Harding, and Perry, three decided evangelicals.[33]

Eden dutifully reported Thornton's opinion that all "would make good colonial bishops." They were each "earnest good men, of good sense, and with habits of business." The letter also carried a warning that although Thornton considered Davis the best of the three, as one of the secretaries of CMS he might be considered too evangelical by Howley and the SPG. Here is the first evidence that churchmanship was squarely on the table for political consideration. Perry was described "as being a very earnest man, with considerable practice in the management of men; & accustomed to hard work," but it was unknown if he would quit England for the Colonies. Interestingly, Eden adds at the end of his letter this assessment of the trio:

> They are if any thing more inclined to the low church party than to the high but very far from being men of extreme opinions.

31. Grey to Howley, 27 January 1847, Grey Papers.
32. Grey to Howley, 15 September 1846, Grey Papers.
33. Eden to Grey, 14 December 1849, Grey Papers.

This was clearly a qualification commending their nomination. Eden describes them as "low church," but Thornton and Venn would have seen them as clearly evangelical. Grey acted swiftly in writing to Howley that same week, complaining that it had been "a considerable time" since he had heard from him and commending Harding and Perry for Melbourne and Newcastle. He took Eden's advice leaving out the unacceptably evangelical Davis.[34] Howley's immediate response, within three days, indicates a degree of panic—especially since he had been sitting in silence on the name of Hamilton since early September when they were only negotiating for Melbourne. But now it was evident that Grey was seeking to influence not just Melbourne, but both appointments. It is clear that in mentioning Newcastle, Grey was not convinced that Allwood's appointment there was finalized, as indeed it wasn't. There was still an opportunity to appoint evangelicals to both Australian sees.[35]

Howley's letter of 21 December is long and verbose compared to Grey's terse correspondence. He attempts an explanation of the glacial pace of progress by way of recounting the particulars of Allwood's appointment, the largesse of Broughton in giving up so much of his stipend, the necessity of any nominee to be able to work with the bishop of Australia, and then finally, the all-important qualification: "not liable to objection from connections with any extreme party in the Church."

And then Howley plays his card, saying, "such men are to be found— but for different reasons—these to whom I have applied have declined the offer. Of the number is Mr. Hamilton . . . " Grey's own nominee had also declined, and hence the problem was not finding suitable men, but willing ones. It was a tactic designed to forestall Grey's initiative in bringing forward evangelical names by introducing the element of needing first to gain the nominees' agreement to go.

It would have been clear to Howley that the busy and energetic Colonial Secretary could not scrutinize each candidate's views and then obtain their agreement to go. He had to act through his agents, just as Howley did. But he was not a cleric or bishop with the connections and undivided focus on ecclesiastical politics. Grey is renowned for his workload and ethic in this period, and the matter of appointing bishops was but one of many tasks for the man administering all of the affairs of the colonies. Howley clearly played this to his advantage.

Howley wrote again two days later, saying that he had considered that Allwood was all but confirmed for Newcastle, except that now he had

---

34. Grey to Howley, 18 December 1846, Grey Papers.
35. Howley to Grey, 21 December 1846, Grey Papers.

heard from Broughton that Allwood had declined to be nominated. Further, Broughton had not suggested any other names to Howley. That seems to have been the extent of local influence on the nomination process. Howley also wrote the following:

> I have the satisfaction of stating that the results of my enquiries respecting Mr. Perry have so fully corresponded with the opinion which your Lordship has formed of him, that I shall have no difficulty in communicating with him on the subject of an Australian Bishopric—with respect to Mr. Harding who is I am told a very excellent Clergyman I must take a little more time.[36]

Perry had passed Howley's investigations and all that remained was for him to indicate his willingness to go. Perry the remote Cambridge academic was favored over Harding who had an impeccable evangelical heritage. Harding was an Oxford graduate and the rector of St. Andrew-by-the-Wardrobe and St. Anne's Blackfriars, whose line of prominent evangelical rectors went all the way back to William "Willy" Romaine. He was also linked with evangelical expansion through his role as Secretary of the Church Pastoral Aid Society and was increasingly seen as a leader among the growing group of evangelical London vicars. Compared to him, Perry was relatively innocuous. So, Perry's nomination was let through to the keeper, while Howley stalled for time over Harding.

From here, Harding's name disappeared from contention, evidently too evangelical for Howley to accept. Five years later, in more favorable times for evangelicals, Harding was appointed bishop of Bombay by the next archbishop of Canterbury, the evangelical John Bird Sumner.

As events unfolded, Eden secured a glowing written reference from Venn, Perry's compatriot at Cambridge, which he forwarded to Grey. Unaware of Howley's prior acquiescence to Perry's nomination, Eden wrote, saying, "I could also point out the way to make him acceptable to the Archbishop." He shrewdly anticipated that the issue of Perry's low churchmanship or evangelicalism might be problematic.[37] Venn's reference itself indicates that the Secretary of CMS understood the politics of the situation perfectly. He had secured Perry's willingness to go, and he offered his opinion that Perry's legal education and experience in dealing with "many perplexed and delicate questions & negotiations connected with . . . ecclesiastical arrangements" would be an important asset.

---

36. Grey to Howley, 18 December 1846, Howley to Grey, 23 December 1846, Grey Papers.

37. Venn to Eden, 24 December 1846, Grey Papers.

From the CMS perspective, Perry was a proven evangelist: "He set himself, even while Tutor of Trinity to evangelize the outlying suburbs of the University containing from 4000 to 6000 inhabitants." He was a leader, enabler, and hard worker: "peculiarly suited to take the lead and get others to work, and to be a laborious leader in the work himself." The founding vicar of St. Paul's Cambridge was just the sort of man to send to the colonies; just the sort of investment the CMS contribution to the Colonials Bishoprics Fund was intended for. Venn ends by commending the whole matter to "Divine Direction"—Robertson notes that this is the first time in the whole affair when mention of spiritual matters occurs.

The next name to come up was a Mr. John Ley, evidently a Howley nominee that Grey had Eden investigate. The report was that he was "a high churchman—while not altogether adopting the forms and every extreme view of Dr. Pusey"[38]; and that "Mr. Ley is a high churchman—but not one that commits extravagancies: and for the rest a good sort of man."[39] The letters were dated 29 and 30 December 1846. On 31 December Grey had had a face-to-face meeting with Howley, which he followed up the next day in writing:

> Since the conversation I have had with you about Mr. Ley I have come to the conclusion upon thinking over what was said by Your Grace in his favor that it will be better to consider it as settled that he and Mr. Perry should be recommended to Her Majesty for the two vacant Australian sees, and I will accordingly submit their names to the Queen . . . [40]

Grey knew that Ley was a high churchman, and it seems that it gave him pause in his meeting with Howley. However, on reflection, he saw that it was necessary to compromise and have Ley the high churchman with Perry the evangelical. Ley subsequently withdrew because of a bad report from his medical check-up.[41]

Howley then put forward the Reverend G. W. Huntingford, Fellow of New College Oxford whom he declared as "not attached to any party in holding extreme principles in the Church."[42] However, despite his earlier acceptance of Ley, Grey rejected Huntingford within a week, having found out from his sources that "he is very far from answering the description

---

38. Eden to Grey, 29 December 1846, Grey Papers.
39. Eden to Grey, 30 December 1846, Grey Papers.
40. Grey to Howley, 1 January 1847, Grey Papers.
41. Howley to Grey, 14 January 1847, Grey Papers.
42. Howley to Grey, 27 January 1847, Grey Papers.

of 'not attached to any party holding extreme opinions in the Church.'"[43] For Grey, there was a real difference between the high-church Ley and the unacceptably Tractarian Huntingford. Just as Howley had ditched Harding previously, Grey now struck out Huntingford.

Perry remained the only nominee to have passed both Grey and Howley, obtained a positive physician's report, and accepted his nomination. In that same letter of 2 February 1847 Grey was able to confirm that the Queen had approved Perry for Melbourne.[44]

In late January, Miss (later Baroness) Burdett-Coutts had agreed to endow Adelaide and Cape Town, and so two more bishops had to be found.[45] It had taken more than half a year to find one candidate to fill two sees; now they had to find four! Pressure was building on both Howley and Grey.

They seemed to have acted more expediently, as by mid-March the high churchman Augustus Short was confirmed for Adelaide, leaving Newcastle and Cape Town to be filled. On balance, at least one of those should have been an evangelical. The preceding correspondence indicates that this was the main point of negotiation Howley and Grey. The manner of William Tyrrell's appointment indicates that Eden either played falsely with Grey, or was himself misinformed, in advising that William Tyrrell "subscribes to the Church Missionary Society" and by association was an evangelical.[46] The first bishop of Newcastle was in fact a subscriber of the SPG and Tractarian, as his subsequent ministry abundantly demonstrated.

Grey was characteristically impatient and by this stage in a hurry to fill the posts. He evidently did not check the details of Eden's advice. He knew that the nominee for Cape Town, Robert Gray, was a high churchman, and if William Tyrrell subscribed to CMS then he was an evangelical, and so the balance would be kept. Hence, he swiftly approved both.[47] In his mind, he was appointing the evangelicals Perry and Tyrrell to balance out

---

43. Grey to Howley, 2 February 1847, Grey Papers.

44. Grey to Howley, 2 February 1847, Grey Papers.

45. Widely regarded as Anglo-Catholic by historians, it is interesting to note that in her will the Baroness expressly mentions the "Protestant Church of England."

46. Eden to Grey, 18 March 1847, Grey Papers. Eden had investigated both Gray and Tyrrell and found evidence that both were possibly connected to the Tractarians. On Tyrrell he wrote, "He comes from the neighbourhood of Dr. Moberly which makes one suspicious of him," Eden to Grey, 16 March 1847, Grey Papers. On Gray, he wrote, "the only blot that can be hid in him is that he voted forward in that from an Oxford context: he may therefore have strong tendencies to the Tractarians," Eden to Grey, 18 March 1847, Grey Papers. It seems that he was convinced that Gray was high church and that Tyrrell seemed neutral, except that a CMS subscription would certainly push him toward the evangelical side.

47. Grey to Howley, 22 March 1847, Grey Papers.

the Tractarians Short and Gray. In fact, in late March 1847, high churchmen came to take three of the four new bishoprics. Grey through his initiative and proactivity may have secured the first bishopric for the evangelicals, but Howley and a vital mis-assessment of Tyrell's churchmanship secured the other three positions for high-church Tractarians.

An Assessment

Grant and Robin's argument that Melbourne came to have the evangelical Perry because of the need to balance out the churchmanship of the other previous appointments has been unchallenged except by Robertson and has been remarkably persistent in Australian Anglican historiography.[48] However, the examination of the Grey correspondence shows that this prevailing narrative is flawed in at least three ways.

First, and most obviously, it is chronologically incorrect: Perry was appointed first, and not last. Second, the description of "the evangelical Perry" is potentially misleading because it implies that Perry was the preferred evangelical candidate "balancing out" the other episcopal appointments. Perry clearly was not the only, nor the strongest, evangelical candidate. That would have been Harding, or the even more strongly evangelical Davis, whose name was never put to Howley for that very reason. Politics is the art of compromise; neither party was able to get their preferred men at the time and compromise was necessary. It is evident that Grey, Howley, and Eden understood this and played their parts in the process of political negotiation.

The importance attached by both sides to excluding anyone of "extravagant notions" or "extreme views" is telling, for it indicates that a prime concern was for the maintenance of a kind of Anglican unity that avoided the extremes that had driven the nation to civil war not so many centuries before. However, in this negotiation, the extremity most commonly in view was towards Pusey and unacceptably high-church practices in the Protestant Church of England.

Third, and most significantly, the prevailing analysis is incomplete: the language of "the need to balance churchmanship" puts the issue too gently and generically. The correspondence shows that there was a power struggle between personalities and philosophies. Howley was determined to stymie evangelical appointments and put forward *only* high churchmen like Allwood, Ley, Huntingford, Gray, and Tyrrell. His early acquiescence to Perry seems to have been out of the shock of having a new and unexpectedly

---

48. It is followed, for example, in Breward, *Australian Churches*; Piggin, *Spirit of a Nation*.

proactive Colonial Secretary. But he subsequently failed to show any enthusiasm for Grey's other nominees, pushing hard for his own instead. The manner of Tyrrell's approval shows that misinformation played its part in the process. Howley's aim was not to achieve balance, but to achieve dominance—and in 1847, he was successful.

Grey, for his part, was forthright and persistent in seeking to promote evangelicals. He was unafraid to break with convention. Not only did he not rubber-stamp Canterbury's nominees, he was also proactive in putting forward evangelicals like Harding and Perry and actively responsive in rejecting candidates recommended by the archbishop. However, he had to be careful not to overstate the case for evangelicals, given that the Colonial Bishoprics Fund was endowed mainly with high-church money and administered by an almost completely high-church episcopate led by Howley and the very capable Blomfield, bishop of London. He saw the need to compromise, as seen in his acceptance of Ley and Gray—known high churchmen.

Curiously though, Grey failed to double-check his facts. He relied too heavily on Eden, who was not an evangelical, to do his homework for him. Even more curious is the lack of cooperation and direct correspondence between Grey and known evangelicals like Venn or Thornton. No correspondence relevant to this or subsequent rounds of appointments exists in the Grey Papers collection between Grey and Venn or Thornton. There are certainly no known letters between Grey and Harding or Hamilton.

At one level, it is easy to put this down to the Colonial Secretary's incredible workload and prodigious output of correspondence as evidenced by the Grey Papers collection. He simply did not have the time to scrutinize every piece of advice. However, on another level, it reveals something of the relatively low priority evangelicals placed on the strategic importance of episcopal appointments in the colonies. They were unable to achieve a balance of churchmanship in the round of four founding appointments made in 1847, and there is little evidence to show that they made a concerted effort to lobby Grey or encourage their candidates to accept nominations. Evangelicals, then as now, put their energies into parochial ministry (such as Perry did at Cambridge) or into the many voluntary societies (such as the CMS) that have usually proliferated in periods of evangelical strength. There may have been a failure to recognize how determinative episcopal leadership was, and is, in shaping the nature and character of a diocese. Or, more likely, this was recognized, but evangelical piety prevented leading men from seeking advancement for themselves.

Henry Venn's reference for Perry is especially telling. His focus was on Perry's suitability for the work, not on his acceptability. Perry was, to Venn, "just the man for such a situation," an evangelist, leader, hard worker, and skilled negotiator in delicate matters. In concluding his letter to Eden, he gives us a glimpse of evangelical piety of the time; he writes saying, "Leaving the matter in your hands under the divine direction."[49] Venn trusted Eden—who was not an evangelical—to promote Perry on his merits, under God.

The circumstances around the founding of the Diocese of Melbourne, which finally came to effect when Perry was consecrated and received the Royal Letters Patent, illustrate the intensity of the competition between parties within the Church of England. Contrary to the relatively genteel and civilized narrative put forward by Grant and Robin, the evidence points to a powerful contest between high and low churchmanship in the Church of England in the mid-nineteenth century. The Tractarian movement, energized by Keble's Assizes sermon in 1833, was increasing in power and influence. The effect of Newman's infamous Tract XC, published in 1840, was reverberating through the Church of England and steadily gaining adherents. That Perry himself understood the robust politics surrounding his own appointment is beyond doubt. Perry's early biographer, George Goodman, records that "the friend of Henry Venn never ceased to find satisfaction in being the nominee of Charles James Blomfield."[50]

The Evangelical Perry's Priorities in Ministry

Recruiting and Preaching Prior to Departing England

Perry's priorities while still in England awaiting his consecration and departure were to typify the kind of evangelical ministry and industry that he was later to be renowned for in Melbourne. Perry realized that he was going to a diocese roughly the size of all the British Isles with only three active clergy present. His top priority was to secure resources—"men and means"—for the work in the colonies. His parish ministry experience at Cambridge, initiating and then rapidly expanding the work of St. Paul's, had taught him that these were crucial to the successful discharge of his pastoral responsibilities and evangelistic mission.

On the Sunday after his consecration, Perry preached a commencement sermon at his *alma mater*, Cambridge. The university had conferred on him the degree of Doctor of Divinity on the occasion of his appointment. Perry's sermon was later published under the title, *The Christian's Light Shining to God's Glory*. It was accompanied by an appeal to help provide clergy for the "spiritually destitute colonists" of Melbourne, not to mention some 4000

---

49. Venn to Eden, 24 December 1847, Grey Papers.
50. Goodman, *Church in Victoria*, 475.

"aboriginal inhabitants" of whom "no account had been taken." Perry hoped for "the blessing of God to be enlarged abundantly so as to preach the Gospel of Christ to the heathen also." The appeal illustrates Perry's twin priorities of pastoral care to the white settlers and evangelism of the nations found at the ends of the earth. He hoped to raise £6000, or enough to get nine men to the colony with him and keep them there for up to five years.[51]

By mid-September he wrote to the SPG, confident in having secured the services of seven or eight men, but only five eventually sailed with him on the *Stag*: Macartney, Hales, Newham, Bean, and Tanner.[52] Perry used the outward journey of three-and-a-half months to get to know the men and their families, leading them in daily readings of the Greek New Testament and in services and prayers. They entered Port Philip safely on 22 January 1848, landing at Melbourne on 24 January.

The Office and Duty of a Minister of the Gospel

Perry had ample time on the journey to work out his manifesto for ministry. This should not be seen as stemming from new insights he acquired post-consecration, but rather as the methods and priorities already formed through his previous and substantial ministry experience. Perry's industrious leadership, business acumen, and organizational abilities were the very qualities that had Venn commended so highly to Eden. Upon arrival, Perry used the occasion of his first sermon to deliver a charge on *The Office and Duty of a Minister of the Gospel*. It was delivered in St. James' Church on 28 January 1848. At the request of the members of his church, the sermon was published and distributed with their welcome address and Perry's response.[53]

The Office and Duty of a Minister of the Gospel set out Perry's program and priorities for ministry in the Diocese of Melbourne. It resounds with evangelical fervor, biblical clarity, and humble devotion. Although based, as sermons typically were in that time, on just one verse, the entire sermon is steeped in Scripture. The one verse was 2 Corinthians 5:20: "Now then we are ambassadors for Christ, as though God did beseech you by us; we pray you in Christ's stead, be ye reconciled to God." But there are no less than twenty different Scriptures cited from both Old and New Testaments and numerous other allusions besides. Phrases from the *Book of Common Prayer* (BCP) are woven in throughout.

---

51. Robin, *Charles Perry*, 36.

52. Robin, *Charles Perry*, 37, cites a letter from Perry to Hawkins dated 13 September 1847, SPG Letter Book, vol 1, 7.

53. Perry, *Office and Duty*.

Perry makes two requests for prayer close to the beginning of the sermon:

> Pray for us, and pray for yourselves and fellow-countrymen in this colony, that the word of the Lord may have free course and be glorified.
>
> ... pray for the success of our labours, that ... we may so prepare and make ready the way of the Lord Jesus, by turning the hearts of the disobedient to the wisdom of the just; that, at his second coming to judge the world, we may be found an acceptable people in his sight.[54]

These reflect his emphasis on an evangelical doctrine of Scripture, on the necessity of personal conversion, and on the reality of the judgment to come. Each of these evangelical tenets framed the sermon and his ministry manifesto.

For Perry the office of a minister of the gospel was clearly delineated in his chosen text:

> They are ambassadors for Christ. They are commissioned by Christ, as His representatives, to deliver the message, with which He has entrusted them, to the people, to whom He sends them.[55]

The message was nothing other than the "declaration of God's will" concerning those people and the urgent need for the people to act on that message so proclaimed to them. Informed by the Scriptures and his views of humanity as sinful and God as fundamentally gracious and merciful, Perry emphasized the ministry of the "proclamation of peace" and "reconciliation" between humans and God. There was no room for cheap forgiveness or latitudinarian humanism in Perry's theology. He held strongly to, and was direct in proclaiming, the evangelical doctrine of penal substitution in his first sermon to the elites gathered in Melbourne's pro-cathedral church of St. James.

Perry went on to emphasize the two chief means of discharging the minister's duty: public preaching and private instruction of the Word of God. For Perry the content of these ministries of the Word was Christ: "if we preach not Christ, and him crucified, it will avail nothing to the salvation of our hearers." He was quick to counter potential criticism by adding that the two sacraments were "a most important and pleasing part of a minister's duty" but nevertheless subordinate to preaching and teaching the Scriptures.

---

54. Perry, *Office and Duty*, 6.
55. Perry, *Office and Duty*, 7.

Further, Perry concluded that it was his, and his incoming fellow ministers', "assured conviction" that if preaching and private teaching were carried out faithfully and diligently, the people could hope that "the Lord will own, and bless us in our work. On the contrary, if we neglect or pervert [public preaching of the Word and private ministerial teaching], we cannot expect His blessing."[56] For the evangelical Perry, all blessing and success in ministry was linked to the preaching and teaching of the Scriptures.

The sermon reveals Perry's humble desire to serve his Lord Jesus Christ, his dependence on the grace of God, his clear theology of the atoning death of Christ, his passion for evangelism and the conversion of souls for Christ, the strategic importance he placed on preaching and teaching in ministry, and his commitment throughout to prayer and to his fellow laborers in the Lord. This was the brand of principled and passionate evangelicalism that Melbourne's first bishop brought to, and sought to establish in, his new diocese.

Passage on "Not Knowing Any Parties in the Church"

Published as an appendix to his sermon is a formal address from the townspeople to their new bishop, welcoming Perry and expressing their gratefulness for his arrival and looking forward to his ministry of diffusing peace, order, and goodwill in the diocese. Perry's response was also included. It yields insight into the new bishop's strength of theological conviction, for he took the opportunity to declare again that there would be no true peace without reconciliation with God; no reconciliation without repentance and faith towards the Lord Jesus Christ; no happiness without holiness; no holiness without the indwelling of the Holy Spirit given through the Lord. He further stated: "My desire is to contend for the faith, which was once committed to the Saints . . ."[57]

Some writers have quoted the first part of the following portion of his reply as evidence that Perry was a decided nonpartisan evangelical. But the passage, when cited in full, reveals that Perry was nonpartisan only to the extent that unity in the gospel of Christ and the Word of God—as he, the evangelical, understood them—was not compromised:

> When I entered upon my late parochial charge in England, I determined to know no party, and to interfere in no political matters; but to fulfil towards all my people alike the office of a

---

56. Perry, *Office and Duty*, 18.
57. Perry, *Office and Duty*, Ibid., 21.

Minister of Christ in simplicity and faithfulness. The experience of five years confirmed me in the wisdom of this determination; and I trust, that all of you, gentlemen, will approve of my purpose to adopt the same rule of conduct here. I do not know anything of the parties, which may exist in this City and Diocese; I do not know, what seeds of disunion and discord may have been sown amongst you; nor what amount of bitter fruit they may have produced; and, God helping me, I shall endeavour to know as little of them as possible. I wish to recognise no distinction of persons, *except that which the Word of God requires of me*; and I shall shun no man's society, *except he be known to be profane or immoral, or teach doctrines, which I believe to be subversive of the Gospel of Christ*. This is my purpose; and I pray God, that I may have grace and strength to act it out; and that I may see the same beneficial results from it, which I was permitted to see in England.[58]

This principled nonpartisanship was further enumerated two years later in the inaugural edition of the *Church of England Messenger*, the official diocesan paper started by Perry with himself as editor. He wrote:

Its object will simply be to promote true religion and piety among the inhabitants of this province . . . The principles upon which it is wished to carry on the Church of England Messenger, are those of Christian charity, but not of latitudinarian indifference. The Conductors desire never to forget, that, as Christians, they are fellow members with all that belong to the spiritual body of the Lord Jesus. With all such, therefore, they would "to keep the unity of the spirit in the bond of peace." They would not exaggerate minor difference, nor anathematise those, who do not in all particulars agree with themselves. But they desire also to remember, that, as clergymen of the Church of England, they are bound to set forth, and to defend, her peculiar doctrines and constitution. They cannot regard the differences, which exist between the various Protestant Denominations, as unimportant, although they are thankful to be able to regard them as of subordinate importance. While therefore, they hope always to think and to write in the spirit of love; they purpose, if the Lord shall enable them, to bring distinctly into view, each of the characteristic principles of their own Church, and to show the Scriptural evidence on which it is grounded.[59]

---

58. Perry, *Office and Duty*, 22. Emphasis added.
59. COEM, January 1850, 1–2.

In a further passage, Perry outlined the editorial team's view of the Roman Catholic church:

> They regard the latter (the Church of Rome) as an apostate and idolatrous Church. They believe her to be the subject of the prophetical denunciations of Daniel, St. Paul, and St. John. They believe, that every true Christian must come out of her, if he would not partake of her sins, and so receive of her plagues. But they would not therefore the less, in their writings as well as in all their conduct, show due courtesy and kindness to her members. On the contrary, they would cherish, and in every way evince, the most tender compassion towards those, who are the victims of this, which they regard as a Satanic delusion.[60]

The passage, in hindsight, goes some way to explaining his treatment of the Catholic priest, Patrick Geoghegan, who paid him a courtesy call at the St. James' vicarage upon Perry's arrival in Melbourne. The incident has been used to characterize Perry as a stern, uncompromising evangelical, but this is an unfair reading, for William Broughton in Sydney similarly refused to attend a government reception in protest against the recognition of the Roman Catholic Bishop, John Bede Polding.[61] Such was the strength of sectarian feeling in the colonies.

Perry was simply not in when Geoghegan called by, and subsequently wrote in response to his calling card declining any private social intercourse between them as it would, in his view, "occasion . . . pain rather than pleasure" because of their theological differences. The press was filled with letters denouncing Perry's prejudice, and the correspondence between the two was published in full by the *Argus*.[62] Perry explains that he did not want to hurt feelings but could not, as a matter of principle, do Geoghegan the discourtesy of not replying frankly. Perry's courteous but principled response is captured in this quote:

> Nothing but a sense of obligation, which is laid upon me to contend earnestly for the faith once delivered to the saints will, I trust, ever induce me to say, write or do anything which may give you pain.[63]

For the evangelical bishop, his public rejection of the Roman Catholic priest was based on his higher obligation to publicly defend the gospel faith as

60. COEM, January 1850, 3–4.
61. Whitington, *William Grant Broughton*, 192–96.
62. 15 February 1848. See also Robin, *Charles Perry*, 46–47.
63. Cited in Robin, *Charles Perry*, 46–47.

he understood it. However, Perry was not averse to working with Geoghegan or other Catholics in a broader context that did not imply his approval—tacit or otherwise—of other faith systems. For example, the Melbourne Committee of the Caroline Chisholm's Family Colonization Loan Society was set up in 1852, with Perry as president and Geoghegan as a member. Caroline Chisholm, herself a Roman Catholic, had been castigated by the Presbyterian John Dunmore Lang for allegedly spreading Catholic teaching in the colony through her social work, but Perry's willingness to be involved is evidence of his breadth of sympathies and spirit of cooperation.[64]

Charles Perry and His Early Clergy

Thomson, Wilson, and Collins

At the time of Perry's arrival, the Diocese of Melbourne covered the entire colony of Victoria—equivalent to the present state of Victoria. There were three "parishes," if the wide areas of responsibility that fell to the three clergymen could be described as such. Melbourne, at the time, stretched all the way to Albury and through to Gippsland—wherever there were known settlers. Geelong covered an indeterminate area from Geelong out to the northwest towards Ballarat. Portland covered the coastal townships up to Warrnambool and the interior settlements up to Hamilton. The three clergy at each of these centers were Adam Thomson in Melbourne, Ebenezer Collins in Geelong, and James Wilson in Portland. Despite the prevalence of evangelicals among the early colonial chaplains, none of these three was in fact evangelical. This did not stop Perry from exercising oversight to encourage them towards more evangelical priorities in ministry.

Subsequent to his arrival, Perry had many occasions to attend services at St. James' Melbourne and hear Thomson's preaching. He had cause to write to Thomson with suggestions on how to better prepare his sermons, including advice that he keep his "particular subject in view throughout" and to express himself "with simplicity and clearness, avoiding useless repetitions." Perry noted the "thin attendance" at St. James' and the fact that at the time of his writing attendances had fallen off again. He declared:

> I have made the above remarks upon the arrangement and composition of your sermons, because I believe that the public preaching of the Gospel is the most important part of

---

64. Kiddle, *Caroline Chisholm*, 179. The committee met once a month through 1852; assuming their attendance, Perry and Geoghegan would have been working quite closely together.

a minister's duty; and because I thought that the last sermon that I heard you preach at St. James' might have been much improved, in all the points which I have noticed, by a careful revision of the whole.[65]

Perry was forthright in his constructive criticism. However, he was also as encouraging as possible and communicated a sense of his understanding the difficulties and challenges of colonial ministry. Nevertheless, Thomson resigned in 1850 to take up a smaller parish in Tasmania.

Preaching the gospel was not the only priority for Perry. He was just as concerned about the quality of pastoral oversight provided by his clergy. Hence, Perry made this assessment of Collins in Geelong:

> Here, as at Melbourne, I found our Church in a very low condition. The Rev. Ebenezer Collins is quite incompetent to fulfill, without assistance, the duties of his arduous and responsible position. His health and energy seem to have been much impaired by a residence in the West Indies, and at Sierra Leone; so that, although his charge is not so onerous as that of Mr. Thomson in Melbourne, he is not more able to exercise an efficient pastoral oversight of his flock.[66]

Collins proved completely unsuitable and a source of great conflict for Perry and Archdeacon Macartney. Matters deteriorated to the extent that Perry wrote to him offering to pay for his passage home to England.[67] Collins eventually departed the diocese in 1852, leaving a legacy of friction in his parish.[68]

Wilson's ministry in Portland was hardly more successful. Attendances were poor with hardly any communicants and no confirmations. There were no Sunday or day schools. In addition to this, Wilson had amassed a personal debt of some £800, which Perry took on himself to repay. Wilson remained at Portland for over two decades, despite repeated attempts by his vestry to have him removed. Perry seems to have been reluctant to eject him, possibly because he had nowhere else to go and Perry would have felt duty bound to care for him. The vestry finally succeeded by refusing to pay Wilson until Perry accepted his resignation. At any rate, Wilson's ministry was nondescript and quickly overshadowed

---

65. Goodman, *Church in Victoria*, 62.
66. Goodman, *Church in Victoria*, 63.
67. Perry to Collins, 25 January 1850, Bishop's Letter Book No. 1, 15.
68. Robin, *Charles Perry*, 49.

by two energetic evangelical Irishmen, Peter Teulon Beamish and Francis Thomas Cusack Russell, who arrived in 1850.

The fate of the three clergymen who predated Perry in Melbourne indicates how difficult the conditions were in the colonies and the stress placed on Perry to secure able and willing evangelical clergy for his diocese.

Macartney, Hales, Newham, Bean, and Tanner

Perry prioritized the recruitment of like-minded and able evangelicals to bring with him to Melbourne. Their ministry and fate after landing in Melbourne is instructive. Of the group, the oldest and most experienced was to become Perry's "beloved brother" and long term "fellow-labourer in the Lord"[69]—Hussey Burgh Macartney.[70]

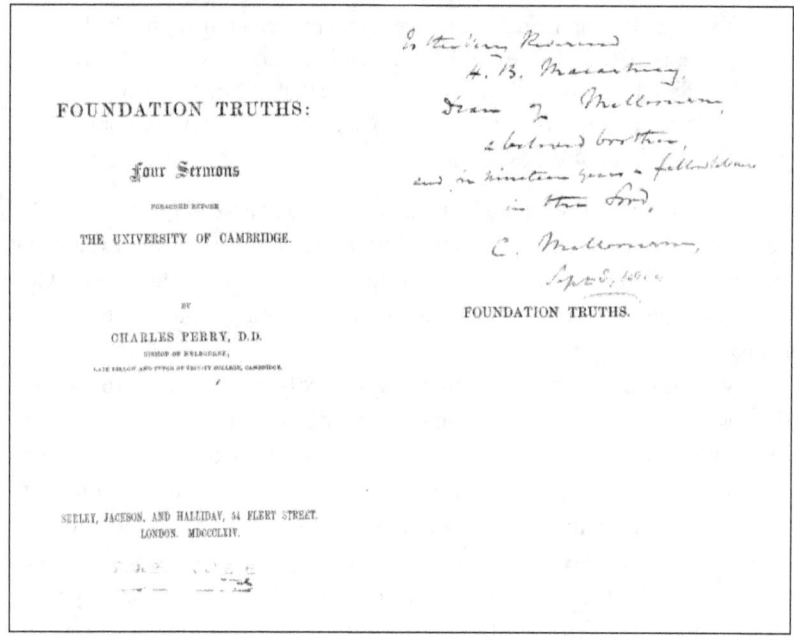

Inscription from Charles Perry to H. B. Macartney

69. From the inscription in Macartney's volume of Perry's *Foundation Truths*. This volume is in the Ridley Archives.

70. See ADB and ADEB entries for "Macartney, Hussey Burgh." Macartney's unpublished memoirs, authored between 1889 and 1890, are held in the Melbourne Diocesan Archives (*Memoirs*). Several volumes of his and his wife Jane's diaries are held by the Royal Historical Society of Victoria.

Macartney was born in Dublin in 1799, studied at Trinity College, and was ordained priest in 1823. He was almost fifty when he arrived with his family in Melbourne, where he was to serve as a vicar, first archdeacon and first dean of Melbourne, and on three occasions vicar-general in charge of the diocese in the absence of the bishop. He was, without doubt, Perry's right-hand man and coworker in expanding the gospel mission throughout the state. Churches were being rapidly planted, and ministers had to be found, appointed, and managed. Macartney was an able and hardworking leader and administrator, fearless in preaching the gospel and defending it against opponents. He was a staunch and vocal defender of the authority of Scripture and the Bible as God's word against the onslaught of "new" or "higher" criticism. And he was a missionary at heart: at the age of ninety-two he chaired the inaugural meeting of the Victorian CMA, declaring proudly that he was born in the same year that the English CMS was founded, 1799. Goodman, a contemporary observer, wrote of him, "his knowledge of the Bible is accurate and complete."[71]

He had held the living at Creagh, County Cork, but the combination of a one-third reduction of income from the living and having eight children to feed, exacerbated by his poor health, led him to seek the relatively warmer climate of the south, at Kilcock in County Kildare. However, the income situation did not improve there. Macartney was related to prominent Irish emigrants to Melbourne, men who were a significant example of the kind of prosperity and status attainable in the colonies: William Foster Stawell, John Fitzgerald Leslie Foster, and Charles James Griffiths. It was Griffiths, later appointed the first chancellor of the diocese by Perry, who encouraged Macartney to emigrate. While as yet unknown to each other, Macartney asked for an interview with Perry and was accepted for colonial service. The reason of poor health for migrating south was ironic because he ended up serving three bishops of Melbourne, was vicar-general on no less than three occasions, and lived to ninety-four, dying in office as very much *the* elder statesman of the diocese, the widely respected and beloved Dean Macartney. His son, the Reverend H. B. Macartney Jr., was himself a leader of evangelicals in Melbourne, heavily involved in supporting world missions and a founding member of the CMS in Australia.

Daniel Newham had been Perry's curate at St. Paul's and therefore well known to him. He had engaged in business pursuits before training at Cambridge and being ordained as Perry's curate. They had then participated together in the energetic start-up work of that large parish, where Newham's business and organizational skills were put to good use planting

---

71. Goodman, *Church in Victoria*, 39.

churches, building at least two new buildings, starting Sunday Schools, a lending library, a District Visiting Society, and a Young Men's Society. These skills would be vital in the new diocese where the same start-up work would be required, only on a much larger scale with even fewer resources. Perry persuaded Newham to follow him to Melbourne to participate in the great work, which Newham launched into with gusto, helping to start four schools across the state within as many years.[72]

Newham's untimely early death in 1851 while vicar of St. Peter's Melbourne was a great loss to the evangelical cause—not least because of the way his successor was to eventually take that leading city parish away from its evangelical heritage. Perry's sermon at his funeral was printed in full in the *Church of England Messenger* and also published separately.[73] The sermon expressed clearly the sense of a great loss of both a friend and leader, but its overwhelming purpose was to commend Newham's firm evangelical faith and ministry. Perry's concluding exhortation was to remember Newham and to follow his example of faith in Christ alone.

Of the remaining men who came out on the *Stag*, Willoughby Bean distinguished himself by serving faithfully across the diocese, notably in the harsh conditions in Gippsland, for twelve years, before returning to Melbourne where he died in 1877, still affectionately known as "Parson Bean." Writing in the *Messenger* in 1851, Perry commended Bean's ministry while saying that the work in Gippsland really demanded four centers of ministry—and by implication, four men. Less enduring was Edward Tanner, who served for five years before moving to Queensland. Francis Hales proved to be a difficult character, unable to bear the harsh conditions on the colony, clashing with his lay leaders, and publishing a protest against Perry and Macartney before leaving for Tasmania.[74] The difficult conditions in the colonies were only too well known in England. Perry himself was subject to a medical examination before his appointment was finalized—and indeed, the Grey correspondence reveals that a number of candidates for colonial bishoprics failed at that hurdle. Perry wrote in rather understated and pointed language in the very first edition of the *Messenger* in 1850 on the difficulties, especially in the bush:

> There is likely to be more difficulty in procuring suitable clergymen; for a minister of a Bush Parish must unite great energy,

---

72. Robin, *Charles Perry*, 116, refers to a report of the Victorian Legislative Council noting these schools at Belfast, Kilmore, Geelong, and Barrabool Hills.

73. COEM, August 1859, 85, also contains a parish history which recounts in detail Newham's contribution.

74. Hales, *Tell it to the Church*. Robin, *Charles Perry*, 150.

and power of enduring fatigue, with much Christian wisdom and experience.[75]

Handfield

A subsequent vicar of the important parish of St. Peter's was also on the *Stag*. Henry Hewett Paulett Handfield was born in Dublin and orphaned before he was eleven. He was subsequently put in the care of his grandfather and later, through a Trinity College connection, came under Perry's guardianship. He was nineteen years of age when he came out with the childless Perrys to Melbourne. He was an assistant master at the Diocesan Grammar School for three years while preparing for ordination under Perry's supervision. Perry did not mention Handfield in his letter to the SPG about the men he had recruited, probably because he regarded him as part of his own family, and any future in ministry may at that time still have been uncertain.

The current and predominant understanding of Handfield's ministry is that he developed into a thoroughgoing Tractarian and established St. Peter's character as the leading high-church parish of the diocese. However, the *Victorian Churchman*, an evangelical newspaper distributed throughout Victoria between 1890 and 1913, carried Handfield's obituary in 1900 and gave this intriguing assessment:[76]

> On August 8, there passed away one of the venerable links of the past with the present of our Victorian Church life. Canon H. H. P. Handfield, after a ministry of nearly fifty years as incumbent of St. Peter's Church, Eastern Hill, went to his rest and reward.
>
> . . . many of the clergy will remember the courteous and brotherly treatment received by them at their ordination in old St. Peter's, ere St. Paul's Cathedral was consecrated. Those who knew him best knew him as a lovable, cultured English gentleman, always ready to find points of contact rather than points of difference with those who differed from him. In his courteous humble deference to other men's cherished convictions, he was an example for the younger men who hold neo-Anglican views, and whose supercilious cocksureness and thinly veiled contempt does so much to create and embitter party feeling.
>
> For many years Canon Handfield's ministry was an earnest evangelical force in Melbourne, and there are not a few who look back with regret to those days as the best days of St. Peter's.

75. COEM, January 1850, 43.
76. VC, 24 August 1900, 288.

> Of late the character of the church has been transformed, but it is to be borne in mind that the many modern innovations which St. Peter's of today are due rather to the activity of curates than the initiative of its deceased incumbent. Old-fashioned High Churchmen regard such playthings as the Stations of the Cross, Sacramental Confession, Children's Eucharists, etc., as alien to the true spirit of English Christianity. They know too well that they are part of the machinery of the Roman propaganda . . . Canon Handfield was an English Churchman, and his sympathies were never fully given to the sensuous ritualism which has crept into St. Peter's.

Rather than describing him as a thoroughgoing Tractarian leading the charge towards ritualism, the evangelicals who produced the *Churchman* regarded Handfield as having begun as an earnest evangelical but certainly having moved towards high churchmanship. In 1860 for example, collections were being taken at St. Peter's Eastern Hill on the third Sunday in Advent for the evangelical CMS of Victoria.[77] Handfield spoke the introductory words, the Reverend R. B. Dickinson of Emerald Hill, Honorary Secretary of the Society, preached in the morning, and another noted evangelical, the Reverend S. L. Chase of St. Paul's, preached in evening. There was a further Wednesday meeting, thinly attended, at which Dickinson spoke of the need to preach the gospel to Chinese immigrants in Victoria.[78] Forty years later, St. Peter's was a very different place that would not have had that connection with evangelicals and the CMA. Yet, the *Churchman* regarded Handfield as still faithful to the English Church of the Reformation. His failure was in not restraining his more radical young curates, whom the editors of the *Churchman* had obvious disdain for as seen in the quote above.

The fate of these shipmates is instructive. Of the six men who came out with Perry, only three lasted more than a few years in Melbourne. Of those three, Handfield moved away from clear-cut evangelicalism, leaving just Bean and Macartney as Perry's long-term fellow-workers in the evangelical cause. It was a continuing challenge to secure the right men for the work, and to secure the funding for them. Perry found himself walking the tightrope between appointing the right men with his preferred theological

77. In 1860 this had no official connection to the evangelical CMS founded in 1799—other than the obvious imitation of the name. The CMS of Victoria was formed by mission-minded evangelicals in Victoria in 1854 and raised funds for the support of missionaries. It existed in parallel with the Victorian Auxiliary of the English CMS until they merged (also with the Church of England Zenana Mission Society and the Macartney Missionary Fund) in 1892 to form the Church Missionary Association of Victoria (CMA). See Cole, *History of the Church Missionary Society of Australia*, 13.

78. *Church Record*, January 1860.

and ministry perspective—that is, evangelicals—and finding enough men who were simply willing to come and able to endure the conditions.

Conclusion

The founding of the Diocese of Melbourne took place in the pioneering colonial context of the nineteenth century District of Port Philip. Evangelicalism was present and encouraged in the colony through the presence of civic leaders like Lonsdale and La Trobe, and ministers like Orton, but there was no concerted evangelical church ministry to or for the whole colony. Despite the prevailing narrative of how Melbourne got the evangelical Charles Perry as its first bishop, the evidence shows that, besides the proactive stance taken by Earl Grey, there was no deliberate or sustained political approach by evangelicals either in Melbourne or England to secure an evangelical bishop. Thus, the process of Perry's appointment and conduct of the various parties exemplified the tension between high churchmen and evangelicals in this period.

Once appointed, Perry's clear evangelical priorities were evident both in England and upon arrival in Melbourne. His first priority was to secure men and means for the diocese, to build the church and society in Melbourne. Securing an evangelical character for the diocese was a more secondary concern, for Perry was determined to be a bishop for his whole diocese and not partisan to the extent that theological orthodoxy was not compromised. He was first a loyal churchman, albeit a convinced evangelical one.

However, Perry's principled evangelicalism, especially his deeply held views on ministry method and aims and recruitment of many able evangelicals, meant that a strong core of evangelical parishes and men were built up in the diocese from the outset. This chapter shows that Perry made a vital contribution as a solidly evangelical bishop in the critical foundation period of the Diocese of Melbourne.

4

Evangelical Energy, 1847–1875

Unless the LORD builds the house, those who build it labor in vain.
Unless the LORD guards the city, the guard keeps watch in vain.

PSALM 127:1

Introduction

THE EARLY PART OF 1847 to 1875 was marked by evangelical energy in the establishment of the diocese, its parishes and agencies. Evangelicals were ably led by Bishop Perry and a host of clergy and laity that he encouraged in ministry and effort. From just three clergy and a few buildings, the diocese grew largely as a result of evangelical efforts and resources to two separate dioceses, with some 200 buildings used for divine worship and nearly 150 clergymen. Naturally the incredible economic and population growth following the gold rush years of the 1850s was critical for such progress.

Through this period, Melbourne remained predominantly low church with a strong evangelical foundation. However, as the quarter-century progressed, two significant pressures came to bear on evangelicalism, one external the other internal: externally, the increasing influence in wider society of scientific method and the attendant skepticism towards received notions of biblical authority and reliability; and internally, the rise of the Tractarian movement within the church.

With Bishop Perry at the helm, a firmly evangelical bishop was in place, and evangelicals were brought into the diocese and appointed to positions of seniority. Evangelicals within the diocese and across denominations in Melbourne drew strength, confidence, and inspiration from Perry's leadership, and so distinctly evangelical—as opposed to simply low-church—Anglican parishes and interdenominational societies began to flourish. These two vital contributors increased in strength throughout Perry's episcopate, and there was increasing confidence about the evangelical movement in Melbourne.

This chapter describes Perry's struggle to establish parishes and provide for parochial needs. It demonstrates that the early leading evangelical parishes of Richmond, Prahran, and Caulfield were established by energetic evangelical activism on the part of both laity and clergy. The chapter also provides evidence of evangelical societies' role as outlets for lay energy and enthusiasm, as highlighted by the history of the founding of the British Foreign and Bible Society and missionary societies, which reflected evangelicals' biblicism and conversionism—two key aspects of early evangelical identity in the diocese.

The chapter then demonstrates the vital contribution made by Perry's leadership in two areas, theology, and administration. In particular, it is argued that his philosophy with regard to the style of ministry leadership he expected in his clergy, and his determination, as far as possible, to appoint firmly evangelical men to ministry in Melbourne, were extremely significant. In the matter of appointments, Perry perfectly illustrated the vital contribution of a determinedly evangelical diocesan bishop.

Finally, the vital contribution of a firmly evangelical college—or lack thereof—is shown for the period 1847 to 1874. Melbourne lacked a theological school, and despite local pressure to establish one, Perry preferred and supported the evangelical Moore College in Sydney.

Building Parishes and Communities

Perry struggled to find able clergy who were suitably evangelical and who could endure the harsh colonial conditions in Victoria. At the time of the diocese's foundation in 1847 there were three ministers, officially chaplains, at Melbourne, Geelong, and Portland. These three centers of ministry were akin to parishes; between them, they provided for the pastoral ministries of the entire colony of Port Philip. Maps of this period show settlements at Melbourne, along the west coast from Geelong to Portland, and in remote farm locations throughout Victoria.[1] There were few roads to the interior, and the entire population numbered around 10,000.

None of the three clergymen present before Perry were known evangelicals; prior to Perry's arrival, Anglican church services in Melbourne were characteristically low church rather than evangelical. There were, however, strongly evangelical laymen, not least the Superintendent of the Colony Charles Joseph La Trobe, who exercised a powerful influence on local congregations and volunteer societies. Perry's influence and the evangelical clergy he brought with him on the *Stag* soon moved the ministry in most parishes in a firmly evangelical direction.

There were a few buildings at Perry's arrival in 1848, including St. James' Melbourne (1839), a stone building in Brighton (1839), Christ Church Geelong (1843) and St. Peter's Melbourne (1846). Services were being read by committed evangelical laity like Joseph Pickering in Doncaster, who had been preceded in the foundation years of the settlement by other evangelical (or at least certainly devout) laymen connected with the city parish: William Lonsdale, James Smith (later the Manager of the Savings Bank), and George Langhorne (Superintendent of the Aboriginal Mission Station on the banks of the Yarra at what is now the Botanic Gardens).

The city of Melbourne itself had been divided between St. James' to the west and St. Peter's to the east. Perry's first sermon was preached at the former, where he was formally enthroned and the parish church building declared a pro-cathedral. His Royal Letters Patent were read out on the front steps of the latter. By 1850 these buildings were joined by St. Paul's Swanston Street and six other buildings in the suburbs, including New Town (Fitzroy), Collingwood, Richmond and Heidelberg. Each of these was led by evangelical clergy recruited by the bishop.

The pace of church growth was rapid, but even so struggled to keep pace with the population—especially after the discovery of gold in 1851. The diocese grew to 373 parishes in the first fifty years—excluding those parishes that formed the Diocese of Ballarat in 1875. Virtually all were low church in worship style, with most evangelical in theological orientation.

Much of the early growth in parish ministries was driven by laity. Laypeople were keen on securing religious services, a resident clergyman, and schools for the growing numbers of children. Melbourne's pioneer church of St. James' had started in 1837 as a result of demand from the settlers for a place of worship and education. Christ Church in Geelong (1843) and St. Peter's (1846) on the hill on the east side of Melbourne were similarly begun

---

1. See, for example, the remarkable contemporary map attached to the back inside cover of Goodman, *Church in Victoria*.

by laity keen on securing a church building and school facilities. Perry recognized the importance of the city parish of St. Peter's, assigning his trusted former curate, Daniel Newham, to serve there.

Newham followed the church and school planting model that had worked successfully for him and Perry in Cambridge. Newham's premature death meant that Perry's vision and perseverance have been credited with the founding of Melbourne Grammar. Classes had in fact commenced at St. Peter's in 1849 under Newham. A subsequent colonial land grant south of the river in 1858 meant that the school could move to larger premises and expand.[2] Newham was also remembered for his role in leading the process of planting St. Stephen's Richmond, and the schoolroom at St. Mark's Collingwood, and his active part in the founding of the city's Benevolent Asylum.[3] He and other leading evangelicals were also active in the Mechanics Institute, which functioned as a venue for public lectures and discussion of topics of importance to building Melbourne's sense of community and strengthening its social fabric. Evangelical activism in and through parish life meant not just spiritual services, but attention to education and practical social helps.

Women were especially active in the latter, with Charles's wife, Frances Perry, remembered for her role in founding the Lying-in Hospital for Poor Women in 1856, subsequently known as the Royal Women's Hospital. The hospital was the first of its kind in Australia, focused on underprivileged women, often pregnant without a husband or support. She was president of the hospital for twenty years, until the Perrys' departure from Melbourne. In 1970 a wing of the Royal Women's Hospital was named in her honor.[4]

St. James' first building was a modest wooden structure capable of housing about a hundred. It doubled as a schoolhouse, so church and school were combined from the start. John Batman was one of the first subscribers, putting in a generous £50. However, it was, in the words of a contemporary description, "A mere wooden shell, and incapable of keeping out the cold."[5] The building stood on the corner of William and Little Collins Street, and by January 1838 discussion arose of the need for a more permanent structure. Broughton visited that Easter and appointed Grylls as the first resident clergyman. He arrived in October 1838. Meanwhile, lay leaders had begun the subscription fund, and building works started

2. Bate and Penrose, *Challenging Traditions*.
3. COEM, August 1859, 85.
4. See ADB and ADEB entries for "Perry, Frances." See also https://www.frances-perryhouse.com.au/About-Us/History. Last accessed 31 October 2018.
5. Harmer, *St. James Old Cathedral*. No page numbers. Harmer and subsequent others seem to have sourced this quote from Goodman, *Church in Victoria*, 21.

by 1839, with the building opening in 1842. By this time, Grylls had been succeeded by Adam Thomson. Neither of the first two ministers were evangelicals, but by virtue of being Perry's pro-cathedral and as a result of Macartney's first incumbency from 1852 to 1860, St. James' was firmly established as an evangelical center for the whole diocese, remaining thus up to the latter part of the twentieth century.

There were more decidedly evangelical laity in other places. Thomson officiated at the opening of a little stone building on 30 November 1839 in Brighton. The date was St. Andrew's Day, and the parish church was subsequently consecrated with that name. The building had been paid for by Henry Dendy and Jonathan Binns Were. The duo, with Robert Dunsford and George Were (J. B.'s brother-in-law and brother) also gave to the church a ten-acre site, which includes the present St. Andrew's Church grounds, the adjoining historic cemetery, and the Brighton Grammar School buildings.[6]

Services were read by Dendy and Were, and probably some of the others as well. Of the group, Were was the leader with characteristic evangelical social activism: he was, for example, a president and founder of the local British and Foreign Bible Society auxiliary, along with Chief Justice William Stawell and Judge Robert William Pohlman as his vice presidents.[7] His evangelical energy and commitment made the establishment of the local Brighton parish possible, although it was not until 1849 that Brighton received a cleric, when Perry deaconed a local schoolmaster William Brickwood for the task.[8] Brickwood was educated and dutiful rather than fervently evangelical, and the parish never took on the spiritual outlook of its real founder, Were.

---

6. The 10-acre land grant was part of Dendy's notorious "Special Survey" lands of 1841, and by the time of the 1843 conveyance to the Church of England was probably wholly owned by the Were family. The story of the survey and the uproar it caused in colonial Melbourne can be found in Ellis, *House of Were*, 32–38. Other parcels of land from the Special Survey were conveyed to church authorities to become sites for St. Mark's North Brighton (1849) and St. John's East Brighton (1868).

7. As cited in Sturrock, *Fruitful Mother*, 11. The 8th annual report of the Melbourne Auxiliary is lodged in the State Library of Victoria. This suggests a founding date of 1841. See ADB entries for Stawell and Pohlman.

8. Brickwood was local to the area and had arrived from England to become the Master of St. Ninian's School in 1841. In 1844 he was listed as the Head Master of the Port Philip Academy Institute, and records show that he continued running a school while undertaking pastoral duties at Brighton. See Cable et al., *Index of Australian Clergy*. The Index represents decades of labour and is a faithfully updated collection of cards currently in the possession of Leonie Cable in Sydney. A duplicate set belonging to Noel Pollard exists but ceased being updated upon his death.

Charles Perks, St. Stephen's Richmond

Perhaps the pre-eminent example of evangelical energy in the parishes in the early history is that of Charles Perks. A testimonial to his forty years of ministry at St. Stephen's Richmond was published in 1893.[9] It notes that parishioners had wanted "to present a Testimonial to Mr. Perks expressive of the esteem in which he was held by his Parishioners."[10] But the committee soon learnt that Perks was opposed to any gift to himself, suggesting instead that something could be done in or for the church. The results were the stained-glass windows in St. Stephen's, illustrating St. Stephen before the Sanhedrin (Acts 6 and 7) with a memorial inscribed to "Chas. T. and Martha Perks, 1892."

The bishop of Goulburn, the Reverend Canon Chalmers, delivered a brief address on the occasion of the dedication of the Memorials. He noted, among other things, that Perks was the driving force behind the Widows' and Orphans' Fund, by which the widows and orphans of clergymen were cared for, and that he also played a "prominent and active part in the erection of St. Paul's Cathedral." On the same occasion, Miss Henty (of the prominent settler family, who were close friends of Perks and long-term parishioners) delivered an illuminated address to Perks. Even the substantially aged Dean Macartney came out to the evening celebrations—"only the second time in the last two years that he had ventured out in the night air, but he could not resist the impulse to come out to Richmond and take part in the congratulations to his friend and coworker, Mr. Perks."[11] He testified especially to Perks's valuable work in the Councils of the Diocese. Perks was being rightly feted for a long and energetic ministry at St. Stephen's and in the diocese.

That ministry had begun when Perks was recruited by one of Perry's commissaries in England, namely Henry Venn of the CMS. While at King's College, London, as part of his preparations to go to India as a missionary, Perks received an unsolicited offer to go to Port Philip as a clergyman. He accepted on the condition that he was ordained in England prior to departure.[12] Venn had no doubt been attracted to Perks's firmly evangelical heritage and missionary mindset.

---

9. St. Stephen's Richmond, *Forty Years' Ministry*.
10. St. Stephen's Richmond, *Forty Years' Ministry*, 5.
11. St. Stephen's Richmond, *Forty Years' Ministry*, 15.
12. St. Stephen's Richmond, *Forty Years' Ministry*, 25. Sturrock, *Fruitful Mother*, 12, points out that the Subscription Book of the Diocese of Melbourne shows that Perks was in fact priested in Melbourne in December 1854. He may have been deaconed in England prior to departure.

Perks's grandparents were part of the Wesleyan movement during the Evangelical Revival. His mother desired that he and his brother become "ministers of the gospel," and as Perks grew up, he became interested in ministry, particularly in overseas mission work. After both his parents died, when he was relatively young, Perks wrote to Oxford and Cambridge seeking study and ordination. The vice chancellor of Cambridge replied saying that it was not necessary for him to "go up" to either if he were fixed on ministry career, and so Perks went to King's in London instead. Perks left England in 1850, landing first in Adelaide, where he made such a strong impression during his layover that the dean of Adelaide urged him to return if Melbourne did not work out for him.

St. Stephen's Richmond, the parish in and from which Perks was to exercise the bulk of his ministry, was itself planted out of St. Peter's Eastern Hill by Newham. Newham and Perry saw that the expanding Richmond area to the east of the city would require its own church and ministry. As usual in that period, contributions from local laity was needed to ensure that buildings could be constructed and the clergyman's stipend raised. Among the early contributors were Perry himself and the evangelicals La Trobe and Pohlman—the latter was a leading layman of the parish.[13]

On 16 November 1851, St. Stephen's was opened, with Perks and Bloomfield as the appointed clergymen. Bloomfield could not take up his appointment as vicar, and the job fell to Perks. The parish was defined as that area "bounded by Gertrude and Hoddle Streets and south of the River Yarra, then 'extending infinitely beyond' to the east."[14] Soon after, St. Andrew's Brighton was opened, and Perks had to travel to Brighton as often as he could to take services there also. The following passage from a contemporary source illustrates the pioneering work of those early days:

> At that time there was no church as far as Brighton on the one hand, and Nunawading on the other. A mud hovel was procured in Hawthorn at 30s. per week, and a church opened there. Subsequently Mr. Fenwick presented to the people of Kew a piece of land and the Kew church was erected. Thus Hawthorn, Kew, Brighton, and other places were offshoots of St. Stephen's.[15]

By 1853, Perks was running services in South Yarra, Prahran, Malvern, Hawthorn, and Camberwell. Perks's energetic ministry across the eastern and southern regions of the colony led to a string of ministries, buildings, and separate parishes being birthed from St. Stephen's. These included

---

13. Sturrock, *Fruitful Mother*, 5–7.
14. Sturrock, *Fruitful Mother*, 7.
15. St. Stephen's Richmond, *Forty Years' Ministry*, 16.

- Hawthorn school, 1852; church, 1853 (subsequently Christ Church)
- St. Matthew's Prahran, 1853
- Holy Trinity Kew, 1854
- Holy Trinity Doncaster, 1868
- North Richmond in Simpson's Road, 1856; formed into the separate parish of St. Matthias in 1881
- St. Thomas' South Richmond in 1855, the building in Cremorne Street opened on Easter Day 1857
- St. Bartholomew's Burnley in January 1885, enlarged in 1889, declared a separate parish and further enlarged in 1890

These were challenging times for church fundraising, and the onset of the gold rush only made money and resources for church expansion harder to come by. Parish historian Morna Sturrock notes that some of the practical expenses for this ministry expansion were paid for by Perks himself. The parish accounts noted that a substantial portion of its debt was owed to their vicar![16]

Additionally, Perks was a member of the first Council of Diocese, handpicked by Perry; the Honorary Secretary of the Erection Board of St. Paul's Cathedral; a life governor of the Melbourne Hospital, the Benevolent Asylum, the Orphan Asylum and Richmond Free Dispensary.[17] Perks was joined by his parishioner Pohlman in this commitment to social action: Pohlman was himself associated with the work of the Melbourne Hospital and University, a guardian of the Port Phillip Orphan Immigration Committee, a committee member of the Merri Creek Northcote Inebriates Home, and president of the first Early Closing Association targeting pubs and drunkenness.[18]

The Church Assembly of 1892 elected Perks a canon of the cathedral in recognition of his seniority and contribution. Perks is an important example of evangelical social activism later exemplified by the Mission of St. James and St. John.[19]

Perks later revealed that he had wanted to move from St. Stephen's—presumably to take on something less demanding—but the bishop had not consented. Hence, according to Perks, the people at his fortieth

---

16. Sturrock, *Fruitful Mother*, 14.
17. St. Stephen's Richmond, *Forty Years' Ministry*, 30–31.
18. See ADB entry. Pohlman's diary is extant and held by the Royal Historical Society of Victoria.
19. See also Monk and O'Donoghue, *Billylids And "Home Kids."*

anniversary celebrations gave him too much credit for sticking to St. Stephen's. This self-effacing humility was typical of the kind of evangelical spirituality that Perks exemplified.

Canon George Oakley Vance preached the sermon at St. Stephen's, commemorating Perks's forty years. His text was Acts 20:20, where Paul says to the Ephesian elders, "I kept back nothing that was profitable unto you, but have showed you, and have taught you publicly, and from house to house . . . " Vance spoke of Perks and other early ministers coming to Port Philip "in a missionary spirit—true fishers of men; they had obeyed their Master's command to launch out into the deep and let down their nets for a draught, and they had no fear for the result . . . Of such a spirit was the minister who by the good hand of God was appointed to this place"—namely, Perks.[20] Vance asked rhetorically:

> What has been the secret of so much effort?—the chief object of this forty years' ministry? –the true meaning and sustaining principle of the life lived among you, lived in your service and in Christ's, with unflagging zeal and unsparing self-denial, from vigorous youth to failing age? Has it not been, as with St. Paul, the desire to teach publicly and from house to house, and to testify to the eternal necessity of those two twin truths of the Gospel: Repentance towards God and Faith in the Lord Jesus Christ?[21]

It was a testimony to the evangelical leader's gospel character, motivation, and method. Vance ended by urging the congregation, "to value the true word and faithful service," "to give proof that his labour here has not been in vain," and to stay loyal to the "plain words of sound doctrine" until they "stand at last, on the shore of their heavenly inheritance." The evangelical themes of conversionism, crucicentrism, biblicism, and activism were plainly evident in the assessment of Perks's ministry, which laid the firmly evangelical foundation of St. Stephen's and in many of the parishes planted from Richmond.

St. Matthew's Prahran

It would however be a mistake to assume that evangelical expansion in the parishes occurred in a straightforward linear progression. As seen from the example of St. Andrew's Brighton, evangelicalism would not prosper

---

20. St. Stephen's Richmond, *Forty Years' Ministry*, 35.
21. St. Stephen's Richmond, *Forty Years' Ministry*, 37.

in a new setting without able clerical evangelical leadership in partnership with able lay evangelicals. There were great difficulties in obtaining able and willing clergy of any description to come to the colony—much less firmly evangelical clergy. The challenge of increasing scientific rationalism in wider society and the rise of Tractarianism and Higher Criticism movements within the church meant that unless confident and able evangelical leadership was supplied, there was a significant risk that the "natural" adherents to the Church of England—being British immigrants and their progeny—would trend away from evangelical distinctives of faith for lack of adequate instruction.

One of Perks's church plants, in Prahran, illustrates the degree of influence that subsequent leadership would have. Charles Perks may have run the first services in the municipality of Prahran from rented premises as part of his responsibility for the wider area, but as early as 1853 there was a specifically licensed minister to the Prahran mission district, James Brennan. By 1855, the language of "incumbent" and "parish" were used to describe the appointment of John Herbert Gregory to Prahran.

Gregory was sympathetic to the Tractarian movement, and subsequently became its leading proponent in Melbourne. While at Prahran, he held services in a school house. The closest church buildings were those of St. John's Toorak and Christ Church South Yarra. Gregory saw the need for a church building in the municipality and eventually secured the site for All Saints St. Kilda at the bottom of Chapel Street. The plan for the school house congregation to move there never eventuated as a significant proportion of parishioners refused to move from Prahran to St. Kilda. Gregory continued to serve both congregations until the vestry of All Saints insisted that he focus his energies on the parish of St. Kilda, which he then established as Melbourne's leading high-church parish.[22]

Gregory was followed at Prahran by John Watson and John Fulford, but their incumbencies covering the next thirteen years were marked by difficulties and conflict with the church trustees. The operation of both a worshiping congregation and a school in the one building, being the school house, was the primary source of tension. Both men struggled to raise the finances required to build a church building. Both men clashed with the church trustees over fund raising and financial matters, with the trustees resorting to legal action against Fulford at the end of his incumbency.[23] In such circumstances, the church struggled to be firmly established and did not have a distinctly evangelical reputation, although, like most churches

22. Soley, "Highest of the High"; Holden, *Saints, Sinners and Goalposts*.
23. Bride, *Proclaiming the gospel*, 30.

of the era, it was basically low church in style. Fulford's departure in 1875 opened the way for the decided evangelical Barnabas Shaw Walker to take a stronger lead in Prahran, which subsequently developed into an evangelical and missions-minded stronghold.[24]

St. Mary's Caulfield

St. Mary's Caulfield was another example of the impact of a change in clerical leadership on a local church. The first services in the area were conducted by the high-church-leaning Gregory, as Caulfield fell within his Prahran parish. However, the leading family in the area, which donated land from their estate for the building of a local church, was firmly evangelical with links to William Wilberforce and the English anti-slavery campaign. James Wilberforce Stephen had been named after his father George's friend, and was himself later Perry's second diocesan chancellor.

After the creation of a separate Caulfield parochial district in 1864, with St. Mary's as its church, there were two relatively short incumbencies until the appointment of Dean Macartney's able son, H. B. Macartney Jr., in 1868. His appointment was probably due to the influence of James Stephen. Macartney Jr. stayed at Caulfield for thirty years, during which time St. Mary's became a center for the evangelical deeper-life movement and for missionary concern. From 1873, Macartney Jr. produced *The Missionary at Home and Abroad* from Caulfield—a magazine detailing missionary and evangelistic efforts, containing news, inspiring stories of conversion, prayer points, and appeals for support. The long partnership between supportive laity and an evangelical cleric meant that Caulfield was firmly established as an evangelical center in the southern suburbs.[25]

Perry deployed his key clergy carefully to ensure that there were strong evangelical parishes in each region. In 1848, he initially sent the senior Macartney to Heidelberg to establish the work in the north-eastern corridor but recalled him within the year to become archdeacon of Geelong so as to deal with the incompetent Collins at Christ Church. In 1855, another Cambridge evangelical, George Goodman, came to Christ Church and established its evangelical credentials for ensuing decades.[26] Goodman not only inherited a church school but was also involved with Geelong Grammar School, which was founded across the road from Christ Church in 1857 with the Reverend George Vance in charge. The ceremony to lay

---

24. Bride, *Proclaiming the gospel*.
25. Durie, "St. Mary's 150th."
26. See ADB entry, "Goodman, George."

the foundation stone was reported on with much enthusiasm in the *Messenger*.[27] Present were Governor Barkly, Perry, Macartney, and Goodman. School services were held in Christ Church, and in 1863 Goodman became secretary to the school council.

Key parishes and schools throughout the diocese were being deeply affected by evangelical ministry, with its sharp focus on the need for spiritual conversion and social action. Evangelicalism's spread was no doubt made possible by the fact that "many of the most prestigious families of Melbourne shared [this] crusading spirit and evangelical Anglican faith."[28]

Societies

A feature of evangelical activism in the late eighteenth and early nineteenth centuries was the proliferation of evangelical societies in Britain. Most were interdenominational, reflecting the primary allegiance of evangelicals to the brand of vital personal faith rather than to institutional religion. Among them were societies such as the ones listed here with their dates of foundation:[29]

- Society for Promoting Religious Knowledge among the Poor (1750)
- Naval and Military Bible Society (1779) (originally known simply as the "Bible Society")
- London Missionary Society (1779)
- Sunday School Society (1785)
- Society for the Suppression of Vice (1787)
- Society for Bettering the Condition and Increasing the Comforts of the Poor, "The Bettering Society" (1796)
- Church Missionary Society (1799)
- Religious Tract Society (1799)
- Society for the Better Observance of Sunday (1800)
- British and Foreign Bible Society (1804)—later "The Bible Society" and the "The United Bible Society."
- Society for the Mitigation and Gradual Abolition of Slavery throughout the British Dominions (1823)

27. COEM, July 1857, 66–67.
28. Russell, "A Wish of Distinction," 20.
29. See, for example, Bradley, *Call to Seriousness*, chapter 7, "The Age of Societies."

- Society for the Prevention of Cruelty to Animals (1824)

Societies such as these were a context for the expending of much evangelical energy. Many focused on key evangelical tenets: the importance of the Scriptures, the vital work of evangelism and conversion, and the improvement of society as a reflection of the extension of the kingdom of God. Societies provided opportunities for lay leadership and focused effort towards particular ends. Significantly, they were also often interdenominational and independent of diocesan structures and so were more flexible and faster to respond to changing needs.

In Melbourne, much of the activity in the various societies was led by Anglican evangelicals. Loyal Anglicans recognized the potential risk that evangelical energy would be diverted from their denomination, the corollary being that the energy and enthusiasm of the societies could be directed back into revitalizing the denomination. Hence, the CMS was founded in the wake of the success of the LMS, specifically as a Church of England missionary society.[30]

Separate mention should also be made of the temperance movement, which began in America, where it had much greater impact than in British dominions. The British and Foreign Temperance Society was established in London in 1831 and spread to its colonies. John Wolffe notes that while there were strong links between evangelicals and the temperance movement, the relationship was not straightforward, as a number of evangelicals did not support either the temperance or total abstinence movements. In fact, at least two noted evangelical families were brewers—the Buxton and Guinness families.[31] In Melbourne, although agreeing with the potential evil of alcohol abuse, Perry refused to sign on to the Temperance Society, citing the principle of freedom, although many other evangelicals—clerical and lay—were avid supporters.

Two aspects of evangelicalism received special attention from Melbourne evangelicals: the importance of the Bible, and overseas evangelistic mission work.

Biblicism: The British and Foreign Bible Society

Among the first societies in Melbourne was the British and Foreign Bible Society. The BFBS was not the first Bible Society in the United Kingdom. That

---

30. See Stock, *History of the Church Missionary Society*, vol. 1. For discussion of the Australian CMS and the determination of its founders to receive episcopal and denominational status, see Cole, *History of the Church Missionary Society of Australia*.

31. Wolffe, *Expansion of Evangelicalism*.

was founded twenty-five years earlier by Methodist laymen "for purchasing Bibles to be distributed among British Soldiers and Seamen of the Navy, in order (by the blessing of God) to spread abroad Christian knowledge and reformation of manners."[32] This society was simply known as the Bible Society. Although being Methodist in origin, according to Roald Kverndal it had an interdenominational evangelical flavor and enjoyed sustained evangelical support from such Anglicans as Wilberforce and Newton—and, in all probability, their large network of evangelical colleagues.

Demand outstripped supply of Bibles, and in 1804 the BFBS was founded with a wider purpose. It was clearly more prestigious, having been gestated in the committee of the Religious Tract Society with an eye on the upheavals on the Continent. There were thirty-six laity on the founding committee, including Wilberforce. It was also in a position to learn from the experiences of previous interdenominational societies so that its constitution maximized support and minimized cause for controversy—it would focus on the publication and distribution of Bibles for the promotion of their common faith.[33]

The Bible Society was thereafter renamed the Naval and Military Bible Society. The two societies worked together, being careful to not usurp each other's roles. However, by 1808 the BFBS was distributing Bibles to "convicts sailing for New South Wales" and the crews of various ships en route to the colonies.[34] By 1817, through the instigation of Governor Lachlan Macquarie and with Samuel Marsden's involvement, there was a BFBS Auxiliary in NSW.[35]

By 1840, there was an auxiliary in Port Philip, with the retired East India Company Presbyterian Chaplain, James Clow, who as one of the two founding vice presidents (and later third president) moved the motion to establish it. Other significant leaders of civic society were involved. Edwin James Brewster, the Chairman of Court of Petty Sessions and Commissioner of Court of Requests in Melbourne, was the other founding vice president. James Dredge, who moved the election of officers at the first meeting, was Assistant Protector of Aborigines, and later a Wesleyan Minister in the city and then Geelong.

32. Kverndal, "Sowing by Sea," 329.

33. A point well noted by the editors in their Introduction. Batalden et al., *Sowing the Word*, 2.

34. Kverndal refers to Reports of the BFBS from the period.

35. Thompson, *Australia and the Bible* is a general history of the BFBS in Australia. However, it contains inaccuracies about the founding of the Melbourne Auxiliary, corrected later by Massey, *Sowing and Reaping*.

Another member of the original committee was Jonathan Binns Were, mentioned briefly already in connection with the founding of St. Andrew's Brighton. In 1842 he was elected the second president. He had arrived in 1839 from England and is remembered as the founder of J. B. Were and Sons Stockbrokers and the first member for Brighton in the Victorian Legislative Assembly. Were was also involved in the first hospital to be established in the old police station in 1840, and a member of the committees of the Melbourne Hospital in 1846, the first Botanic Gardens in 1841, the Philosophical (later Royal) Society.[36] Were was a prime example of evangelical activism in this period.

The founding president of the BFBS Melbourne Auxiliary was Captain William Lonsdale, and later the first patron was Superintendent Charles Joseph La Trobe. La Trobe had in fact brought with him a supply of Bibles from London when he arrived as Superintendent of Port Philip in 1839. One hundred Bibles and three hundred Testaments were given as a gift by the London Committee of the BFBS for distribution in his new field of work. It was noted that La Trobe's missionary father was a warm friend of the Society.[37]

La Trobe himself was a subscriber to the local auxiliary but, being busy with public duties, could not attend as many meetings as he liked. However, he lent his prestige to the Society, maintained an active though indirect interest, writing on one occasion to the Secretary expressing his regret at not being able to attend meetings but affirming his interest and support:

> It is both my duty and my pleasure to be a member and look forward with exceedingly great gratification to the prospects opening to us of a very important accession both to our number and strength. The enclosed is not my subscription, but what I should, if present, have added to our evening's collection."[38]

In 1848, the year of Perry's arrival, La Trobe chaired the BFBS Melbourne Auxiliary's Eighth Annual Meeting. The meeting elected him their first patron, and Bishop Perry their third president, with James Clow and William Lonsdale as vice presidents.[39] The Society was in good shape. That year they reported the establishment of a depot for sale of Bibles in an Elizabeth Street bookseller's premises, from which five hundred and sixty Bibles, three hundred and ten Testaments and three Psalters were sold –nearly

---

36. Ellis, *House of Were*, 39.
37. Thompson, *Australia and the Bible*, 27–28.
38. Massey, *Sowing and Reaping*, 31.
39. The Eighth Annual Report of the Auxiliary Bible Society for Australia Felix, 1848.

double the number of volumes sold in the previous year. The social impact of more than a thousand Scripture books being held and read in private hands in the fledgling city should not be underestimated. Forty pounds was remitted to the parent society in London against their purchase account, and an additional fifty pounds was remitted as a "free contribution" to the wider work. The Report ended with these words:

> The Bible is the bulwark of any nation; it exalts any people, and it proves their defense. It is their sun and their shield. Let all that fear God and wish well to this their adopted country, see that nothing be wanting on their part to place a copy of the Bible in the hands of every inhabitant, and thus shall be laid deep, the foundations of a great and mighty nation, secure in the enjoyment of civil and religious liberty, exalted in righteousness, and diffusing on all the Isles around the fragrance of pure genuine Christianity![40]

The BFBS remained a key outlet for evangelical energy in the nineteenth century. Part of the secret to its longevity lay in its deliberate interdenominationalism and determined focus on the narrow aim of Bible publication, sales, and distribution. In this way, it avoided the internal conflict that arose within groups with more complex goals and activities. It also enjoyed a measure of prestige because the value of the Bible was held by more than evangelicals alone. The desirability of biblical literacy and the civilizing influence of religion on society were concepts valued by wider society and culture—especially among the ruling classes in Christianized Europe. Hence, the parent BFBS cultivated the patronage of elite members of civic society in order to raise funds and profile, and further its aims. The Melbourne Auxiliary's action in appointing La Trobe its first patron and Perry its president at the first opportunity after their arrival in the colony was consistent with this thinking and approach.

---

40. The Eighth Annual Report of the Auxiliary Bible Society for Australia Felix, 1848.

> 5. Moved Mr. by J. W. Bell, seconded by Mr. George Cooper—That the following individuals be elected Officer Bearers and members of the Committee for the ensuing year:—
>
> *Patron*—His Honor C. J. La Trobe.
> *President*—The Right Rev. the Lord Bishop of Melbourne.
> *Vice-Presidents*—Rev. James Clow, Capt. Lonsdale.
> *Treasurer*—Robert Smith, Esq.
> *Secretaries*—Rev. Messrs. Morison and Ramsay.
>
> *Committee:*
>
> | | |
> |---|---|
> | Mr. Sidney Stephen | Mr. Samuel Crook |
> | Mr. John M'Gregor | Mr. J. W. Holloway |
> | Dr. Wilkie | Mr. J. W. Bell |
> | Mr. J. R. Pascoe | Mr. P. Davis |
> | Mr. A. Ross | Mr. H. Budge |
> | Mr. W. Williamson | Mr. John Lush |
> | Mr. W. Everist | Mr. Henry Langlands |
> | Mr. Joseph Richardson | Dugald Fletcher, Esq. |

Image from the Eighth Annual Report of the BFBS Auxiliary of Australia Felix.

In 1872, Perry was still president, with Sir William Stawell and Justice Robert Pohlman as his vice presidents.[41] Their public status as leaders in civic society was important. That each of these men was personally an evangelical was probably incidental, but not insignificant for the ethos and strength of the BFBS in the Melbourne. Also significant is the absence of clergy and the complete dominance of laity on the committee, as seen in the image provided.

Late in the century, in 1898, perhaps the foremost evangelical leader of his generation, H. B. Macartney Jr., left Melbourne to take up his final ministry posting as the General Secretary of the BFBS in London. The BFBS

---

41. See introduction to a lecture delivered by Perry in aid of funds for the Melbourne Auxiliary in Perry, *Evidences, Characteristics and Effects*.

was certainly "evangelical enough" for him and was to remain a gathering point for evangelical activism well into the twentieth century.

Conversionism: Missionary Societies

If the strength of the interdenominational BFBS was indicative of the evangelical commitment to the Scriptures, then the strength of the missionary societies was indicative of evangelicals' commitment to evangelism and conversion. Membership of the Anglican CMS was a key indicator of evangelical self-identification. The Australian church had been originally established by CMS chaplains sent by the parent body as "the best way of planting and promulgating the Gospel in Botany bay."[42] Perry himself owed part of his appointment to CMS Secretary Venn's positive reference to his evangelistic and church- and school-planting abilities.

The evangelical Perry maintained this focus on evangelism and mission in Melbourne. Perry held firmly to the reasoning that involvement in overseas mission was a key to spiritual prosperity at home. In 1851, he spoke at the founding meeting of a diocesan Board of Mission, which was chaired by Charles La Trobe. Also present at the meeting were Daniel Newham and H. B. Macartney. The meeting was held in response to a resolution of the inaugural Australasian Bishops' Conference of 1850, calling for the formation of a joint Board of Mission—today the Australian Board of Mission. Perry took the lead in the implementation of that resolution on a local diocesan level.

The *Messenger* reported Perry saying that:

> Activity in missionary undertakings was one of the means best calculated to promote the general prosperity of a Church and the edification of her individual members. This was true in the way of natural consequence. The cultivation of a missionary spirit, tended perhaps, more than anything, to produce that enlargement of heart, which was so great, and alas! so rare an ornament, both of an individual and of a community. The record of the self-denying labor of missionaries, was calculated also to stir up their brethren at home to emulate their zeal and diligence, and self-devotedness to the work of their high calling. What minister could read of the heroic zeal of a Swartz, a Brainerd, a Henry Martyn, without feeling his sense of ministerial responsibility deepened, and without being animated to increased diligence and to greater exertions in his sacred duties.

42. Cole, *History of the Church Missionary Society of Australia*. 4.

> In like manner the faith, zeal, self-denial, knowledge, and joy, manifested by those who had recently been converted from the darkness and wickedness of heathenism, were often made, by the grace of God, effectual to put to shame, the selfishness and sluggishness of members of Christian Churches at home, and to provoke them to an holy emulation, in the bold profession of the faith, and the consistent practice of the precepts of the gospel. Thus in the way of natural consequence might we expect a blessing to revert on the Church, in proportion to the zeal it displays in the missionary work; and we might expect a blessing also in the way of direct reward from God. Unworthy as our services are, God vouchsafes for the sake of his beloved Son to reward them; and the saying "He that giveth to the poor lendeth to the Lord, and look that which he layeth out shall be paid to him again," is true in respect to spiritual as well as to temporal benefits.[43]

It was a reasoned and passionate call for increased involvement in the work of overseas mission and in the still new colony. At the end the speech, this first motion of the meeting, called to form the diocesan Board of Mission, was moved by Perry and seconded by Newham:

> That in the opinion of this meeting it is the duty of every branch of the Church of Christ to take an active part in the evangelization of the world and that in proportion to the zeal and energy which it exhibits therein, a church may expect the blessing of God to be manifested in its own general prosperity and enlargement, and in the edification of its individual members.[44]

The motion was passed unanimously, and the new committee included Newham, Redmond Barry, and the city's mayor William Nicholson[45]. In March 1851, the *Messenger* ran a lead article on the formation of the Board of Mission, outlining its three objects:

1. conversion of the Aborigines of the colony (Port Philip);
2. cooperation with the Provincial Board of Mission established in Sydney at the 1850 Bishops' Conference (the ABM);
3. receiving and forwarding subscriptions to particular missionary societies or special projects.

---

43. COEM, February 1851, 52.
44. COEM, February 1851, 48.
45. See ADB entries for Barry and Nicholson.

The objects indicate that the strategy was to focus on local work (conversion of the Indigenous peoples within the diocese) and to act as a financial clearing house to support other independent societies and projects. The evangelical focus on eternal salvation was foremost: lamenting the fate of the Victorian Aboriginal peoples, the editor wrote, "If the aborigines should finally disappear, might the last . . . die in the hope of a glorious immortality."[46]

Even prior to departing England, Perry had in mind the fate of the unevangelized Aboriginal peoples. The need for effective evangelism among colonists and Indigenous peoples was locally apparent in early 1851, but gold would soon be discovered and the opportunities for evangelism and mission at home multiplied many times over.

In 1859, there was an interdenominational Chinese Evangelization Society that had as its agent Lo Sam Yuen, who was working among the Chinese miners in Ballarat. Perry had encouraged the work of the society and organized for the bishop of Victoria (Hong Kong) to send Lo over as a missioner. The bishop had been Lo's teacher in Hong Kong and was later invited by Perry to visit and assess the missionary endeavor in Victoria. Public meetings in Ballarat and Geelong drew 400 and 600 people respectively. There did not seem to be a shortage of interest in Chinese evangelization. The report of the visit in the *Messenger* ended with this plea directed towards the cause of overseas mission: "Let us not forget to pray for China with its Christ-less millions."[47]

Much of the energy for evangelism was initially expended in local home missions and on the goldfields rather than overseas, but as early as 1854 there was a CMS of Victoria—no connection to the English CMS—of which Perry was president. Although it had essentially the same aims and structure as the English society, it was completely independent from it. There was also an active auxiliary of the English CMS and an active Church of England Zenana Mission Society. The latter was intimately connected to H. B. Macartney Jr.'s independent missions work based at St. Mary's Caulfield from 1868. These societies and the Auxiliary to the English CMS operated in parallel until 1892, and their very existence speaks of the independent and committed, though at first uncoordinated, support for missions work among evangelicals in the diocese.

46. COEM, March 1851, 73.

47. COEM, August 1959, 88–89. There was, however, a falling out between the interdenominational mission and Perry, who felt it necessary to publish the correspondence between them in a supplement to the COEM in February 1860 in order to clarify the reasons behind his decision to withdraw Lo from the Mission in Ballarat.

Bishop Charles Perry

Perry's leadership was fundamental to providing a deep and broad foundation for evangelicalism in the diocese. His leadership across several key areas inspired both clergy and laity to confident evangelicalism in the first thirty years of the diocese and helped to establish Melbourne's long-term character as low church and evangelical.

Leadership—Theological

The first key area was that of theological leadership. Perry's intellectual ability is almost universally recognized. He had been Senior Wrangler of his year at Cambridge, and his sermons read as carefully and logically prepared scripts, with the force of deep scriptural, theological, and pastoral reflection applied throughout. Perry took every opportunity to speak evangelistically, pointing out the reality of human sin, the need for Christ the Savior, and the attendant grace and love of God, who spared not his only Son. He preached, wrote, and lectured on topics such as science and the Bible, religion in schools, duties of parents and children, and the threat of Higher Criticism.[48]

Perry's ability to reflect theologically within an evangelical framework on issues facing the church and society gave evangelicals confidence in the veracity and intellectual rigor of their faith. They were armed with confidence about their interaction with wider society. In the nineteenth century, largely positive attitudes towards organized religion and its role in society gave evangelicals a natural hearing, which a bishop like Perry did not hesitate to leverage for the cause of proclaiming the gospel of repentance and salvation. His example inspired other evangelicals to follow suit. Indeed, Perry's leadership in this area extended beyond evangelicals in the diocese to the wider Protestant and evangelical cause in Victoria. In 1872 there were several hundred signatories to a handsomely illustrated address from evangelical churchmen, thanking Perry for his quarter of a century of leadership in the evangelical cause in Melbourne.[49]

Perry's firm evangelical stance was clear from the first sermon he preached in the diocese and was made clearer still at the first regional bishops'

---

48. Perry, *Office and Duty*; Perry, "School and Schoolmaster"; *Foundation Truths*; "Science and the Bible"; "Parents and Children"; *Evidences, Characteristics and Effects*.

49. Held in the Melbourne Diocesan Archives. It seems clear that the persons collecting signatures got carried away as even the local rabbi's signature is to be found in the address. However, the document still reflects the high esteem in which Perry was held by a sizeable group of religious leaders.

conference a few years later in 1850 when he issued the sole dissenting view of baptismal regeneration. This was a key moment that marked Perry out as willing to rock the bishops' boat for the sake of his evangelical beliefs.

The 1850 conference was held in the wake of the Privy Council's judgment in what has become known as the *Gorham* case. The high-church bishop of Exeter, Dr. Henry Phillpotts, had declined to license the evangelical George Gorham to a position within his diocese on the grounds that Gorham's views on regeneration—that it did not occur simultaneously with baptism—were incompatible with the Prayer Book's teaching. Litigation ensued, the Privy Council found no such incompatibility, and hence the bishop's decision to decline Gorham's appointment had no legal standing. It was a highly contentious issue within the English church and became a long-running, dispute-fueled conflict that bred rancor between low- and high-church Anglicans. Ultimately the evangelical archbishop of Canterbury, John Bird Sumner—who was himself on the Privy Council— ended up instituting Gorham into his living and Phillpotts responded by pretending to excommunicate Sumner on the grounds of trespassing on his episcopal jurisdiction.[50]

As the national and Established church, the Church of England's constitutional documents and legal provisions were—and indeed still are—tied up in the civil institutions of Parliament and the courts of law. The *Gorham* case confirmed the power of English civil authorities over the bishops—even over matters of interpretation of theology. This did not sit well with the high church and subsequent Tractarian view of episcopal office and authority which viewed bishops as spiritual leaders above any other authority, save God. After *Gorham*, the charge of "Erastianism" was commonly laid on evangelicals and others who approved of the outcome of the case. "Popish" or "a Rome-ward tendency" were the charges laid on those who sided with Phillpotts.[51]

Gorham had international ramifications, as the Church of England had spread with British colonialism all across the world. At stake were not just issues of sacramental theology and churchmanship, but also of the relationship between church and civil authority. Questions as to the legal standing of the church in relation to state in the various colonies were unresolved, and *Gorham's* applicability was uncertain.

---

50. "Sumner, John Bird," in Lewis, *DEB*.

51. Peter Williams has recently argued that the Church of England's connection with civil authority has basically served since to maintain its identity as comprehensive, inoffensive, and evangelistically ineffective. Williams, "'Pragmatic, Comfortable and Unobtrusive.'"

At the 1850 Australasian conference, *Gorham* served to focus the bishops' minds on the legal and constitutional basis of the church in their colonies. These discussions did not result in a uniform response, and different bishops chose different courses to determine the constitutional basis of their dioceses.[52] It seems they were not driven primarily by theological commitment on this point. Perry was in favor of securing a legislative enactment, believing strongly that the courts and the documents of Reformation settlement of the Church of England—including the Prayer Book and Articles—were the guarantee of future doctrinal and ecclesiological orthodoxy. Many evangelical Anglicans held the same conviction well into the twentieth century.[53]

The other Australian bishops, plus Bishop George Augustus Selwyn from New Zealand, were more united in their eagerness to issue a strong statement in support of their fellow bishop's view of the issue at stake in *Gorham*, baptismal regeneration. Robin helpfully reproduces their Minute on Holy Baptism alongside Perry's independent statement, comparing passages with parallel themes.[54] As he observes, only Perry grappled with the theological issues, the Prayer Book, canons, and Scripture. Perry alone attempted a definition of regeneration and set it into its context with baptism and the only other sacrament, Holy Communion. The other bishops were briefer and did little more than restate the words of the liturgy and assert Phillpotts's position without further argument or evidence.

Through his close examination of these statements, Robin has demonstrated convincingly that Perry's theological mind and theological leadership were the more convincing and robust.[55] For evangelicals, Perry's championship of the cause gave them confidence about their place in Victoria under his leadership.

---

52. See Davis, "Continuity and Change"; *Australian Anglicans and Their Constitution*.

53. Indeed, the theme of Anglican identity in the twenty-first century is still being debated along the lines of fidelity to and the meaning and purpose of the documents of the Reformation settlement. Evangelical Anglicans still maintain that fidelity to the plain words of those documents are the best guarantee of orthodoxy: see for Okoh et al., *Being Faithful*.

54. Robin, *Charles Perry*, Appendix I.

55. Robin, *Charles Perry*, Appendix I. This appendix reproduces the Bishops' 1850 minute on Holy Baptism in parallel with Perry's independent statement. Perry's statement is much longer, setting out his stance in eight propositions, substantiated from the Articles. The Bishops' minute states their beliefs, with virtually no argument or substantiation. Pages 65–66 contains Robin's assessment.

Leadership—Administrative

Perry's gifts in a second key area, that of administrative leadership, were also critical for the establishment of evangelicalism in Melbourne. The size and scale of the administrative challenge facing the founding bishop of Melbourne would have seemed insurmountable to a less energetic and committed man. Perry wrote to the SPG in 1851, seeking more funds for the work in Melbourne.[56] He detailed the progress at the time of the discovery of gold. The buildings in Melbourne, St. James' and St. Peter's, could hold 450 and 700 respectively, the latter still in the process of completion. St. Paul's on Swanston Street was still being built. There were various buildings—churches, school houses, and cottages—at Collingwood, Richmond, St. Kilda, Brighton, Williamstown, Heidelberg, Pentridge (Coburg), Kilmore, Ballan, Geelong, Belfast (Port Fairy), Portland, and "the port in Gippsland." There were still just twenty-four clergymen serving an estimated 77,000 residents—double what the population had been three and a half years before at Perry's arrival.[57] The want of pastoral care and resources for evangelism was staggering. Melbourne did not have the resources and status of Sydney, but its growth was steady and persistent.

Perry's lasting legacy was the invention of synodical government in Melbourne, a new structure of governance that spread quickly through the Church of England in the colonies. Perry saw that without historic and substantial endowments of the sort in England, the church in Melbourne was reliant on the goodwill and financial giving of its laity. He thus sought to devolve the absolute episcopal authority vested in him as a colonial bishop and share that authority to govern with those who would actually raise the financial resources to pay for clergy and buildings and ministries.[58]

Perry's presidential addresses to a succession of Church Assemblies begin by presenting a report of clergy numbers and appointments, losses in the previous year, and church building works. He was focused on the need to deploy pastors into the field and provide adequate places of worship. He was constantly in search of new "men" and "means" to pay for ministry.

In 1861, Perry announced that eight vacancies in the year were all filled, but there were still great needs. He also reported that he expected two more men from England, and one from Sarawak, Borneo, shortly. Perry was focused on getting men into the field, and the record shows that he made

---

56. Goodman, *Church in Victoria*, 152–54.
57. Goodman, *Church in Victoria*, 152–54.
58. See Grant, *Anglicans in Victoria*.

steady progress over the entire length of his episcopate.[59] Not all were as well qualified or theologically oriented as he might have liked, but the great majority were low-church evangelicals.

In 1869, he noted that the 114 clergy from the previous year had increased to 117. There were thirty-four consecrated churches (free of building debt), and eighty-five licensed places of worship. Eleven new places of worship had been licensed in the past year. However, Perry lamented that there were only four clergy in Gippsland, and he wanted this number to increase. Plans for an endowment fund for a Ballarat bishopric were reported to the Assembly, but no progress had been made.

Albert McPherson, writing in the official sesquicentenary history of the diocese, credits Perry with building no less than seventy-one church buildings between 1847 and 1874, at roughly the pace of thirty per decade.[60]

Even in retirement, Perry was working for the expansion of ministry in Victoria. The 1879 Ballarat Assembly noted that Bishop Perry, in retirement in England, was still mindful of the church in Victoria and actively supporting it. The Assembly heard that Perry had pledged to personally give £500 to the diocese, provided £1000 could be raised locally. This promised amount was not his first generous gift to the new diocese. It was further reported that Perry had written in strong support of a £1000 grant for the diocese from the Society for Promoting Christian Knowledge (SPCK). The news was greeted with applause.[61]

But Perry was never focused merely on numbers and buildings and money. In the annual report of 1869, he grieved over the death of two clergy wives in the year and noted it "strange that during 15 years only 6 or 7 clergymen had died while no less than 16 or 17 had had their wives taken away."[62] The colonial experience was extremely trying for many.

Perry's determination to establish an evangelistically effective church laid deep foundations for evangelicalism in Melbourne. He successfully engaged leading laity through the innovation of synodical government, creating an important context for vital partnership between laity and clergy to develop. Perry however, retained his episcopal prerogative in the critical area of clergy appointments. He was also highly influential in the appointment of his two successors. It was the exercise of this episcopal authority and influence in particular that was so determinative for the diocese.

---

59. COEM figures show 20 clergy in 1851, 67 in 1860, and 122 in 1870 close to the end of Perry's episcopate.

60. McPherson, "Architecture," 51–54.

61. COEM, 5 May 1879.

62. COEM, 25 February 1869.

Leadership Appointments—Perry's "Rules"

Perry was committed to finding able evangelical clergy to serve in Melbourne, which remained in need of clergy throughout the century. Faced with persistent demand for clergy, and laity who at times puzzled over his disinterest in their recommendations, Perry found it necessary to comment in the COEM on his rules with respect to licensing of clergy in the diocese.[63] These were that they had to supply their letters of ordination and letters testimonial from three beneficed clergymen, countersigned by their bishops—a requirement that still stands in the Diocese of Melbourne to this day. Additionally, because of the distance from England, Perry appointed three commissaries to examine the "character and fitness of all candidates for employment in this Diocese"—including any candidates from either the SPG or the Colonial Church Society. These were men he knew he could trust to assess not just character and fitness, but also theology. They were three staunch evangelicals, and long-term friends of Perry's: the Reverends John Scholefield, Henry Venn, and John Cooper. Scholefield was at Cambridge, Venn with CMS, and Cooper was a vicar and Perry's brother in law.[64] Candidates had to have letters of commendation from all three commissaries.

Noting his own stringent requirements, Perry wrote:

> I am placed in a very difficult position from the want of additional clergymen to occupy various stations in the country... Pray then that the Great Head of the Church would supply us with a body of faithful and zealous laborers in this portion of His vineyard.[65]

It seems that his prayers were answered. Acceptable men were found, and in increasing numbers. In December 1850, there were nineteen clergy and five lay readers licensed in Melbourne. By 1861, there were seventy-five clergy, rising to 117 in 1869 and more than 120 by the time of Perry's departure in 1874.

Perry shied away from the use of partisan labels like "evangelical," but his choice of commissaries made it clear that he was looking for men of evangelical persuasion. Over the foundation period of the diocese, he was able to import such men in significant numbers from England and Ireland. Dean Macartney's own *alma mater*, Trinity College Dublin (TCD), was an important source of evangelical clergy for Australia. Many Trinity

---

63. COEM, 23 August 1850.

64. On Perry's relationship with each, see Robin, *Charles Perry*, 10, 15, 36. For Scholefield in particular, see Bullock, *Ridley Hall, Cambridge*, vol. 1, 52.

65. COEM, 23 August 1850, 234.

graduates were heavily influenced by the Irish Evangelical Revival, which peaked in 1859. Macartney's personal connections, along with those of two other early evangelical clergy, Beamish and Russell, further assisted in sourcing men from TCD.[66] Perry's willingness to use Moore College as the primary training college for his clergy also provided a steady source of evangelical clergy for Melbourne.

However, Perry's first priority was getting faithful men able to work in colonial conditions. So, for example, Perry ordained John Herbert Gregory to the position of bush missioner, a position in which he served with distinction and indefatigability—especially as the gold rush set in.[67] Gregory was later to emerge as a leading high churchman, but Perry kept him within the diocese where he established All Saints St. Kilda as a leading and perhaps original center of Melbourne high churchmanship.[68]

Perry summarized his own attitude towards appointing and dealing with clergy who did not share his evangelical views in his address to the Church Assembly of 1868:

> So long as I retain my present office so long shall I, God helping me, endeavour to keep out of the ministry of the church all persons who will not unite with me in resisting the movement which I regard as calculated to pave the way for a return to the doctrine and practice of the church in England previous to the Reformation.[69]

In 1873, a few months before his final departure for England, Perry wrote in the *Messenger*:

> I esteem it the bounden duty of every Bishop . . . to use the greatest possible care in preventing the entrance into his diocese of clergymen who have the least tendency to what are commonly known as ritualistic or rationalistic opinions; but if some do (and some always will) find entrance, then, instead of driving them from him, and strengthening them in such a tendency, by expressing any censure or indicating any distrust of them, to show towards them all brotherly kindness, and to believe and hope the best concerning them. This—however I may have

---

66. There were more than 100 men originally ordained in Ireland, many from TCD, serving across Australia from the mid-nineteenth century. See Cable et al., *Index of Australian Clergy*. Their influence and contribution to Australian church and society has yet to be adequately acknowledged.

67. Goodman, *Church in Victoria*, 131–33.

68. See, for example, Soley, "'Highest of the High.'"

69. *Church News*, 1868, 31.

failed in carrying it out—has been my rule of conduct during my episcopate, and will continue, with God's help to be so long as that episcopate shall last.[70]

Perry was determined to use his authority to prevent the entry of high-church and liberal-leaning clergy into his diocese, but accepted the reality that some would find entry, or once within the diocese might adopt such views. Towards such men, the bishop's duty, according to Perry, was clear. He was to be a pastor to all his clergy, not just to those who agreed with him.

In fact, Perry and Gregory continued corresponding after Perry's retirement from Melbourne, and their still extant letters bear evidence of the fondness that both men had for each other despite their theological differences. They shared in common a love of learning and intellectual pursuits, the bond of having labored long and hard from the early days of the diocese, and a passion for evangelism among the poorer and less educated of the city.[71] Despite sometimes heated differences over churchmanship, the genuinely warm relationship between the two outlasted their individual involvement in the diocese. This particular relationship exemplifies Perry's principled pastoral leadership and relational style towards all his clergy—not just those who shared his evangelical convictions.

Perry recognized that he was powerless to prevent men from changing their theology after they had gained entry into the diocese, but so long as they remained committed to the biblical gospel, he would not withdraw their license to minister. In fact, because of the need for competent leaders and workers, Perry promoted able men like T. C. B. Stretch and T. H. Braim to archdeaconries, despite their churchmanship. The pursuance of this policy meant that Perry—not his successors—laid the foundations for Melbourne's comprehensive character.[72] Perry created a situation where clergy with views different to their bishop's were nevertheless pastored by him and able to continue in their ministry largely unimpeded. He might not have approved of the high-church ritual in St. Peter's or All Saints, but he did not withdraw licenses to minister or threaten to do so unless the practices were unorthodox or heretical. This was effectively his practice in the controversy around church music in the decade beginning in 1857.

70. COEM, 4 December 1873.

71. See State Library of Victoria, Charles Perry, Box 28/9, for examples of their correspondence. Also Bride, *Proclaiming the gospel*, 18–21.

72. Prevailing historiography wrongly caricatures Perry as the narrow-minded evangelical, in contrast to his successor James Moorhouse, the broad-minded liberal. Moorhouse is thus credited with establishing the Diocese's comprehensive character, and Perry's contribution—if any—is limited to his vision in appointing his successor. See for example, Sturrock, *Bishop of Magnetic Power*, 36–38, and Grant, "Overview," 7.

Church Music Controversy

Perry is sometimes caricatured through this episode as being colorless and completely amusical in his preferences for services and a contributor to the hardening of divisions between evangelicals and Tractarians,[73] but in fact, his objections related to his understanding that sung responses and the intoning of parts of the service were illegal in terms of the prescribed form of the Book of Common Prayer.

Upon returning from a trip to England, Perry found it necessary to issue a circular letter to all clergy prohibiting the intoning of parts of the service and also the response, "Glory be to Thee, O Lord" after Gospel readings.[74] These practices had been introduced during his absence, and he noted in his letter that he had been reluctant at first to speak out against them because he recognized that variety in liturgical style could be justified on two grounds: first, local custom, and second, for the maintenance of diocesan unity:

> ... although requested to do so, I was reluctant to interfere, except in the way of private advice: first, because I do not regard an absolute uniformity in all particulars as at all essential to the well-being of the Church, and some variety (provided the spiritual character of the service is not affected by it), may be considered as justified by custom; and second, because I am very unwilling to recognize, and thus perhaps promote among the members of the Church, both clerical and lay, a division of opinion and feeling upon matters of ritual.[75]

The same circular letter also contained Perry's prohibition of the response to the gospel reading noted above, on the same basis. Despite the strength of his views, Perry did not gain widespread support from either leading clergy or laity, and he later largely accepted these liturgical developments in his own diocese. Significantly, he did not act to de-license offending clergy; rather, as in the case of Gregory and Handfield, he maintained a deep personal affection and ongoing gracious relationship with them.[76] However, any hesitation to introduce further innovation certainly weakened after his departure.

---

73. See, for example, McPherson, "Architecture."

74. Circular letter to all clergy dated 23 June 1857, reproduced in COEM, July 1857 and in Appendix III. See Robin, *Charles Perry*, 135–38, and Sturrock, *Fruitful Mother*.

75. COEM, July 1857.

76. Robin, *Charles Perry*; Grant, "Overview," 37.

Russell and Beamish

If Gregory and Handfield are examples of the evangelical Perry's willingness to accommodate able men who took on divergent views after entry into the diocese, then Peter Beamish and Francis Russell are examples of his willingness to actively recruit men from the opposite theological extreme. Peter Beamish was born in Cork in 1824. Francis Russell was born a year earlier, the son of the rector of Killarney, County Kerry. The two had met at Trinity College Dublin, where they began a life-long friendship. Together they offered for missionary service in New South Wales with the Society for the Propagation of the Gospel (SPG). However, their youthful, energetic, even "Irish" protest against the Tractarian direction that St. James' College (based at St. James' King Street and led by Allwood) was taking earned them the anger of Bishop Broughton, who suspended them for three months and refused to priest the two deacons.[77]

In spite of support for the duo from leading laity of their parishes, Broughton refused to budge. The two eventually offered their services to Perry, who was reluctant to take them without their bishop's approval. Later believing that approval had been given, Perry invited them to move to Victoria where they distinguished themselves by their hard work, faithful preaching of the gospel, dedicated pastoring and able strategic leadership in what is now the Diocese of Ballarat. Russell was known as "The Apostle to the Western District." For over twenty-five years, he traveled on horseback doing pastoral visiting, preaching, and taking services in more than a dozen churches, six of which he planted himself. Russell wrote to a friend that Perry had offered him at several times "every desirable living in his gift," but he remained committed to the region.[78] Beamish similarly had responsibility for an area 110 miles across with more than twenty centers. He was described by a contemporary as "a man of determination and a man of work," and a leader "of foresight and determination."

Russell and Beamish played a leading role in ensuring that the first bishop of Ballarat would not be a high churchman, by eliminating themselves—known local evangelicals—from consideration. This led to the leading local high-church candidate's withdrawal and paved the way for

---

77. *Correspondence between the Right Reverend the Lord Bishop of Sydney and Metropolitan and the Reverends F.T.C. Russell and P. T. Beamish, Deacons.* Moore College Australiana Collection.

78. Kiddle, *Men of Yesterday*, 445. Kiddle cites Russell's correspondence with Sir Charles Nicholson, dated 19 October 1867, archived in the Winter Cooke Collection, Murndal, the Western District.

a compromise candidate from outside the diocese, Samuel Thornton, to be selected.[79]

Senior Clergy

A bishop's power of appointment also extends over a range of senior clerical and lay leadership positions. Perry's key leadership team were committed evangelicals, perhaps none more so than H. B. Macartney. Macartney's first posting upon arrival was Heidelberg, but Perry, faced with the difficulty of the incompetent incumbent E. C. Collins in Geelong, hit upon a solution that involved the appointment of the diocese's first archdeacon. The pastoral care of the many residents was lacking, and there was only one church, Christ Church, which Collins was unwilling to resign. Further, there was no prospect of building another. Perry's solution was to move Macartney from Heidelberg by appointing him archdeacon of Geelong in October 1848. His seniority would be recognized by his title and the ministry in Geelong would take place under his leadership.[80] Macartney was later archdeacon of Melbourne and Geelong and the first—and longest serving—dean.

The first archdeacon of Melbourne was Thomas Hart Davies, who came out from Trinity Hall Cambridge to replace Daniel Newham after his sudden death in 1851. Handfield, whose first curacy was under Davies, wrote that he was not a scholar, but well-read and "a studious reader of the Puritan divines." He was an evangelical who was suspicious of the new scientific theology and whose favorite themes were the necessity of repentance by the unconverted, the joys of redemption, and the glories awaiting the redeemed.[81] Handfield further wrote that when Davies "perceived that the Lord was calling him to preach the gospel, he resolved that such ministry was to be exercised in the Church of England." Davies was therefore just the kind of evangelical that Perry would have been keen to promote: a Cambridge man like himself, focused on proclaiming the gospel for conversion and sticking to the old truths of the Scriptures. Unfortunately for the diocese, Davies found that he and his family could not handle the climate and conditions and returned to England after a year. His departure in 1852 saw the return of Macartney to Melbourne as the first dean.

Davies used his influence back in England to recruit men for Melbourne, and as a direct result of his appeals another long-serving evangelical

---

79. See ADB "Russell, Francis Thomas Cusack"; ADEB "Beamish, Peter Teulon." See also Spooner, *Golden See*.

80. Goodman, *Church in Victoria*, 88–89.

81. Goodman, *Church in Victoria*, 173–74.

stalwart of the diocese, George Goodman, offered for service in Melbourne and arrived in December 1853.[82] Goodman was immediately appointed an examining chaplain by Perry—a position of influence he held for fifty years. He was among the first canons of Melbourne, elected by the Church Assembly in 1879. Goodman went to Heidelberg briefly before going to Christ Church Geelong to replace Collins. He was to stay there, declining offers of preferment, until his retirement in 1906.[83]

Geelong remained without an archdeacon for a period after Macartney's return to Melbourne, until Perry's appointment of T. C. B. Stretch in 1854. Stretch had graduated from Worcester College, Oxford, in 1841, worked in parish ministry in Northamptonshire, and had been an association secretary for CMS for three years before coming to Geelong.[84] It seemed at the time of his appointment that Stretch was a capable, missionary-spirited evangelical. He is, however, now remembered as a capable leader of the Tractarian movement. Prior to the late twentieth century, the rule of "once an archdeacon, always an archdeacon" applied in the diocese and so Perry either could not or did not reverse Stretch's promotion. In any case, Perry was keen to use Stretch's financial and organizational acumen for the service of the church.

The movements of Macartney to Melbourne, and Goodman and Stretch to Geelong, illustrate how Perry was careful and strategic with his senior appointments, placing able men—preferably evangelical allies—across the diocese in the key population centers.

Lay Leaders

As described in the chapter above, there were significant evangelical lay leaders present in the district before Perry's arrival, and Perry was able to give them leading roles in the development of the diocese. One in particular was charged by Perry with a significant role in relation to the church's constitutional development: William Stawell was a relative of Macartney's and a key lay leader for Perry and subsequent bishops. He had in fact been converted under Perry's preaching in St. James' church in 1848.[85] Stawell was a leading proponent of the division of the diocese for the sake of mission and involved in evangelical societies like the BFBS.[86] Stawell's

82. Goodman, *Church in Victoria*, 199.
83. See "Goodman, George" in ADB.
84. Goodman, *Church in Victoria*, 200.
85. Robin, *Charles Perry*, 87, cites Stawell, *My Recollections*.
86. Goodman, *Church in Victoria*, 215. See also Stawell's entry in the ADB and

standing in society and civic life, and his substantial leadership contribution to the church, are especially noteworthy. However, on his death in 1889, the eulogy delivered by Bishop Goe was underscored by a telling focus on the vitality of Stawell's faith in Christ as Savior and consequent dedication to church and society:

> Sir William Stawell never spared himself in the conscientious discharge of the onerous trust imposed upon him, and was always guided by a strong sense of his duty to God and to the community in which he lived. The history of his life as a judge, a man, and a politician, was a splendid example to us all. He was a just man, and, more than that, he was a sincere believer in the Son of God as the Savior of the world . . . he was a diligent worker for the Church, teaching in the Sunday school morning and evening. He was also for many years a prominent member of the Church Assembly and a loyal supporter of the former Bishops of Melbourne in promoting the glory of God and the good of the Church.[87]

Perry's first chancellors were also men with an evangelical heritage. The first was another relative of Macartney's, Charles James Griffiths, and the second was James Wilberforce Stephen, whose connection with the English evangelicals has already been noted.

Evangelicalism was energized by Perry's own personal ministry and by the ministry of those he promoted and appointed. Yet, Perry's unwillingness to be party-spirited to the extent of demoting those whose theological views changed after their entry into the diocese or promotion to senior ranks meant that the seeds of diversity and later conflict were sown in this period and not, as is often asserted, in the subsequent broad church Moorhouse era.[88]

Colleges: Training Clergy

Colonial dioceses for most of the eighteenth century had no choice but to import clergy trained in the British Isles, but the pattern gradually changed towards training clergy locally. Part of the reason for this was the low retention rate among imported clergy used to less harsh physical conditions. Notable exceptions were men like Macartney, Beamish, and Russell, all

---

ADEB.

87. Goodman, *Church in Victoria*, 234–35.

88. For this view see Sturrock, *Bishop of Magnetic Power*, and Grant, "Overview."

Irishmen who trained at Trinity College Dublin. Trinity was not a specifically evangelical college, but it nevertheless attracted Protestant low churchmen. Many of these were used to hardship, further accentuated for some by The Great Famine, which began to set in from 1842 onwards. This resulted in, among other things, the huge Irish diaspora, as people left in search of food and better fortune. This meant that Irish clergy in the colonies had substantial numbers of Irish, with whom they could naturally connect in ministry. Their impact and contribution was significant for Australia.[89]

Perry's experience of men returning to England, unable to cope in his diocese, was not uncommon. As early as 1845, Broughton had founded St. James' College in Sydney as a theological training center to raise up local men for the ministry on the correct premise that they were more suited to local conditions and less likely to leave. In 1855, the estate of Thomas Moore enabled Bishop Barker to set up an evangelical theological college specifically for the purposes of training clergy for his diocese. It was a priority he attended to as soon as he arrived in Sydney in 1855.[90]

Perry's personal preference was for a university college where men could gain higher qualifications—he was no doubt colored by his own Cambridge experience. However, in the absence of this in Melbourne, he was more than happy to rely on Moore College to train clergy for Melbourne. He was no doubt personally assured of Moore's ethos by his friend and fellow evangelical, Barker, who had been instrumental in appointing Perry's own old friend William Hodgson as founding principal.

Additionally, Perry innovated by using lay readers to make up for the lack of clergy. These readers were licensed to read Morning and Evening Prayer, the Litany, and Homilies. Perry trusted in these to be the safeguard of doctrinal orthodoxy. The scheme expanded rapidly: from four lay readers in 1850, numbers increased to fifty-eight lay readers (including Trinity College students) plus another 308 honorary readers in 1896. Many would go on to be ordained.

The scheme was not universally popular; one bishop described it as "miserable makeshift."[91] Perry was well aware of its limitations but saw its usefulness. Perry's examining chaplain, George Goodman, wrote that: "he

---

89. See, for example, the conference proceedings edited by James Grant and held at the Mollison Library of the Diocese of Melbourne: "Victoria's Debt to the Irish Church." Judd and Cable, *Sydney Anglicans*, 76, argues that the Church of Ireland produced more clergy than it could employ, hence the emigration of clergy and the stronger possibility of remaining in the colonies.

90. Kaye, *Anglicanism in Australia*, 59–60. Judd and Cable, *Sydney Anglicans*, 74–75. Loane, *Centenary History of Moore*.

91. Attributed to Arthur Green in Nash, *Forward Flows the Time*, 115.

(Perry) turned the evangelistic efforts of young laymen to a double purpose, the maintenance of Church ministration on the one hand, and the testing of pastoral fitness on the other."[92] Ministry apprenticeship was the means by which evangelistic enthusiasm was tested for pastoral ministry.

By 1859, it was reported that, despite the objections of some leading laity who decried Moore's narrow theological focus, Perry intended to confine the ordination of men in his diocese to persons who had been educated at Moore.[93] He correctly surmised that men trained in Australia were more likely to stay in Australia upon completion of their studies, although a certain percentage preferred to stay in Sydney rather than Melbourne, so the situation was still less than optimal for Melbourne. By 1866, there were sixteen Moore College graduates serving in Melbourne and another six Melbourne men in training at the college.[94]

A decade later, in 1869, Perry still preferred to keep using the well-endowed and evangelical Moore College. A lengthy cover story for the *Messenger* dealt with the issue squarely. The diocesan paper had been re-founded that year, with evangelicals R. B. Dickinson, George Goodman, and G. O. Vance[95] forming the editorial board under the chief editorial control of Perry himself, so there is little doubt that the following were Perry's convictions:

> There is undoubtedly at present in the minds of some members of our Church a strange prejudice against Moore College; but notwithstanding all that has been said and written in jest and in earnest about it, we avow ourselves to be its staunch advocates. We believe that the Church in this diocese has derived great benefit from it; and we hope that, when the Church in Victoria contrives "to have a divinity school of its own," it will not be "very different from what Moore College" *really is*.[96]

The editors were responding directly to those who were campaigning against the influence of the "narrow party-spirited" Moore College, and calling for Melbourne to have its own college reflecting its own

---

92. Goodman, *Church in Victoria*, 474.
93. Church of England Record, 1859, 86–88. As cited in Robin, *Charles Perry*, 157.
94. *Church News*, 1866, 19.
95. Vance's theological position appears to have changed over time. He was chosen to give C. T. Perk's farewell address from St. Stephen's Richmond, which contained solidly evangelical themes (see above); however, he was later the offending vicar of Holy Trinity Kew whose drift towards high-church liturgy sparked the founding of St. Hilary's East Kew (see below).
96. COEM, 25 February 1869, 1. Emphasis in original.

self-perceived broader, more generous culture. Their article argued strongly against the anti-Moore sentiment, citing a variety of reasons including the witness of Moore graduates working in the diocese: "Many of those who have passed through Moore College are now parochial clergymen, highly esteemed not only for their personal piety and diligence in their work, but also for their ministerial ability."[97]

Perry, seeking to avoid unnecessary conflict and potential hardening of party lines, responded to the objectors by issuing a statement to the following Church Assembly of 1869, declaring that he would no longer draw from the Diocesan General Fund monies to support students from Melbourne at Moore. Instead, Perry set up a special association for collecting funds for this purpose, stating that it was a better outcome than "to give occasion to anything like a party conflict in the Assembly, and much better than to lose the benefit of a collegiate training, imperfect as it may be, for our students for the ministry."[98]

Perry fully recognized the danger in founding a college in Melbourne without sufficient assurance that it would not lose its evangelical character. One of the assurances Perry was seeking was an independent endowment fund for the principal's salary, which would give a measure of security to the position.[99] While that was not forthcoming, he preferred to risk that men training in Sydney would be tempted not to return to Melbourne or to other regional postings. This was a very real risk in times of severe shortage of qualified clergy nationally. Perry also banked on his good relationship with the evangelical Bishop Barker. Remarkably during Perry's episcopate, more Moore graduates were ordained for ministry in Melbourne than for any other diocese, *including* Sydney.[100] In fact, according to Judd and Cable, a significant percentage of men trained at Moore during Barker's episcopate were ordained in Melbourne and Ballarat: sixty-three out of 142. Goulburn, Bathurst and North Queensland, offshoots of Sydney, took twenty-seven; and Sydney itself took forty-two.[101] There was a strong and close relationship between Australia's most evangelical diocese and its most evangelical college, with Perry declaring thus:

---

97. COEM, 25 February 1869, 1.
98. COEM, 25 February 1869, 1.
99. Goodman, *Church in Victoria*, 461. COEM, February 1869, 2.
100. Loane, *Centenary History of Moore*, 180–82.
101. Judd and Cable, *Sydney Anglicans*, 75.

> I consider the establishment of Moore College, New South Wales, to have been one of the greatest blessings God has provided for the Church among us.[102]

Perry's ultimate aim was to have an evangelical diocesan training college in Melbourne. He therefore founded Trinity College in 1872, with the intent that the diocese would eventually have a theological school within the university college context, but he refused to open such a school until the necessary resources were available. It seems likely that another reason for Perry's refusal to start a theological school immediately, despite the urging of some laity, was that he could not ensure its evangelical character by way of the appointment of a suitable principal. The school eventually opened under his successor, Moorhouse, with low-church Protestant Alexander Leeper as its founding warden.

Interestingly, in retirement in England, Perry worked tirelessly to found Ridley Hall, Cambridge, which opened in 1881. Ridley was, unlike Trinity in Melbourne, a private college of the university with distinctly evangelical foundations. As a result of Perry's work, both Wycliffe Hall in Oxford and Ridley in Cambridge maintained a degree of independence from the universities and required their trustees and members of council to sign an assent to doctrinal statements designed to preserve evangelical and Protestant distinctives.[103] Perry may have felt unable to assert such a strongly partisan stance while needing to be bishop of the diocese, but had no hesitation once he was in retirement.

This model of an evangelical theological college with effective independence, close association to a university, and doctrinally assured trustees and council members was later adopted in Melbourne by evangelicals who founded Ridley College in 1910. The choice of college name and structure indicates that, three decades after his death in England, the leadership of Charles Perry was still being looked to in Melbourne.

Conclusion

This chapter has argued that the vital contribution of Charles Perry's leadership resulted in the Diocese of Melbourne being founded and established as the most identifiably evangelical of the Australian dioceses. This chapter has demonstrated that the prevailing narrative of Perry's contribution to early Melbourne history has not been adequately nuanced. Melbourne historian

---

102. Goodman, *Church in Victoria*, 460.
103. Robin, *Charles Perry*, 183.

Alan G. L. Shaw, for example, characterized Perry and Macartney as "militant low churchmen."[104] Manning Clark's monumental *History of Australia* focused almost exclusively on Perry the sectarian, using characteristically emotive language: "Charles Perry rejoiced as much in denouncing the errors of Rome . . . as he did over the return of one sinner to the flock."[105]

James Grant, in his chapter in the Diocese of Melbourne's official sesquicentenary history, described Perry as having a "reputation as a narrow-minded bigot in matters of churchmanship."[106] In the same volume, David Hilliard described Perry's opposition to the Tractarian movement and his steadfast refusal to ordain or admit entry to Melbourne of men with such inclinations.[107] However, both writers failed to properly account for the warmth of relationship between Perry and both Gregory and Handfield.

This chapter has demonstrated that Perry was neither militant nor bigoted, but rather that he operated on the basis of strongly principled theological and pastoral convictions. Two factors meant that it was Perry, not Moorhouse, who planted the seeds for future diversity in the diocese: first, Perry's acknowledgement that he was powerless to prevent clergy from changing their views after they had gained entry into the diocese; and second, Perry's conviction that it was the bishop's episcopal duty to care for all of his clergy, no matter what their views. In fact, Perry allowed Gregory and Handfield and others to continue in ministry in the diocese so long as he regarded them as remaining theologically orthodox and pastorally competent.

104. Shaw, *Port Phillip District*, 225. In this characterization, Shaw focuses on Perry and Macartney's "sectarianism" and anti-Catholicism and completely fails to recognize that the root cause of their attitude was not churchmanship, but theology. They were, first and foremost, evangelicals.

105. Clark, *History of Australia*, vol. 4, 365. It is far from certain that Perry rejoiced as such. Instead, his published writing and sermons indicate that his passion was to defend Protestant orthodoxy against what he perceived as Catholic error. In this, Perry was demonstrating his considerable intellectual capacity, for which he was routinely admired by both contemporaries and later historians. Clark's words on page 366 comparing Perry with his successor Moorhouse reveal Clark's prejudice and set the tone for much future historiography: "Perry was not renowned for his intellectual power; Moorhouse had a fine mind. Perry had frowned on pleasure; Moorhouse smoked a pipe in public. Perry had frequented the society of the great; Moorhouse, like his Savior, sought out the society of the publicans and the sinners. Perry set his face against the secularization of life, and the equation of human happiness with titillation of the senses; Moorhouse believed that Christ had come into the world so that men might have life and have it more abundantly. Perry was obsessed with asking how sinful man could enter at the narrow gate; Moorhouse entertained the larger hope of reconciling the Sermon on the Mount with the Rights of Man."

106. Grant, "Overview," 7.

107. Hilliard, "Intellectual Life," 28.

The conclusion of Robin's biographical account recognizes Perry's administrative leadership but fails to adequately account for how his evangelical theology informed his ministry priorities.[108] This chapter has demonstrated that Perry's policies and senior appointments reflected the priority he placed on evangelism and pastoral care. These priorities were shared by the evangelical clergy and laity he led and expressed in energetic church and school planting. Additionally, evangelicals were committed to the notion that gospel activism properly expressed would lead to the general betterment of society, hence their work in the founding of social institutions such as hospitals, asylums, and gathering points for learning and discussion like the Mechanics Institute. This chapter has also argued that the two causes that excited the most support among Melbourne evangelicals were the Bible and overseas missions, as expressed by the growth of the BFBS and various missionary agencies. Perry and other leading evangelicals were public supporters of both.

At the beginning of the life of the diocese, three of the four vital contributors identified by this study were present. There was a strongly evangelical bishop, there were vibrant and vital evangelical parish ministries, and there were also—though in their infancies—well-supported, active evangelical societies. There was not, however, a distinctly evangelical training college in the diocese. However, Perry's determination to keep sending his ordination candidates to Moore College, in the face of local resistance, indicates that he fully understood the vital contribution of a firmly evangelical theological college in forming future leaders for the movement within his diocese.[109]

---

108. Robin, *Charles Perry*, 191.

109. Robin, *Charles Perry*, 191. Robin correctly identifies in his conclusion Perry's emphasis on tertiary level education but fails to address and note Perry's main priority in retirement: the founding of a distinctly and constitutionally evangelical theological college within a university context. Perry was certainly not of the view, as Robin implies, that general tertiary education was adequate for clerical formation. See especially Perry, *Clerical Education Considered*.

5

Mission at Home and Abroad, 1876–1900

> You will receive power when the Holy Spirit has come upon you;
> and you will be my witnesses in Jerusalem, in all Judea and Samaria,
> and to the ends of the earth.
>
> ACTS 1:8

Introduction

THE LAST QUARTER OF the nineteenth century was a period of continued numerical growth for the Diocese of Melbourne. Beginning with around 200 buildings used for worship and 150 clergymen, by end of the quarter (in 1902) there were four separate dioceses and some 1200 buildings used for divine worship and nearly 300 clergymen.[1] However, after the departure of Bishop Perry, evangelicalism lost momentum for lack of a strongly committed and able diocesan bishop and leader.

Perry's successors were either not committed to evangelical priorities or not willing to elevate those priorities to the point of making difficult and painful decisions. Moorhouse was not an evangelical: although he used the language of "the gospel" and the necessity of "evangelism" and "conversion," he was not intently biblical in his sermons or lectures and he held modern views of the atonement that were unacceptable to contemporary evangelicals. Goe, who followed Moorhouse, was a good-hearted and mission-minded evangelical, but a poor leader. He avoided conflict and did little to restrain

---

1. Diocese of Melbourne Yearbook, 1903–4, 10.

the rise of ritualism in the diocese. It seems he was captured by the agendas of the powerful senior clergy appointed by Moorhouse.

By the turn of the century, evangelicals were more marginalized from the central structures of the diocese and more energetically involved in parishes and societies, especially those with a lively and committed focus on missionary endeavors sparked by the rise of Keswick spirituality. In Melbourne, a succession of missions by George Grubb and the Torrey-Alexander Crusades of 1902 and 1909, alongside the Chapman-Alexander Crusade of 1912, were extremely influential.[2] However, a great deal of this energy was interdenominational in character and not directed towards the renewal of the evangelical movement within Melbourne Anglicanism. Further, the lack of a firmly evangelical theological college able to produce evangelical Anglican clergy and train missionary candidates was a weakness that became increasingly apparent through this period.

In this chapter, the social context to these developments is outlined, highlighting some of the wider trends affecting evangelicalism in Melbourne. It will be shown that Perry's departure and the episcopates of James Moorhouse and Field Flowers Goe resulted in the loss of the vital contribution of the diocesan bishop. Evangelicals' response to this loss was demonstrated and expressed through the founding and continued publication of the *Victorian Churchman*.

This chapter shows that evangelical energy continued to be focused in local church ministry, as exemplified by the vitality of evangelical parishes at East Kew, Prahran, and Caulfield, as well as in Bendigo. These demonstrate that strong and vibrant evangelical parishes continued to be vital contributors to Melbourne Anglican evangelicalism. This chapter then examines how evangelical societies grew in their importance as vital contributors to the movement in Melbourne. The continued growth and development of the Church Missionary Society, and the founding of evangelical work among children and youth through the Children's Special Service Mission and Scripture Union, illustrate this. Towards the end of the nineteenth century, the influence of evangelical societies increased in importance relative to the other three vital contributors. Finally, this chapter notes the continued lack of the fourth vital contribution, a firmly evangelical theological college.

Social Context

The last quarter of the nineteenth century was the age of modern science. "Scientist" was a term coined by a teacher of Charles Perry's, William

2. See Evans, "Evangelicalism in Victoria in 1910."

Whewell, a polymath, philosopher, Master of Trinity College Cambridge, and ordained Church of England minister. Whewell had also coined the terms "cathode," "anode," and "ion" for Michael Faraday and influenced Charles Darwin and other major scientists of the day.[3] But by the mid-1870s, science was moving out of the laboratory. Alexander Graham Bell founded the Bell Telephone company in 1877, and the world's first commercial telephone exchange opened in New Haven, Connecticut, the next year. In the early 1880s, electricity was available in London houses and streets and was quickly spreading to the rest of the country.

These developments were part of a Technical or Second Industrial Revolution, when advances in steel, petroleum, chemical, and electrical industries built on earlier advances in steam, coal, and iron ore industries. Except for a few countries such as Japan, it was wealth accumulation in this period that established the foundations for long-lasting economic prosperity in the so-called developed nations of today. In North America, the period fell within the Gilded Age of the Rockefeller, Vanderbilt, Carnegie, Mellon, and Morgan families.[4] Wealth from tremendous industrial and financial earnings gave many of those families opulent lifestyles but also enabled philanthropic work which founded universities, museums, art galleries, other important social institutions, and immense trust funds for similar ends. This largesse reflected the powerful residue of Enlightenment trust in the value of civilizing education for the masses and higher education for leaders of society. The maxim of progress through education affected religious life as well, with some church leaders emphasizing the message of further education rather than the message of the gospel of forgiveness for repentant sinners.[5]

Opulence also reached "Marvelous Melbourne," whose wealth from gold production and trade was on show in the city, which became filled with new buildings made of solid stone rising seven stories off the street, stately mansions for the rich in surrounding localities, and an expanding tram and train system.[6] Melbourne was at the peak of its wealth, vitality, and

---

3. It was to Whewell that Charles Perry dedicated his 1864 volume of Cambridge sermons, *Foundation Truths*, which sought to defend the authority of the Old Testament Scriptures against "certain skeptical philosophers and critics of the present day." See forward to Perry, *Foundation Truths*.

4. The term is taken from the title of an 1873 satirical novel critical of the materialism of the times, *The Gilded Age: A Tale of Today*, by Mark Twain and Charles Warner. See http://www.gutenberg.org/ebooks/3178. Last accessed 31 October 2018.

5. For a detailed treatment of the Gilded Age, see Edwards, *New Spirits*.

6. The nomer "Marvelous Melbourne" is credited to the visiting English journalist George Augustus Henry Sala, writing in 1885. See Tout-Smith, *Melbourne*, 49, from which much of the Melbourne city information has been sourced.

influence, surpassing Sydney as the nation's premier city in terms of both population and progress. At one stage during the gold rush, Melbourne led the world in economic growth rates. The Melbourne International Exhibition of 1880–1881 and the Melbourne Centennial Exhibition of 1888–1889 were housed in the purpose-built Exhibition Buildings and took in unprecedented millions of visitors. Both exhibitions showcased the city's achievements on an international scale and further stimulated trade and economic activity. Perhaps more significantly, they engendered a sense of pride in the relatively young city's modern accomplishments and abilities.[7]

More mundane advances were nevertheless socially significant: this was the era in which Melbourne's roads and pavements were constructed, and telephone, gas, water, and electricity infrastructure were developed and extended into the suburbs. Melbourne's bishop began an ambitious cathedral building project. Growth was stimulated in part by a massive boom in land prices, with suburban plots changing hands in 1887 at up to twenty times the price from three years earlier.[8] By 1889, prices in Melbourne were equivalent to those in central London. The crash came in 1891, and the subsequent depression lingered for a decade.

Britain's colonial empire was at its zenith. On the European scene, German nationalism was on the rise, backed by rapid industrialization that was able to leapfrog Britain's earlier heavy capital investment and take advantage of newer technologies. However, it did not have a vast colonial empire, and this combination of nationalistic ambition and lack of access to primary raw materials laid the foundation for future aggression. Nationalistic ferment was in evidence elsewhere, too. Between 1894 and 1895 Japan and China were at war, with Japan taking control of Taiwan and Korea. China suffered further unrest in 1899 in the Boxer Rebellion against the encroachment of colonial values and control. In Africa, there were two Boer Wars, in 1880 and in 1899, between independence-minded Boers and their British rulers. Australians still viewed themselves as part of the British Empire, and some 16,000 volunteered *en masse* to serve Queen and country in South Africa.

The disparity between the modernizing nations and the rest of the world was stark. Between 1875 and 1900, famine in India claimed an estimated twenty-six million. Half that number, a still staggering thirteen million, perished of similar causes in China in the period between 1876 and 1879. Colonial contact with these regions meant that such news, although slowly communicated, was able to reach centers such as Sydney, London,

---

7. Tout-Smith, *Melbourne*, 39–51.

8. For a description of this, see Cannon, *The Land Boomers*. The impact of the land boom on evangelicals (and vice versa) is another important social theme yet to be adequately explored.

and Chicago. This sort of news, and a heritage of missionary heroism, kept the burden of world evangelization on the minds of evangelical Christians in affluent centers. However, the new urban and industrial centers locally also gave rise to an increasingly prominent home missions focus. By 1872, Dwight Lyman Moody was preaching in Chicago and Charles Haddon Spurgeon was at the height of his ministry in London.

Energy for evangelism was matched in part by energetic contention for the evangelical faith within the Church of England against the earlier Tractarian push and the drift towards a trust in scientific rationalism and the promise of human logic exemplified by the Higher Criticism movement. This was the age of "the Prince of the Tract Writers," John Charles Ryle. Ryle was installed as the first bishop of the rapidly industrializing city of Liverpool in 1880, aged sixty-three. He had already established his reputation as an evangelical leader and writer, publishing tracts collected in *Knots Untied* and *Practical Religion*; as well as *Expository Thoughts* on the Gospels, works reflecting on the reformers and church leaders of the seventeenth century, and his classic title, *Holiness*. His works were widely read in Britain and Australia and provided a robust Reformed and Protestant response to the Tractarian attempt to assert an essentially Catholic understanding of Church of England identity. Importantly, his writings celebrated both the biblical coherence and pastoral—especially evangelistic—effectiveness of the faith of the Thirty-nine Articles, thus providing inspiration for evangelical Anglicans to persist within their Church.[9]

In 1875, the first of the annual Keswick conventions was held in the Lake District of England. The Keswick movement had its origins in another annual conference organized by the Reverend William Pennefather in his London parish of Mildmay. The Mildmay conferences, like Keswick, were interdenominational, evangelical, and suffused with a strong concern for personal holiness, evangelism, and—later at Keswick—world mission.[10]

The twin themes of personal holiness and mission at home and abroad were to suffuse evangelicalism over the following decades. The first Protestant missionaries entered Korea in 1884, and by 1892 the Australian CMS Auxiliaries were organized into a single sending agency. The Irish evangelist and Keswick speaker George Grubb preached in Sydney and Melbourne in 1890 and 1891, resulting in a fresh wave of offers for missionary service.[11] His latter visit inspired a Keswick-style convention in

---

9. See the introduction by Gervase Duffield to Ryle, *Knots Untied*. Also, Harley, *J. C. Ryle*.

10. Bebbington, *Dominance of Evangelicalism*, 194–6.

11. Paproth, "Upwey Convention."

Geelong, the first of many in Victoria and Australia at which there would be regular calls to commit to serving the Lord wherever he might dictate. The rise of Keswick spirituality meant that a passionate commitment to mission was a hallmark of interdenominational evangelical life at the latter end of the nineteenth century.

Moorhouse and Goe

Under Perry, Melbourne became the most evangelical diocese in Australia. But it was not uniformly so. The advancing tide of theological liberalism and ritualist liturgy continued unabated, and even as convinced an evangelical as Perry was powerless to prevent their growth in Melbourne. Perry may have tolerated a certain degree of ritualism because he knew that he could not easily replace high-church clergymen. Further, there was clearly some grassroots demand for more color and ceremony in liturgy, despite the bishop's own views about the legality of sung responses, for example.

Perry was also a strong proponent of the independence of the bishop in his diocese and, correspondingly, the vicar in his parish. He was thus reluctant to exercise discipline unless there was heresy or a clear dereliction of pastoral duty and loss of parishioner support. Nevertheless, at the time of Perry's departure for England in 1874 the Diocese of Melbourne was easily identified as the most evangelical of the Australian dioceses.

Perry's power of appointment extended to bishops as well—a real power that is still retained by Anglican bishops more informally today as they act as referees and provide references and opinions on candidates' suitability. Perry was one of a small committee of four authorized by the Church Assembly to select the first bishop of Ballarat in 1875. The other members were William Stawell and the archbishops of York and Canterbury. As evangelicals and Melbourne "locals," Perry and Stawell had a decisive role in the selection of the first bishop of Ballarat, Samuel Thornton.

Perry also played a similar role in selecting two successive bishops of Melbourne, Moorhouse and Goe. He was popularly regarded as the founder of the church in Melbourne and widely respected as a father figure for the province, so it is not surprising that his opinion was regarded very highly by fellow nominators and by the diocese while he was still alive in an active retirement in England.

James Moorhouse

When Perry resigned in 1876, he was followed by the broad churchman James Moorhouse (1876–1886). Moorhouse was clearly an intellectual and able public speaker. His public lectures would pack the Melbourne Town Hall, and his proclamations ranged from education policy to water reform. He had thoughts on a Victorian North-South water pipeline in the nineteenth century, a century before its eventual construction. He was engaging and popular—"magnetic," to quote his biographer Sturrock.[12]

But Moorhouse is universally recognized as a broad churchman and not an evangelical. Under him, the diocese's movement towards diversity accelerated. It was still mainly low church but no longer distinctly evangelical. Perry had been classically evangelical: clearly biblical, clear on the atoning work of Christ on the cross for sin, focused on the gospel of forgiveness and salvation following the repentance of sins, stressing the need for conversion, and possessed of an activism based on the gospel imperative. By contrast, Moorhouse was an intellectual whose activism was based on liberal ideals. He was, relative to Perry, only incidentally biblical and only occasionally used the evangelistic language of conversion. His speeches and sermons focused on the importance of education and the improvement of society through reading, lectures (which he encouraged in church buildings) and schooling. The authorities he appealed to were invariably logic and human reason rather than divine revelation through the Scriptures.

Why the evangelical Perry chose the broad churchman Moorhouse to succeed him is an important historical question that, for lack of source documents, may never be satisfactorily answered.[13] Perry had no official authority to choose a successor, but his recommendation was decisive for the selectors in Melbourne. Moorhouse came highly recommended, his own successful ministry at Paddington spoke for itself, and there is clear evidence that he was deeply spiritual and shared the evangelical perspective on the need for repentance from sin and conversion to Christ.[14] But he never self-identified as an evangelical and was not connected to evangelical societies like the CMS or Church Pastoral Aid Society (CPAS).

Perry might have considered that it was more important for Melbourne—by this stage a leading city of the Empire filled with cultured, able, and powerful citizens—to have a man of intellectual and oratorical ability to

---

12. Sturrock, *Bishop of Magnetic Power*.

13. Sturrock, for example, suggests that Perry saw in him "a firm evangelical," *Bishop of Magnetic Power*, 41. In this she follows the lead set by Curry, "Moorhouse and Melbourne," 4–5.

14. Curry, "Moorhouse and Melbourne." 5.

lead and unite the diocese. Perry was considered by the Melbourne press to be impressively academic, godly, and an able administrator, but also (unfairly) as colorless and dour. If Perry was at all party-spirited, then this would have been the key opportunity for him to prove it. Instead, Perry seems to have placed his trust in someone considered orthodox and not necessarily clearly evangelical. It is likely that Perry saw in Moorhouse a man of ability and commitment to the church, someone able to combat the internal threat of Tractarian theology and the external threat of scientific rationalism, and someone able to make stronger connections to Melbourne society.

However, Moorhouse's ministry would seriously erode Perry's evangelical legacy. Under Moorhouse, the diocese slid inexorably away from being distinctly evangelical in theology. The priority of local evangelism began to give way to other, more church-centered projects. For example, Perry had steadfastly refused to give active support to a cathedral building project, citing the infancy of the diocese and more pressing needs at the parish level. While there were churches and schools to be built, Perry stalled on the question of a cathedral. But Moorhouse immediately gathered support and finances and commenced building.

In the Moorhouse period, evangelicalism was beginning to be affected by the Keswick movement. In Melbourne, there was strong expression of this form of evangelicalism, expressed particularly in the missionary effort and revival missions. A good record of this exists in the journal *The Missionary at Home and Abroad*, edited by H. B. Macartney Jr. between 1873 and 1898. The journal focuses on missionary stories in Victoria and reports from missionaries serving abroad with the CMS Victoria Auxiliary, CMS of Victoria, and the Church of England Zenana Mission Society (CEZMS), as well as other missionaries associated with other missions and groups.

One of the consequences of Keswick spirituality was a gradual withdrawal from diocesan engagement. Evangelical energy went into missions and their own societies instead of into diocesan committees and affairs. Evangelicals prioritized mission and gravitated to those groups that were most active. Some missionary societies, like the CMS, were Anglican, but many others were interdenominational or independent. This trend, combined with Moorhouse's lack of evangelical fervor, made it easier for evangelicals to withdraw from diocesan affairs.

Dean Macartney's assessment of both of Perry's successors is telling. His unpublished memoirs contain this assessment of Moorhouse:

> He was a thoroughly masculine man, but he combined that with all the charm of a woman. He belonged to the Broad School, but his wife was an extreme Sacerdotalist. He boldly condemned

her views whenever she expressed them and imagined that she had no influence over his conduct in his diocese, just as a strong rower might imagine that the little girl with a stick in her hand at the stern of the boat, had no power over his strong arm. The consequence was that while men who held the doctrines of the Church of England were allowed to be hewers of wood and drawers of water—all that was worth having went to those who were called Broad or High.[15]

I knew that his episcopate had lowered the spiritual tone of the Church, while it had greatly added to her popularity—so that I could not but hope that God would send us one more entirely guarded by His Word and Spirit—but there was a halo of sympathy about him—of all that is attractive in man that led to a mingling of contradictory feelings such as I never experienced in any other event in my life—He went—and his going was almost like the setting sun. I was again left in charge of the diocese, but it was a very different diocese from that which I had watched with so much pleasure and thankfulness from 1874–1877.[16]

Macartney was certainly correct about Mrs. Mary Moorhouse, whose favorite place of worship was the ritualist St. Peter's Eastern Hill.[17] Macartney clearly regarded Moorhouse's popular and intellectual ministry as detracting from the scriptural and vital spirituality so valued by evangelicals. Further, Macartney understood the "doctrines of the Church of England" as expressing and safeguarding this spirituality. For him the opposite of men who were true and loyal to the Church were those "called Broad or High"— including Moorhouse.

His assertion that evangelicals were passed over for promotion is true at least of his own son, H. B. Macartney Jr., and Henry Langley.[18] Macartney Jr. was without doubt the pre-eminent leader among the evangelical enthusiasts of the 1875–1900 period. He had been sent to his father's *alma mater*, Trinity College Dublin, for studies, and was ordained in Melbourne by Perry upon his return. In 1868, he began a thirty-year association with St. Mary's Caulfield, which became one of the leading evangelical parishes in Melbourne—and certainly the diocese's leading missions-focused parish.

---

15. Macartney, "Memoirs," 321–2. Original MS held in the Melbourne Diocesan archives.

16. Macartney, "Memoirs," 348.

17. Sturrock, *Bishop of Magnetic Power*, 251, notes that Moorhouse chose St. Peter's as the last place of his public ministry in Melbourne, celebrating communion there the morning of his departure.

18. See ADEB entries.

Macartney was at the height of his ministry influence during the Moorhouse period, proving to be an able leader and organizer, and initiator of new developments like bringing Scripture Union's reading notes to Australia. However, his focus was interdenominational evangelicalism and never merely or even primarily on the Church of England. He was never given wider responsibilities within the diocese until his appointment by Bishop Goe to the Council of the Diocese in 1895, just a few years before his departure in 1898 to take up a leadership role with the BFBS in London.

Similarly, Henry Langley, who exercised an energetic evangelistic ministry at St. Matthew's Prahran from 1878 onwards, turning it into the leading evangelical parish of the diocese, was passed over until Goe appointed him archdeacon of Gippsland in 1890 and then archdeacon of Melbourne and Geelong in 1894. Under his care, St. Matthew's had come alive with well-attended services, conferences for the deepening of spiritual life, open air services, and increasing numbers of young men converted. He also started the work that eventually led to the planting of St. Alban's Armadale as a separate parish. Parish historians describe his ministry as "living power," through which others were inspired to work hard for God; a contemporary account describes his "intense spiritual force."[19] Langley had come to Melbourne after a successful ministry in Sydney, including a stint as acting dean, during which time attendances of men in particular increased. He was a recognized leader, eloquent preacher, evangelist, energizer of spiritual lives, and popular parish missioner among his colleagues—but ignored for wider service by Moorhouse. A comparison of Moorhouse's and Goe's appointments of canons is revealing: the former appointed the high churchman Robert Potter in 1883, the latter the vociferous evangelical Digby Berry in 1895.[20]

Macartney's assessment of Moorhouse's successor, Field Flowers Goe, provides an interesting contrast. Moorhouse had been translated to Manchester and is the said bishop of Manchester mentioned in the following extract. Tellingly, Macartney does not use his name in the second half of the first sentence or in the paragraph that follows.

> When Bishop Moorhouse resigned the Board of Electors took the miserable course of leaving the decision to the Archbishop

---

19. Bride, *Proclaiming the Gospel*, 62.

20. An exception is Moorhouse's promotion of the evangelical John Christian MacCullagh in 1885. MacCullagh's outstanding ministry was in the Bendigo region and very highly regarded, so it is likely that Moorhouse did not have much of a choice and MacCullagh's influence would have been limited to the region. See *Statistics of the Diocese of Melbourne*, 11 (held in the Diocese of Melbourne Archives).

of Canterbury, Bishop Perry and the Bishop of Manchester & two others.

The bishop of Manchester was anxious to appoint someone of his own vision—if any very extreme man was named Bishop Perry objected and they did not like to go against his protests. Some to whom the offer was made refused to leave England and after one or two ineffectual meetings the Archbishop proposed Mr. Goe, a truly excellent & enlightened man, an admirable parish clergyman but without any idea of colonial work or the connection of Episcopal authority with representative institutions. His Grace did not again call the new nominators together but wrote notes to each proposing Mr. Goe—and they all answered—yes.

We thus regarded him as sent to us by a succession of providences and blessed God for providing us a man who knows the truth and loves it.[21]

Macartney's frank assessment was that it was better to have a less administratively competent evangelical who knew and loved the truth, rather than a popular and powerful public speaker less "entirely guarded" by God's Word and Spirit.

Field Flowers Goe

Melbourne's third bishop, Field Flowers Goe, was publicly identified as an evangelical. He was a member of the CMS and a speaker at the evangelical Islington Conference.[22]

Goe inherited a diocese that in 1887 was a mix of high- and low-church parishes. Moorhouse had allowed both to coexist and thrive in his ten years, weakening the decidedly evangelical foundation laid by Perry. Evangelicals, sidelined by Moorhouse, continued to focus much of their energies in the missionary societies, fostered in large part by the growth of the Keswick movement.

Goe was at least a supporter of evangelical initiatives: he hosted the Keswick evangelist George Grubb during his 1891 mission and encouraged the merging of the CMS of Victoria, the CMS Victoria Auxiliary, and the CEZMS into the single Victorian CMA in 1892.[23] In his 1896 address to

---

21. Macartney, "Memoirs." 360-1.
22. Bebbington, "Very Essence of Evangelicalism."
23. See Cole, *Sharing in Mission*; Cole, *A History of the Church Missionary Society of Australia*.

the Church Assembly, he declared: "The most important event which has occurred in this diocese during the past year, from the spiritual point of view, was the General Parochial Mission in Melbourne and the suburbs held in July and August last."[24]

However, to the disappointment of some, Goe did nothing to restrain ritualists: in fact, he had earlier, as a clergyman in England, signed a memorial against their persecution by more extreme Protestants like John Kensit of the Protestant Truth Society, who had threatened to disrupt ritualist services.[25] Goe prioritized good order and amenable relations, and so evangelicalism and ritualism both continued to grow in Melbourne.

Goe was dutiful, faithfully completing the cathedral project started by Moorhouse. He did this just in time, before the arrival of the 1893 bank crash. Another measure of his sense of personal duty and conscience was his decision to take a £500 cut in his stipend as a result of the financial hardship caused by the crash. He declared that he and his wife had no children and could live very simply.[26] Financial difficulties for the church and wider society dogged Goe's time: the severe drought from 1895 to 1903 further depressed the local economy.

The Victorian Churchman

Significantly, it was during this time that *The Victorian Churchman* first appeared in print in January 1890. The *Churchman* was an evangelical and low-church newspaper. It was started out of dissatisfaction with the existing paper, the *Church of England Messenger*, and bemoaned the rise of ritualism and the tolerated proliferation of high-church practices in the diocese. The *Messenger* had been edited by Canon Vance since 1877. He had been on a renewed editorial team headed by Perry in 1869 and displayed some sympathy to evangelicalism, but by 1890 his ministry at Holy Trinity Kew showed that he had clearly shifted in relation to liturgical matters considered touchstones of evangelical identity.

The *Argus* published a pseudonymous letter of protest, which reported the presence in Vance's church of a "high culture party . . . gloveless hands and swinging crosses . . . altar and super-altar, with the cross appearing to rest upon it (which is illegal) . . ." The "gloveless hands" referred to manual acts or gesturing with the hands during the Eucharistic prayers, which was regarded

---

24. Diocesan Year Book, 1896–7.

25. James Grant, "Right Reverend Field Flowers Goe," 9. See also COEM, 8 December 1886.

26. COEM, 8 December 1886.

as ritualistic by evangelicals. The correspondent further reported that these developments, and the illegal cross on the altar in particular, were "an offence to many . . ." and, "All these things have come about bit by bit, and evangelical part of the congregation do not know when they will stop, and so the desire for another church and a minister of their own choosing."[27]

One such appointee was the originator of the idea of founding the *Churchman*. He also happened to be the minister appointed by Goe to the church formed in protest against Vance's practices at Holy Trinity Kew: he was Henry Stanley Mercer, the young incumbent of the fledgling St. Hilary's East Kew. St. Hilary's had been birthed in protest by convinced evangelical laity who were determined to have their own church and a minister of their own choosing.

Mercer edited the first edition of the *Churchman*, but then the reins were taken up by another young minister, Alfred Charles Kellaway, who would be editor for the next twenty-three years.[28] The *Churchman* was a protest by younger, emerging evangelical leaders of the next generation against the perceived laxity of their elders. The idea for the paper was itself hatched in an evangelical stronghold:

> A gathering of evangelical clergy held at St. James' parsonage in the year 1889 saw the first steps taken toward the publication of a church newspaper, which should distinctly represent the view of the evangelicals of the Church of England in the Melbourne Diocese, and when necessary voice their protests and their needs.[29]

For twenty-four years, the *Churchman* was the voice of evangelical churchmen within the diocese and indeed the province. It was distributed throughout the state, from Portland to Bairnsdale to Mooroopna, and in 1900 had some 2000 subscribers.[30] Underneath the title banner for each edition were the words, ἀληθεύοντες δὲ ἐν ἀγάπῃ αὐξήσωμεν εἰς αὐτὸν τὰ πάντα. Readers were left to discern that they were a quote from Ephesians 4:15a— "Speaking the truth in love, we will in all things grow up in him." It was a declaration of the paper's purpose and method, with the untranslated biblical

27. *The Argus*, 25 September 1888. Incorrectly cited as 24 September in Behan, *St. Hilary's Anglican Church Kew, 1888–1988*, 7, although the letter itself is dated the 24th.

28. VC, 1901, 25 January 1901 article featuring St. Hilary's Kew and its first incumbent Henry Stanley Mercer noted that "he may be regarded as the founder of the *Victorian Churchman*, the suggestion of starting this journal having first come from him."

29. VC, 1913, 26 December 1913, 834.

30. An appeal for each subscriber to get another subscriber was published on 14 September 1900 noting that if every present subscriber did this they would, "with very little effort," reach their target of 2000 new subscribers.

Greek emphasizing the primacy of serious attention to the Scriptures. A typical edition contained an editorial lead, which in later editions became comments on latest news; English Church news, Diocesan and Parochial news, notices and news from the Evangelical Church Association and CMA, missions reports and letters, and other articles and lectures. The premillennial fascination of many evangelicals of the period is revealed in long-running series by Digby Berry expounding Revelation and Daniel.

The *Churchman* dates the beginning of strong, publicly voiced opinion in the evangelical camp against the general direction of the diocese—and this during the episcopate of the evangelical Goe. So although there was confidence about the strength of evangelical parishes and agencies, there was a loss of confidence in the ability of the diocese to safeguard doctrinal orthodoxy and promote evangelical priorities. Goe did not or could not arrest that trend which had gathered so much momentum under Moorhouse.

An early feature in the *Churchman* that did not continue with any real degree of consistency was the publication of a portrait and brief biography of a noted church leader. These were not necessarily evangelical heroes, but loyal churchmen who, in the estimation of the editors, served the church beloved by the evangelicals well. The first portrait was that of the then elderly Dean Macartney. There were subsequent portraits of the Archdeacons T. C. B. Stretch and H. A. Langley, which may have served more political purposes, given that they were published at the same time as discussions around the founding of new dioceses. Both men were mooted for promotion to episcopal rank; Stretch had previously been a candidate for Ballarat, and Langley was subsequently appointed to Bendigo.

The immediate past bishop of Melbourne, James Moorhouse, was also featured in the series. The editor noted the influence of his "presence and speech," praised his advocacy of the Bible in state schools and his work on "our magnificent Cathedral." It was noted that "under his eloquence the income of the Bishop of Melbourne's Fund was largely augmented, with the result that the work of the Church was greatly extended, more particularly in the sparsely populated portions of the diocese." The final assessment was frank. The editor was explicit in saying that the *Churchman* could not accept his views on the atonement, the inspiration of Scripture and on the future punishment of the wicked, yet admired his "great intellectual gifts" and ended the portrait on a positive note: (we) "heartily appreciate the many noble qualities for which he is justly famous."[31]

These portraits reflect the way some evangelicals of the period related to the diocese. Although formed in protest, these evangelicals sought

---

31. VC, 1891, 8 May 1891.

engagement with the diocese, not disengagement. They recognized that there was variety in churchmanship and sought to be as inclusive as possible, while excluding extreme high-church ritual and Tractarian and liberal theology. So, while they lauded the energy and commitment to the church of men like Handfield, Stretch, and Moorhouse, they could at the same time lament their lack of clarity on distinctive evangelical tenets such as the authority of Scriptures, a penal substitutionary view of the atonement, and the necessity of conversion.

The *Churchman* also sought to encourage Goe's independence and strong exercise of authority in denying unsuitable men entry into the diocese. It did this in a way that echoed Goe's own evangelical and Keswick spirituality, appealing to the language of that spirituality in an editorial of 15 January 1892, in which the editor sought to defend Bishop Goe against criticism published in letters to the secular press. Apparently, Goe had declined to appoint certain men to ministry in the diocese, and their supporters had written letters of complaint outlining their eminent qualifications for ministry. Goe could or would not defend his decisions in public, and so the *Churchman* took up his case. The editor encouraged Goe to keep being a bishop unswayed by popular opinion, declaring, "We desire not a puppet but a Bishop."[32]

> This we pray and believe, that his Lordship will do what, in God's sight, he believes to be his duty. Of course he will offend many, and some may bring railing accusations against him, and he may, being human, make mistakes; but still we believe that this independent action will result in the greatest good to the Church as whole, for, after all, the Bishop's responsibility is not to the Church but to the Church's Master.[33]

By 1892, the diocese as a whole was beginning to move away from its earlier distinctively evangelical character. Evangelicals, or at least the editor of the *Churchman*, recognizing the strategic importance of appointments, tried to encourage their evangelical bishop to exercise his authority in such a way as to maintain an evangelical witness in the diocese. In parishes where able and decidedly evangelical clergy were appointed and where a core of evangelically minded laity were present, a strong evangelical ministry flourished.

32. VC, 1892, 15 January, 13.
33. VC, 1892, 15 January, 13.

Parishes

Four examples of evangelical activity in the parish sector during this period are St. Hilary's East Kew, St. Matthew's Prahran, St. Mary's Caulfield, and St. Paul's Sandhurst (Bendigo), which was still part of the diocese of Melbourne.

St. Hilary's Kew

St. Hilary's East Kew—later simply St. Hilary's Kew—was an example of evangelical lay activism in the face of unacceptable liturgical or theological drift. Two principles were significant in the creation of this parish: first, evangelicals' belief in their right to freely associate and act according to their convictions; and second, their assertion that as they paid for their minister, they would determine the person they would appoint. A correspondent to the *Argus* put it more bluntly:

> With no state church here the clergy ought ever to remember that those who pay the piper have a right to call the tune.[34]

The correspondence in the *Argus* had been sparked by a letter complaining about the preferment of younger clergy to city parishes, ostensibly because such appointments diminished the privileges of older men who had done their time in the more difficult conditions in the rural churches. The correspondent considered that this sort of action would alienate country church members and lead to "further impoverishment of church funds."[35] It was perceived as an attack on the independent evangelical action at East Kew in securing the appointment of the young, capable evangelical Stanley Mercer as their first incumbent. Mercer's four years of service in Ballarat as a curate and a vicar before coming to Prahran to be Langley's curate was conveniently discounted by this correspondent.

Yet another correspondent wrote in defense of Mercer's appointment:

> In discussing the recent appointment to the new parish at Kew your correspondent seems to imagine that the laity have no rights, and that the church exists for the clergy. The East Kew people do not agree with him. They have rights, and have asserted them effectually. They say in effect, "We are able and willing to build a church and to support a clergyman, but we

---

34. *Argus*, Tuesday 25 September 1888, 13, letter from "Carthusian."

35. *Argus*, Saturday 22 September 1888, 14, letter from "A Member of the Church Assembly."

will do neither one nor the other unless we have a voice in the appointment of the clergyman who is to minister to us."[36]

It was lay evangelical dissatisfaction with the ritualist trend at Holy Trinity Kew that agitated and organized for the creation of a separate parish and minister of their own choosing. Among them was Captain Edward Dumaresq, a successful land speculator in Tasmania and then Melbourne. He owned and then subdivided lands in the Kew junction area, giving a portion to the diocese. However, the diocese decided to sell the land, at which point he bought it back for £500.

In July 1888, the organizing committee, of which Dumaresq was an original member, decided to buy the parcel of land for the establishment of their new church, which for a while was known as St. Helier's, after the Dumaresq ancestral home on the Channel Island of Jersey.[37] However, the committee could not find any such saint's name, and the parish was later renamed St. Hilary's. Parish historians McCullagh and Rodda record the substantial founding efforts of "Mr. John Wilkinson," "Mrs. Fred Wilkinson," and "Mr. and Mrs. Albert Purchas"—all members of the original committee. At the time of his death in 1898, the parish Guardians regarded the layman John Wilkinson as "practically the founder of the church."[38]

The importance of evangelical laity is more clearly seen when it is observed that the first incumbent, Mercer, stayed only two years. The Cambridge graduate had indicated his desire to return to England from the outset, for reasons unknown. Mercer had come to Australia in 1884 and served in Ballarat, then became Henry Langley's curate at Prahran for less than twelve months before his appointment to East Kew. At Prahran, he was said by an observer to have held the attention of "700 or 800 people who listen to him with pleasure and profit Sunday after Sunday."[39] The same correspondent to the Argus declared Mercer to be "an unusually effective preacher . . . and has shown proofs of being a most successful priest in, perhaps, the most successful parish in the diocese," referring to St. Matthew's Prahran. At East Kew, Mercer would have a much smaller congregation of around fifty and a smallish building that the bishop refused to consecrate, even after it had been fully paid for, on the grounds that it was only made of wood.[40]

---

36. *Argus*, Monday 24 September 1888, 10, letter from "A Lover of the Church."

37. The spelling of St. Helier's itself was varied. For example, "J. G. Mickelburgh, Honorary Secretary of the St. Hillier's Church Committee, East Kew" was one of the correspondents to *The Argus*, 24 September 1888, 10.

38. Rodda and Behan, *St. Hilary's*, 8.

39. *The Argus*, 24 September 1888, 10, letter from "Fairplay."

40. Rodda and Behan, *St. Hilary's*, 9.

That St. Hilary's laity were able to secure the services of the talented young curate is testimony to their persuasive abilities and influence, not just with Mercer but also over the bishop. Among some of the powerful early laity were John and James Griffiths, the successful owners of Griffiths Brothers Tea, and Edwin Lee Neil, the Managing Director of Myer's Emporium.[41] Their evangelicalism led them to commit to the fledgling evangelical St. Hilary's rather than to the established but theologically suspect Holy Trinity. All three men were leading Melbourne evangelicals who gave generously, not just to their local parish but also to a variety of other evangelical causes—especially those connected with their deep and abiding interest in missionary work. Half of their children went on to serve as overseas missionaries in Bolivia, Egypt, the South Seas, and Roper River.

The Griffiths and Neil families were committed to St. Hilary's because they had chosen to live in the Kew area, which experienced a population boom in this period. Stately Victorian homes rose from the farmlands and orchards that previously dotted the area. Most church people were committed to the idea of attending the local parish church; traveling across parish boundaries to attend another church was rare. Marriages and baptisms were certainly only ever conducted within the parish, and permission for cross-parish services still had to be sought well into the mid-twentieth century. The presence of these decidedly evangelical and certainly capable laity who were committed to their local parish meant that, even from small beginnings, St. Hilary's stood a good chance of developing an enduring evangelical ministry—provided the right clergyman could be found.

St. Matthew's Prahran

The arrival in 1875 of a new vicar, Barnabas Shaw Walker, marked a strong turning point in the life of the parish of St. Matthew's Prahran. Parish historians Graham and Margaret Bride note that the parish became more lively as a result of Walker's leadership. Seat-holders increased from 132 to 320. Special evangelistic services and church events were widely advertised in the district to increase the church's profile and connection to the local community. Walker brought the evangelical Methodism of his childhood, his training to be a Methodist minister, and his evangelistic ministry in Gisborne to bear on urban Prahran.[42] An extant handbill advertising a service with a

---

41. See entries in ADEB, ADB and further below.

42. Bride, *Proclaiming the Gospel*, 32–42. Walker's Methodist career was interrupted because of he got married and had to leave his training per the rules of the Methodist church for student ministers. He then offered to Perry for ordination and

"Sermon having reference to young men," but nevertheless with an invitation to "young men and women . . . specially invited to the service," illustrates his concern for the young people of the parish and his innovation in using cheaply printed materials as tools of evangelism and mission.

In the wake of the passage of the 1872 Education Act mandating secular instruction in state schools, St. Matthew's Sunday School ministry expanded greatly to provide religious education to the faithful. The seriousness of the Sunday School regimen at Prahran was lightened once a year by the Annual Sunday School Treat—on one occasion a picnic outing to Brighton Beach. The theme of evangelical seriousness was not uncommon through the 1800s; indeed, it was a marker of evangelical culture both in Britain and her colonies.[43] Part of this seriousness was applied by Walker to his call for young people to consider ordained ministry and missionary service. It is testimony to Walker and the parish's successive ministries that many who were influenced by him later went down the path of full-time ministry work.

Walker's unexpected death in 1878 paved the way for a succession of notable evangelical vicars who firmly cemented St. Matthew's evangelical character, which may have been in danger of being lost if the wrong appointments had been made. Bishops Moorhouse and Goe did not interfere with the parish's desires in this regard. Henry Archdall Langley followed Walker and remained at Prahran till his promotion to archdeacon of Gippsland in 1890. Langley's family had emigrated from Ireland to Sydney in 1853, and both Henry and his older brother John Douse entered ordained ministry. Both trained at Moore College and took their first ministry postings in that diocese. However, both found their way to Melbourne and were eventually successive founding bishops of Bendigo. The Langleys were key evangelical leaders of the era, and Henry Langley's ministry at the flagship Prahran parish was particularly remembered:

> When the years Langley spent at St. Matthew's are examined, his energy and his many and diverse interests both in Prahran and in the wider church are quite breathtaking. His ministry in Prahran was indeed *living power*. He also had the capacity to inspire other men to work hard for God . . . He was an eloquent preacher, usually speaking without any apparent reference to notes.[44]

Langley started Saturday night prayer meetings in the parish, which he regarded as the most important parish meetings outside of Sunday

---

was accepted and posted to Gisborne.

43. See for example, Bradley, *Call to Seriousness*.
44. Bride, *Proclaiming the Gospel*, 62.

services. He cleared the church's large building debt and raised more funds for further extensions. He particularly encouraged young men to participate in church services and encouraged those he thought suitable to offer for ordained ministry. In 1887, Langley ran a special mission to men in the parish. This ministry to young men, which included encouraging appropriate ones into ordained ministry, is a key ministry of leading evangelical clergy across the period of our study. In this, Langley followed the example already set by his predecessor, Walker. One of Langley's curates, for example, was Henry Stanley Mercer, mentioned already as the instigator and founding editor of the *Victorian Churchman* and the first incumbent of St. Hilary's Kew. Under Langley, open air evangelistic preaching became a feature of the parish and Prahran became known as one of the most lively and active parishes in the diocese.[45]

Langley was also involved in wider efforts at evangelism, most notably the 1888 Centennial Mission. He was one of two signatories to the Mission's final report to the diocese and one of the chief organizers. The Mission itself ran for a week from 15 July that year and was focused in the thirty-five parishes that had agreed to be involved. Each received a dedicated missioner from outside the parish, who spoke evangelistically on most evenings and then on the Sunday. It was Langley who had suggested this diocese-wide parochial mission take place in conjunction with a wider interdenominational Centennial Mission already being organized by the Evangelisation Society of Victoria (ESV)—of which he was an executive member.[46] Despite opposition from other members of the Church of England, who were reluctant to be associated with such evangelical enthusiasm, the support of Bishop Goe meant that the Anglican mission went ahead, albeit only in the more firmly evangelical parishes.

The diocese's overall response to the Mission is important. Although many viewed evangelical enthusiasm with suspicion, the *Messenger*, edited by George Vance, still carried a full report. Evangelicals were gradually losing ground in the diocese, but persons in positions of seniority within the establishment like Vance, who by this stage was not considered an evangelical, were still sympathetic, or at least viewed the place and contribution of evangelicals in the diocese as important.

Langley was promoted to archdeacon of Gippsland in 1890. He was later archdeacon of Melbourne and Geelong before his consecration as the first bishop of Bendigo—further testimony to his ability. Arthur Blackett

---

45. Bride, *Proclaiming the Gospel*, 52–57. See also ADEB entry for "Langley, Henry Archdall," 214–5.

46. See Paproth, "Centennial Mission."

followed Langley in Prahran. They were certainly well acquainted with one another. Both had trained for ministry at Moore. Both had been involved in the 1888 Mission, when Blackett had been the missioner to Prahran, while Langley himself was missioner to Carlton. That both men were missioners speaks of their evangelistic and preaching gifts.

Both men were also possessed of the evangelical commitment to world missions. Blackett and Langley had been among the forty evangelicals, lay and clerical, who gathered in Sydney in 1889 to consider changes in the constitution of the Church Missionary Society in Australia to make it separate from the English CMS and enable it to send its own missionaries overseas. Other Melbourne leaders present were Arthur Pain, John Langley, and H. B. Macartney Jr.[47] It was a sign that evangelicals in Australia were growing in confidence, strength, and passion for world evangelism. The same men were later key members of the Victorian CMA, which formed in 1892 and united at least three separate evangelical missionary societies.[48]

Leading Prahran laity like John Henry Maddock became highly involved as well. Maddock, a prominent Melbourne lawyer and mayor of Prahran, was the first honorary treasurer and a long-term trustee of CMS. His wife was secretary of the Women's Missionary Council.[49] The importance of world mission was certainly preached from the Prahran pulpit. In 1889, for example, Langley preached a monthly series on "aspects of missionary effort and fields of operation."[50] In May 1889, the subject was Japan. Leadership of this sort was not merely in words: Blackett himself eventually resigned from Prahran to serve as a missionary in Persia in 1895. He and his wife were the fourth set of CMA missionaries to depart for overseas service.

By this time, Prahran's evangelicalism was firmly established and typical of Melbourne Anglican evangelicalism in this period. It had a lively conversionist ministry with strong links to the CMA. In 1894, the parish hosted a week-long Convention on the Deepening of Spiritual Life.[51] The list of speakers reads as a who's who of Melbourne evangelicals. They included the bishop of Melbourne, Field Flowers Goe, the aged dean of Melbourne, H. B. Macartney, his son H. B. Macartney Jr., Canon Septimus Lloyd Chase, and Digby Berry. The president of the convention was the past incumbent, Archdeacon Langley. It was noted that the Convention was not distinctly evangelical in the sense that not all of its topics would have met with the approval of

---

47. Johnstone, *History of the Church Missionary Society*, 250.
48. Cole, *History of the Church Missionary Society of Australia*, 19.
49. Bride, *Proclaiming the Gospel*, 48.
50. Bride, *Proclaiming the Gospel*, 48.
51. See report in the VC, April 27.

those labeled as part of the Evangelical Party in the "old country."[52] Rather, the Prahran Convention was affected by Keswick spirituality and its impetus to press on into deeper personal piety and more effective world mission. Some charismatic spirituality was also in evidence, with Digby Berry noting that there were "many indications that the Church was groping her way back into the possession of the gift of healing."[53]

Prahran had suffered along with Melbourne during the depression of the 1890s, but was still a strong manufacturing, commercial, and residential area. The church itself had large functional buildings clear of debt, a thriving Sunday School, and an active congregational life. Blackett had struggled to step into the large void left by the highly capable Langley, and the bishop and nominators would have been anxious to make a wise choice in the next incumbent. William Townsend Cooper Storrs, the young curate of St. Stephen's Richmond, would not disappoint them. He was a Cambridge graduate and already on the committee of the CMA. His thirty-one-year incumbency at Prahran not just maintained but grew Prahran's evangelical ministry and witness through a period of momentous social and demographic change. He would serve as a key leader of Melbourne evangelicalism for more than fifty years.

St. Mary's Caulfield

The parish with perhaps the strongest interest in mission was St. Mary's Caulfield, largely because of the personal ministry of its vicar, H. B. Macartney Jr. Caulfield had begun as part of the parish of Prahran, with J. H. Gregory as its vicar. By this point, Gregory had developed his definite high-church inclinations, but the strength of the evangelical laity at Caulfield meant that a high-church culture did not establish itself there. Interestingly, the first services held in the parish, though under Gregory's oversight and by his instigation, were conducted by "Revd Samuel Taylor (from St. Andrew's Brighton) and Revd David Seddon (of Christ Church St. Kilda) on a Sunday afternoon in Park Street, just around the corner from the future site of St. Mary's."[54] Christ Church was another strongly evangelical parish of the period.

The influence of evangelical laity at Caulfield was significant. The church's lands were given by Sir George Stephen, who emigrated in 1854 with

---

52. VC, April 27, 98.
53. VC, April 27, 98.
54. See the parish booklet commemorating Caulfield's 150th anniversary. Durie, "St. Mary's 150th."

his wife, daughter Mary, son James Wilberforce, and James's wife. Sir George had been knighted for his role in the Clapham campaign to abolish slavery, a campaign in which his father, James Stephen, was intimately involved. Sir George had married a niece of William Wilberforce and was related to him by marriage. In the wake of the gold rush boom, Sir George built and lived in the Caulfield mansion Helenslea, and it was from a portion of that estate that the church lands were subdivided in the late 1860s. By 1871 a church building was opened with the Stephen family firmly ensconced as leading laity and refusing to follow the high-church trend set by Gregory.

Bishop Perry had come to trust and rely on the Stephen family. James Wilberforce Stephen was appointed by Perry in 1864 to be the second chancellor of the diocese, taking over after the death in office of Charles James Griffiths. He was one of the founding trustees of Trinity College and was appointed a judge of Supreme Court in 1872. Goodman calls him "a man of remarkable ability;" he was fourth wrangler of St. John's Cambridge in 1844, then was called to the Chancery Bar in London before emigrating in 1854.[55] James Stephen was yet another leading evangelical layman who was Attorney General before being elevated to the judicial bench.

After the first two relatively short incumbencies, Dean Macartney's son, H. B. Macartney Jr., began a thirty-year stint at St. Mary's, developing a particular focus on Keswick spirituality and one of its key features, a commitment to world mission. From Caulfield, Macartney single-handedly edited *The Missionary at Home and Abroad*, a journal detailing missions efforts and providing missionary news and prayer notes. Its motto was 1 Corinthians 2:2: "Not to know anything among you, save Jesus Christ and him crucified." The *Missionary* ran from 1873 to 1898 when Macartney left Caulfield to become the Home Secretary of the BFBS in England. It was interdenominational and international in scope, appearing monthly with news from and about the parish missions in Victoria, missions by Victorians throughout Australia, the Chinese work, the work among Jews, the CMS, the CEZMS, the Aborigines Mission, the Condah Aboriginal Mission, the Australian Mission to South Africa, Lovedale Mission South Africa, the Bible Union, and the Children's Scripture Union—just to name some of the recurrent items.[56]

It is claimed, and highly probable, that Australia's first three Church of England overseas missionaries came from St. Mary's:

---

55. Goodman, *Church in Victoria*,187. See also ADB entry.

56. The almost complete collection of the MAHA has been lodged by CMS Victoria with the State Library of Victoria.

Sarah Davies, Annie Slaney and J. Henry Davies, who all went to India in 1875–6. Annie was from one of the founding families of St. Mary's congregation: she tragically died from cholera within months of arriving. The third to depart was Henry Davies but he was compelled to return in 1878 due to ill health. His sister Sarah, who was the first to go, received her call while singing a holiness hymn "I am coming to the cross" during the second Christian conference at St. Mary's in 1875. Sarah was to stay in South India for 59 years, marrying another missionary John Cain, and working in Dummagudem until her death in 1934.[57]

The Saunders sisters, who had preceded the Blacketts as CMS Victoria's first missionaries, were also sent out from Caulfield. Their story links two strongly evangelical parishes in Melbourne at the time. They had earlier been converted under the ministry of Henry Mercer at St. Hilary's Kew when they were living in that area. They subsequently moved to "The Willows" in Caulfield and attended St. Mary's where under H. B. Macartney's influence their passion for overseas mission was fanned into flame. They were active teachers in St. Mary's Sunday School and started a Monday night prayer meeting—presumably focusing on missionary prayer points. The Saunders sisters and mother began to take an active and supporting interest in the Church of England Zenana Mission Society, which focused on women's work in India and then China.

It was Macartney who brought the Children's Scripture Union to Australia within months of it starting in England. He recruited an energetic woman of the parish, Mrs. J. W. Veal as secretary—thus beginning a long association between Scripture Union and Caulfield. The forceful and dominant Mrs. Veal was followed by her daughter Alice in this role: two further examples of women being empowered by opportunities in evangelical ministry.[58]

Not surprisingly, the children's ministry at Caulfield was energized. The connection between church and school and mission was also strong; Macartney encouraged Joseph Henry Davies to establish the nearby Caulfield Grammar School. Davies subsequently went to Korea as a Presbyterian missionary, where he is regarded as one of the founding fathers of the Korean church. E. J. Barnett, headmaster of Caulfield Grammar, was appointed the first Honorary Secretary of the CMA in 1892.[59] One of Caulfield Grammar's alumni was subsequently the parish's longest serving incumbent:

---

57. Durie, "St. Mary's 150th." 7.
58. See below. Also Prince and Prince, *Tuned in to Change:* 13–15, 33f, 42f.
59. Cole, *Sharing in Mission.* 17.

Henry Thomas Langley, son of Henry Archdall Langley.⁶⁰ St. Mary's may not have been as large and vibrant as Prahran, but Macartney's organizational skill, consummate ability to network, and enthusiasm for mission and the deepening of spiritual life meant that Caulfield developed into an organizational center for evangelical life in Melbourne.

Macartney's interest in the deeper life movement led to the first ecumenical Australian Christian Conference, held in St. Mary's in 1874—a year before Keswick and twenty years before the Prahran Convention of 1894 mentioned previously.⁶¹ He was also instrumental in convincing George Grubb, who was visiting Australia under the auspices of the Keswick movement, to stay in Victoria for a fortnight's mission in 1890, and then to return for a highly successful mission between May and September the next year.⁶²

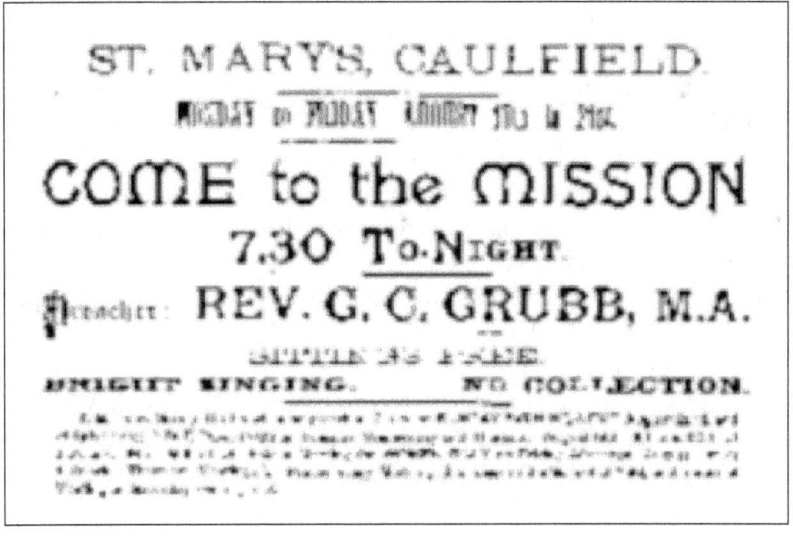

St. Mary's Caulfield Advertisement for the G. C. Grubb Mission

For a week in 1891, the Grubb mission was based in Caulfield with evening meetings from Monday to Friday, 17–24 August, advertised with a handbill containing the words, "Come to the Mission ... BRIGHT SINGING ... SEATING FREE ... NO COLLECTION"⁶³—three aspects designed to lure prospective listeners within the doors of the church who might other-

60. H. A. Langley served at Caulfield from 1911 to 1942.
61. Paproth, "Hussey Burgh Macartney Jr."Also MAHA 1874, 174, where Macartney reports on the deeper life and baptism in the Spirit movement in St. Aldate's Oxford.
62. See Paproth, "The Upwey Convention."
63. See reproduction in Durie, "St. Mary's 150th."

wise be put off by dull singing, pew rents, and the pressure to put something into the collection plate.

Caulfield also birthed a number of other parishes in the region: many with evangelical beginnings. St. Clement's Elsternwick commenced in 1886 as a chapel of ease to St. Mary's, with its first service being taken by Dean Macartney. Joseph Davies preached there in the first two years before a curate was put in charge; in 1890, the evangelical George Sproule was appointed first incumbent. Sproule and Macartney Jr. were both on the inaugural CMA committee. Under Sproule, St. Clement's built on the evangelical foundations inherited from St. Mary's Caulfield. Sproule laid "a deep and firm foundation . . . within the parish for missionary activity," which remained recognizably evangelical into the latter part of the twentieth century.[64] He was also a leader in wider evangelical causes and was subsequently one of the founding members of the council of Ridley College.

The Reverend J. Lacy Winn, a curate of St. Mary's, was given charge of St. Catherine's South Caulfield in 1892. It subsequently became a separate parish in 1907. Macartney Jr. was also remembered by St. Stephen's Elsternwick (later Gardenvale) for the "tremendous amount of time and energy spent . . . on their affairs" in helping them plant the church and achieve independence.[65] The first incumbent of another St. Mary's church plant, St. John's East Malvern, was another member of the evangelical CMA committee: John Boyle Gason, appointed in 1888. Macartney Jr. also took services and helped to found St. Agnes' Glenhuntly and St. Paul's North Caulfield.

This sort of parish expansion was a characteristically energetic evangelical response to the needs of Melbourne's growing population. While all churches recognized their duty to provide religious services and saw the opportunities in school-building and education, the remarkable industry and organizational power of the evangelicals, and the persistent evangelical culture that they engendered in many parishes, is especially notable. A parish connection to the CMA or CMS, for example, demonstrated a cultural value of commitment to evangelical missions; such a connection often remained after other signs of evangelical life in a parish might have died out.

From Caulfield, Macartney Jr. raised up women and men for overseas mission and interdenominational ministry like SU and BFBS, but the parish in this period was not noted for supplying men for ordained ministry within the diocese. At least three factors were at work. First, following their vicar's passion, many of the most committed Sunday School teachers and young people of the parish ended up in overseas missions work. Second,

---

64. Covey, *Our First 100 Years*, 5.
65. Durie, "St. Mary's 150th," 16.

the deeper life and missions movement within evangelicalism was from the beginning markedly interdenominational, so the relative importance of diocesan affairs was lowered. Third, Bishop Moorhouse's refusal to promote the able Macartney Jr. served to keep Macartney Jr.'s energies directed towards non-diocesan evangelical efforts.

Hence, despite the active church planting in the region, the emphasis on overseas missionary service and cooperation with other like-minded evangelicals meant that there was less energy for focusing on denominational affairs. As much as the *Churchman* focused on the shift in the diocese away from its evangelical foundations, *The Missionary at Home and Abroad* focused attention on the needs and glorious efforts in the sphere of mission and evangelism. Faced with a negative narrative and a positive one, many evangelicals chose to focus on the latter and pour their energies into mission rather than engagement with the diocese. This trend would mean a decrease in the supply of able evangelical clergy from evangelical parishes and evangelical societies. In the future, this shortage of qualified and able clergy would have a detrimental effect on maintaining vital evangelical piety in even the movement's leading parishes.

Bendigo Parishes—John Christian MacCullagh

Evangelicalism was also prevalent in parishes outside of the immediate surrounds of the city of Melbourne. The diocese covered all of Victoria until the creation of the Diocese of Ballarat in 1875. An example of evangelical energy in the regions is the ministry of John Christian MacCullagh. MacCullagh was yet another evangelical Irishman and Trinity College Dublin export to Australia. He had entered into CMS training in Islington but was subsequently rejected on health grounds—too much study was ruining his eyesight.[66] MacCullagh came to Sydney to start afresh. Ironically, the long sea journey improved his eyesight and, having won a scholarship to Moore College in 1863, he resumed study with a view to ordination.

Keith Cole calls MacCullagh a "pronounced evangelical all his life." His favorite text was 1 Corinthians 2:2, "I determined not to know anything among you, save Jesus Christ and him crucified." This was the central verse of three verses placed in the Moore College chapel in memory of MacCullagh's principal, William Hodgson. It was MacCullagh's central text as well, featuring in his first sermon at St. Paul's Bendigo and inscribed on his gravestone. He was ordained by Perry at St. James' Melbourne in 1864 and posted to Lancefield and Romsey, north of Melbourne, as its first clergymen

---

66. Cole, *Men of Faith and Vision*, 21.

in 1865. It was a large district of twenty by fifteen miles in size with only one small weatherboard building. MacCullagh threw himself into the work, preaching three times each Sunday, teaching in two different Sunday Schools, conducting services twice a week, and spending the rest of the time visiting and helping parishioners.

Cole notes that the "church grew rapidly in membership wealth and importance" through his ministry. Fourteen acres of land was purchased in Lancefield as an endowment, and a brick church was built. Another building went up in Rochford and land for another bought at Romsey. Another clergyman, Rev J. H. Williams, was appointed—all within six years. By the time of MacCullagh's departure in 1870, there were ten places of worship and as many Sunday Schools.

MacCullagh had earlier married Elizabeth Ince of Camberwell at Christ Church Hawthorn on 26 December 1865. He was ten years older than his young wife of twenty-three at the time. She threw herself into parish work, but tragically died in October 1870, aged twenty-seven. Her gravestone states that she was "a faithful, gentle, self-denying follower of the Lord Jesus. Her delight was to be engaged in teaching in the Sunday Schools; in conducting Bible Class; in relieving the distressed; and in every other good word and work." A tablet in Christ Church Lancefield reads:

> This tablet was erected by the teachers, children and lady friends of the Lancefield Sunday School in memory of their beloved friend Elizabeth MacCullagh who went in and out among them for nearly five years, speaking of the Kingdom of God and teaching those things which concern the Lord Jesus Christ, and who ceased from her labor and entered into rest October 20th 1870 aged 27 years. "Looking for that blessed hope and glorious appearing of the great God and our Saviour Jesus Christ."[67]

MacCullagh was so devastated that he resigned from the parish in which there were so many memories of his wife. He contemplated resigning from ministry altogether, but Cole credits Perry's pastoral ministry as the key to MacCullagh subsequently resuming his ministry at St. Paul's Sandhurst in November 1870.

The parish was not an easy appointment. The church building was incomplete, and there was a very large debt of £3,800; "The congregation lacked enthusiasm and leadership."[68] Cole cites the local paper the *Bendigonian*'s assessment of MacCullagh:

---

67. Cole, *Men of Faith and Vision*, 24–25.
68. Cole, *Men of Faith and Vision*, 29.

> By the most natural of all means, that of unobtrusive kindness and good deeds, he immediately gained a warm place in the hearts of his flock . . . He imparted much spirit into the young church and he was helped by prominent Bendigo residents who were delighted to assist him.[69]

MacCullagh never remarried and threw himself again into the work of pastoral ministry. He was remembered as a loving and hardworking pastor. Archdeacon J. E. Herring gives this first-hand assessment:

> Nobody of the parish and beyond was properly baptized, married, or even laid to rest unless MacCullagh officiated. His sympathy and human touch won all hearts . . . With the poor, the needy and the bereaved he was generous to a fault.
>
> It is said that the dean was a great worry to his housekeeper, as he often returned home late at night without his overcoat or shoes, having given them to some needy person in the course of visiting. He refused to take any credit for his generosity. He used to say, "I am able to do it because I have no wife and family; my fellow ministers are not able to do it, because they have wives and families. Therefore I am not entitled to any particular credit, and I cannot, if I would, boast of anything that I have done in that way."[70]

MacCullagh was also personally committed to the work of evangelism. Bendigo had a sizeable Chinese community that had come into the area with the gold rush. He organized English and Scripture classes at St. Paul's for the local Chinese, conducted baptismal instruction classes for them, and baptized a number of adults and children. MacCullagh was a known supporter of the later Torrey, Chapman, and Alexander missions of 1902, 1909, and 1912, and of the CMA and subsequent CMS. He enthused the people of St. Paul's for the work of overseas mission, and his laypeople helped with the establishment of a CMA Depot in Bendigo.

MacCullagh's evangelicalism also held steady against the assaults of higher criticism and scientific rationalism. The *Bendigo Advertiser* noted the themes of evangelical faith in his life and ministry:

> It might be thought amidst all these activities and cares Dean MacCullagh had no time for study, but such an idea would be on the opposite pole to actual fact. Night-workers who passed the Deanery frequently saw a light burning in the study right

---

69. Cole, *Men of Faith and Vision*, 29–30.

70. Cole, *Men of Faith and Vision*, 40–41. Citing Herring's unpublished MS, "A History of the Diocese of Bendigo."

into the early hours of the morning. It was thus that Dean MacCullagh kept abreast of modern theological thought and excursions into often dangerous tracks. His profound knowledge of the Bible and of man, and more than both, of God caused him to cling with unquestioned loyalty to the verities of the Christian religion, and expound them with no uncertain or temporizing note. "For I determined not to know anything among you save Jesus Christ and him crucified" was the first text that the Dean preached from in St. Paul's on the 13th November 1870, and while other clergymen might have been shaken by the winds of "the higher criticism," that was always the Dean's message, and he delivered in the optimism and confidence born of inward experience."[71]

MacCullagh was a Freemason, and a chaplain of the Golden and Corinthian Lodge No.7 in Bendigo for several years. He was also the attending chaplain when the foundation stone of the View Street Masonic Temple Hall was laid on 24 June 1873.[72] However, unusually among low-church masons, his membership of the lodge did not seem to interfere with his crucicentrism or emphasis on evangelism and conversion.[73]

MacCullagh's work and worth was acknowledged when he was appointed a canon of St. Paul's Cathedral in 1879 and archdeacon of Sandhurst in 1883. As one of the four archdeacons of the diocese, he had responsibilities for pastoral care and administration over the north western portion of the state—excluding Ballarat, which was a separate diocese from 1875. As the local dean and archdeacon, he was a leading contender for the post of bishop of Bendigo at that diocese's foundation in 1902, narrowly losing out to Henry Langley due to the preponderance of Melbourne voices on the selection committee as opposed to ones from Bendigo. MacCullagh was nevertheless fiercely loyal to Langley, who had been his peer at Moore College, publicly declaring his intent to serve faithfully during the celebrations welcoming the new bishop to Bendigo.

71. Cole, *Men of Faith and Vision*, .43, where Cole cites the *Bendigo Advertiser* but without a date.

72. Cole, *Men of Faith and Vision*, 44.

73. The theme of the connection between Melbourne Anglican evangelicalism and Freemasonry is not unimportant, especially given the wide influence of the long-serving layman Dr. George Bearham, who led evangelicals and the Low Church party in the Synod and served as the Chairman of Ridley College Council and its executive over several decades in the middle of the twentieth century. Masonic connections also influenced a number of parish appointments, some of which led to the decline in evangelical vitality—for example at St. Mary's Caulfield. Interview with John Moroney, 4 June 2007.

Raising up Future Leaders—John Christian MacCullagh

MacCullagh understood the importance of evangelical succession and the need to train younger men for ministry and was especially noted for his ability to train up curates. Among his curates was William Charles Sadlier from 1892 to 1899, who was quick to pay tribute to his training under MacCullagh. Sadlier had a fine academic record from the University of Melbourne, graduating with a B. A. in 1894 and an M. A. two years later. He came to St. Paul's after curacies in Pyramid Hill and Macorna, also in the region. In Bendigo, he was appointed the part-time principal of Perry Hall (1897 to 1899) while MacCullagh's curate. In 1899, he was given the incumbency of Holy Trinity East Melbourne, and in 1910 he became the acting principal of Ridley College while serving as vicar of Christ Church St. Kilda. From there he was elected bishop of Nelson, New Zealand, in 1912.

Another prominent MacCullagh curate was Herbert Smirnoff Begbie.[74] Begbie had been converted in Sydney during the George Grubb mission of 1891 when he was aged twenty. He trained at Moore College and then came to St. Paul's to work under MacCullagh for three years, from 1899 to 1902. He exercised an exciting evangelistic ministry in Bendigo, then later in North Melbourne; here, Begbie trained other men for overseas missions through a men's training home—a progenitor of Ridley College. He later moved to Gippsland, then back to Sydney, where a succession of Begbie clergymen were noted evangelical leaders.[75]

The leader of the founding party of CMS missionaries who started the Roper River Mission at Ngukurr in July 1908, J. F. G Hutchnance, was another MacCullagh curate.

Raising up Future Leaders—Digby Berry

Digby Berry's relatively short incumbency at Holy Trinity East Melbourne was also notable for the men he influenced into ministry—in particular, three sets of brothers: Eustace and Arthur Wade, who went on to be principal and acting principal of the evangelical Ridley and Moore Colleges respectively; Charles and Arthur Young, who were noted evangelical clergymen in Melbourne; and Brooking and Horace Hannah.[76] Brooking Hannah went with the China Inland Mission to Western China, where he worked with Howard Mowll. Horace Hannah married Berry's daughter,

---

74. See ADEB entry.
75. Loane, *Mark These Men*.
76. See ADEB entry for Digby Berry.

Catherine "Kitty," and together they applied to join Brooking and his wife but were refused on medical grounds. Horace became a Melbourne banker and highly influential evangelical leader.[77]

There is little doubt that Berry was "a man of pronounced, even pugnacious, evangelical convictions," as Len Abbott describes him in the ADEB. He ministered in a succession of Melbourne parishes: All Saints' Northcote, St. Thomas Moonee Ponds, and Holy Trinity. In each, his decidedly evangelical ministry left a deep local legacy. His vigorously premillennial Bible study series in the *Churchman* identifies him as a respected Bible teacher for that generation of evangelicals. Further, he had no hesitation in resigning his post as examining chaplain to Bishop Goe when the bishop acted against his advice in ordaining a man with Anglo-Catholic views. This further highlights the importance Berry placed on ensuring a succession of clearly evangelical clerical leaders.[78]

The strength and vitality of evangelical parishes and ministry, focused on the work of evangelism, church planting, and overseas mission, reflected the priorities of evangelicals in this period. However, most local congregations were strictly parochial, and congregations often contained a mix of people with different spiritualties. The majority of churches remained outwardly low church and strictly Prayer Book in liturgy. For evangelicals, the local parish was becoming less important than their volunteer societies and the growing convention movement, which increasingly became the main contexts for evangelical activism and conversionism.

Societies and Mission

Missionary Societies: The Church Missionary Association and the CMS

Macartney Jr.'s missionary enthusiasm is the prime example of the kind of interdenominational and extra-parochial expression of evangelical energy in this period. He reportedly raised close to £2,000 a year for missionaries in India and China, and the energy and vitality of his work and personal commitment was noted by Eugene Stock in his monumental four-volume

---

77. See ADEB entry and below.

78. Berry was a man for a fight, for when he was unwell and in South Africa for health reasons in 1907 he was exposed to the persecution of evangelicals by the Tractarian Church of the Province of South Africa. Although almost 60, he volunteered to stay on and minister to the Church of England congregation at Christ Church Hillbrow, Johannesburg, which he did for the next fifteen years. Berry died and was buried at sea on the way back to Melbourne in 1922.

history of CMS.[79] It is also attested to by the long running *The Missionary at Home and Abroad*. *The Missionary* contained a special focus on CMS work in Africa and the Middle East, and Zenana work in India and China, reflecting Macartney's Church of England heritage. There were missionary letters, stories of conversion, cultural notes, and sections on children's ministry. It was a persistent call for active involvement in the work of evangelism and conversion: personal involvement through prayer and financial giving, and participation in home missions. It was a phenomenal achievement, representing years of sustained reading of missionary correspondence, obtaining necessary intelligence, editing, and production—Macartney did this while engaged in a full range of other local parish and wider ecumenical and interdenominational evangelical activities.

However, he did not hand the baton on. He failed to train and encourage successors for his various ministry roles. When he left in 1898, *The Missionary* ceased, and of his interdenominational evangelical work, only the ones that had been institutionalized to some degree, like the CMA, Scripture Union, and Zenana Bible and Missionary Mission,[80] persisted in the longer term.

The presence of *The Missionary* and its wide subscriber base, alongside these societies and the level of support they received, were indicative of the energy and commitment of evangelicals within the colony for the cause of evangelism and mission. It was a perfect illustration of what was possible when the principle of independent action and subsequent organization of independent societies was given free course. This principle had been established and encouraged by Perry, who did not see any need to control or make "official" the activities of independent evangelicals, and indeed, lent them his personal support. This policy resulted in points of tension and even conflict at various points of history after Perry's departure, especially around the status of the CMA (later CMS).[81] Nevertheless, all branches of the Australian CMS have been long recognized as missionary agencies of the Anglican Church.

Evangelical independence saw the birth of several societies in the mid-nineteenth century, and a coordinated approach came about later. In 1889, a group of about forty evangelical clergy and laity were invited to a "Missionary Breakfast" in Sydney by the Prothonotary of the Supreme Court of NSW, Mr. Walsh, a member of St. John's Darlinghurst. Among the attendees

79. Stock, *History of the Church Missionary Society*, vol. 2, 408; vol. 3, 184, 568–9, 673.

80. The Zenana Bible and Missionary Mission was later renamed the Bible and Medical Missionary Fellowship, and later yet, Interserve.

81. See Cole, *History of the Church Missionary Society of Australia*, 18–19.

were Arthur Pain, John Langley, Arthur Blackett, and H. B. Macartney Jr. The meeting considered the question of changing the constitution of the CMS Auxiliaries so that an Australian society could send out missionaries in its own right, rather than through the English parent society.

This constitutional change happened in 1892, when the Church Missionary Association (CMA) was formed in both NSW and Victoria, largely as a result of the visit by a deputation of the English CMS. This came to Australia due to the increased interest in missionary work in both countries as a result of the spread of Keswick spirituality. George Grubb had returned to England after his missions of 1890 and 1891 reporting the rise of missionary enthusiasm in Australia to the Parent Committee of the CMS, which resolved that:

> . . . the Secretaries be instructed to enquire if a suitable clergyman and layman can be found to go as a Deputation to the Colonies, and that the Deputation be sent with the hope of stirring up a missionary spirit, and to consult with friends on the spot as to the best means of bringing them more closely into sympathy and united action with the Parent Committee and as to finding suitable candidates for missionary work . . .[82]

Additionally, a group of Keswick enthusiasts had written an open "Keswick Letter" appealing for a thousand new missionaries to come forward, including from Australia. This letter reached Bishop Saumarez Smith of Sydney, who responded by inviting the CMS to send a delegation to Australia.[83] The layman Eugene Stock and the Reverend Robert Stewart were sent in 1892. The visit was an unqualified success, with the NSW and Victorian Auxiliaries of CMS being reconstituted as Church Missionary Associations in their own right. Eugene Stock, reflecting on the deputation, insisted that it had been the spiritual climate produced by the earlier Grubb missions that had enabled the reorganization and revitalization of the mission societies in Australia to take place.[84]

The first three Victorian CMA missionaries were Harry Tugwell, Eleanor Saunders, and Elizabeth Saunders—the latter two sisters who were better known by their nicknames, Nellie and Topsy. Tugwell was in fact from Tasmania but offered through the Victorian CMA. He left Melbourne in 1893 after a period of training with the Reverend E. J. Barnett

---

82. Cole, *History of the Church Missionary Society of Australia*, 15.

83. Metropolitan bishops gained the honorific "Archbishop" by General Synod resolution in 1897.

84. Stock, *History of the Church Missionary Society*. See also Paproth, "Upwey Convention," which contains a description of the impact of the Grubb missions.

at Caulfield Grammar School and died of malaria in India in 1896. Keith Cole, the historian of the Australian and Victorian CMA/CMS, was fond of quoting a letter written by Dr. John Ludwig Krapf to the CMS Secretary in London. Krapf was the pioneer CMS missionary to East Africa whose wife Rosina and baby died in Kenya of tropical disease soon after their arrival. He was himself so sick that he could not even rise from his bed to confirm her death. He later wrote to the Secretary:

> Tell them, my dear Sir, that there is on the East African Coast a lonely grave of a member of the Mission cause connected with your Society. This is a sign that you have commenced the struggle with this part of the world, and as the victories of the Church are stepping over the graves and death of many of her members, you may be the more convinced that the hour is at hand, when you are summoned to the conversion of Africa from the East.[85]

Martyrdom was the fate of the first Victorian missionaries, the Saunders sisters. In 1889, Mrs. Eliza Saunders and her daughters, Nellie and Topsy, heard Hudson Taylor speak during his visit to Melbourne to publicize his work with the China Inland Mission. It was a visit largely organized by their vicar, H. B. Macartney Jr. As they heard Taylor, they felt called to offer for overseas missionary service. Three years later, during the 1892 deputation of the English CMS, they spent time conversing with the Reverend Robert Stewart, an English CMS missionary to China for over sixteen years. The conversations led to a firm commitment on the part of both sisters and their mother to offer for service in China with the newly formed Victorian CMA. They were to partner with the Stewarts in Ku Cheng. Although they desired to go as self-supporting honorary missionaries, the economic depression meant that they could not realize enough value from the sale of their home in Caulfield, "The Willows," for all three to go. Nellie and Topsy went ahead, leaving their mother behind—although she was desirous of joining them as soon as practicable. Nellie, Topsy, the Stewarts and two of their children, a carer, and four other female Zenana missionaries in their group were murdered by Chinese brigands on 1 August 1895.[86] Mrs. Eliza Saunders was nevertheless determined to remain faithful to her calling and subsequently served in China as a self-funded missionary, dying there of natural causes in 1915.

The sisters' horrendous deaths were mourned in Melbourne, but leading evangelicals did not hesitate to reflect on them as a clarion call to more

---

85. As cited in Cole et al., *Servants for Jesus' Sake*, 9.

86. Nellie and Topsy Saunders' story is told in Cole et al., *Letters from China*. Cole edited and abridged the more contemporary original work: Berry, *Sister Martyrs of Ku Cheng*. See also chapter 10 of Hattaway, *China's Christian Martyrs*.

sacrificial missionary effort. Bishop Goe, in his presidential address to the Melbourne Church Assembly just a month after their deaths, said:

> ... the interest felt among us in missions to the heathen is evidently increasing. It receives, I trust, a mighty impulse from the martyr-deaths of those devoted servants of God at Ku Cheng, who counted not their lives dear unto them, so that they might finish their course with joy.[87]

It was Digby Berry, by then at Holy Trinity East Melbourne, who rushed into publication the letters written over the course of the sisters' eighteen months in China to their mother in Melbourne. The 320-page book was published within four months of their death. Berry wrote in his preface that:

> The profits, if any, from the sale of this work will be devoted entirely to missionary objects, and the single aim which the bereaved mother has in view, in allowing these sacred treasures to go forth into the world, is, that they may be some help in arousing the Christian Church to a fuller sense of its opportunities and responsibilities, in relation to those millions of our fellow-creatures who are sitting in darkness and in the shadow of death.[88]

In his epilogue, Berry reflected on the problem of why such a tragedy had been permitted, asking why a few minutes warning had not been given, or even why a shower of rain had not stopped the brigands' advance. He declared that:

> This terrible thing was permitted by Him without Whom not even a sparrow falls to the ground ... Beyond all human and secondary considerations we believe He had some all-wise reason for this, but what was it? Was it in order that the Cause for which they fell might be conspicuously brought before the eyes of the civilized world? Was it in order that a lukewarm Church might receive another electric shock to rouse her from the slumber of indifference towards the perishing heathen? ...
> It may be that the Lord will use these letters to carry a thrilling and effectual message to many souls, who would otherwise never have known what can be done, what may be done, what ought to be done by Christians in vast, dark, unhappy China.[89]

---

87. Report of the Church Assembly, 1895.
88. Berry, *Sister Martyrs of Ku Cheng*.
89. Berry, *Sister Martyrs of Ku Cheng*. 319–20.

As the close of the century approached, the missionary enthusiasm that had been generated by successive Grubb missions, the Keswick movement in Melbourne and Geelong, and the activity and organization of evangelistic societies and groups was reaching a peak. Between 1892 and 1902, the Victorian CMA and CEZMS sent out forty-three missionaries to China, Japan, India, Persia, Palestine, Egypt, Kenya, Canada, and Lake Tyers (Victoria).[90]

The role and enthusiasm of women for missions was significant. Women were not able to be ordained or even elected to church vestries, so missionary work was an important channel for the energy of evangelical women during this period. Three out of Victoria's first four missionaries were single women. Twenty-nine out of the forty-three missionaries mentioned above left Victoria as single women.

Membership of the CMA was burgeoning: there were 480 missionary box holders in 1893; by 1896, when E. J. Barnett resigned from his position as headmaster of Caulfield Grammar School to become the full-time Organizing Secretary of the CMA, there were 4,280 members of Gleaners' Unions, 1,786 members of the children's Sowers' Bands, and 6,000 missionary periodicals being sent out monthly.[91]

It was at the evangelical stronghold of St. Matthew's Prahran that the idea of having an "Our Own Missionary" (OOM) emerged. This meant that the parish would take on the responsibility of raising funds and support for their own missionary. Early adoption of this scheme is indicative of strength of commitment to overseas mission and evangelical character. Other early adopters of the OOM scheme were St. Stephen's Richmond, St. Paul's Ballarat, St. Clements' Elsternwick, St. Mary's Caulfield, St. Alban's Armadale, and Holy Trinity East Melbourne.

---

90. See CMS Victoria document, "List of CMS-VIC Missionary Personnel in Full Connection 1892–2009," CMS Victoria Office.

91. Cole, *Sharing in Mission*. 24–25. Gleaners' Unions were founded in England in 1886 and were effectively a missionary interest group with their own magazine, *The Gleaner*. Members committed to *glean* from the Bible God's message about salvation and mission, *glean* information about the non-Christian world, *glean* the monetary offerings of young and old, rich and poor, and *glean* the blessings of the Lord in this work. In Melbourne the Honorary Treasurer was J. H. Maddock, the leading layman from St. Matthew's Prahran. The Sowers' Band was an equivalent organization for children that became very popular in Australia.

Children's and Youth Ministry: CSSM and Scripture Union

Another evangelical society that had its origins in this period was the Children's Special Service Mission, later Scripture Union. The genesis of Scripture Union (SU) is to be found in a passion for evangelism among children, with clear and engaging Bible teaching and the necessity of a personal response to Christ at its core.[92] Summer beach missions and a commitment to daily Bible reading and were also integral from an early point in SU's history.

In the summer of 1867, an American, Payson Hammond, started running services especially for children in London. Instead of preaching from a pulpit, he engaged in dialogue from a platform. He used stories and contemporary, lively music. At the end of services, believing that young children could have a personal and vital relationship with Christ, he asked any who wanted to stay behind for counseling or prayer to do so. Hundreds professed faith in Christ for themselves. Importantly, a few among the adults present began to be convinced by his philosophy and methods.

Among them was the young office worker and Sunday School teacher Josiah Spiers, who was already engaged in ministry to young children. Spiers quickly founded special services for children in London following the same model. The following summer, Spiers followed the relatively new fashion of the time and went to the beach on holidays. At Llandudno in Conwy, North Wales, Spiers observed children making a garden in the sand with pebbles and seaweed, and thought, "These children could be making a text of Scripture with the stones." He organized materials and the children into making the words "God is Love." After this, the children demanded a story, and Spiers obliged with a children's Bible talk, and found himself telling many more Bible stories in response to their requests. Thus, the first Seaside Service was held—the progenitor of the SU beach missions. Demand from the children was so great that Spiers repeated the service every day for the rest of his stay. On the final Sunday, a more formal beach service was organized and announced by the Town Crier. Spiers stood in a boat surrounded by children and spoke to some three or four hundred gathered on the shore.

Spiers returned from his holidays energized, and with a group of friends founded the Children's Special Service Mission, formally adopting that name on 30 May 1868. The recently passed Special Services Act authorized Anglican churches to use non-Prayer Book services for special purposes, and the official name sought to take advantage of this new legal coverage. However, CSSM was an evangelical interdenominational group

---

92. The sources of the history of SU used are Sylvester, *God's Word in a Young World*; Prince and Prince, *Lighting the Lamp*; Prince, *Tuned in to Change*.

from the outset. Their weekly services drew children from some twenty different churches, chapels, and Sunday Schools.[93]

Another key figure in the early history was Tom Bishop. He was a founding member of the CSSM in 1868 and provided the strategic leadership and administrative and organizational skills to complement Spiers's gifts in public speaking. It was Bishop who managed the growth and internationalization of CSSM. In 1878, Bishop was approached by Anne Marston, a Sunday School teacher in Keswick, where the Convention movement was in its early years. Marston had been writing out Scripture reading lists to aid her Sunday School girls in daily Bible reading, but some of the girls wanted to keep reading after they left her class or moved away. Lists would have to be prepared for longer periods, and Marston wondered if CSSM, a children's ministry, could assist. The already busy Bishop was initially disinterested but, while convalescing in bed from an illness, realized that Marston's idea could assist with the challenge CSSM faced in following up children from their summer beach missions. His illness has been described as divine intervention.[94] By the end of that year, the CSSM committee had Bishop's firm proposal to launch "The Children's Scripture Union" from 1 April 1879.[95] By July, they had distributed 30,000 Bible reading cards. The growth was phenomenal and not limited to the British Isles. By 1887 some 350,000 cards were being distributed internationally.

In December 1879, the vicar of St. Mary's Caulfield, H. B. Macartney Jr., received in his mail a card dividing up the four Gospels into nine months of reading, beginning on 1 April. The card announced that, starting 1 January 1880, members would begin a four-year schedule covering the whole Bible. On the cover of the card were the words "The Children's Scripture Union."[96] Macartney Jr. wrote off immediately to Bishop and obtained electroplates of the 1880 card for local printing and distribution, thus bringing SU to Australia. Macartney Jr. immediately organized for separate state secretaries, and within months 737 cards were distributed to members in four states and the movement began to grow. William Shrimpton, a member of the founding committee in London, visited Australia in 1884, enthusing and energizing the movement greatly.

In Australia, the work of the Scripture Union Bible reading notes among both adults and children preceded that of the CSSM beach missions to children. These gained momentum later, with the emigration of

93. Sylvester, *God's Word in a Young World*. chapter 1.
94. Prince and Prince, *Lighting the Lamp*, 4.
95. Prince and Prince, *Lighting the Lamp*, 4.
96. Prince, *Tuned in to Change*, 13–14.

experienced enthusiasts to Australia. The first beach missions were held at Manly in NSW in 1888, and the next year at Brighton in Victoria when H. B. Macartney Jr. conducted a service for "100 children and as many adults" on 9 November.[97] Two months later, a three-week program at Mornington was planned, largely through the inspiration of a recently arrived English CSSM enthusiast, Mrs. Macnutt.

Beach missions and the focus on children's work were significant for two reasons. First, they gave evangelicals access to relatively wealthy families who could afford to go on beach holidays but who were not normally in churches or Sunday Schools. Many of these families would support CSSM financially in years to come. Second, the focus on evangelism and the eventual involvement of CSSM "graduates" meant that the missions became significant training grounds for future evangelical leadership—and that from a relatively young age. Young leaders learnt organizational and communication skills and picked up vital experience in evangelism, witnessing, and using the Scriptures in public ministry.

Macartney Jr.'s organizational ability, and that of the state secretaries whom he recruited, resulted in early growth in the distribution of SU reading cards. It was Macartney Jr. who found secretaries for Victoria, South Australia, NSW, and Tasmania, all of whom worked to popularize and distribute reading cards. The SU was another sphere in which evangelical women could become involved in leadership roles: in Queensland, there was Miss Young[98]; in NSW, Macartney Jr. recruited Eliza Marsden Hassall[99], granddaughter of Samuel Mardsen and evangelical missionary enthusiast; in Victoria, he recruited Mrs. Veal, who was succeeded by her daughter Alice Veal.

However, SU Australia historians John and Moyra Prince credit the accelerated growth of SU from 1884 onwards to the visits of the English committee members and enthusiasts, William Shrimpton in that year and Henry Hankinson two years later.[100] Membership of the SU before its revival in the second half of the twentieth century peaked at 22,500 in NSW in 1892 and 20,000 in Victoria in 1897. All of these were individuals who had committed on their Scripture Union reading cards to a regimen of daily Bible

97. Prince, *Tuned in to Change*, 24.

98. "Miss Young" was one of Charles Ernest and Margaret Young's six children, all of whom were brought up to "belong to God." The Young family, based in Bundaberg where they enjoyed commercial success in the sugar industry, was strongly evangelical, with Brethren roots and strong involvement in mission. See ADEB entries for Charles Ernest Young and Florence Young.

99. See ADB entry.

100. Prince, *Tuned in to Change*, 17–20.

reading and who were on that basis admitted into membership. Underneath their signatures was featured this verse of Scripture:

> From a child thou hast known the Holy Scriptures which are able to make thee wise unto salvation through faith which is in Christ Jesus. 2 Timothy 3:15.

In an open letter to Australians commending the Young People's Scripture Union (sometimes shortened to Young People's Union), William Shrimpton wrote that among the duties of local branch secretaries was "to always remember that . . . the distinct aim of the Scripture Union is 'to bring to present decision for Christ, and to feed and strengthen those who have eternal life in Him.'"[101] Hence the biblicism of the SU was from the outset inextricably linked to its conversionism and evangelistic enterprise.

The decline of membership numbers at the end of the century owed as much to the limits of what volunteer secretaries could achieve as to "the fearsome problem of geographical dispersion throughout a sparsely settled continent."[102] In Melbourne, efforts slowed after Macartney Jr.'s departure for London and the BFBS, yet Victoria maintained around 20,000 members at the turn of the century, when the largest branch at St. Stephen's Richmond had 700 members. Local leadership and enthusiasm was critical. When H. M. Gooch visited from the London SU headquarters in 1901, he found that at St. John's Footscray, where Miss Kerr was the new branch secretary in 1901, numbers had risen from fifty to 400 in quick order. At Sandringham beach, Gooch conducted a CSSM-style service for up to 100 children and adults with the vicar of Sandringham, Henry Howell, the evangelical layman Edgar Shelley, and the redoubtable Mrs. Veal present. A highlight of his tour of the country regions was a meeting in Bendigo with 1,000 children present.

However, Mrs. Veal's restricted Church of England bias and consequent inability to maintain Macartney Jr.'s interdenominational networks, her lack of interest in the CSSM work, and her intransigence with respect to allowing others to share in the organizing work and to have access to membership lists meant that the Victorian work stalled until a way forward was negotiated by C. H. Nash in 1905.

The preponderance of Church of England leadership and membership in the Australian CSSM and SU work is significant. In Victoria, it indicated that there was a high and healthy number of Anglican evangelicals for whom the priorities of Scripture reading, conversion to Christ, and evangelistic

---

101. William Shrimpton, 30 October 1884—reproduced in Prince, *Tuned in to Change*, 16.

102. Prince, *Tuned in to Change*, 29.

children's and young people's work resonated. The SU was an example of a society that invigorated and energized parishes rather than depleting them, for through its ministry of encouraging Bible reading and beach missions, it provided vital training in Scripture and in evangelism that young people could take back into local church ministry and life.

College

Although founded by Perry in 1872, Trinity College was not primarily purposed to be an evangelical training institution. Perry's reluctance to open a theological school there has already been noted. He rather prioritized the importance of having a Church of England college of residence attached to the University for the advancement of Christian development among the natural future leaders of society. The Latin inscription on a scroll in a bottle under the foundation stone of the college (laid by Perry in 10 February 1870) declared that the college would be:

> ... for the spread and support of the Christian religion, for the increase and continuance of the practice of devotion ... for the education of youth in piety, virtue and discipline as well as in humanities and science ...[103]

However, after Perry's departure, any hesitation to found a local theological school in preference to Moore College was discarded. Moorhouse opened the school in 1878, with Trinity's incumbent warden, Alexander Leeper, in charge. The Trinity College Dublin-trained Leeper was staunchly low church, but no evangelical. Like Moorhouse, the successful schoolmaster of Melbourne Grammar prioritized the value of an advanced liberal education.

Trinity was the only Church of England theological school attached to the University, and so the only destination for matriculated men training for holy orders. However, it was poorly resourced. The report of Trinity College Council in the 1896–7 Diocesan Yearbook observed that that the Presbyterian Ormond College was able to spend £2000 on the salaries of its theological professors alone, whereas Trinity only had £160 to spend on all five lecturers, among whom were Leeper, Potter, Handfield, and Goodman.[104] It was a mixed group, with only Goodman able to lay claim to evangelical credentials. However, it seems that the combination of

---

103. Grant, *Perspective of a Century*, 5.
104. Diocesan Yearbook 1896–7, 68, 120.

Leeper and Goodman did not prevent the college from producing mainly broad to high churchmen.

An *Argus* correspondent in 1888 stated that "Trinity College produces a large majority of men belonging to one party or school in the church," meaning the High Church party. Further, the correspondent identified the dynamic that "the more earnest and the more able" the teacher, the more likely they were to reproduce their opinions in those taught by them. "One of the Laity" declared that what was wanted was that " in the church of England ... all parties should be fairly represented, and above all, that we should have not only an earnest and a pious ministry, but an intellectual and cultured ministry, to combat, among other things, cultured unbelief."[105]

It was a thinly veiled criticism implying that Trinity graduates were unable to do the work of evangelism and of combating the rise of scientific criticism.

Potter replied, identifying the parties alluded to by the previous correspondent as the "high," "low," and "broad," associated with the names "Keble, Bickersteth, and Stanley." Further, he declared, "I do not think any churchman is worth his salt who has not distinct sympathies with all three; and further I hope that Trinity College, as well as the Church of England, will always include them."[106]

Potter went on to describe his personal acquaintance of the nine men ordained up to 1888 from the college. In his opinion, two were "low," two were "high," two were "broad," two were "broad to high" and one "low to high." Going on his assessment, it was a full spectrum but nevertheless biased towards the "high" end. Potter was not interested in identifying if any were distinctly evangelical.[107] In its first two decades, Trinity produced forty-eight ordained men, with thirty-five serving in the diocese. The only evangelical of note was William Sadlier. While Bishop Goe was in office, it seems that evangelicals were content not to agitate for a more distinctly evangelical training process or theological college; however, that was soon to change.

105. *Argus*, Thursday 10 May 1888, 5, letter from "One of the Laity."
106. *Argus*, Saturday 12 May 1888, 14.
107. Armstrong is listed in the ADEB, but his ministry legacy at St. Columb's and lack of support for the founding of Ridley College are seen by John Moroney as indicators of the lack of vital evangelical spirituality. Interview with John Moroney, 4 June 2007.

Conclusion

The period 1875–1902, for evangelicals in the Diocese of Melbourne, was dominated by the concern for evangelism and mission at home and abroad. This mood was no doubt fueled by the influence of Keswick spirituality, in particular the influence of the George Grubb visits and missions of 1890 and 1891, which led to the reorganization and energizing of the Australian CMA, later CMS.

This chapter has argued that the absence of the vital contribution of episcopal support and leadership meant that evangelicals increasingly poured their energy into local parish work and the work of their societies. Macartney Jr. was the key leader of the convention and missionary society movements in this period, effectively founding the Scripture Union work in Australia and gathering evangelical activism around these causes. However, he was repeatedly passed over for ecclesiastical preferment. This chapter has also argued that societies such as the SU, with their emphasis on conversionism and biblicism, tended to strengthen instead of weaken parishes. In particular, the SU provided vital training in Scripture study and the CSSM in evangelism, which young people then carried back into and through parish life.

Of the four vital contributors of interest to this study, two—parishes and societies—continued to gain strength. The founding of St. Hilary's East Kew on firmly evangelical principles by firmly evangelical laity, and the continued strength of evangelical missionary fervor at St. Matthew's Prahran and St. Mary's Caulfield, show that there was much vitality located in evangelical parish life. The work of Digby Berry and John Christian MacCullagh in actively encouraging younger men towards ordained ministry was part of this parish-based vitality that made an important contribution towards evangelical continuity in the diocese.

The vital contribution of a supportive diocesan bishop made by Perry evaporated under his successors Moorhouse and Goe. The diocese as a whole may still have been predominantly low church, but under Moorhouse, men considered broad or high were promoted into positions of seniority. Goe, though dutiful, did not reverse this trend substantially, and in this period the diocesan bishops offered little to no encouragement to evangelicals and their priorities in ministry. This, combined with the general shift towards a preference for more color and ritual in ceremony reflecting Melbourne's more "advanced" culture, gave evangelicals cause for concern. The relative success of their long running newspaper, the *Churchman*, reflected the fact that such concern was widely shared.

However, this chapter also shows that evangelicals were increasingly inclined to focus their energies in missionary work at home or abroad rather than in efforts to achieve diocesan reform or arrest the diocese's drift towards high-church practice. The vital contribution of a firmly evangelical theological college continued to be missing from Melbourne Anglican evangelicalism. This remained a critical weakness, for it meant that even with growing work among children and youth, and even with growing enthusiasm for overseas missions work through the mission societies, future evangelical leaders had no context for theological formation and preparation for ordained ministry in a firmly evangelical tradition.

6

Entrusted with the Gospel, 1901–1937

> That which was from the beginning,
> which we have heard, which we have seen with our eyes,
> which we have looked at and our hands have touched—
> this we proclaim concerning the Word of life
>
> 1 JOHN 1:1

Introduction

IN THE EARLY YEARS of the twentieth century in the Diocese of Melbourne, evangelicalism's center of gravity continued shifting away from the diocesan bishop and, to a lesser extent, flagship evangelical parishes. Evangelical energy was to be found in the newly restructured CMS—especially in its vibrant new youth wing, the League of Youth. It was also centered around the new and staunchly evangelical college formed in protest against the theological drift of the diocese. By the end of the period of this study, immediately prior to World War II, Ridley College had emerged as perhaps the most important vital contributor to Melbourne evangelicalism.

Flagship evangelical parishes remained important centers of vital ministry and rallying points for leaders, conferences for the deepening of spiritual life, and local missions work, but the effectiveness of their engagement with local communities was adversely affected by the war and subsequent economic depression. Demographic changes in their localities also had an important impact on parishes. The rise of individualism and philosophical liberalism had a generally negative effect on local churches' ability to connect with younger people in ways that made a life-long sacrificial commitment to Christ meaningful.

This chapter demonstrates that evangelical parishes continued to make a vital contribution to Melbourne Anglican evangelicalism, examining the histories of St. Matthew's Prahran, All Saints' Northcote, and St. Columb's Hawthorn during the period 1901 to 1937 and noting the shift in focus from diocesan affairs and evangelicalism within the life of the diocese to overseas missions work and the work of the CMS in particular.

There was a sustained absence of the vital contribution of a supportive diocesan bishop in this period. In 1902, the creation of the three new dioceses of Bendigo, Gippsland, and Wangaratta greatly reduced the size of the Diocese of Melbourne, but also created the possibility of a vital contribution from these diocesan bishops, filling the void left by the bishop of Melbourne. The chapter demonstrates that each of the three new provincial dioceses began independent life as predominantly evangelical, due in large part to the founding influence of Charles Perry on their parishes and clergy. The evangelicalism of each of the three founding provincial bishops is described. The chapter then argues that the distinctly anti-evangelical decisions and policies of Bishop (later Archbishop) Henry Lowther Clarke resulted in a significant evangelical response: the founding of Ridley College. The college's hoped-for vital contribution to evangelical continuity in Melbourne was explicitly stated by its founders, among whom were the bishops of Bendigo and Gippsland, the vicars of Melbourne's leading evangelical parishes, and the key lay leaders of the CMS. All were keen supporters of overseas and missions work.

Finally, the chapter reveals the vital contribution made by evangelical societies, in particular the CMS League of Youth. The League's ability to gather and focus young evangelicals' energy, enthusiasm, and leadership skills for the work of evangelism and overseas mission was critical for engaging a new generation of evangelical leadership. The chapter discusses the mixed nature of the impact of the League's activity and success on local evangelical continuity.

Social Context

The first day of the new century was marked by the birth of the Commonwealth of Australia, whose Parliament would be opened in the temporary capital of Melbourne in May 1901. It was an occasion marked by a sense of optimism and bursting with new-found national pride. Some 12,000 people crowded into the Exhibition Buildings to witness HRH The Prince of Wales open proceedings. A distinctly Australian identity was being formed, with the choices of the kangaroo, emu and wattle as emblems on the new coat of arms. However, the first Act passed by Parliament was the Immigration Restriction Act 1901, which limited the entry of non-European immigrants into the Commonwealth. Descendants of Chinese gold miners who might leave the country would experience difficultly re-entering the land of their birth. Aboriginal Australians were also denied voting rights by the Parliament, and so it was clear that the national vision was about the forging of a white Australia, protected from the Asian hordes of the north and leaving the indigenous people to perish as many felt certain they would.

As Australia and the world celebrated the dawn of a new age, the Victorian era came to a close with the death of the Queen on 22 January 1901. Aggressive imperialism, sometimes labeled the New Imperialism, continued unabated as the industrialized powers competed for raw materials and foreign trade markets, spurred on by national pride and the push for continued technological and manufacturing progress. Motor vehicles became cheaper and private vehicle ownership, more commonplace. Department stores carrying an increasingly wide range of consumer goods and gadgets became common in major cities. Electric kettles and toasters had just been invented and mass produced. In Melbourne weekend trips by the dressed-up family to the Myer Emporium—run by the evangelical Edwin Lee Neil—were an anticipated event. The temperance movement was gathering strength internationally, and in Melbourne multi-level coffee palaces such as those owned by the evangelical Griffiths brothers sprang up to provide refreshment for day visitors who came from the suburbs and further afield on the train network.

Advances in science and engineering were awaited with eager anticipation and witnessed with wonder by an amazed population. Many products were aimed at the average consumer—the modern age of consumer-driven capitalism was moving into full swing. The Model T Ford and the first small portable camera by Kodak—the "Brownie"—came on the market, as did radio broadcasting and relatively cheap receivers. Other advances represented the progress of human ingenuity and the promise of an assuredly glorious future: two men took the air in a winged machine in 1903—the Wright brothers aboard the *Kitty Hawk*. It was the age of romantic sea travel in modern luxurious ships, exemplified by the launching of the so-called "unsinkable" *Titanic* in 1912. Her disastrous loss was met with such universal shock and horror precisely because it challenged the overwhelming narrative of unstoppable human triumph and progress so prevalent at the time.

Among the European powers, this progress was combined with an aggressive military build-up, as the technology of weapons of war and the means of producing them both advanced. Many of the same nations were also wracked by internal political tensions, as old monarchies struggled to deal with new aspirations of a post-feudal and increasingly affluent, educated and politically-active population. Social power structures based on primogeniture were beginning to give way to new, more populist structures, especially as economic power shifted away from old families to new industrialists.

The 1914 assassination of Archduke Franz Ferdinand, heir to the Austro-Hungarian monarchy, in Sarajevo was the catalyst that unleashed the pent up tensions between heavily militarized, nationalistic and factionally-aligned forces in Europe and across the world. Within weeks World War I had begun, unleashing the destructive power of the new industrial war machines, including modern heavy artillery, machine guns, tanks, aircraft, submarines and chemical weapons. In excess of seventy million militants were mobilized. By the war's end some fifteen million combatants had perished. Some 400,000 Australians enlisted, drawn from a total population of just under five million.[1] More than 60,000 lost their lives. Some 150,000 were wounded in battle—including by chemical warfare. The statistics were grim, but the ongoing social impact and cost were as sobering. Whole towns and villages across Europe, Canada, New Zealand and Australia lost or saw maimed more than half of the young men of the generation. There was a depressing effect on society and on social institutions like churches, as confidence and leadership was sapped. Apocalyptic sentiment towards the end of the war was fuelled in part by the rapid spread of the Spanish influenza pandemic of 1918. It spread across the world in the closing stages of the war, taking at least fifty million lives worldwide. In Melbourne, the Exhibition Buildings were turned into a 4,000 bed temporary hospital. Nearly 2,500 lives were lost in Victoria.[2]

In the wake of the war several European monarchies were dissolved and revolutionary movements gained the ascendancy in Russia and Mexico. Other European nations were radically restructured, notably the Ottoman, Balkan, Austro-Hungarian and Polish states. The post-war Treaty of Versailles left Germany humiliated and embittered, laying the foundations for future nationalistic fervor and more conflict. The same treaty ensured

---

1. Linder, *Long Tragedy*, 145–52. Linder cites official Australian War Statistics and regards Australia's population as 4M at the time. Australian Bureau of Statistics information states that by 1914 the nation's population was already 4.9 million. See ABS publication 3105.0.65.001 Australian Historical Population Statistics, 2008.

2. Tout-Smith, *Melbourne*. 61.

favorable terms for the victors, contributing to the post-war economic boom in the rest of Europe, which took up from where it had left off at the beginning of the War. In Australia a similar post-War mini-boom occurred as the government poured funds into retraining war veterans and restarting the economy. Returning war hero General, by then also Sir, John Monash took charge of the State Electricity Commission and major works began in Victoria's brown-coal rich Yallourn Valley working towards the electrification of almost the entire state.

The church experienced a similar checkered forward movement in the opening quarter of the century. An idea first suggested for Cape Town by William Carey finally came into being a hundred years later in Edinburgh in 1910.[3] The World Missionary Conference was perhaps the most significant international meeting of the church yet held. Its stated focus would be on evangelizing unreached people groups throughout the world, with no discussion of work among Latin American Roman Catholics or traditionally Eastern Orthodox peoples. The conference gathered nominated representatives of the influential missionary agencies—predominantly North American, British and other Europeans—determined in proportion to the agencies' contribution to the overall missionary enterprise. Australia sent a small delegation, which included Bishop Arthur Pain of Gippsland. Plans and information were exchanged, valuable interpersonal contact established, and a predominantly evangelical Protestant international network for missionary cooperation was strengthened. The Great War halted much work, but exposed other opportunities for missionary endeavor, like the Sudan, to which evangelicals embarked upon cessation of hostilities.[4]

Two important features of church life were developing in this period. First, evangelicals developed a series of responses to growing theological liberalism. The Five Fundamentals issued in 1895 by the Evangelical Alliance at Niagara Falls were at one level completely orthodox and unremarkable, but it associated the word "fundamentals" with the evangelical movement.[5] The Evangelical Alliance's response to theological liberalism

---

3. Gairdner, "*Edinburgh 1910.*"

4. An early notable example was the Ridley collegian, Arthur Riley, who served in Sudan from 1926 to 1960. See Riley, *No Drums at Dawn*.

5. The Five Fundamentals considered essential to orthodox Christian faith were the inerrancy of Scripture, the divinity deity of Jesus, the Virgin birth, Jesus' substitutionary death on the cross for human sin, and Jesus' physical resurrection and impending return. Subsequent fundamentalism would gravitate towards increasingly literal and schematized ways of reading the Bible, culminating in the dispensational schemes of biblical theology with their concomitant fascination with identifying elements of premillennial prophecy in international events. These were often married to nationalistic pride, identifying enemy combatant states as the "other" and agents of evil. See,

in founding their own seminaries, colleges and journals were important strategic moves that paved the way for evangelicalism to build and gain intellectual respectability and credibility.

Second, the period saw the development of the "social gospel" of Walter Rauschenbusch.[6] Rauschenbusch had lived and ministered for eleven years in one of the worst New York slums. He was later appointed a professor of church history and argued that sin was endemic in the social and economic structures of the day through which the poor were often victimized by the rich, and that the gospel should mean working for justice in these areas as well. Rauschenbusch's ideas later gained popularity and acclaim, including among evangelicals—especially those who self-identified as liberal evangelicals, including two principals of Ridley College.

Parishes

At the beginning of the twentieth century the vast majority parishes in the diocese were low church in character. Services conformed to the Book of Common Prayer, clergy took the north-end position at the table and wore the cassock, surplice and black preaching scarf only. Colored stoles were unknown except in the few Anglo-Catholic leaning parishes, such as Christ Church Brunswick, St. Peter's Melbourne and All Saints East St. Kilda. Candles on the table were similarly limited to those parishes. Stoles, candles and departures from the BCP liturgy were viewed as outrageous innovations well into and past the middle of the century.

However, outward conformity to low-church practices should never be confused with evangelical piety or fervor. Most parishes were not energetically evangelistic in their ministry orientation and were satisfied to keep offering parochial services to a predominantly Anglo-Saxon populace. Even though the CMA/ CMS enjoyed widespread parish support, this affiliation did not correlate with vitality of local missions activity in the parish. The key centers of evangelical health in the parishes were naturally associated with the CMA, but the telling difference between them and the low-church parishes was that their leaders were also directly connected to the founding of Ridley. This affiliation with Ridley was a key indicator of decidedly evangelical and strategic leadership. Parishes that

---

for example, Digby Hannah's long-running series in the VC, 1895 to 1900. The most important disseminator of dispensational theology was the Scofield Reference Bible, published by Oxford University Press in 1909 and still in print today.

6. Rauschenbusch, *Christianity and the Social Crisis*; Rauschenbusch, *Theology for the Social Gospel*.

had this double association with the CMA and Ridley tended to be have high levels of missions activity in their local sphere, and a high level of support for national and international missionaries.

But even these parishes came under incredible pressure with the rise of Higher Criticism, the devastating impact of WWI, and the economic Depression of 1929. The Great War in particular had a disproportionately large impact on the relatively small Australia populace. Quoting official Australian war statistics Robert Linder noted that of the more than 400,000 Australians recruited, 60,000 perished and 213,061 returned wounded or maimed in some way. For a country of only four million, the social impact of the war was immense.[7] Of the youthful vitality that remained in evangelical churches, most focused their activities and efforts on the CMS League of Youth (LOY) and its overseas missionary concerns. Few evangelical clergy with notable Melbourne ministries were raised up out of parishes in this period, a weakness that affected evangelicalism adversely in the subsequent middle period of the century.

The record of three evangelical parishes may be taken as illustrative: St. Matthew's Prahran, All Saints' Northcote and St. Columb's Hawthorn.

St. Matthew's Prahran

The parish of Prahran was, at the turn of the century, the leading evangelical parish of the diocese. The firm evangelical foundation laid by Henry Langley was further strengthened and widened by the long incumbency of William Townsend Cooper Storrs from 1895 to 1926.

Prahran itself was an inner-city locality, just south of the Yarra and within five kilometers of the city center. This meant that it was soon populated after the city's founding and densely packed housing was constructed in the suburb. Population growth meant that there was demand for religious services: the first Church of England services in the locality were held in 1853 with regular services commencing the year after. The foundation stone for the permanent church building was laid by Bishop Moorhouse in 1877 on land donated by a Mrs. Chomley.[8] By the end of the Victorian era, the locality was filled mainly with laborers, but as the twentieth century progressed small business owners and traders came to dominate the population.

The combination of a long succession of missions-minded evangelical vicars from 1875 onwards, and the presence of able like-minded laity like John Henry Maddock meant that St. Matthew's reputation and strength as

---

7. Linder, *Long Tragedy*.
8. VC, 9 March 1906, contains a brief history of the parish.

a leading evangelical parish was well established by 1895, when there was some public murmuring about the appointment of a young curate from St. Stephen's Richmond to the incumbency of such a significant parish ahead of more senior clergymen.[9]

W. T. C. Storrs was a Cambridge graduate and was ordained in England. He had served curacies in Cumberland and Surrey before emigrating to Melbourne and a curacy at St. Stephen's. He was deeply influenced by his father, who was also a clergyman and a CMS missionary in India. Indeed, two of his uncles and his brother were also CMS missionaries, so there was no doubting the family's missionary and evangelical convictions.[10] Storrs's own daughter Christabel married a son of the Prahran parish, Lionel Bakewell, while he was home on furlough from Tanganyika. Together they served with CMS Victoria in Tanganyika for a total of seventy-nine years between them.[11]

Storrs's two other daughters, Enid and Geraldine, also had missionary jobs.[12] Geraldine married William Frederick MacKenzie, and together they served with distinction as Presbyterian missionaries in Aurukun on the Cape York Peninsula for some forty years. MacKenzie was subsequently Moderator of the Presbyterian Church in Queensland and awarded an MBE and CBE.[13] Enid's daughter, Jean Guy, served in Africa for more than twenty years, the first four and half with CMS in Tanganyika. In an interview she spoke of her mother as being "always known as Mr. Storrs's daughter, Mrs. Bakewell's sister and Miss Guy's mother," but asserts that it was Enid's selfless service that enabled much of that family's ministry to take place: Enid left school at eighteen to look after the Prahran vicarage when her mother's long illness set in, enabling her father's ministry to continue.

9. VC, 19 July 1895.

10. See Storrs' entry in ADEB. Further information from an interview with Jean Guy, Storrs' granddaughter, 28 May 2007.

11. See Cole et al., *Servants for Jesus' Sake*, 39–45. Lionel served forty-three years, Christabel, thirty-six. Interestingly, Jean Guy recounted in an interview of 8 July 2010 that "Uncle Lion was converted on the missions field" during his first term and had told her so. When she asked, "How did you go out with CMS Uncle Lion?" he answered, "I think I answered the question, 'Jesus was the Savior of the world,' but I didn't say Jesus was *my* Saviour." From his second term onwards, Lionel Bakewell became very involved in the East African Revival and "everything was about the blood of Jesus." As he had matriculated, he trained at Trinity College and always remembered it, but "he became a great Ridley supporter after his conversion."

12. Bride, *Proclaiming the Gospel*, 87. Also, interviews with Jean Guy, 28 May 2007 and 8 July 2010.

13. See William Mackenzie's entry in the ADB. http://www.adb.online.anu.edu.au/biogs/A150286b.htm?hilite=william%3Bmackenzie, last accessed Friday 16 July 2010.

On the invitation of Alfred Stanway, Enid joined Jean Guy in Tanganyika, running a guest house for missionaries in Dodoma for two and a half years. She later accompanied Jean for six of her ten and a half years serving with Wycliffe Bible Translators in Nigeria.[14]

Jean Guy described the two great loves of her grandfather's life as first, CMS and second, evangelicalism in Melbourne—especially the establishment of an evangelical training college. Storrs served on CMA and CMS committees for more than 50 years. In 1892, while still a curate, he was invited to meet with the deputation from the English CMS in Sydney and became a founder member of the Australian CMA Committee that year. He was one of the first members of the CMS Federal Council in 1916. Storrs was intimately involved in the birth of Ridley College, participating in the earliest recorded meetings in 1908. He was on the council until his death in 1953 and the minute books bear ample evidence of his sustained efforts on the part of the college, where he also lectured. Remarkably, Storrs was also the Chairman of the Katoomba Convention, based in the Blue Mountains outside Sydney, for fourteen years. However, according to Keith Cole, it was his thirty-one-year incumbency of St. Matthew's Prahran which was his most outstanding ministry achievement.[15]

One of Storrs's first innovations was to begin the publication of St. Matthew's *Church Notes* for distribution to every dwelling in the parish as a means of connecting people with the local church community. Some six to eight hundred copies were printed of each edition for distribution by up to fifty visitors—parish volunteers who would hand deliver these to every home in the parish as a means of evangelism and an expression of local mission. Storrs trained his visitors to speak an appropriate word to the householders and take every opportunity to commend Christ to them.

A near-complete run of *Church Notes* has survived, thanks in large part to the family of William Davies, an active member of the church and local business owner, who was mayor of Prahran in 1891.[16] Storrs's vicar's letter on the cover of issue No. 1, which was published on 1 July 1897 makes the evangelicalism of the parish evident: he wrote that he was "most anxious . . . that it (*Church Notes*) shall be a spiritual blessing in the houses where it is left by the visitors."

The evangelical concerns of the parish were also advertised. Storrs also announced an upcoming ordination of Godfrey Smith to the curacy

---

14. Interview with Jean Guy, 8 July 2010.

15. See ADEB, 356.

16. See Bride, *Proclaiming the Gospel*, 77. The volumes, bound by the Davies family, are now held in the City of Stonnington archives.

of the parish, and noted in particular that it was Smith's intention to go "in time to the Foreign Missions Field." He wrote further that, "We would ask all to pray that his ministry among us may be a real blessing." That same month "an excellent paper from Miss Walker on the Japan Mission" had been heard at St. Matthew's, and among materials distributed by request in the parish were 250 copies of *The Gleaner*, the CMS Gleaners' Union magazine, and 135 copies of *Children's World*, another evangelistic publication aimed at children.

Church Notes was aimed at informing the population of the parish of the kinds of opportunities and resources available through the church to strengthen Christian faith. Storrs commended the Christian faith as a great transformative and positive power: in his second vicar's letter he wrote, "There is really only one thing that can make the home really truly sweet, and that is the presence of Christ in the hearts that make up the house."[17]

It was unashamedly evangelical in commending Christ. A subsequent vicar's letter contains an example of his bold call for commitment to Christ and illustrates the brand of evangelicalism of the parish. Storrs opened with these words:

> My Dear Friends
>
> What are we living for? This world or the next? Who are we living for? Christ or ourselves? Have we ever fairly answered these questions?

Storrs then went on to explicate the Christian life in the following terms:

> Heaven which is to be unspeakably blessed, so unutterably holy, so perfectly happy, if it is to be gained, must be sought for, lived for, struggled for, or we shall never see it. I do not mean indeed that our struggles or efforts can win Heaven. No, the Lord Jesus has bought it with His own blood; the full price has been paid, by laying down His life for us; but paid for though it be, there is some fitness needed for it; there must be a life leading up to it; there must be an ever increasing likeness to Him now, if we are to be like Him there; and with such a heaven to gain, who of us can afford to be slothful, or negligent, or half hearted? No: we must have one object and only one, if that Heaven is to be enjoyed. Let us live for Heaven, and that means living for Christ.[18]

---

17. *Church Notes*, No. 2, August 1897.
18. *Church Notes*, No. 3, September 1897.

Storrs taught that the Christian life was to be founded on a firm understanding of the doctrine of justification by faith alone, by grace alone, by the atoning blood and sacrifice of Christ alone. Even as he emphasized the sufficiency of Christ's work, Storrs insisted that the consequence of "the Lord Jesus . . . laying down His life for us" was that there should be a determined and concerted effort on the part of his parishioners to live for Christ in the present. This was classic evangelical crucicentrism combined with classic evangelical activism.

Not surprisingly, the parish was noted as a hive of evangelical activity, especially missionary activity. Parish historians Graham and Margaret Bride note that it is difficult to substantiate the claim made in 1887 that thirteen members of St. Matthew's had gone to the mission field, but there is no difficultly in confirming a similar number who went overseas with CMS from St. Matthew's in the period 1895 to 1926.[19] The parish actively raised support for their missionaries, with the headline banner of *Church Notes* throughout the Storrs era proudly advertising their "Our Own Missionary." During the period 1895 to 1937 these were Naomi Dines, Sophie Anne Dixon, Florence Biggs, and Lionel and Christabel Bakewell.[20] They served in India, Kenya, Uganda and Tanganyika respectively.

Concern for evangelism and mission was further expressed through local missions. Open air preaching was conducted opposite the Town Hall in the lead up to Christmas, although it was not always universally or enthusiastically supported:

> The number of listeners was encouraging; but there were very few to speak or sing, and it was the same on the following Thursday. We hope that many will rally around this work. We believe that there is hardly any work so needful and so really rewarded.[21]

In December 1914, Edmund Clark of the CSSM took a "A Brief Mission" for children in the parish. He spoke at morning and evening Sunday services, as well as in the Sunday School in the afternoon. From Monday to Thursday he took meetings at 6.30pm for children and at 7.45pm for young people and adults. It was a full schedule for a mission described as "brief." Storrs later noted that it had been:

> . . . a time of real helpfulness and blessing. His sermons of Sunday were effective appeals, especially in the evening on

---

19. Bride, *Proclaiming the Gospel*, 67–69.

20. *Church Notes*, No.1 1897; No. 275, May 1920; No. 347, April 1926; No 459, July 1937.

21. *Church Notes*, January 1910.

the things which will last. The addresses to the children on the four week days were very clear and simple presentations of the gospel for young minds. The talks to young people and adults were very earnest and searching and we know that some were deeply impressed. We shall ever remember the happy Scripture choruses, one which Mr. Clark called the Prahran chorus . . .[22]

Home missions were also an important outlet for evangelistic endeavor. For example, Storrs took a mission at Stawell in 1912 and was able to report that a highlight was having three hundred men at the mission's men's service, where there were "some won for Christ and others brought back."[23]

Melbourne evangelical clergy also regularly swapped pulpits and invited leading evangelical clergy and laity to speak as a way of increasing interest, attendance and eliciting a positive response to the gospel message. Among the preachers and speakers at Prahran were Arthur R. Ebbs of the CMS and Eustace Wade the principal of Ridley College, who had earlier been Storrs's curate.[24] In 1905, during Storrs's absence overseas, E. I. Gason, H. Collier and A. R. Ebbs preached at Prahran. H. E. Warren of the Roper River Mission preached in March 1915. Storrs also asked laypeople to speak at St. Matthew's, especially if they could speak evangelistically.[25] Mrs. Griffiths was a regular at women's events, for example.

St. Matthew's also featured in the early twentieth century evangelicals' focus on prayer bands for revival[26] and conventions for the deepening of the spiritual life. Two conventions were held in 1905: a first was planned for St. Silas' Albert Park, on 27 March and a second for St. Matthew's Prahran, on 13 June.[27] In April 1905, Storrs announced the start of a revival prayer meeting at St. Matthew's, following the encouragement of the Reverend T. B. Tress and a similar meeting he had started at St. Stephen's Richmond, where Storrs had been a curate. These were held on Wednesday evenings for an hour in the Upper Room of St. Matthew's School.

Storrs wrote to the parish warning that revival could not be "organized," insisting that it would be a sovereign work of God, not an excitement of human passion:

22. *Church Notes*, January 1915.

23. *Church Notes*, August 1912.

24. Eustace Wade was followed as the curate by his brother Arthur in 1904. Arthur subsequently married the daughter of the honored St. Matthew's vestryman, J. P. Holmes, in 1910.

25. Interview with Jean Guy, 28 May 2007.

26. See Evans, "Evangelicalism in Victoria," in which the activity of revival prayer bands is discussed and highlighted.

27. *Church Notes*, No. 93, March 1905.

> I would remind you there has been no organization about the Revival in Wales—there has been no working up a Revival. It has been spontaneous above all things. If out here we attempt to manufacture a Revival, the result will be disastrous. It will leave us more discouraged, the careless more careless and indifferent, the worldly more immersed in their worldliness. There must be no organization but that of united, fervent, continuous prayer ... God has his own time for Revival, His own way of bringing it about, His own instruments to use, and we must abide His time. A Revival without ethical results is an empty hollow sham. A Revival which consists in shouting Hallelujah, and a great deal of excitement, without definite forsaking of evil lives, evil occupations, will only be so much froth. A true Revival will make men and women better husbands and wives, better sons and daughters, better masters and employees. Pray that there may be a Revival such as will influence the whole of society, public opinion, and reach all classes—the worldly rich, the political leaders, the socialistic mass, and the sham Christians.[28]

This statement reveals at least three things about Storrs's thinking on revivals. First, revivals could only be caused by God. By "spontaneous" he meant that God would be the cause of revival, not human passion or planning. True revival could break out in spite of the lack of prayer, or by means of the fervent prayers offered up corporately as the parishioners were encouraged to meet and pray and call on God. Second, because God would be its cause, true revival could reach anyone within God's sovereign rule—that is everyone, all classes of society, rich or poor, "true" or "sham" Christians. Third, true revival resulted in true ethical results both at the personal and corporate levels. An attempt to manufacture a revival was, by implication, a sin against the divine prerogative and would lead into further discouragement and worldliness, but a true revival would mean personal repentance from personal sin that would lead to a transformed society. Revival for Storrs and this generation of evangelicals meant the sparking of a passionate and deep spiritual life focused on Christ, the need for repentance, personal holiness, and proclaiming the gospel. The handbook for revival living would be the Bible.

Hence, at the same time as focusing on revival, there was a concerted effort at rebuffing the advance of Higher Criticism and its attack on the divine inspiration, and hence authority, of the Scriptures. While the preaching and attitude to the Bible in St. Matthew's held firmly to the Bible as authoritatively the words of God, the local church was not isolated from the drift towards

---

28. *Church Notes*, No. 93, March 1905.

more liberal attitudes towards Scripture. Storrs's academic and intellectual gifts, his interest in theological education, and, most of all, his perception that this was a touchstone issue for his generation, led him to speak out and offer leadership from an evangelical perspective.

In a 1904 number of *Church Notes* Storrs quoted J. C. Ryle on the inspiration of Holy Scripture at length and with approval.[29] The following year, reflecting on a lengthy series of correspondence in the *Argus* responding to the publication of an English Clergy Manifesto on Higher Criticism, Storrs noted that:

> ... we may say that a copy of the proposition and signatures referred to reached us by post from England. As far as memory serves me, for after reading it through, the paper was consigned to the waste paper basket, there was not a name of any of the Clergy on it who are prominent in Home or Foreign mission work, whether among High Churchmen or Evangelicals. The names of all such were conspicuous by their absence. A great deal of fuss is being made over a very hole and corner affair. We were intensely grateful to read the remarks of our Bishop, and also for once to find ourselves so heartily in accord with Prof. Rentoul. Until the formularies of the Church of England are altered, there cannot be any legal standing in the Church for men who reject the Virgin-birth, the Incarnation, or the Atonement.[30]

Conspicuous in his logic was the rejection of Higher Criticism on the basis that its proponents, high church or evangelical, were not committed to mission or evangelism. Storrs had no time for those who were not busy with the Great Commission.

The "remarks of our Bishop" referred to were those of Henry Lowther Clarke's sermon reported in the *Argus* on Monday 1 May 1904. Clarke was forthright and uncompromising in his declaration that this sort of assault by "false liberality" on the fundamental tenets of the faith was nothing new—they had come against St. Paul himself—and were therefore to be expected and resisted. The *Argus* reported thus:

> Preaching yesterday evening at St. Paul's Cathedral on the words, "If Christ be not risen, then is our preaching vain, and your faith is also vain." (1 Corinthians, xv, 14) the Bishop of Melbourne spoke of the manifesto of some English clergymen in reference to the Higher Criticism and the correspondence in "The Argus" on the subject. They must not be surprised to

29. *Church Notes*, No. 89, November 1904.
30. *Church Notes*, May 1905.

learn, he remarked, that some of the fundamental articles of the Apostles' Creed were now called in question. The church was militant here on earth, and she had made good her standing in every generation against the false liberality which would give away her system and sacrifice some portion of her message. St. Paul was dealing with people who said exactly what some were saying now:– "After all the resurrection is only one article of the creed; if we give this up we can still hold to the other parts. We love Jesus in His adorable character as much as you, and we only want to cast away something said of Him which we do not regard as important." But, the Bishop asked, if Christ died and did not afterwards burst the fetters of death; if His body was long ago mingled with the dust of that land where trod His human feet, then what revelation has He for us more than other men, and what salvation from sin and despair or how could they rejoice in the hope of the glory of God?[31]

Such commentary from Clarke was unexpectedly forthright and supportive of the evangelicals' conservative position on the centrality of the whole gospel message of Christ's crucifixion, death and resurrection, hence Storrs's public gratitude. But Clarke's views did not translate into wholehearted support for evangelicals, and the relationship between bishop and evangelicals remained cool.

Storrs's lengthy incumbency at St. Matthew's took in the years of WWI, when faith in general was battered by the horrific realities of war.[32] Storrs reacted to the declaration of war by commencing a daily prayer meeting in the church at noon. He bemoaned the fact that the main theatre of war was in the Christian nations of Europe.[33] As the war progressed, Storrs, like other clergy, became the bearers of the dreaded pink envelopes from the Department of Defence, informing families of the death of their sons and husbands. Storrs wrote to his parish:

> I almost dread coming home lest I should find another pink envelope, containing another message of death, that has to be taken to another heartbroken mother or wife. Our best men are perishing, the flower of our land is being cut off...[34]

---

31. *Argus*, 1 May 1905, 6. The correspondence around the Clergy Manifesto appeared in the *Argus* from 20 April into June, and included letters from Christians of various denominations.
32. See Linder, *The Long Tragedy*.
33. Bride, *Proclaiming the Gospel*, 80.
34. *Church Notes*, October 1916.

In the midst of these sorrows and horrors, he urged repentance from sins and "triflings" and a turning to Christ. No complete record of St. Matthew's parishioners who died in the theatre of war survives as an honor board was destroyed in the church fire of 1982. Six choir members who perished are listed in a surviving stained-glass window. However, in common with every other Australian locality, the percentage of young men who died was probably tragically high and led to a decrease in the life and leadership of the parish in the generations to come.[35] For St. Matthew's, the war marked the beginning of a decline in congregational attendance, finances, and spiritual vitality. Even its commitment to supporting their "Our Own Missionary" would not go unaffected. In the post-war years Prahran could not afford a curate, although deaconesses served working mainly with women and children and for little monetary recompense.[36]

By 1926, Storrs was exhausted and ready to lay down the demanding ministry at Prahran which had developed into a busy inner city, business district. Archbishop Lees was slow to act on his request for a less demanding parish, so Storrs organized a parish swap with Rochford Brady of St. John's Heidelberg. Parish nominators and the archbishop swiftly followed in agreement and by March that year Storrs's thirty-one years at Prahran had come to an end. His departure marked the start of a slow decline in the parish's identity as a leading evangelical center. Storrs's personal connection to CMS and Ridley was not mirrored in his successors, who kept up a parish connection but did not see the missionary connection or the supporting and strengthening of an evangelical theological college as key priorities.

Rochford Brady's tenure at Prahran was not especially noteworthy. It seems that he was less firmly evangelical than Storrs, which begs the question of whether Storrs was alert to this at the time of the parish swap. Brady discontinued the vicar's letter in *Church Notes* within a few months of his arrival and the publication, which had originally been a vehicle of local mission, became more predominantly focused on notices of church-based activities which Brady was adept at organizing and growing. Several new clubs and activities were started in his incumbency, including the tennis club and associated newly constructed courts. Interestingly, the October 1929 issue of *Church Notes* carried a feature entitled "What is Christianity?" which made no reference to Christ, the cross, repentance, sin or the Bible.

---

35. See Linder, *The Long Tragedy*, 145–52.
36. Bride, *Proclaiming the Gospel*, 84–85.

> # What is Christianity?
>
> ---
>
> In the home, kindness.
>
> In business, honesty.
>
> In society, courtesy.
>
> In work, fairness.
>
> Toward the weak, help.
>
> Toward the penitent, forgiveness.
>
> Toward the strong, trust.
>
> Toward God, reverence and love.

"What is Christianity" Pew Sheet Notice for St. Matthew's Prahran

While Brady kept up the missionary connections to CMS and maintained a parish "Our Own Missionary," it seems that there was a winding down of the evangelical spiritual capital of the church, its priority on conversion to Christ, deep personal spirituality, and energetic evangelistic faith. *Church Notes* certainly became more focused on internal church issues. Brady published "A Simple Catechism on the Catholicity and Continuity of the Church of England" in several parts from June 1931. It does not read as "simple" today and was probably not simple to the average parishioner in 1931 either. It contained at least twenty-nine questions and answers including, "Q. 27: What more do we know of this British or Celtic Church before the coming of Augustine?" It was an interesting choice of topic for the parish paper perhaps reflecting interdenominational tension in the parish or the growth of the local Catholic congregation. But it was not designed to call readers to conversion or to deeper commitment to Christ. Neither did it address any of the key touchstone issues for evangelicals, namely the doctrine of the Scriptures or the atonement or the cross or the necessity of conversion.

Brady left for England in 1932 and was replaced by P. W. Robinson who was noted as a man of zeal and action.[37] Robinson had been involved in founding CEBS, the Church of England Boys' Society, and championed its ongoing activities. When the impact of the Depression on Prahran became increasingly clear, he issued "A Call to Service" in *Church Notes*, announcing that the church hoped to provide a hundred dinners a day to children of needy families struck by unemployment.[38] Robinson called for volunteers to work and friends to give. At a June vestry meeting the vicar reported that 612 children had been fed in three days. By July the figure had risen to 7,000. The scale of this social action was remarkable, but it did not pass without some question as to its spiritual value. Robinson dealt with this in the August edition of *Church Notes*:

> I was asked recently if the children who come to dinner received a spiritual message of any kind. My reply was that the action of providing the dinners was a message in itself... I am convinced that the greatest way of championing the cause of Christ is by life and action and not so much by talking...[39]

The clear and plain presentation of the gospel message in words, whether from the pulpit or in *Church Notes*, was increasingly no longer a part of the culture of St. Matthew's. St. Matthew's status as a leading evangelical parish, according to Robinson, was not linked to doctrine or preaching or the gospel message but to its functioning in the wider activities of the church.[40] So while the activity of the local parish increased in line with its provision of activities and services for the growing local population of families and workers, and the range of people it served and connected with increased, its spiritual vitality in terms of the evangelicalism of Storrs and Langley was ebbing away. The question with regard to the spiritual value of Robinson's social action highlighted above indicates that there were some "old time evangelical" laity left in the congregation, but the changed clerical leadership meant that the parish's evangelical character was at risk.

This change could easily be attributed to Brady and Robinson, but their leadership has to be set in the wider context of shifts in evangelicalism internationally. The rise of the liberal evangelical movement outlined in the section above meant that there was an almost irresistible pressure in this direction. Even Storrs's curate, E. W. Wade, was not immune as his record

37. Ibid., 92–109.
38. *Church Notes*, May 1933.
39. *Church Notes*, August 1933.
40. See quote attributed to Robinson in Bride, *Proclaiming the Gospel*, 93.

at Ridley illustrates. Two other notable future leaders who passed through Prahran in its heyday as "a leading evangelical parish" further illustrate the point. Geoffrey Sambell, later archbishop of Perth, was licensed as a Reader during Robinson's tenure, "to help the vicar in the parish generally but particularly in the work among boys."[41] Despite this connection and training at Ridley, in his subsequent career he could not be mistaken as an evangelical.[42] Neither could that of the long-serving Archdeacon Stan Moss, who was a child of the parish having grown up there, serving as a choir boy and being involved in a full range of parish activities.

Prahran's most notable evangelical progeny from this period were its missionaries: all three of Storrs' daughters, Lionel Bakewell, the Good sisters, and Florence Biggs. All except Bakewell were women. All served overseas where there was greater room for their evangelical ministry impulses. Almost all served in East Africa where the priorities of preaching the gospel message of repentance from sin, forgiveness in Christ, conversion to Christ, living in holiness and working at evangelism were high on the church's agenda—especially during the East African Revival.[43]

Although Prahran's evangelicalism weakened in the post-Storrs period, the demographic changes in the area with increased population and numbers of younger people and families, meant that even with the shift in theological emphasis, the ministry to young people and families continued to prosper and keep the parish busy and a center of activity. Robinson's successful CEBS ministry was a notable example of this. However, the spiritual capital of the parish was winding down because of the loss of focus on conversionism and evangelistic mission, and this would lead to an eventual loss of the parish's status as a leading evangelical center by the middle of the century.

By contrast, in another evangelical parish of the period, All Saints' Northcote, there was a succession of firmly evangelical mission-minded clergy who were invariably connected with the CMS. However, they seemed powerless to reverse a gradual decline in parish vitality in the face of demographic changes in an opposite direction.

All Saints' Northcote

It was the lack of transport infrastructure that devalued its lands and characterized Northcote as a working-class suburb. As such is was regarded as:

---

41. Bride, *Proclaiming the Gospel*, 100.
42. See Challen, *Sambell*.
43. See Reed, *Walking in the Light*. See also Reed, "East African Revival."

> ... an appropriate site for the location of noxious industries and institutions requiring isolation, like the Yarra Bend Asylum (1848), the Inebriates Retreat (1883) and the Fairfield Hospital (1904). By the 1870s the smells from piggeries and boiling-down works regularly offended the growing residential population...[44]

By the start of the twentieth century the area still lacked essential services, but the population had increased dramatically. Most new housing in the area were small, spartan workers' cottages, typical of Melbourne's northern suburbs. From the 1920s more substantial homes were being built in the surrounding areas as population continued to grow, but the locality maintained its working-class character.

The building consecrated All Saints' in Northcote South was opened for divine service in August 1860 by Charles Perry. It had been planted out of Christ Church Brunswick, but unlike its mother church, did not go down the path of high-church liturgical innovation. A brief account of its history in a 110th anniversary edition of the monthly parish bulletin declared that:

> ... in 1865 the parish was cut off from Christ Church, Brunswick. The Rev. W. Hall was the first vicar. In 1869, the year the Suez Canal was completed, the first missionary meeting was held there. There has always been a strong missionary interest at All Saints.[45]

The incumbency of Digby Berry from 1873 to 1885 established All Saints' evangelical culture, which was cemented over several incumbencies leading up to the late twentieth century. In 1901, Alfred Charles Kellaway came to Northcote. Kellaway was a prominent and outspoken evangelical, having served for a decade as the editor of the *Victorian Churchman* and as a leader in the councils of the CMS. He remained at Northcote for three decades, until 1930. His family were a noted part of the parish: his wife Annie Carrick Kellaway was active and had herself trained for Christian ministry under Henry Langley at Prahran[46] and his daughter Gwendoline Kellaway

---

44. The Encyclopedia of Melbourne, online edition accessed at http://www.emelbourne.net.au. Last accessed Thursday 15 July 2010. Site maintained by the University of Melbourne. Print edition published by Cambridge University Press, 2005.

45. All Saints' Northcote South monthly bulletin, "News and Views from the Pulpit and Pews," special 110th anniversary edition, August-September 1970.

46. All Saints' Parish Paper, November 1926, carried this eulogy: "On Sunday, October 10, the Rev. C. H. Barnes, of St. Hilary's, East, Kew, unveiled a memorial tablet in All Saints' Church, in memory of the late Mrs. Kellaway, in the presence of a large congregation. Speaking as one who had known her for over forty years and recognized her true worth, Mr. Barnes outlined her character in a few well-chosen words, and

became a long-term CMS missionary after making a commitment to do so in her mid-teens. She served some thirty-five years in South India.[47] Throughout this period she was linked to All Saints' and the parish bulletins carried a steady stream of her letters, prayer news and information about her movements. Northcote invariably hosted a program of activities during her times of furlough back in Melbourne.

Kellaway himself was a strong proponent of the ministry of evangelical societies within parish life. Upon arrival he immediately founded a Young People's Scripture Union in the parish. By 1903 this had over 200 members. His 1905 incumbent's report mentioned the founding of another new group in the parish:

> ... a Society of Christian Endeavour for young men and women, to train them for lives of Christian usefulness, was inaugurated towards the close of the year, and gives promise of great blessing. I commend this Society, the Gleaners' Union, and the Young People's Scripture Union to our young people.

In the same year the Sunday School reported regular meetings of the Sowers' Band, another CMA-related group, and the starting of a Boys' Missionary Band in the hope that, "a missionary spirit will be instilled into our lads." A Girls' Missionary Band was also started. A Sunday School Mission was held that year with the Reverend A. R. Ebbs of the CMA and Miss Shrapnell as missioners:

> ... many of the scholars handed in their names as having accepted Christ as their Saviour and Friend and expressed their desire to he His faithful soldiers and servants to their life's end. We pray that these young people may be daily renewed by divine grace, and may be kept by the power of God through faith unto salvation.

In 1906, Kellaway again praised the "excellent work" of the Societies attached to the church:

---

pointed out that she had been trained in Christian work under the late Henry Langley (afterwards first bishop of Bendigo), at St. Matthew's, Prahran; that she was thoroughly established in the truth which she loved; that she was a diligent student of the Word of God, and a most capable teacher, who influenced many lives; and that she was always zealous for the salvation and edification of others, as well as a help and a blessing in her own home."

47. Gwen Kellaway served in India from 1912 to 1947, CMS Victoria Branch, "List of CMS-VIC Missionary Personnel in Full Connection 1892–2009." Her life and missionary career is celebrated in Cole et al., *Servants for Jesus' Sake*. 143 onwards.

The Gleaners' Union has cemented together those who desire to see Christ's Kingdom extended throughout the whole world. The Sowers' Band, under Miss Groom's careful management, has continued its work among the young in fostering a missionary spirit, and working and praying for the children of heathen lands. The Christian Endeavour Society has held meeting regularly during the year, and is training our young people for lives of Christian usefulness in the years to come.

This focus on "fostering a missionary spirit" among young people was also seen in the visits of Edmund Clark, a pioneer of the CSSM work in Australia.[48] Clark was instrumental in the conversions and discipling of, among others, C. Stacey Woods, the Bendigo boy who became the leader of the North American Inter-Varsity and then International Fellowship of Evangelical Students movements; and Marcus Loane, a future archbishop of Sydney.[49] Clark's CSSM ministry, is a good example of an evangelical society affecting other evangelical societies and parishes and denominations positively in terms of encouraging and training leaders. This was not specifically targeted, but because the CSSM work was so widespread it affected so many and so much. Much of the activity around the Evangelical Revival was similarly widespread.

Edmund Clark visited the parish in 1913 and was invited back to run another week-long mission in December 1922, which was entitled "Good News for Everybody." Evening week day meetings were held in the parish hall, and two Sunday services were given over to Clark. Special services and picture talks were held, and "attractive new choruses" were promised for every evening. Clark visited again in 1927, speaking at a Sunday School prize-giving.

---

48. Prince, *Tuned in to Change*; Pollock, *Good Seed*; Sylvester, *God's Word in a Young World*.

49. Reid, *Marcus L. Loane*;. Macleod, *C. Stacey Woods*.

> **GOOD NEWS FOR EVERYBODY AT**
> ## All Saints', Northcote,
> From SUNDAY, DECEMBER 3rd, to
> TUESDAY, DECEMBER 12th.
>
> **Mr. Edmund Clark,** of the Children's Special Service Mission, will address Young People and their Friends on Sundays at 11 a.m. and 7 p.m., in All Saints' Church, and at 8 p.m. Week-days in the Parish Hall.
>
> **Boys and Girls' Picture Talks, every afternoon at 4 o'clock.**
>
> **Special Services on Sunday afternoon, at 3 p.m.**
>
> EVERYBODY WELCOME! Come and bring your Friends.
>
> **Attractive New Choruses each Evening.**

"Good News for Everybody" Advertisement, 1922

Evangelical missionary endeavor also focused on the Australian mission field. Writing in July 1908 to parishioners, Kellaway called for hearty support of the new Aboriginal mission in the far north as a matter of justice for the indigenous inhabitants of Australia:

> This month will witness a forward movement in Australian missionary enterprise. The Church Missionary Association has decided to form a mission to the aborigines on the Roper River in the Northern Territory. The South Australian Government has granted them facilities for carrying on the work, and next week the first party is leaving Melbourne to commence work among the wandering tribes of the north. Good success has attended similar efforts in North Queensland, at Yarrabah and at Mitchell River, and it is hoped that the labors of these devoted workers will be crowned with God's richest blessing. We owe a debt to the aborigines of Australia; and the Church has been very slow in seeking the spiritual welfare of the people whose land we possess, and who are dying rapidly before the advance

of civilization. We trust that now the work is commenced it will be heartily supported by all churchmen.[50]

This interest in Aboriginal missions was evidenced again in January 1922, when the noted South Australian Aboriginal Christian leader David Unaipon lectured in the Parish Hall. His subject was "the claims of the aborigines to the Gospel message."[51]

The parish was also active in local mission. The All Saints' Mission Sunday School was opened in the Northcote State School, with nineteen children and four teachers, in March 1907. By the following year's annual report, superintendent J. H. Turner was able to report that it had an average attendance of seventy students, with nine teachers. Land with forty feet of frontage on Hawthorn Road had also been purchased and paid for in preparation for the building of a Mission Church to serve the area.

A wide view of mission, in partnership with traveling evangelists and other local churches, was another value that Kellaway sought to establish in the parish. The Parish Paper often carried notices such as the following:

> Another Simultaneous Mission has just been held in 30 different parts of the metropolitan area. At Clifton Hill a large marquee was erected on Mayor's Park, and Mr. James McKendrick, a Scottish evangelist, was the missioner. Day after day he proclaimed the gospel message with simplicity and force, and attracted large congregations, which listened with rapt attention to his clear and vigorous expositions of the Word of God. It is a very great privilege to have the message of the Gospel put so winsomely.[52]

The strong Church of England evangelical network meant that there was no shortage of available visiting preachers and missioners for the parish. In April 1908, H. S. Begbie spoke at the Sunday School Annual prizegiving, delivering a "stirring and helpful address." The Begbie link persisted, with H. S. Begbie's son, Alan, returning to Melbourne from Sydney to study at MBI under C. H. Nash in 1928, simultaneously undertaking a student ministry placement at Northcote.[53] The connection was probably the rea-

---

50. All Saints' Parish Paper, July 1908. See also, for accounts of the early partnership between the Victorian CMA and the Aboriginal mission in Australia's Northern Territory, Seiffert, *Refuge on the Roper*.

51. All Saints' Parish Paper, January 1922.

52. All Saints' Parish Paper, May 1912.

53. Alan Begbie returned to Sydney to continue his studies at Moore College and to pursue ordination there. He was replaced in the parish by MBI's senior student, W. T. Hewlett. See All Saints' Parish Paper, January 1929. Also Loane, *Mark These Men*. The family was also remembered in an announcement in July 1929 congratulating Charys

son for Canon H. S. Begbie's return to take a Ten Days' Mission at Northcote in the April of that year.[54]

The list of visiting preachers in Holy Week of 1912 further illustrates the operation of the evangelical network of the time. Kellaway reported that:

> During Passion Week, clergy from other parishes addressed us on the sufferings and death of our Lord Jesus Christ; Mr. Deasey, from St. Philip's, Collingwood; Mr. Storrs, from St. Matthew's, Prahran; Mr. Miller, from St. Saviour's, Collingwood; and Mr. Weir, from Heidelberg. There were good attendances at most of the services, and we were brought face to face with the fact of the supreme love of God to us sinners, and with the self-sacrificing love of our Lord Jesus Christ, who willingly gave Himself to rescue us from the ruin which sin brought upon us, to restore us to the favour of God, to bring us into the family of God, and make us sharers of His eternal glory.[55]

As at Prahran, such evangelistic work was not carried out exclusively by clergy. In April 1924, a range of evangelical laymen gave Sunday evening Lent addresses in the parish. Edwin Lee Neil, Walter Buntine, Horace Hannah, and Frederick Homan[56] gave "excellent addresses to men on the great truths of our holy religion from a laymen's standpoint," reported Kellaway, who urged parishioners to attend the remaining Lent lectures by "Mr. F. R. Adams, M.A. and the Hon. W. H. Edgar M.L.C."[57] Adams was a Ridley council member and college alumnus, and the Sunday School superintendent at St. Hilary's Kew until 1930, when he was appointed the headmaster of Launceston Grammar School.[58] The Lent lectures were an attempt to engage the men of the parish by using the gifts of prominent laymen. It was relatively successful and continued for a number of years.

The list of visitors to the parish for various events and preachers in the parish reads as a veritable roll call of key Melbourne evangelical leaders. Neil spoke to their Gleaners' Union in May 1912. Mrs. Neil performed the opening ceremony to the parish Sale of Gifts fundraiser in November 1923, with Mrs. Buntine officiating the following year. At some stage, Walter Buntine, the owner of Caulfield Grammar School, had transferred his membership to Northcote; by December 1928 it was able to be reported that he had been

---

Begbie, sister of Alan, on the conferral of an MBE on her for her work in Kenya.

54. See All Saints' Parish Paper, March and April 1929.
55. All Saints' Parish Paper, May 1912.
56. Buntine, Hannah, and Homan were all long-serving Ridley Council members.
57. All Saints' Parish Paper, April 1924.
58. St. Hilary's Parish Notes, No. 190. February 1930.

their Synod representative for a number of years. The principal of Ridley, Eustace Wade, was another regular visiting preacher. Evangelical leaders were honored, with the aged bishop of Bendigo J. D. Langley preaching at Northcote in his eighty-ninth and ninetieth years.[59]

From the parish emerged at least three long-term missionaries: Gwen Kellaway, Harry Wittenbach, and Jean Meyer. Wittenbach's father was a long-serving vestryman in the parish. Wittenbach wrote that "Eustace Wade recruited me for the ministry." Wittenbach was present when Wade was preaching at St. Hilary's Kew, and was introduced to him after the service by the vicar Charlie Barnes. Wittenbach was at the time in the first year of his university studies, intending to be a teacher. Wade invited him for "a cup of tea, and there he challenged me with the possibility that God might have other plans for my life."[60] Wittenbach entered Ridley College and was influenced by the focus on missionary work evident in the college at the time.[61] One of his best friends at College was Ernest Panelli, who became the Bush Church Aid Society's first mobile missioner in 1924, driving around outback NSW and Queensland in a motor van dubbed "Tin Lizzie." Wittenbach himself settled on a missionary career after ordination, going to a school in South China and Hong Kong, and eventually retiring to England.[62]

Meyer was originally from Bright and had come to Melbourne for further study when she was brought into the fellowship of the CMS League of Youth. She was converted and began serving in the All Saints' Sunday School, before committing herself to missionary service. After twenty years in Tanzania, she returned to Melbourne where she was active in reaching out to Turkish immigrants.[63]

Despite the activism and energy within the parish, some weaknesses in parish ministry, in conversion growth and raising up a new generation of evangelical leaders, was becoming increasingly clear. Enthusiasm for local missions was not always as high as Kellaway hoped. Parish missions and meetings with visiting speakers were sometimes poorly attended, leading

---

59. All Saints' Parish Paper, January 1926 and February 1927.

60. Ridley Report, No. 48, October 1982, reproduces a letter from Wittenbach detailing his call to ministry and ministry career.

61. See *Ridley Annual Reports*, 1919–1921, which consistently mention with pride the college's alumni on the mission field. See also early Ridley College publications: *The Ridley Collegian* (1920–1932) and *The Ridley Monthly* (1921 only, replaced by *The Ridley Quarterly*, 1922 only). Held in Ridley Melbourne Archives.

62. *Ridley Annual Report*, 1945.

63. Cutler, *Bearers of the Torch*, 18.

Kellaway to vent his frustration on more than one occasion. Speaking of a visiting evangelist's ministry, he wrote:

> It is a very great privilege to have the message of the Gospel put so winsomely. Our one regret is that more of our people did not avail themselves of the privilege of hearing him. Those who did so, thoroughly appreciated the missioner, his message, and the way in which he delivered it.[64]

Sunday School numbers remained steady throughout the period of Kellaway's long incumbency, which meant that they did not keep pace with the growth in local population. The parish was already in slow decline. Further, Harry Wittenbach remained the sole example of home-grown talent raised up for ordained ministry—but he served overseas.

Kellaway died while in office at Northcote in February 1930. A "who's who" of evangelical leaders officiated at his funeral and assisted in the parish in the interregnum. They included Arthur Riley, CMS missionary on furlough from Yambio, Africa[65]; Mr. Arthur Lumsden, in charge of the men's hostel at the Melbourne Bible Institute; E. C. Frewin of St. Stephen's Richmond; P. W. Stephenson of the CMS[66]; W. T. C. Storrs, and C. H. Nash.[67] There could be no doubting the parish's evangelical credentials under Kellaway, but the Northcote context made for difficult ministry, and signs of decline were present.

Although a succession of vicars after Kellaway were CMS enthusiasts or returned missionaries with an evangelical heart for mission, the parish failed to raise up any other home-grown missionaries or clergy of note. In common with other social institutions and inner-city Melbourne parishes in the interwar period, Northcote went into decline. Evangelicalism may have persisted, but the parish's inability to engage outsiders with the claims of the gospel meant that conversion rates were low to negligible.

Two factors were significant to this. First, the missionary enthusiasm and the energy of the parish's younger people were centered around the CMS LOY, and much of the most enthusiastic talent, like Wittenbach and Meyer, went overseas. The impact of directing the enthusiasm and energy of the parish's most talented and motivated young people overseas was, and is, complex. On the one hand, their example and the continuing connection to an "Our Own Missionary" helped to inspire evangelism and mission

---

64. All Saints' Parish Paper, May 1912.

65. See again the biography of Arthur Riley by his wife Grace Riley, *No Drums at Dawn*.

66. See Cole, *Sincerity My Guide*.

67. All Saints' Northcote Parish Paper, February and March 1930.

locally. On the other hand, there was the serious negative impact of not having the newer, younger leaders' passion, energy, and talent available for local parish work.[68] An active interest in overseas mission may have served to invigorate enthusiasm for local evangelism. However, local evangelistic effort could sometimes be less fruitful, and hence, less encouraging and exciting than overseas work. So a parish like All Saints' could be simultaneously generous in support of the CMS and relatively unsupportive of local visiting missioners, as demonstrated. It could be easier to be excited about the conversion of faraway exotic people groups than to be industrious and creative about local evangelism to neighbors.

Second, the locality's firmly working-class character meant that there was a relative absence of capable, professional men to help and partner with the vicar in his ministry. Kellaway relied on leading laity from outside his parish when he used them as speakers—there were few or none, except for Walter Buntine, from within. The absence of longstanding and powerful laity seemed to have impaired the persistence of evangelical witness in the parish. A contrasting demographic situation was to be found in another evangelical parish of the early twentieth century, St. Columb's Hawthorn.

St. Columb's Hawthorn

Parish historian Jane Carolan describes St. Columb's as an "infill" parish, founded in 1880 in response to tremendous population growth in the area in between Christ Church Hawthorn, Holy Trinity Kew, and St. John's Camberwell. Originally part of Christ Church, St. Columb's occupied the now more central position in Upper Hawthorn close to the relatively recently constructed Municipal Hall (1860) and Post Office (1872) where the bulk of the population now resided. This saw the new church plant grow numerically beyond the size of its mother church.[69]

The opening decades of the twentieth century were Hawthorn's boom years as significant homes and institutions were established. The population in Hawthorn had almost doubled from 5,000 to nearly 10,000 between 1883 and 1901. The economic depression of the 1890s slowed growth, but by 1916 there were just under 28,000 residents in the area.[70] The 1904 Melbourne Municipal Directory described the locality as "a popular and pictur-

---

68. See section on the CMS LOY below.

69. Carolan, *St. Columb's Hawthorn*.

70. Hawthorn Heritage Study, Volume 1A Main Report, 56–60. Available at http://boroondara.vic.gov.au/sites/default/files/2017-05/Hawthorn-Heritage-Study-Main-Report-Vol1A.pdf. Last accessed 31 October 2018.

esque city . . . (with) well laid-out public gardens and reserves, connected with the metropolis by two cable tram lines and the handsome bridges over the Yarra."[71] The subsequent establishment of the Swinburne Technical College, with the support of the local council, next to the local train station and nearby Municipal Offices, further enhanced the desirability and importance of the suburb.

The first vicar, given charge of the new parish in 1880, was T. H. Armstrong, later bishop of Wangaratta.[72] The liberal evangelical Armstrong was energetic, an engaging speaker, and a good administrator. He was followed in 1894 by another disciplined administrator, William Carey Ward. Ward worked within a strict English parochial model of ministry and established the practice of parish visitation by a team of lay visitors. The process included the assiduous maintenance of a register of the names of every occupier of every home in every street of the parish, along with their religious affiliation. There were some 12,000 residents at the time. District visitors would then visit Church of England adherents every month, and all others once every three months.[73] The work seems to have paid off; by the turn of the century, St. Columb's had become established as a leading parish of the diocese:

> With its past record, its present position and its prospects for the future St. Columb's Church, Hawthorn occupies a foremost place among suburban Anglican Churches. The congregation is slightly above the average not only in point of worldly goods but in Christian harmony. All sorts of conditions of men are represented. Both services are well attended. The regular attendances are between 500–600 in the morning and 600–700 in the evening.[74]

Further testimony to the strength of the parish is seen in that the church buildings along with two further substantial extensions in the 1880s were completed and debt-free, and hence able to be consecrated on 28 October 1905 by Archbishop Lowther Clarke.

In January 1900, Clifford Harris Nash came to St. Columb's. He inherited a thriving concern in a growing locality, with around a thousand Sunday attenders, a similar number of registered Sunday School children, and fifty-eight teachers on staff. Nash built on these foundations, starting the Young

71. Melbourne Municipal Directory, 1904. 191.

72. See ADEB, also Holden, *Church in a Landscape*.

73. A form of the practice was still in place some fifty years later, with the register having survived in parts in the parish archives.

74. Carolan, *St. Columb's Hawthorn 1883–1983*, citing the *Southern Cross* newspaper, 7.

Men's Society in 1905, which had adjunct Literary and Debating Societies, a magazine, Bible classes, and cricket, harriers, and ramblers' clubs, as well as a well-attended annual camp. Like many other parishes of the day, St. Columb's was a focus of community activity, except that it was overtly evangelical and sought openly to inculcate faith and discipleship in its members. By the end of that year, the average Sunday School attendance was six hundred, with eight hundred on the roll. However, unlike Ward, Nash also focused his attention beyond the boundaries of the parish.

Nash's mission-mindedness caused him to immediately apply to Archdeacon Langley for permission to carry out home missions work in the Dandenong Ranges to the east, which he visited monthly. Nash's plan was to establish a church there and use it as a base to train young men for preaching ministry. His friends, the capable businessmen and lay evangelicals, John and James Griffiths, had connections to the area as they had their retreat homes in Upwey.[75] This connection led to the founding of the Upwey Convention in that area.[76]

Another plan with similar evangelistic purposes was just as immediately put into action. Services were commenced in an untenanted shop at 178 Auburn Road on 2 September 1900, where they continued until 1 April 1906. It was another attempt at mission and training other men, this time more locally. Nash preached only occasionally, with several laymen of the parish taking turns to preach there. The preachers' book for the services has survived and lists names of lay preachers such as J. C. Langley, Mr. Biggs, Mr. Hookes, Mr. J. P. Bainbridge, and clergy like George Lamble and Colin Campbell.[77]

This focus on reaching those outside the church for Christ, and Nash's ability and popularity as a speaker, meant that extra-parochial engagements encroached upon time and energy that might have been expended in the parish. Carolan noted that St. Columb's members were disappointed at the high number of outside engagements he accepted.[78] Nash was made a canon of St. Paul's in 1903 and preached in the cathedral bimonthly. From 1906, Nash was also teaching at Clarke's fledgling St. John's College. In later years, Nash also took studies at the City Men's Bible Class, where he gathered and energized an incredibly influential group of evangelical Melbourne businessmen, the chief part of a network described by Stuart

75. See Wehner, *Tea and Charity*, for a description of the retreat homes, the chief of which, "Ferndale," was offered to clergy, missionaries and Christian workers to use (complete with house staff). See also Griffiths family papers held by Kathleen Malone.

76. Paproth, "Upwey Convention"; Patterson, *A Pioneer Church*.

77. St. Columb's Hawthorn, parish archives.

78. Carolan, *St. Columb's Hawthorn*. 12.

Piggin as "the strongest, the best-organized, and the most determined network of lay evangelicals in Australian history."[79] From 1930 onward, he was a regular teacher at the League of Youth Bible class in the cathedral's crypt, having been an instigator and founder of the movement.[80] He was also a regular speaker at the Upwey Convention, and numerous other occasional conferences and events.

However, as with his work in the Dandenong Ranges and with the Auburn Road preaching point, Nash was most interested in missions and raising up missionaries. In 1901, Nash founded a deaconess training house in Fitzroy that later merged with St. Hilda's Women's Training Home for missionaries. Two of the earliest students were Maud Henniker and Clare Wallen, daughters of the parish who became missionaries in India.

St. Columb's monthly newsletter of September 1904 reported that since Nash started in the parish in January 1900 three women had "given up their lives entirely to missionary service." Minnie and Eliza Clark were two further examples of parish women spurred on by Nash into the mission field.[81] The twins were born into a wealthy family touched by tragedy. Their father died of a heart attack aged thirty, the family fortune was lost in the depression of the late 1890s, and their young mother of six succumbed to alcoholism aged forty-six in 1902. Nevertheless, they did well at school and developed a strong Christian faith. They attended St. Columb's regularly and were students at the local Tintern Church of England Girls' Grammar School. They were young women of ability. Minnie was the first president of Tintern's Christian Union in her final years of school. In 1896, the twins placed first and second out of 676 entrants in the Senior Division of the diocese's Sunday School exams. Two years later they were equal first in the Sunday School teachers' exams. In 1898, Minnie became president of the Gleaner's Union—she was twenty years old.

Minnie taught Scripture in schools for a few years before offering for missionary service in the hope of being sent to China. China was very much in the news at this time, due to the publicity around the 1895 murder of Nellie and Topsy Saunders, Victoria's first missionaries, at the hands of Chinese

---

79. Piggin, "Challenging but Glorious Heritage." These lay leaders included Edwin Lee Neil, William Buck, Alex Eggleston, James and John Griffiths, Horace John Hannah, Leonard Buck, Ralph Davis, Will Renshaw, and Charles Alfred Sandland. They were interdenominational, although a significant number were Anglicans.

80. Cutler, *The Torch*; Cutler, *Bearers of the Torch*.

81. Much of this information is from the unpublished paper by Hart, "'An Unshakeable Faith.'" Hart is a descendant of the Clark sisters and had access to first hand testimony. Paper held in the St. Columb's archive and in the Ridley Melbourne Archive.

brigands in Ku Cheng.[82] Their deaths were held up as martyrdoms and used to call for more sacrificial efforts to bring the gospel to China.

Evangelistic activity among the local Chinese had a long history.[83] Earlier waves of Chinese immigration during the Victorian gold rush meant that there were already large numbers of Chinese in Melbourne and Victoria. There were Chinese market gardens in Urquhart Street close to St. Columb's, and there were substantial numbers of Chinese residents in the area. In 1886, pew number eighty-seven, towards the rear and against the south wall of the nave, was specially designated for Chinese—apparently so that youthful louts could not pull on their pigtails during services![84] There were seventy Chinese at a special Chinese hospitality evening in September 1898.[85]

Minnie trained under Nash at St. Hilda's in Fitzroy, graduating after four months at the top of the class. She departed for China on 28 October 1904. There was a constant stream of correspondence between the twins, and Eliza entered St. Hilda's just fourteen months later, sailing for China to join her sister on 11 October 1906. They were to remain there for forty years, finally returning in mid-1947 when China ejected all Western missionaries.

The twins, along with Maud Henniker, Clare Wallen, and the parish's "Our Own Missionary" in the 1930s, Miss Adams, were five examples of the kind of evangelical missionary leadership that was raised up in the parish. They were all women who took up the challenge of bringing the gospel message to difficult faraway contexts. Overseas as missionaries, they had opportunities for ministry and leadership that were not available to them in Australia, where they were not yet able even to be elected on to local church vestries.

The theme of available opportunity was thus common to two evangelical activities. It was true of the involvement of women in the overseas missionary task and of men in the work of local mission. The relative moribund state of the diocese meant that it was comparatively easy for enthusiastic evangelicals to focus their energies on international and interdenominational mission through the work of evangelical societies, rather than on diocesan affairs. There was also little incentive or encouragement for young men to enter ordained ministry. Inspirational leadership and worthwhile evangelism were located outside the parochial and diocesan structures. Evangelical energy was

82. See Berry, *Sister Martyrs of Ku Cheng*; Cole et al., *Letters from China*.

83. See Welch, "Pariahs and Outcasts." See also Paproth, "Character of Evangelism."

84. During a recent re-fit of St. Columb's, pews were removed, sold, and replaced by chairs; but according to the present vicar, Michael Flynn, "No. 87" was retained for posterity.

85. Carolan, *St. Columb's Hawthorn*, 22.

being focused on the work of the missionary societies and evangelical organizations. Laity like Edwin Lee Neil, who were capable and energetic both in mission societies and in diocesan affairs, were rare.

After Nash's departure, his successor Henry Frederick Mercer could only be described as a failure. He had been recruited from England, largely on the recommendation of Nash's predecessor at St. Columb's, William Carey Ward, who had retired there. Carey Ward had also been instrumental in selecting Nash to succeed him, and the vestry wrote in flowery terms thanking him for his discernment in both cases.[86] However, the *Argus* reported that "leading clergymen and laymen" expressed surprise at his appointment, for Mercer was a relative unknown who had never had charge of parish. He had served several curacies and was resigning as Metropolitan Secretary of the Church Army. He was thirty-five years old. Nevertheless, four out of the seven nominators on the board of patronage, being Carey Ward and all three parochial nominators, voted for him.

Carolan's parish history is generous towards Mercer, describing his success with the Sunday afternoon men's services started by Carey Ward, which swelled the ranks in the pews with four to five hundred men regularly.[87] However, according to a contemporary source, Mercer's difficulties were in part due to a strong residual sympathy in the parish for Nash. Mercer was the one to bring accusations against Nash to the archbishop's notice in September 1907, a move which alienated those who supported their much-loved previous vicar—especially the man Nash described as his truest friend, the church organist, choirmaster, and powerful businessman Edwin Lee Neil.[88]

By January 1908, eighteen months after his arrival, Mercer was asking for the resignations of Neil as organist and choirmaster and of Walker the curate for the greater good of the parish.[89] The papers reported that this action created "much surprise amongst the parishioners of the church and others interested." Neil, however, was reported saying that he was not surprised, as relations had been strained for some time, but he had stayed for as long as he could "for the sake of the church." When pressed, Neil told the reporter that the sackings:

---

86. Carolan, *St. Columb's Hawthorn*, 13.
87. Carolan, *St. Columb's Hawthorn*, 23.
88. See *Argus*, 18 June 1912, 7–8, and 20 June 1912, 13–14.

89. *Argus*, 31 January 1908, 5. The report noted that both men had been given the formal period of notice according to the letter of the law—a month for Neil, three months for Walker.

... had nothing to do with my church work. I am certain it must have been solely on account of my openly expressed sympathy for Canon Nash. I believe that the Rev. Mr. Mercer found he could not live up to the ideals established by Canon Nash at St. Columb's.

Mr. Walker has offended by sticking up for Canon Nash. The action against him is monstrous. It will break up the church here altogether. The parishioners are trying to get up an agitation against our removal, but I am doing all I can to put it down. It can do no good.[90]

Additionally, according to Carolan, Mercer had a reputation for running up accounts in Glenferrie Road with traders. She recalls that he eventually left the parish under a cloud, with many unpaid debts.[91] Mercer was subsequently dean of Perth and later returned to England, where in 1933 he was imprisoned for eighteen months on the account of thirteen charges of fraud against him. An *Argus* report mentioned an additional 195 charges, and a history of fraud in Zurich, Switzerland and Southport, England.[92]

Mercer was succeeded by Denis Murrell Deasey in 1912. Deasey had been Nash's curate at St. Columb's and was already well known and accepted. He enjoyed a twenty-year incumbency at St. Columb's, a period noted for his evangelistic ministry to both the rich and poor in the area. Deasey evangelized regularly in the open air in Grace Street, and his Good Friday services were so well attended that they had to be held in the Town Hall or the local Palace Picture Theatre. His preaching was noted as "powerful."

Deasey also managed the activities of the parish well, growing groups and Bible classes in the difficult WWI period and its aftermath. During the war Deasey established a tent ministry to soldiers next to the cathedral and compiled a book of daily Bible readings and prayers for soldiers, *The Warrior's Way*.[93] The 1927 Annual Report noted that the men's afternoon services were enjoying large attendances under Deasey's leadership and that there were many active groups including a Mothers' Union, Girls' Society with monthly Bible talks by Miss McQuie, Young Men's Bible Class, and Young Men's Gymnastics Club. St. Columb's Scout and Cub packs and ministries to young people were "encouraged and sustained" by Deasey's preaching. The Chinese connection in the area remained, with a Miss Yeo's

90. *Argus*, 1 February 1908, 19.
91. Written notes by the Reverend Neil Bach of a conversation with Beryl Ashton, a long-term parishioner from the time of Nash and Mercer. Lodged in the St. Columb's archives.
92. *Argus*, 7 December 1933, 10.
93. Deasey, *Warrior's Way*.

arrival noted as "strengthening the teaching staff at the parish's south Auburn Sunday School" in the following year's report.

After twenty years, Deasey transferred in 1932 to Christ Church Geelong. His legacy was a parish that weathered the post-WWI challenges relatively well.[94] From 1900 to 1937, the priority on evangelism and youth ministry meant that the parish enjoyed a high degree of enthusiasm from recent converts and youthful vitality. The ministry to men in particular meant that there was a high level of active engagement by men in the life of the parish. Leslie Perriman's experience of coming to revived faith through a mission, then attending the men's service, from where he felt led to ask for confirmation and began to attend the regular Sunday services, was typical.[95]

By 1937, the vicar was Archdeacon John Herring, and the assistant minister was William Lloyd—later credited as the vicar who laid the foundations for late-twentieth century growth at St. Hilary's Kew.[96] During the year, Nash returned as a guest preacher, as he had often done since leaving. Other evangelical leaders like A. R. Ebbs,[97] C. W. T. "Hundredweight" Rodgers,[98] and P. W. Robinson were also visiting preachers. That year the Sunday School had 180 scholars, with an average attendance of 111, a relatively healthy number. The Sunday School anniversary preachers were P. W. Robinson and Bishop Banerjee of India—both men who would have brought an outward focus to the church. Miss Clark was the parish's "Our Own Missionary," and £144 was raised for her in the year.[99]

In common with other evangelical parishes of the period 1901–1937, St. Columb's was focused more on parochial and overseas mission than on diocesan affairs. It did not have a sharp focus on raising up future clergy, preferring instead to encourage young talent towards missionary work. This emphasis was laid down by Carey Ward and Nash and further nurtured by Deasey, and it meant that the parish was fruitful in raising up long-standing missionaries like the Clark sisters, Verlie Lawrence, Clara Wallen, Alf Dyer, and Leslie Perriman. However, only one future clergyman, George Hall, came through the parish in this period.[100] The impact of evangelicals' focus on overseas mission

94. Interestingly, Deasey followed Nash in going from St. Columb's to Christ Church Geelong in successive incumbencies.

95. Cole, *Perriman in Arnhem Land*, 9–10.

96. Interview with Peter Corney, 30 May 2007.

97. See ADEB entry; also, Cole, *Sharing in Mission*, and Seiffert, *Refuge on the Roper*.

98. See ADEB entry.

99. St. Columb's *Monthly Notes*, Vol XXVI February 1937.

100. For the Clark sisters see Hart, "'An Unshakeable Faith.'" Verlie Lawrence was married to Tom Lawrence, founder of the CMS LOY. See CMS, *Lawrence of Lira*. Clara

meant that in the subsequent generation there would be a serious lack of able evangelical clergy to take up vacancies in parishes. This problem was further exacerbated by developments at the diocesan level.

Bishops

From 1902 to 1937 there were three bishops of Melbourne, but by the time of Lowther Clarke's departure in 1920 the context of the diocese and the changed relationship between bishop and evangelicals meant that evangelicals had largely ceased to look to their archbishop for anything more than symbolic leadership in either the pursuit of their mission or the preservation of their cause. The movement's fundamental individualism, expressed most clearly in its insistence on the necessity of personal conversion, meant that relationships between recognized evangelical leaders and within evangelical networks were far more influential than bishops or other officers of the church.

Following Clarke were two archbishops, Harrington Clare Lees and Frederick Waldegrave Head, who self-identified as evangelicals.[101] Both were noted Cambridge scholars who wrote and published numerous works of Christ-centered piety.[102] Head was especially noted as an able administrator. However, despite having evangelical diocesan bishops, the movement was not reproducing leadership for subsequent generations; this endemic weakness within evangelicalism meant that there were no noteworthy younger Melbourne evangelical clergymen to appoint to parishes.[103] Both Lees and Head did not seek to impose their evangelicalism on their diocese, and effectively steered a broad-church middle course in matters of senior appointments and diocesan ministry strategy. For this reason, they hardly affected the movement as a whole in their time.

Wallen served in China. Dyer and Perriman served in North Australia. See Cole, *Perriman in Arnhem Land:*.Cole, *Oenpelli Pioneer.*Carolan, *St. Columb's Hawthorn*, 39, contains a list of clergy and missionaries produced by the parish up to 1983.

101. See entries in ADB and ADEB. Also, Head, *Frederick Waldegrave Head*; McKie, "Four Archbishops of Melbourne." According to his ADB entry, Lees was a founding member of the Old Melburnians Masonic Lodge.

102. See for example Lees, *Promise of Life*; Lees, *Divine Master in Home Life*; Lees, *St. Paul's Friends*; Lees, *Eyes of His Glory*; Lees, *Sunshine of the Good News*; Lees, *Joy of Bible Study*; Head, *Six Great Anglicans*; Head, *Fallen Stuarts*.

103. All of the diocese's main leading evangelical clergy in this period were trained outside of Melbourne and licensed in the diocese before 1910.

New Bishops, New Dioceses

In 1902, just as Australia was forging a national government and structure, the Diocese of Melbourne radically reduced in size as it sought to devolve authority down to more local levels for the sake of more effective ministry and mission—a strategy envisaged by Charles Perry. Melbourne was further subdivided, with the creation of the Dioceses of Wangaratta, Gippsland, and Bendigo joining the previously created Diocese of Ballarat. Together these made up the province of Victoria. Moorhouse had envisaged the creation of two new dioceses during his episcopate, but Goe had hesitated—somewhat fortuitously, because the arrival of the bank crash and depression of the 1890s would have made financial provision for the new dioceses quite impossible. Subdivision subsequently occurred at the turn of the century when economic conditions had improved. Archdeacon W. G. Hindley steered through the legislation and negotiated the thorny issue of the division of the diocese's endowment funds. Some fifty years after the foundation of the diocese, there was still sufficient evangelical heritage in the province that each of the three new bishops, who were selected by a combination of local and Melbourne electors, were identified as evangelicals.

Wangaratta

The first bishop of Wangaratta, Thomas Henry Armstrong, was born in Dublin but arrived in Geelong with his parents as an infant. His father was for many years a Crown Prosecutor in Victoria. Armstrong attended Geelong Grammar School and came under the influence of the evangelical George Goodman at Christ Church Geelong. Following in his father's footsteps, he joined the Victorian Law Department after school, then attended the University of Melbourne, during which time he was a resident in Trinity College. It seems that Armstrong received his call into ministry at this time. Upon graduation he was ordained and served curacies in the evangelical parishes of Christ Church St. Kilda and Christ Church Hawthorn, before becoming incumbent of the evangelical St. Columb's Hawthorn in 1883. From there he was appointed archdeacon of Gippsland in 1894, then Beechworth in 1900.

Armstrong has been credited with building up the ministry of St. Columb's, a historically evangelical parish, and is listed in the ADEB. Both connections are *prima facie* evidence of his evangelicalism. Holden, in his history of the Diocese of Wangaratta, acknowledges that during

Armstrong's episcopate "the general tone of the diocese was evangelical."[104] However, by the time of his arrival in Wangaratta, Armstrong had moved to the liberal end of evangelicalism, if not into a broad church position similar to Moorhouse's. Holden emphasizes the liberalizing influence Moorhouse and Trinity College had on Armstrong during his training for ministry in the 1880s. Moorhouse's first biographer, Edith Rickards, publishing in 1920 when Armstrong was still alive, cites Armstrong's reflections on his relationship with Moorhouse:

> I first met him at a reception held by him . . . immediately after coming to Victoria. I was then a young undergraduate . . . Later on, he became my ideal of what a Bishop ought to be, and a great influence in the moulding of my life . . . To me personally Bishop Moorhouse was more than a friend. From the first he must have taken a fancy to me; for from the day I met him until at his departure ten years afterwards he left me in charge of one of the most important city parishes (St. Columb's), he was my guide, philosopher, and second father. My admiration for him was unbounded; but so was that of most others.[105]

As a liberal evangelical, Armstrong cherished the Moorhouse example of reasoned engagement with the world but downplayed the central importance of a propitiatory understanding of the cross. He consequently underemphasized the necessity of repentance from sin and conversion to Christ. Archdeacon John Moroney, who was a successor of Armstrong's at St. Columb's Hawthorn, considered Armstrong to be "flat church" rather than evangelical in his convictions.[106] Key to Moroney's assessment was Armstrong's lack of support for Ridley College and his experience of inheriting a busy but essentially spiritually moribund St. Columb's, where there was little passion for evangelism.[107]

Upon arrival Armstrong announced his conviction that all shades of broad, high, and low were merely "looking at the great Christian verities from different points of view"; and although throughout his episcopate he maintained the strictly low-church north-end position when celebrating

---

104. Holden, *Church in a Landscape*, 75.

105. Rickards, *Bishop Moorhouse*. 74–75. Also cited subsequently by Moorhouse's second biographer: Sturrock, *Bishop of Magnetic Power*, 15–16.

106. By "flat church," Moroney meant low-church in ritual, uninspiring, boring and inward-looking towards the Prayer Book liturgy, rather than outward-looking towards the unconverted masses in society, contemporary, engaging, exciting, and obeying the vernacular and missional principles of the Prayer Book. On the missiological thrust of the BCP, see Null, *Conversion to Communion*.

107. Interview with John Moroney, 4 June 2007.

communion, he broke with this and moved to the east end for his final service in Wangaratta "in order to help ease the way for his successor," the Anglo-Catholic John Stephen Hart.[108] At the founding of Ridley College in 1910, he was conspicuous by the absence of his support. Ridley developed into a locus of evangelical effort in this period, and support for the college became a key indicator of evangelical identity, hence Armstrong's lack of enthusiasm is telling. Three reasons may be advanced for his lack of support for Ridley.

First and chiefly, his energies would have been focused on his own diocesan college of St. Columb's Wangaratta, which was opened in 1906 just as conflict between Lowther Clarke and evangelicals was about to erupt in Melbourne. The college was probably named in memory of his old parish and for the inspirational value of the Celtic missionary saint. Armstrong's instincts for the college were initially inclined towards evangelicals: among his first appointments to staff were the evangelicals George Lamble and J. Eakins Stannage. However, St. Columb's was founded as a diocesan college and not as an explicitly evangelical one. Its diocesan focus, small staff size, and close episcopal control over appointments meant that its ethos was easily changed by the bishop of the day. Lamble and Stannage did not stay beyond 1910, and the character of the college quickly changed.

Second, Wangaratta's relative distance from Melbourne would have made it more difficult for Armstrong to attend college events and meetings and be actively involved. However, the choice of Wangaratta over Beechworth as the episcopal seat for the new diocese was made in part on the basis of better access to the rail network, as it was expected that the bishop would have to travel.[109] Also, a similar challenge facing the bishops of Bendigo and Gippsland did not stop their active involvement with Ridley.

On balance, it therefore seems most likely that a third reason was determinative. Armstrong, as a bishop, no longer held to the distinctive evangelical emphasis on the absolute and desperate necessity of conversion and attendant responsibility for evangelism that so characterized evangelicals of the period. Ridley had been founded on those premises and was considered by its supporters to be of strategic long-term importance to the evangelical cause, whether locally in the province or more widely throughout the world. Coming off the back of a quarter century when Melbourne evangelicals distinguished themselves in evangelistic activity at home and missionary

---

108. COEM, March 1902, 51, and COEM, 8 October 1925, 400, cited in Holden, *Church in a Landscape*, 76–77.

109. Holden, *Church in a Landscape*, 63.

endeavor abroad, it is telling that Armstrong maintained a strictly diocesan and local approach to training men for ministry.

Armstrong was clearly out of step with the main focus of evangelical efforts in this period. His legacy was a visibly low church but one that was essentially inward looking, without an evangelistic and conversionist edge. Moroney considered that this "flat church" culture spread to become the norm in the diocese for most of the middle part of the twentieth century. By "flat," he meant boring, traditional, and disconnected from contemporary culture, having a form of godliness but without the power to convert and change people.[110]

Commitment to the authority of Scripture (biblicism) and a rigorously evangelical understanding of the atonement (crucicentrism) without the attendant energetic focus on conversion and evangelism meant that evangelicalism eventually faded out of the Diocese of Wangaratta. Armstrong's successor, Hart, was certainly high church at the time of his appointment and moved towards an increasingly Anglo-Catholic position in liturgy and theology. Evangelicals distrusted him, and within six years of his appointment the *Church Record*, alarmed by the possibility of his translation to the Diocese of Goulburn, claimed that he was intolerant towards low-church clergy and appointed only Anglo-Catholics to vacant parishes.[111] The claim was unduly polemical, but the absence of a clearly evangelical diocesan bishop to model confidence in the authority of the Scriptures, highlight the importance of evangelism and conversion, and prioritize the appointment of clearly evangelical clergy meant that Wangaratta's dramatic shift away from its earlier evangelical character under Armstrong was largely completed by Hart.

Gippsland and Bendigo

Quite unlike the Diocese of Wangaratta, there has been no hesitation among historians about the robust evangelical identity of the dioceses of Gippsland and Bendigo and their founding bishops. Both dioceses enjoyed a close link with Ridley College: their bishops in 1910 were among the founders of the college, and the grand majority of the college's earliest students were from and for these dioceses.

Arthur Wellesley Pain, the first bishop of Gippsland, was English-born and a graduate of Cambridge. He served a curacy in Suffolk before emigrating to Sydney in 1868, where he was appointed to succeed one of the evangelical heroes of the early years of that diocese, Thomas Hassall.

110. Interview with John Moroney, 4 June 2007.
111. *Church Record* cited without ascription by Holden, *Church in a Landscape*, 86.

Hassall was the son of LMS missionaries to Tahiti and the son-in-law of Samuel Marsden. He had served in the evangelical parish of St. Paul's Cobbitty for forty-one years, dying in office. In 1902, just before he was consecrated the first bishop of Gippsland, Pain was a senior Sydney evangelical cleric: the rector of the prominent parish of St. John's Darlinghurst, rural dean of East Sydney, chaplain to the bishop of Sydney, and a canon of St. Andrew's Cathedral.[112]

Pain refused offers to move from Gippsland, stating that his duty was to stay with the people of the diocese, which he served until 1917 when he retired for reasons of ill health.[113] He retired to Sydney, where he was active as an Honorary Secretary of CMS for his remaining years. Unlike Armstrong, there was no shift in Pain's theology or evangelical self-identity through to the end of his life. Despite pressure to admit a broader theological outlook in his diocese, Pain was resolute in his evangelical convictions. His archdeacon, W. Hancock, recounted Pain's gracious but firm response to a paper he delivered: "I am sorry to differ from my dear friend the Archdeacon . . . but I am sure he is wrong."[114]

Mission and evangelism were constant priorities for Pain. Despite his intimate involvement in Ridley College's founding, he was not present for the opening in March 1910. Instead he was overseas as an Australian representative at the World Missionary Conference in Edinburgh.

Similarly, Henry Archdall Langley, the first bishop of Bendigo, was a life-long evangelical. Langley was thirteen when his Irish family emigrated to Sydney in 1853. As a young layman, he was in charge of the Sunday School at St. Barnabas' Sydney and a noted open-air preacher. His early work was in a merchant's office, where he gained the administrative skills that were subsequently to prove helpful in his episcopal work. Langley then trained at Moore College and served in Bathurst, Orange, and Sydney.

Langley was a gifted evangelist, much in demand among other ministers in both Sydney and Melbourne as a leader of parish missions. He moved to Melbourne to take up an appointment at the leading evangelical parish of St. Matthew's Prahran in 1878, where he served with distinction for twelve years. In that time, parish attendances grew markedly, debt on the property was erased, a new church plant was established (St. Alban's Armadale), and younger men were raised up to positions of ministry leadership. "His ministry in Prahran was indeed *living power*," write the parish

---

112. See ADEB entry. See also the brief family memoir Pain, *In the Master's Service*. Pain's papers are held in Rye, Victoria by the bishop's great-grandson, Professor Michael Pain.

113. Maddern, *Light and Life*, 26.

114. Nash, *Forward Flows the Time*, 200.

historians. A contemporary wrote at his death, "His best spiritual work was done at St. Matthew's Prahran. His intense spiritual force has left its mark indelibly printed on thousands of men and women."[115]

In 1890, Langley was appointed archdeacon of Gippsland, and in 1894 he was promoted to archdeacon of Melbourne and Geelong. He was therefore the senior archdeacon of the diocese and naturally in line for one of the new bishoprics in 1902. He was preferred ahead of the local favorite, Archdeacon John MacCullagh, for the seat of Bendigo. Nevertheless, the evangelical MacCullagh was publicly and fully supportive of his old Moore College compatriot, speaking at an occasion welcoming Langley to Bendigo to voice his support—and by implication encouraging any disappointed local supporters to get behind Langley.[116]

Tragically, Langley died suddenly just four years later in 1906 of a stroke, aged sixty-six. In his funeral address, Archbishop Lowther Clarke spoke of his "simple, unfaltering faith . . . The theme of his preaching was ever the same . . . the story of Jesus and his love."[117] Arthur Pain was offered the promotion to the larger and wealthier diocese, but he declined. Pain felt duty bound to establish the work in Gippsland rather than desert it after four years. Petitions from Gippsland church members appealing to him to stay also swayed his thinking.[118] The Bendigo electors were more successful in convincing Langley's elder brother by five years, John Douse Langley, to come from Sydney.

J. D. Langley was already seventy years old and a well-established Sydney evangelical, as had been his younger brother. He was less charismatic but no less able an administrator and leader. J. D. Langley was a strategist as well, with a deep interest in training men for ministry and missionary work, and for evangelistic and discipling ministry among men. He had completed studies at Trinity College Dublin before emigrating and subsequently trained at Moore College. Langley recruited clergy for Bendigo from both Ireland and Sydney. His interest in training led to his reviving of Perry Hall in Bendigo after it had gone into abeyance following the able William Sadlier's return to Melbourne in 1899. Langley was a key member of the CMA and intimately involved in the founding of Ridley College. Despite his advanced age at the time of his appointment, he went on to serve Bendigo for twelve years, retiring aged eighty-three in 1919. From the dioceses of Bendigo and Gippsland

---

115. Bride, *Proclaiming the Gospel*, 62.

116. Cole, *Men of Faith and Vision*.

117. See ADEB entry.

118. The petition is in the possession of the bishop's great-grandson, Professor Michael Pain.

came the sort of leadership that evangelicals in Melbourne wanted, but lacked in their own new bishop, Henry Lowther Clarke.

Melbourne

Clarke's appointment to Melbourne marked the beginning of a period of active disengagement by evangelicals from the diocese. They simply ceased to view it as an effective vehicle for mission, preferring to focus on their local churches or societies.

Bishop Goe never recovered from the death of his beloved wife Emma, and it is telling that the baptismal pool in St. Paul's Cathedral is dedicated to both bishop and wife. They were childless and formed a close ministry partnership.[119] He resigned within four months of her death in August 1901, leaving Melbourne in April the following year. The Bishopric Election Board, rather unusually, sent two leading laymen to England to consult with the archbishops of Canterbury and York about a successor. The previous two appointments had been by an England-based committee comprising of the two leading English archbishops, previous bishops of Melbourne, and a leading Melbourne layman. As described above, the committee that selected Goe had Perry, Moorhouse, and Stawell on it, with Perry's voice standing out in the final decision.

However, Perry was no longer on the scene and evangelicals were largely disengaged from the political processes of the diocese. The same could not be said of those opposed to evangelicals. Canon Godby and Dr. Leeper (the warden of Trinity) both wrote in the *Messenger* of their initial attendance at meetings called to organize voting tickets to ensure that "the pending vacancy in the See of Melbourne should be filled by a man of different views to that of Bishop Goe's."[120] Leeper and Godby wrote giving reasons for their refusal to take any further part in these clearly anti-evangelical meetings. Evangelicals did not respond with their own ticket or political machine. In the matter of Clarke's appointment, the response to high-church party moves may have come from members of the masonic network.

Darrell Paproth suggests that the increasing influence of the low-church masonic movement in the Melbourne Synod may have been the reason behind the change in the selection process. He wondered if the two

---

119. Interestingly, each of Melbourne's first three bishops were married but childless, a factor adding to their ability to persevere in trying conditions, doing the hard, pioneering work in the diocese that involved difficult travel across the state on episcopal duties.

120. COEM, 15 November 1918, 538.

men sent to England, William Morris and Frederick Grimwade,[121] were in fact masons, pointing to the later allegation reported in the *Argus* that "Masonic influence had helped Archbishop Clarke to preferment."[122] The allegation was first contained in an article in the anti-establishment paper the *Truth*, entitled "Clarke, the Nark," over which Clarke sued for libel and £5000 in damages. The same report in the *Argus* contained opening remarks from Clarke's own lawyer, stating that Clarke was, in fact, a mason. He had become one in 1899 and had attained the level of "Master," but his lawyer denied that this link had anything to do with his appointment or indeed his "career as a clergyman."[123]

Whether masonic influence was involved or not, the reduction in size of the committee and the absence of clear evangelical sympathies in Grimwade, Morris, and both archbishops meant that the chances of an evangelical nomination were negligible. Canon Lowther Clarke's name was put to Morris and Grimwade in such terms that they immediately communicated with the Melbourne Board for permission to make an offer. They were so empowered by cable from Melbourne and, extraordinarily, only subsequently interviewed the vicar and rural dean, who quickly accepted.

Despite his position as the rector of the historic evangelical parish of Huddersfield, Clarke was no evangelical—a fact acknowledged by the *Messenger* at the time of his appointment.[124] After the irenic and dutiful but unexciting Goe, the laymen selected "a sound churchman," noted for his preaching and strong public leadership. It was a return to the Moorhouse style of episcopal leadership, perhaps in the hope that Clarke would raise the profile of the church in the city the way Moorhouse had. Clarke certainly brought the church into the news, but not in the positive way that may have been envisioned.

Within a few years of Clarke's arrival in Melbourne, any sense of optimism that the diocese could be trusted to promote evangelical priorities in ministry and church life was largely destroyed. There were three reasons for this.

First, Clarke failed to restrain or discipline the Tractarian vicar of St. Peter's Eastern Hill, E. S. Hughes. There were repeated calls from concerned clergy and church members for him to act against Hughes's ritualist and illegal

---

121. See ADB entry.

122. Paproth, *Failure Is Not Final*, 54. *Argus* 18 June 1912, 7. No determinative evidence has yet been uncovered as to whether the two were or were not masons.

123. *Argus*, 18 June 1912, 8. The court proceedings of Clarke v Norton were reported daily between 18 and 22 June 1912. The case was finally settled by John Norton, who also agreed to withdraw the article and issue an apology.

124. COEM, 1 October 1902, 133.

practices in that parish, in particular his leading of services that strayed outside the bounds of Prayer Book liturgy and incorporated such things as taking an westward position to the table, calling the table an "altar," using incense, elevating the host and mimicking the hand actions of the Catholic mass during the prayer of consecration—the so called "manual acts." The complaints culminated in a call in 1906 for the archbishop to take direct action. Clarke received a petition signed by clergy and some 1,300 laypeople, but still steadfastly refused to discipline Hughes.

Second, Clarke was a broad-church centrist, whose policies on theological education managed to disappoint both evangelicals and middle-churchmen. In 1906, he closed the theological school at Trinity and founded his own St. John's College, originally to be based at the cathedral as a sign of its central and important status as a place of worship and education. Trinity's able and well-regarded warden, Dr. Alexander Leeper, rightly felt disenfranchised, disappointed, and frustrated. Evangelicals were similarly chagrined.

The clergyman who was perhaps Melbourne's pre eminent evangelical leader of the day, Clifford Harris Nash, was appointed to the mixed faculty at St. John's. However, evangelicals, with Nash probably leading their opinion, regarded the training at St. John's as at best confusing and at worse hopelessly inadequate. On the one hand, it had Nash the evangelical Bible scholar teaching the classic theories of the atonement from his Greek New Testament and the necessity of conversion and evangelism; on the other were the Anglo-Catholics Canon R. Stephen and John Stephen Hart promoting new ideas out of *Lux Mundi*. The college succeeded in pleasing no one. Trinity's theological school was restored in 1912, and St. John's eventually closed in 1919.

Third, and most important, in 1907, Clarke acted directly against Nash, effectively causing his resignation from the diocese and removal from diocesan life. Nash was widely recognized as an excellent preacher and teacher of the Scriptures with a successful ministry at St. Columb's Hawthorn then Christ Church Geelong and with influence extending across the diocese through evangelical networks and the missionary societies. He had, however, left England in 1895 under a cloud. Nash admitted, with contrition, that as a curate he had tried to kiss a young woman to whose sister he was then engaged. His supporters describe it as a moment of misunderstood exuberant celebration upon receiving good news about a future position, blown out of proportion by his accusers. His enemies, however, saw it as a gross act of indecency and "grave impropriety," going directly to his character and suitability as a clergyman.[125]

---

125. See Paproth, *Failure Is Not Final*, 41–42. See report of court proceedings,

Similar allegations of improper conduct with a young woman arose in 1907 from St. Columb's, and Clarke acted on them, bringing pressure on Nash to submit to an enquiry or trial or resign. Paproth's biography of Nash covers the events in detail, noting that it was finally at a special meeting of the Cathedral Chapter, called to consider his position as a canon where, without a dissenting voice ("*nemine contra dicente*"), and with great reluctance, the following motion put by Archdeacon Crossley was passed:

> Though there is no proof that Canon Nash has been guilty of any criminal offence or even of any immorality yet he has admitted such grave indiscretions that the Chapter feel reluctantly compelled to call upon him to resign.[126]

Appended to the minute book is Nash's signed resignation note, witnessed by the dean, George Vance. A following note signed by Dean Vance included the comment that Nash had, before the meeting, undertaken before the Chapter to accept their decision and to resign his offices if required to do so. It was clear that Nash resigned in 1907 rather than expose the church to further shame by pressing his case.

As to the question of his guilt or innocence with regard to the charges, a later source reported that one of Nash's closest supporters and friends, the banker and bibliophile Horace Hannah,[127] considered that for all his godliness and giftedness as a teacher, Nash had "no idea about the other sex." In other words, he was incompetent in his dealings with women.[128] However, as Paproth argues, it is far from clear that Nash's accuser, Clarke in particular, acted purely and objectively, without self-interest.[129] Indeed, while Clarke was justified to be concerned about Nash's fitness for ministry, the process of investigation he followed left much to be desired.

The rather sanguine personal assessment of Clarke offered by J. D. McKie in his 1983 Sydney Smith lecture, in which he describes the "lack of bitter party strife in the Diocese of Melbourne" as one of his lasting legacies, should be contrasted to his own earlier words in the lecture:

Clarke v Norton, *Argus* 18 June 1912, 7–8; 19 June 1912, 13–14.

126. Minutes of the Cathedral Chapter of St. Paul's Melbourne, Vol.1, 1870–1907, meeting of Monday 28 October 1907, 569–571.

127. See ADEB and further below for Hannah's biographical details.

128. Interview with Alan Kerr, 24 July 2007. Kerr was close to Hannah, who was an important influence on his early life and subsequent Christian ministry as a leading evangelical layman and leader of evangelical missions agencies. See his autobiography Kerr, *Guided Journey*.

129. Paproth, *Failure Is Not Final*, 70–75.

He had no complexes: he would be unlikely to lie awake all night worrying whether he had or had not dealt properly with some problem. He had none of the suavity of [Archbishop] Lees or the gentleness of [Archbishop] Head. He could be firm; indeed blunt.[130]

A subsequent Sydney Smith lecturer, Robin Sharwood, quoted this same passage with approval, describing Clarke as "a tough, blunt, insensitive Yorkshireman." He highlighted the conflict between Clarke and Trinity's warden, Leeper:

> There was . . . severe personal antipathy between Leeper and Lowther Clarke. They quarrelled constantly . . . It was Dr. Floyd [the cathedral's organist] speaking of Lowther Clarke, who said that in the part of Yorkshire from which he came, it was not that the people had bad manners, they had no manners at all. Miss [Valentine] Leeper tells me that in their household Lowther Clarke was referred to not as "the Archbishop" but as "the Archfiend."[131]

John Poynter's biography of Alexander Leeper describes the conflict between Clarke and Leeper in detail, and noted that Clarke "infuriated Evangelicals . . . but he also worried the whole range of ecclesiastical opinion by high-handedness in action . . . He was certainly tactless."[132]

In Nash, Clarke had another obvious opponent. Nash was a public leader in the movement, calling Clarke to act against Hughes at St. Peter's, and was a popular and effective leader of a large section of the diocese, namely, the evangelicals. Just three months before his resignation, he had spoken forcefully to a crowded Melbourne Town Hall public meeting. The talk was entitled "His Seamless Vesture" and focused on the internal coherence of the Scriptures produced by a single divine author. The content of the lecture was an affirmation of the inspiration and authority of the Scriptures that were being threatened by rationalism and Anglo-Catholic inroads into the church.[133] Nash rejected the views of those who "assail the scientific accuracy, the historical reliability, and the moral elevation of the Bible teachings." Clarke stayed away from that meeting; indeed, the only bishop present was Pain of Gippsland. The editor of the *Messenger*, Vance, criticized it. It simply

130. McKie, "Four Archbishops of Melbourne."

131. Sharwood, "Faculty of Theology at Trinity College."

132. Poynter, *Doubts and Certainties*, 306. Valentine was the daughter of Alexander Leeper, a keen observer of Anglican and national affairs throughout her lifetime, and shared her father's antipathy towards Clarke. See Poynter, *Nobody's Valentine*. 34.

133. The text of the lecture is reproduced in Chambers, *"Tempest-Tost."* 173–81.

did not fit with the new, broad-church program that Clarke had designed for Melbourne. "Broad" did not include "evangelical." It certainly did not fit with Clarke's vision of comprehensive theological education at St. John's. Nash was then the main signatory to a letter to the *Messenger*, criticizing its editorial policy. Two months later, his resignation was requested.

In the wake of his resignation, Nash's evangelical supporters were vocal, active, and sustained in their support of him. Clarke was petitioned by 830 laymen who were protesting over the secrecy of the Chapter meeting at which Nash had resigned and calling for an open trial under the Ecclesiastical Offences Act. He ignored them. Both St. Columb's Hawthorn and Christ Church Geelong, Nash's two most recent parishes, supported him strongly. Christ Church went as far as repeatedly nominating him for the vacancy that his own resignation had created, but Clarke stubbornly refused on the ground of clerical fitness, forcing the non-evangelical F. R. Newton upon Christ Church instead. The ensuing long-running battle between bishop, new vicar, and laity eventually destroyed the evangelical character of the parish when disgusted Nashites migrated to St. Matthew's East Geelong (which retains its evangelical character to this day).

The libel suit brought by Clarke, mentioned above, was precipitated by this case and took place some five years later. The *Argus* carried a daily report of court proceedings, and there were letters to the editor and much discussion—all to the detriment of the church's general standing in the wider community.[134] The expectation that Clarke would be the sort of bishop to bring the church into the news was fulfilled, but it was not the kind of media exposure that his selectors would have desired.

Clarke's personal animosity towards Nash, his stubbornness with respect to the rightness of his conclusions about Nash's fitness for ministry, and his failure to gauge the level of esteem and influence that Nash enjoyed among evangelicals, meant that from the "Nash affair" onwards it was much easier for evangelicals to focus on interdenominational efforts and on action independent of the diocese. Evangelicals rightly recognized that Clarke's centrist and broad-church agenda would be detrimental to their emphasis on the reliability of the Scriptures, the orthodoxy and coherence of the substitutionary theory of the atonement, and the attendant necessity of conversion and evangelism. It had become clear that the bishop of the diocese could no longer be relied on to support evangelical priorities in ministry, and consequently the diocese itself would become less effective as a vehicle for evangelistic mission.

---

134. *Argus*, 18–22 June 1912.

The key move by evangelicals in response to the lack of a supportive diocesan bishop was to act to secure future evangelical clergy by founding their own theological college. They were able to do this as two other provincial and diocesan bishops, Langley and Pain, were publicly supportive and willing to work on both the provisional and founding councils of the college. Their support, and the implied guarantee that college graduates would be ordained into their dioceses, meant that the college could proceed with a degree of confidence. Evangelicals remained loyal to Melbourne and tried to work with Clarke's ideas for theological education for the better part of a decade before they showed that they were ultimately willing to cross diocesan boundaries for the sake of gospel proclamation and evangelical continuity.

Even though Clarke was followed in 1920 by the devotionally minded evangelical Harrington Clare Lees, and Lees in 1929 by Frederick Head, the relationship between evangelicals and the office of bishop had been deeply affected. Although Lees and Head were both respected as evangelical leaders and invited *ex officio* to chair the Ridley College council during their tenures as archbishop, no one could mistake them as the real and effective leaders of the evangelical movement in Melbourne. That leadership role had passed into the hands of those individuals, like Nash, who were demonstrably committed to the cause of overseas mission and demonstrably able Bible teachers and preachers who viewed the Bible as supremely authoritative and focused on Christ and the cross. From this period forwards, evangelical leadership was exercised by the movement's Bible teachers and missionary enthusiasts—and through Ridley College.

Colleges: The Founding and Early History of Ridley College

James Grant argues that evangelicals "torpedoed" Clarke's idea for central training in Melbourne.[135] However, it is more accurate to say that Clarke frustrated and alarmed evangelicals by his dogged pursuit of Nash and his policies at St. John's, and so they eventually responded. Nevertheless, it would be a mistake to regard the founding of Ridley as a purely defensive action on the part of Melbourne evangelicals in response to Clarke.[136]

Clarke launched evangelicals into action, but evangelicalism in the diocese had already become increasingly marginalized prior to his arrival. Melbourne parishes were still outwardly low church—there were generally

---

135. See Clarke's ADB entry by James Grant.

136. See also, for an extended discussion of the theological and political context of Ridley's founding, Adam, "Founding of Ridley College."

no unauthorized liturgies, candles, Eucharistic vestments, copes, or miters. But inwardly, the passionate and principled evangelicalism of Perry and Macartney that was fiercely loyal to the visible church as an agent of evangelism and mission had been replaced by an evangelicalism that emphasized world mission and activism wherever it could be expressed. This meant an attendant weaker sense of connection with the diocese, which increasingly lacked a focus on evangelical priorities in ministry. Under a succession of bishops from Moorhouse onwards, both evangelicalism and other theological and liturgical traditions were allowed to develop without drastic interference from the center. Some evangelical dissatisfaction at the level of tolerance within the diocese for liturgical and theological innovation was expressed through *The Victorian Churchman*, but for the most part evangelicals redirected their energies into parochial work and overseas mission. This ambivalence was to change with the founding of Ridley, which signaled a readiness to act to secure evangelical continuity within the diocese itself.

The founding of Ridley has also to be seen in the light of the "promiscuous founding" of theological colleges in Australia.[137] Although there was a degree of excessive diocesanism in the founding of colleges, partly to be explained by the desirability of training clergy locally, theological difference was another significant factor. Two themes were important to Ridley's founders.

First, there was an increasing need for adequate training of overseas mission workers. Incredible energy and passion for overseas mission came from the rise of the Keswick movement. It was Keswick spirituality that fed the world missions movement. As more and more lay men and women offered for overseas missionary service, demand for a lay training facility rose. The model of training was very much the vocational college one, where men or women (separately) would live and learn together in a shared household environment. Even before Clarke's arrival, evangelicals were already committed to the principle of having their own training structures to raise up men and women for the overseas harvest field. The missions societies provided leadership and resources for these.

In 1892, Dr. and Mrs. Warren were running a CIM women's training home run in Kew. This was closed in 1901, and in 1902 James and Emily

---

137. Adam, "Theological Education in the Diocese of Melbourne." Adam lists the founding of St. James Sydney in 1846, Moore in 1856, Trinity in 1878, St. Barnabas Adelaide in 1880, the Brisbane Theological College in 1897 (renamed St. Francis in 1910), St. John's Armidale (later Morpeth) in 1898, St. Wilfred's Tasmania in 1904, St. John's Melbourne in 1906, St. Aidan's Ballarat in 1903 and St. Columb's Wangaratta in 1903. Additionally, there was Perry Hall in Bendigo in 1894, renamed Langley Hall in 1911, and the Divinity Hostel in Sale.

Griffiths, of the Griffiths Brothers Tea & Coffee enterprise, opened another women's training home at 199 Victoria Parade, Fitzroy. This trained candidates for the CIM and the CMA. C. H. Nash had recently started a deaconesses training home in Elmie Street, Hawthorn, in 1901. It was called St. Hilda's and was modeled on a similar training home set up by Nash's friend, the evangelical leader Mervyn Archdall,[138] in Sydney. Nash and the Griffithses were close associates, and the two institutions soon combined under the name St. Hilda's at the Fitzroy address. Nash was in charge of training. In 1907, St. Hilda's moved to a house provided by the Griffithses in Clarendon Street, East Melbourne, where it remained until 1963, when it was sold and operations relocated to St. Andrew's Hall, next to Ridley College, in The Avenue, Parkville.[139]

By June 1903, the CMA committee noted that a men's training home was also needed, but it was not until April 1906 that it finally opened in North Melbourne—coinciding with the noted evangelical H. S. Begbie's arrival from Bendigo as vicar of St. Mary's North Melbourne and supervisor of the home. When Begbie left St. Mary's for Bairnsdale in 1908, the home was closed, but the importance of having such a training institution remained. The St. Mary's training home for male missionary candidates was thus a progenitor institution of Ridley College. All the men who were party to discussions in 1908 about the desirability of an evangelical college for training men for Holy Orders and missionary service were CMA members who were aware of the St. Mary's experiment and the continuing need for such a facility.

Second, and partly in response to Clarke's antipathy towards Nash and evangelical requests to restrain ritualism, evangelical leaders recognized that there was a need to secure training in evangelical religion for their ministers. The founders of Ridley included the bishops of both Gippsland and Bendigo, Pain and Langley, who saw the strategic importance of being able to secure supply of future evangelical clergy for their dioceses and were open about this need.

Laurence Langley Nash, the son of C. H. Nash and a long-time Ridley council member and author of the jubilee history of Ridley, wrote, "By doing this (founding Ridley) a large section of Church opinion considered

---

138. See ADB entry.

139. The Griffithses had in fact ceded St. Hilda's to the Church of England Evangelical Trust of Victoria (today the Anglican Evangelical Trust), which retains title in St. Andrew's Hall. This was done in accordance with the evangelical strategy of separation of powers so that property and governance would not be vested in the same bodies—in case evangelical character in one was subsequently lost. See Deed of Trust, Anglican Evangelical Trust of Victoria papers.

it must act for itself unless it was prepared to suffer eclipse through compulsory attrition."[140]

The Victorian Churchman published these words in November 1909, when the debate in the diocese regarding the founding of evangelical college—in opposition so it seemed to Trinity—was raging:

> Why should our Church, whose doctrines are so defined as to include within its pale so many varying shades of belief, still be unable to offer a course of training where young men who are loyal to the principles of the Reformation may pursue their studies in an atmosphere which harmonises with their convictions? A thoroughly competent principal, conspicuous for scholarship, who is a student leader and a Christian man of robust type, will be placed at the head of the institution.[141]

In March the following year, when Ridley was opened, the *Churchman* published this statement:

> It is greatly to be lamented that there has been an absolute necessity for such an institution. Trinity College and St. John's College ought (at least in conjunction) to have sufficed for the training in divinity of all students of the Church of England in Victoria. The theological tuition at these two colleges has been quite one-sided and wholly unsatisfactory in its character. Protests have been made, from time to time, but altogether without effect.[142]

The Ridley Council's reasons for founding Ridley were reported or published at least three times in the first two years. On 12 October 1911, a notice was published notifying the public of the lease of the property named "Kooringa" and the college's imminent move out of "Norwood" at 101 Royal Parade to "Kooringa" on 1 November. It also made public the council's resolution:

> That, having in view the prospect of an early commencement to erect suitable buildings for the purposes of the college, and the urgent necessity for energetic and decided action on the part of all supporters of the evangelical cause, this council deems it well to make public the following statement of its aims and intentions:– Ridley College is founded as a church of England evangelical college, and is designed as a place of residence and education for students while pursuing university

---

140. Nash, *Forward Flows the Time*, 20.
141. VC, 12 November 1909.
142. Nash, *Forward Flows the Time*, 19–20.

and theological studies. The aim of the college is twofold—(a) to provide theological training for students who are seeking holy orders, or preparing for mission work; (b) to provide a course of preparation in university work for students who wish to proceed to a degree . . .

Friends and supporters of this cause who desire to see a college where students for the ministry will be given a course of education in keeping with the evangelical principles of the church, are urged to assist at once by their prayers and contributions.[143]

The model of a university college was clearly in mind. It was the case even up to the 1960s that ordinands were only required to take the two-year licentiate in theology (ThL), but students of greater ability were encouraged to go on to take a university degree; typically a BA or MA, hence the second aim of providing a preparatory course in university work. This also meant that in the event that the college's rooms were not fully occupied by ordinands, they could be let to secular students and finances would be kept in the black. Unlike Trinity, Ridley would cater to non-matriculants and thus had a bigger market.

On 14 December 1911, an article was published announcing the purchase of land on The Avenue for the future permanent buildings. It also reiterated the main purpose of the college: "for the training of men for the Anglican Evangelical ministry in the home and foreign field."[144] The land on The Avenue was subsequently sold to finance the purchase of "Cumnock," also on The Avenue.

Finally, on 11 March 1912, the third anniversary of its opening day, the following report was printed: "The college was founded a little over two years ago to provide theological training of an evangelical character for students preparing for the ministry of the Anglican church . . . "[145]

Canon Sadlier, Bishop Elect of Nelson (NZ) and first principal of Ridley, said the aim of the college was to train men who would be faithful to the convictions which were dear to all evangelical people and which had been responsible for much that was greatest and best in the Church of England.

Ridley was clearly and self-referentially an evangelical Anglican training college, founded to raise up workers at home and abroad. It was a college for the training of evangelical men. Women were already being trained at St. Hilda's.

---

143. Newsprint cuttings in the Ridley College Minute Book No. 1.
144. Article news cutting in Ridley College Council Minute Book No. 1.
145. Article news cutting in Ridley College Council Minute Book No. 1.

Provisional Council 1908

The opening words of the first College minute book note that "several meetings of a Provisional Council were held during the early part of 1908, and there was formed a rough outline of the Constitution." The following were elected as the first members of the council proper:

> Revds Canon Sadlier MA, W. T. C. Storrs MA, A. C. Kellaway MA, C. H. Nash MA, A. J. H. Priest, H. S. Begbie.
>
> Messrs John Griffiths, E. Shelley, H. J. Hannah, H. McL. Duigan, E. Lee Neil, W. M. Buntine MA.[146]

Nash and Begbie never attended any meetings. They had moved to Sale and Bairnsdale respectively, and distance and heavy local responsibilities were certainly a factor. More significantly, Nash was discouraged and recovering from the events of 1907. He had sought solace by throwing himself into the local work in Gippsland, where Pain had appointed him archdeacon of Sale. The other council members recognized that he probably wished to disengage from Melbourne and the painful memories of his conflict with Clarke. They wrote to him in July 1908, asking if he wished to withdraw from the council, to which he replied in the affirmative. However, Nash maintained an interest in Ridley, and soon afterwards he forwarded a check for £100 from a generous supporter to the council.[147]

Begbie tendered his resignation in November, but his involvement was still greatly desired. No doubt his high profile as a gifted and popular missions speaker was on the minds of the council when they sought his services to head up a three-month traveling canvass for funds. However, Bishop Pain replied that he could not spare him from the work at Bairnsdale.[148]

Although these were important declensions from the council, the list of elected members above is nevertheless indicative of the group of key clerical and lay leaders of the day expected to be supportive and involved in the work of the college. The fact of Begbie and Nash's election to the founding council shows that they belonged to the group. The other founding council members were no less noted as evangelical leaders in the diocese:[149]

Herbert Smirnoff Begbie, not to be confused with his son Herbert Gordon Smirnoff Begbie, is remembered today as the patriarch of the influential evangelical Begbies of Sydney. His involvement in Victoria was brief.

---

146. Ridley College Council Minute Book No. 1, 1.
147. Nash, *Forward Flows the Time*, 13.
148. Ridley College Council Minute Book No. 1. 29.
149. See generally their entries in ADEB.

He was born in Sydney and was energized by the Grubb Mission of 1891, going on to study at Moore College where he was tutored by Nash, who was much impressed by him.[150] From Sydney he came to Bendigo to serve a curacy under MacCullagh. Begbie had a bright and powerful evangelistic ministry in Sydney, Melbourne and Gippsland. He was heavily involved in missionary and evangelistic societies like the YMCA and Sowers' and Gleaners' Unions and the CMA and CMS. His relatively brief ministry as vicar of St. Mary's North Melbourne from 1905 to 1908, together with the CMA men's training home there, is remembered as a time of evangelistic effectiveness and missionary fervor. From Bairnsdale, Begbie returned to Sydney where he exercised the remainder of his ministry and influenced a remarkable line of evangelical descendants.[151]

William Sadlier was born in County Cork, Ireland—one of many Irishmen to serve with distinction in Australia. He was energetic, able, and a scholar. During his second curacy in Bendigo, he combined his duties with the principalship of Perry Hall, which had been left vacant when his predecessor, Nathaniel Jones, became principal of Moore College in 1897. On his return to Melbourne, he was vicar of Holy Trinity East Melbourne and then Christ Church St. Kilda, completing his BA, MA, and London BD while a busy parish clergyman. He was clearly a person of ability and was appointed canon of the cathedral at the relatively young age of thirty-four by Goe. Sadlier was the founding and acting principal of Ridley, which he combined with his parish work at St. Kilda, until appointed bishop of Nelson NZ in 1912. One of the first students of Ridley, Percy Stephenson, was also subsequently elected bishop of Nelson in 1940.

William Townsend Cooper Storrs, as described above, served as vicar of St. Matthew's Prahran from 1895 to 1926, thirty-one years, during which time it was firmly established as the leading evangelical parish in the diocese. He was a recognized leader of the CMA and later CMS in Australia and a founding member of its committees, on which he sat for over fifty years. Unsurprisingly, St. Matthew's was a key sending church for CMS missionaries in his time. He was also chair of the Katoomba Convention for fourteen years. Outside of the parish, missionary and convention work were

---

150. Judd and Cable, *Sydney Anglicans*, 150–51, asserts that Begbie was energized by the Grubb missions in Victoria, but this is incorrect. Loane, *Mark These Men*, correctly notes that Begbie was born and raised in Sydney, influenced by the Reverend Dickinson in Marrickville, energized by Grubb when in Sydney in 1891, and then went on to train for ministry at Moore College in 1898. Begbie only came to Victoria after his studies.

151. See ADEB entries for A. E. S, H. G. S, H. S., and S. C. S. Begbie. Also Loane, *Mark These Men*.

his main focus, with Ridley's training function tying in with those concerns. He was a notable absence from the councils of the diocese and was never promoted to the ranks of senior clergy.

Alfred Charles Kellaway served at St. James' Melbourne, in Lara, and in Northcote and was another key CMA and CMS supporter. His contribution was recognized by the parent CMS in London, which made him an honorary governor for life for "rendering essential services to the Society." He was also on the National Missionary Council of Australia as the CMS representative, reflecting evangelicals' missionary interdenominationalism. Kellaway was an administrator able to organize people and resources and a loyal churchman with a deep concern for the diocese's drift away from its evangelical heritage. These came together in his chairmanship of the Ridley Council and in his lengthy service as the editor of the *Victorian Churchman* from 1890 to 1913.

Alfred Priest was the CMA secretary and vicar of another leading evangelical parish, St. Mary's Caulfield. After thirteen years in parish ministry, and on the back of successful missions he had recently conducted in Ballarat and in the evangelical parish of St. Alban's Armadale, he was appointed the first traveling "Missionary Missioner" of the CMA of the Commonwealth in 1911. This was one of the first decisions of the newly formed CMA Council for the whole of Australia and part of the beginning of a nationalized CMS structure of which Priest was one of the early leaders.[152] The move to the traveling national position meant that Priest resigned from the council in 1911.

John Griffiths' involvement was similarly brief, due to other heavy commitments, principally his election to the presidency of the YMCA. In June 1909, his resignation was accepted "with regret" by the council.[153] His brother James subsequently featured repeatedly in council minutes.

John and James Griffiths were brothers from Wolverhampton, England, who made good in Melbourne as tea merchants. The Griffiths Tea Company was one of the most successful businesses of the day, an example of the kind of new industrial and trading wealth made possible by the technological and social context of the times. It was this kind of wealth that made philanthropy and the pursuit of private causes possible on the scale seen in this era.

The Griffiths brothers owned teahouses in the city, and the present-day Hotel Lindrum on Flinders Street, near Spring Street, was the company headquarters: it still has "Griffiths Bros" inscribed in the brickwork high

---

152. Cole, *Sharing in Mission*, 32, 37.
153. Ridley College Council Minute Book No. 1, 33.

on the building. They worshiped at St. Hilary's Kew and at St. Columb's Hawthorn and were intimately connected with Nash and H. J. Hannah. It would not be an exaggeration to say that they helped to bankroll a good portion of the evangelical ministry in their time, including the CMA, Ridley, Nash's Melbourne Bible Institute (later the Bible College of Victoria, and, from 2011, the Melbourne School of Theology[154]), and the Upwey (later Belgrave Heights) Convention.[155]

James and Emily Griffiths were tragically killed in an accident at the Bayswater railway crossing on 6 April 1925. Their wills revealed that they had a relatively small personal fortune for a couple as successful as they were in business: less than £80,000.[156] Most had been given away to evangelical causes during their lifetimes.[157]

Another CMA layman, Edgar Shelley, ran the first CMA training home for men in North Melbourne, which H. S. Begbie directed. As described above, this was the progenitor institution of Ridley.

Horace John Hannah was a senior banker with the English, Scottish & Australian Bank, now part of the ANZ Bank. He was a keen reader of theology, with a massive personal library of some thirty thousand learned volumes that was used by Archbishops Mowll and Loane of Sydney.[158] It was considered for a time as perhaps the best theological library in the country. After his death, the library came mainly to Ridley, where for years later students would find one-pound notes used as bookmarks.[159] Hannah was a lay reader of the parish of Rosanna, leading and founding the church there in the absence of a clergyman. He was a close friend of Nash and was instrumental in the conversion of Edwin Lee Neil. Two of his six children were CMS missionaries in Tanganyika. Horace himself, with his wife Kitty,

154. The library of the Bible College of Victoria, now Melbourne School of Theology, is the C. H. Nash library; and it has recently founded the Nash Institute.

155. See ADEB entries. Remarkably, little by way of evangelical biography has been written on the Griffithses; there is a secular local history biography: Wehner, *Tea and Charity*. Among the Griffithses descendants were two Ridley College faculty, his great-grandsons Andrew Malone and Andrew Reid. Reid is married to Heather, a descendant of H. S. Begbie.

156. By contrast, Sidney Myer's estate was sworn for probate at £1M in 1934. A tenth of that was given to philanthropic trusts. See ADB. The theme of evangelicals' use of their money and resources is not unimportant. Myer's business partner, Edwin Lee Neil, similarly left behind a small amount relative to his business success—about the same as the Griffithses. Again, he had given most away to evangelical causes during his lifetime.

157. Wehner, *Tea and Charity*, 39.

158. See ADEB entry, and also Loane, "They Shaped My Life."

159. Related by Stuart Barton Babbage, interview of 11 May 2007.

the daughter of Digby Berry (the outspoken evangelical vicar of Holy Trinity East Melbourne), offered for missionary service in China. His brother, Brooking Hannah, was already serving with his wife in China. However, Horace was rejected on health grounds and instead put his financial and administrative gifts to use by serving for many years on the council of the CIM as well as the councils or leading bodies of Ridley College, the Nurses' Christian Union, Crusaders, the Church of England Evangelical Trust of Victoria, and the diocese's Mollison Library. He was also responsible for founding the Victorian branch of the Mission to the Lepers.

The man Hannah helped to bring to faith, Edwin Lee Neil, was himself instrumental in the conversion of the philanthropist Sidney Myer. Neil became a manager of the Myer Emporium business after Myer bought out his drapery business of Wright & Neil in 1911.[160] The two men were business partners and also lifelong friends. Neil became the managing director of Myer Emporium Ltd when it was formed in 1925. He was an extraordinarily able businessman, exemplifying the connection between Protestant faith and commercial success that marked out Melbourne in this period. His leadership there is remembered as in the style of a benevolent, though firm, Christian patriarch:

> . . . at times severe, at times lenient, he cultivated loyalty and enthusiasm by inspections, lectures and exhortations, stressing the desirability of good health and manners, and the avoidance of strong drink (Myer's did not sell liquor during his lifetime). He installed a doctor and nurses who daily attended staff and customers.[161]

Neil's exhortations were typically from the Scriptures, and he regularly led staff in public prayer. He was also a close friend and evangelical colleague to C. H. Nash and in 1920 was the founding president of the MBI Council. He was the prime mover behind the founding of MBI as a necessary institution for the training of overseas missionaries and as an appropriate avenue for the deployment of the exiled Nash's gifts.[162] Interestingly, early members of the interdenominational MBI Council from 1921 onwards included sitting Ridley council members Storrs and Hannah, one-time member Neil,

---

160. See entries in ADB and ADEB.

161. See ADB entry.

162. Paproth, *Failure Is Not Final*, 53, suggests that Neil was perhaps Nash's closest friend. Paproth quotes Nash's reflections in 1934 after Neil's death: "Such friendship is too sacred for discussion. For me it has been the most formative, inspiring and protective influence in the latter half of my lifetime." See also the 70th anniversary history of MBI/ BCV, Clack, *We Will Go*.

and the great supporter of Ridley, John Griffiths. The same group of Anglican evangelical leaders were active in both colleges.

Despite his interdenominational evangelical interests, Neil was rare in that he was also a committed churchman. A gifted musician, he had been the organist at St. Columb's Hawthorn before leaving because of a dispute with the unsavory vicar at the time, Henry Mercer.[163] Neil was then the organist at St. Hilary's Kew, a synod member, and a lay canon of the cathedral. The missionary cause was closest to his heart. He was heavily involved with the CMS as chair of the general committee, president of the Gleaners' Union, and leader of the Missionary Service League. He was also involved with the China Inland Mission (CIM), joining its council in 1915. He was a leader in the Days of Prayer revivalist movement. Neil was appointed a CBE in 1926 for his leadership as commissioner in charge of the Australian section of the British Empire Exhibition, held in London the year before.

Walter Murray Buntine was another outstanding evangelical lay leader with a great commitment to mission and to theological education. Together with Hannah, he gave decades of unstinting service to Ridley. He was a graduate of Scotch College and Melbourne University and deeply interested in education, becoming the owner and principal of the St. Kilda and Caulfield Grammar Schools in an age when many schools were privately owned and run. His commitment to the cause of education extended to writing histories of Caulfield Grammar School and Ridley College.[164] His contribution is commemorated in The Australian College of Educators' annual Buntine Oration.[165]

Buntine was a member of the nearby evangelical parish of St. Mary's Caulfield and shared its evangelistic and missionary commitments. The vicar for most of the period of his membership was H. T. Langley, the son of the first bishop of Bendigo and nephew of the second. Buntine had a lifelong involvement with the CMS. He was a founding member of the CMA in 1892 and a trustee of the CMS at his death in 1953. He was heavily involved in Ridley as well: he was a founding council member and died in office. Council minutes show that he was a tireless worker for the college,

---

163. Carolan, *St. Columb's Hawthorn*, 13, notes that Mercer's parish administration was not successful: his curate Edward Walker left after nine months, Neil and many of the parishioners left, the choir was split. Subsequently there were allegations of financial impropriety and mismanagement. See above.

164. Buntine, *Caulfield Grammar School Jubilee*. The history is cited in Buntine's ADB entry http://adbonline.anu.edu.au/biogs/A070484b.htm, last accessed Tuesday 9 March 2010. Buntine's brief history of Ridley was published in 1917 by the college and held in the college archives.

165. Among the orators have been Sir James Darling, Sir Zelman Cowan, and Justice Michael Kirby.

attending the majority of meetings and leading a variety of administrative and business tasks for the college in between. The contribution of able lay businessmen like Buntine, Hannah, the Griffiths brothers, and Neil is not to be underestimated.[166]

A common factor that bound all of the elected members of the founding council was their commitment to evangelism and overseas mission, expressed in their membership of the CMA and CMS. Indeed, the majority of early council meetings were held in the CMA rooms in the cathedral, with CMA Secretary Arthur Ebbs often present as a visitor or observer. Clergy and laity were energized for committed and sacrificial action for the sake of world mission. Without this factor, Ridley would have been just an inward-focused political movement seeking to maintain the evangelical party's cause within the diocese. Clarke's antagonism was certainly a factor for the founding of the college, but it was this clear mission focus that supplied the motive and energy to found the college and to build rapidly on its foundation. It was envisaged that missionary candidates studying at Ridley would be ordained and serve overseas with the CMS. Missionary candidates who wanted to serve with the other interdenominational societies such as the CIM could be prepared at the MBI. The interdenominational evangelical focus of many of the council illustrates the point that they were fundamentally mission-minded rather than party-focused. Members and friends of the Ridley Council such as the Griffithses, Neil, and Nash were involved with the MBI as well, illustrating the point that evangelicals in this period were working both within the denomination and interdenominationally to encourage and support world missions.

The Perry Heritage and Ridley's Founding[167]

The energy for mission and concern to maintain an evangelical witness in the diocese led the founders to look back to the heritage left by the founding bishop of Melbourne. Perry's crowning work in retirement had been the founding of Ridley Hall Cambridge, with constitutional arrangements

---

166. The contribution of able business-minded laity is an important theme in evangelical studies. Following this theme in Melbourne, Piggin has argued that in contrast to Sydney, Melbourne evangelicalism has been dominated by laity over clergy—Stuart Piggin, "Pietism, Pluralism and Provincialism: The Divergent Paths of Melbourne and Sydney Evangelicalism, 1848–1988" the Perry Memorial Lecture, St. James' Old Cathedral, West Melbourne, 19 October 1990. The same theme is explored in Hilliard, "How Anglican Lay People Saved the Church."

167. See Kuan, "The Perry Heritage."

designed to preserve its evangelical, Protestant, and Reformed heritage.[168] A number of themes in the founding of Ridley Hall were mirrored in the founding of Ridley College.

First, Ridley Hall's objectives included a close connection with university lectures and the associated benefits of higher learning, which Perry had argued for decades earlier in a pamphlet on clerical education.[169] But they also recognized the need for additional and distinctly evangelical tutoring of the "Protestant Reformed" kind, and they envisaged the provision of residential assistance for quality candidates of lesser means.

Second, Ridley College was founded explicitly on the "principles of the Protestant and Reformed settlement of the Church of England." Council members had to annually sign a declaration "expressing their continued belief in and adherence to the Constructive and Evangelical Principles of the Reformation Settlement of the Church of England."[170] A similar requirement still exists today. Unlike England, there was no expectation in the colonies that clergy would definitely have university degrees. Ridley was open to non-matriculated students who would receive evangelical tutoring but hopefully reach the required standard for university studies. It was to be located in the university precinct so that attendance at university lectures might be possible for men of such ability.

Third, Perry ensured that there was a deliberate separation of powers between the trustees of Ridley and Wycliffe Halls, who controlled the property assets, and the council members, who dealt with matters of governance and—critically—appointments. He believed, as he had shown in Melbourne by his reluctance to found a divinity school at Trinity, that the independence of the controlling authority was critical. Deep within this thinking was an older evangelical commitment: a belief in the right of members of the church to freely associate for the achievement of their chosen ends. This thinking had given birth to a plethora of evangelical societies at the height of the Evangelical Revival, including the CMS.

In the same way, Ridley College's property was held by the simultaneously founded Church of England Evangelical Trust of Victoria.[171] The first trustees were John MacCullagh, Charles Barnes, Alfred Priest, W. T. C. Storrs, and the laymen William Pearson, James Griffiths, and William Buntine. In other words, they were evangelicals, most of whom were also

---

168. See Bullock, *History of Ridley Hall*.

169. Perry, *Clerical Education Considered*

170. Articles of Association of Ridley College under the Companies Act 1915, 17 December 1920.

171. The Trust was settled on 14 June 1910.

founding councilmen of Ridley. Alfred Kellaway became a trustee in 1916. After MacCullagh's death that same year, his place was taken by Horace Hannah, further cementing the Ridley and Trust link. The Trust Deed provided, as Ridley's constitution did, that members had to, and still have to, sign an annual declaration as to their beliefs. In particular, from 1914, they were to acknowledge

a. The supreme authority of Holy Scripture

b. The acceptance of the Reformation Settlement of the Protestant and Reformed Church of England as expressed in the language of the thirty-nine articles taken in their literal and grammatical sense

c. The free access of the individual to God through Christ alone

d. The right of private judgment within the limits of the creeds and articles

e. The right of individuals to take combined action for the extension of the Kingdom of God[172]

Fourth, all of Perry's fellow Ridley Hall councilmen were associated with the CMS and had impeccable evangelical missions-minded credentials: among them were J. C. Ryle, Edward Hoare, William Carus and Henry Wright (Henry Venn's successor at CMS). According to one observer, it was in the meeting rooms of the Church Mission House that the plans for the independent colleges matured.[173] All of the founding councilmen and trustees were CMA men, and almost all of the early Ridley Council and Trust meetings were held in the CMA rooms at Melbourne's St. Paul's Cathedral.

The direct link to England was explicit. The Ridley College Council sought advice not just from Ridley Hall but from the principals of all three English evangelical colleges: Ridley Hall, Wycliffe Hall, and St. Aidan's Birkenhead. Replies to their enquiries about their trust deeds and constitutional arrangements were received in late 1909.[174] Ridley's first full-time principal, George Aickin, came from a lecturer's position at St. Aidan's.[175]

The Perry legacy of a largely evangelical province of Victoria meant that from 1906 onwards, when Clarke's antagonism towards evangelicals in

---

172. Church of England Evangelical Trust of Victoria Minute Book No. 1, header paragraph to the lists of annual signatures. Interestingly the Trust Deed also reflects evangelicals' firmly premillennial eschatology of the age: the property of St. Andrew's Hall cedes to the Chief Rabbi of Melbourne upon the Lord's return.

173. Bullock, *History of Ridley Hall*, 101.

174. Ridley College Council Minute Book No. 1, 44. Meeting of 9 November 1909.

175. See ADEB. Also Paproth, "Principals of Ridley."

Melbourne became increasingly clear, there was a series of firm responses. First, there were sufficient strength in numbers of convinced Melbourne evangelicals concerned about the drift towards "Rationalism and Ritualism" in their diocese. Second, these evangelicals were sufficiently well-informed and strategically minded that they made as their priority the founding of an independent evangelical theological college, mirroring Perry's own priority in retirement. Third, they took as their model and example the founding of Wycliffe and Ridley Halls; and when it came to selecting a name for their college in Melbourne, it seems they chose the one most closely associated with their revered founding bishop.

The result of Perry's founding work meant that the real health and strength of evangelicalism in Melbourne was, as in England, centered around the CMS. This vital interest in missions was coupled with another aspect of Perry's legacy: a robust understanding of the importance of clergy in maintaining the character of the Reformed and Protestant Church of England. Perry, the father of synodical government and architect of the devolution of absolute episcopal power, had said:

> I would remind the laity that, under God, the real well-being of the Church in this diocese depends mainly upon the character of its clergy. I do not depreciate the importance of the laity—God forbid. But the character of the church as a whole will depend under God on the character of the clergy.[176]

Hence, Ridley was founded to train clergy for church and missionary work, and A. W. Pain was able to point to the vital connection between the CMA and the college as the means of creating "greater certainty of evangelical continuity."[177]

Early Support for Ridley College[178]

The founding work of Ridley was also an example of the kind of vital partnership between clergy and laity envisioned by Perry. His thinking was enshrined in the constitution of the college, which provided for equal numbers of lay and clerical members. In the work of the council, bishops Pain and Langley provided a good deal of the strategic-level leadership and advice. Pain is especially prominent in the minutes, and his travel to England in 1910 meant that he could consult with colleagues there about constitutional

---

176. Goodman, *Church in Victoria*, 460.
177. Ridley College Minute Book No.1, 1 May 1908, 3.
178. See Kuan, "Ridley, Melbourne and Beyond."

arrangements and about the appointment of the first full-time principal. Much of the committee work was done by the clergy like A. C. Kellaway, but the commercial and financial work in negotiating for lease of premises, purchase of lands, and managing funds was done by laymen like the long-serving treasurer Hannah, Carre-Riddell, Neil, and Buntine. The Griffiths brothers were especially generous. John Griffiths had offered to cover the costs of the initial canvass for capital mentioned above. James Griffiths promised five payments of £50 per half-year from the opening month of the college onwards.[179] He later offered to give £1,000 if £4,000 could be collected from other sources within the first four months of the canvass. Another similar offer, "£100 each to the Dioceses of Bendigo and Gippsland for the Ridley College Fund" if each diocese could collect £400, was also made by him.[180] The Griffithses were in a position to give—in 1913 they gave £750[181]—but clearly saw the benefit in working with the council to encourage a larger body of supporters for the college.

This vital partnership between evangelical laity and clergy meant that Ridley enjoyed a flying start to life. It was able to grow in both student numbers and property assets through the years of WWI as supporters gave money, gathered at events, and, one assumes, prayed earnestly as they were constantly asked to do by the council and successive principals.

Early growth in student numbers placed pressure on accommodation, but supporters rallied to bring forward funds for continued expansion. The level of support is indicative of the good health of evangelical faith in Melbourne and Victoria and the importance Melbourne evangelicals placed on the training of their future clergy. Writing to the *Argus* in 1911, the honorary secretary Buntine was able to say that:

> In the opinion of a large body of the clergy and laity of the Church of England it is of the greatest importance that candidates for the sacred work of ministry should have the advantage of such a system of theological education as will be in harmony with the principles of the school of thought to which they belong . . .[182]

---

179. Ridley College Council Minute Book No.1, 79. Reported to the meeting of 21 March 1910.

180. Ridley College Council Minute Book No.1, 214. Reported to the meeting of 9 May 1912. Another donation from James Griffiths was received in December 1912, 248.

181. Ridley College: Report of the Women's Committee with Statement of Monies Received, November 1913. Appended to Ridley College Council Minute Book No. 1, 251.

182. *Argus*, 11 August 1911.

Buntine also asserted the importance of such students having the benefit of taking university courses and noted the recent removal of Trinity's theological school and hence the removal of this benefit. He then wrote:

> It is to some extent because of this that the establishment near the Melbourne University of a theological college, where students of the Church of England are being educated on evangelical lines, and where male candidates for the mission field are received for training, has been accorded such widespread support.[183]

Indeed, the level of financial support was unprecedented, and Leeper was right to be anxious about the probability that Ridley would take away resources from Trinity College. As early as 31 January 1911, the Ridley Council was confident enough to authorize the purchase of land on The Avenue, close to the University precinct, for a permanent site. By the end of that year, because of increased student numbers, the college had to move from Norwood, a rented terrace house opposite Trinity College, to Kooringa, a larger rented villa with gardens on the west side of Princes Park. A large gathering of some 150 supporters at its opening unanimously called for its purchase. Council members Alfred Kellaway and Horace Hannah made a successful offer, and the following year extension works commenced with Ridley's long-term friend and builder Clements Langford, also the builder of the cathedral's spires.[184] By 1915, the buildings were free of debt, although operating costs were only half met, prompting principal Aickin to report, "It is a matter for much thankfulness that these premises exist, and stand as a very striking testimony to the self-sacrifice and energy of the evangelical people in our Church."[185]

As the college grew, it had to move in 1921 to larger premises on the corner of Walker Street and The Avenue. The house on the site, Cumnock, was to become Ridley's center of operations for the next eighty-seven years. The following year, the college's support peaked at over 1,100 donors, and it managed to collect promises and cash amounting to £7,000. Building and Endowment Fund Organising Secretary Reg Nichols's report was confident and underscored the spiritual nature of his and the college's work. Speaking of the donors, he wrote, "Our clientele, indeed, is quite a new one on the whole, and this fund of personal interest must be regarded as a spiritual asset to the College."[186]

---

183. *Argus*, 11 August 1911.

184. Langford was an active member of the then strongly evangelical parish of St. Stephen's Richmond. See Sturrock, *Fruitful Mother*.

185. *Ridley Annual Report*, April 1915.

186. *Ridley Annual Report*, 1921.

The list of Ridley's benefactors is indicative of those parishes and people willing to support the independent and clearly evangelical enterprise—perhaps initially in opposition to Clarke's St. John's College, then later, despite the reinstatement of theological training at Trinity. Supporting Ridley was a reasonable barometer of evangelical conviction. Parish donors at the time included the usual evangelical suspects—St. Mary's Caulfield, St. Hilary's Kew, St. Columb's Hawthorn, St. Luke's South Melbourne, and St. Thomas' Essendon—as well as a long list of others, most of which would later lose their evangelical character—St. Stephen's Richmond, Holy Trinity East Melbourne, Elsternwick, Barrabool, Belmont (Geelong), Northcote (All Saints'), St. Philip's Collingwood, St. John's Footscray, and All Saints' Kooyong. Ridley survived and grew because the diocese was largely low church, and many parishes valued having an evangelical college for training clergy and male missionaries.

Also notable is the role of women. The 1920 annual report noted the special contribution of the Women's Prayer Band led by Emily Griffiths. It continued its work of intercession and substantial financial help. Women in this period were increasingly involved in social action outside the home, and their support was crucial for the success of many organizations, particularly ones connected with the church and social welfare. At Ridley, their fundraising activity was of great importance. In 1913, the Women's Committee raised a total of £3,250, although there were a few large donors: £1,000 came from a single bequest, £750 from the Griffithses, and £305 from the Women's Evangelical Guild of Geelong. While this figure represented an enthusiastic high, a succession of principals persistently noted with thanks the significance of women's groups to the life of the college.

Early Growth in Student Numbers and Student Placements[187]

Student numbers grew from three at the beginning of the first year to twelve in 1912: eleven students in residence and one non-resident. The non-resident was the married man, Percival "Paddy" William Stephenson. Stephenson was later a missionary in India, a professor in Canada, and the bishop of Nelson, New Zealand. An earlier bishop of Nelson had been Stephenson's teacher at Ridley: the college's first principal, William Sadlier.[188] All students in 1912 were ordination candidates for either Bendigo or Gippsland. Principal Aickin declared:

---

187. See Kuan, "Ridley, Melbourne and Beyond."
188. Cole, *Sincerity My Guide*.

> The main purpose of the College has been to meet the increasing demand for clergymen trained on the positive and constructive lines in the Evangelical principles of the Church of England. The aim has been to combine the breadth of outlook gained by association with the scholarship and general culture of University life, with a definite and spiritual grounding in the great truths of the gospel. For men so trained there is an unlimited demand in our own State, in the Commonwealth and in the Foreign Mission field.[189]

By 1914, Ridley alumni were incumbents of Alphington in Melbourne and Eaglehawk in Bendigo, and Paddy Stephenson was on the mission field in Peshawar. The list of curate placements was long: St. Mary's Caulfield, St. Luke's Adelaide, St. Mary's Mirboo North in Gippsland, plus others in Gippsland, Footscray, Raywood, and St. Stephen's Richmond (Joseph Booth, later archbishop of Melbourne). Two alumni were serving with the Expeditionary Forces of Australia and in Red Cross work, thus meeting (albeit in a small way) the college's expectation that they would turn out men of high moral principle and service.

Alumni served not just in established centers, but did much pioneering work, helping to establish social cohesion and build community in remote and growth areas. For example, the college magazine celebrated the fact that it was a Ridley alumnus who founded the ministry work in Wonthaggi in 1920.[190] Post-WWI, the electrification of the state was taking place under the leadership of General Sir John Monash, utilizing the resources of returned war veterans. There was desperate need for ministry among the hundreds of State Electricity Commission workers at Yallourn in Gippsland. A Ridley man, Reverend Percy Dicker, was appointed missioner.[191] Part of the willingness of Ridley alumni to work in outlying areas in these early years may be put down to their country placements on weekends as students, when they were exposed to the work and needs.[192] Evangelical mission-mindedness also played a part.

In 1926, the college had opened the year full, and some applications had to be refused. Building works on a second wing of accommodation were begun by Clements Langford. Seven men were listed as on missionary service, including Cyril Chambers in India, Tom Lawrence and W. Hillard in Uganda, Henry Wittenbach in China, L. Hall in Ceylon, and

---

189. *Ridley Annual Report*, 1912.
190. *Ridley Collegian*, October 1920.
191. *Ridley Collegian*, April 1922, 6.
192. *Ridley Collegian*, April 1921, 13–14.

Arthur Riley in Soudan (Sudan). Overseas and country missionary work was constantly featured and championed in college publications, which made heroes out of missionaries like Paddy Stephenson, Tom Lawrence, Alfred Stanway, and Ernest Panelli.

However, that same year "debt" crept into the college's lexicon. Despite the growth in numbers of men sent out as ministers, financial support from parishes and individuals could not eradiate the £5,000 debt—which included £2,000 still owing on the purchase of "Cumnock." An indication of the Ridley's loyalty to the Diocese of Melbourne is seen in that Wade did not appeal for more funds during the year "in order that we should not even seem to distract attention from the Cathedral Spires Appeal."[193]

By 1929, Ridley alumni were serving in Melbourne, Bendigo, Gippsland, Ballarat, Tasmania, Bathurst, Goulburn, Sydney, Willochra, Boggabilla, Werrimull, England and Ireland, India, China, Singapore, Kenya, Tanganyika, and Ceylon. Their locations in Victoria ranged from Wonthaggi to West Geelong, Spotswood to Sorrento, Moe to Maffra, Tatura to Tongala.

In 1931, the principal declared that the majority of men ordained in Melbourne from 1910 up to that year had been trained at Ridley. This caused Wade to wonder aloud about the absurdity of the situation that Ridley was not entered in the official diocesan yearbook.[194] In fact, Ridley had been listed in the Bendigo yearbook in 1910, reflecting the leading role and support of Bishop Langley in its founding, but nowhere else subsequently—a sign of its independence and the delicate relationship between Ridley and the Diocese of Melbourne. It would be 1963 before Ridley was listed.[195]

In fact, Diocese of Melbourne yearbook active lists for each decade between 1920 and 1950 show that an increasing and clearly larger share of clergy was trained at Ridley relative to any other college, and that reliance on overseas-trained clergy (represented in the "other" category) decreased sharply. The five most significant affiliations for the whole period are shown in the graph below, with the Australian College of Theology, Melbourne College of Divinity, and Yarra Theological Union figures being combined. Some of these may have been Ridley students, but even if those figures were combined with the Trinity College total, they would not overtake the final number of Ridley clergy in 1950. It is not always clear from the yearbooks

---

193. *Ridley Annual Report*, 1926.

194. *Ridley Annual Report*, 1931.

195. A few years prior to this, theological students training at Ridley began to be listed, but there was no college listing.

which affiliation should be ascribed, but the trend is clear. Ridley numbers increased steadily.[196]

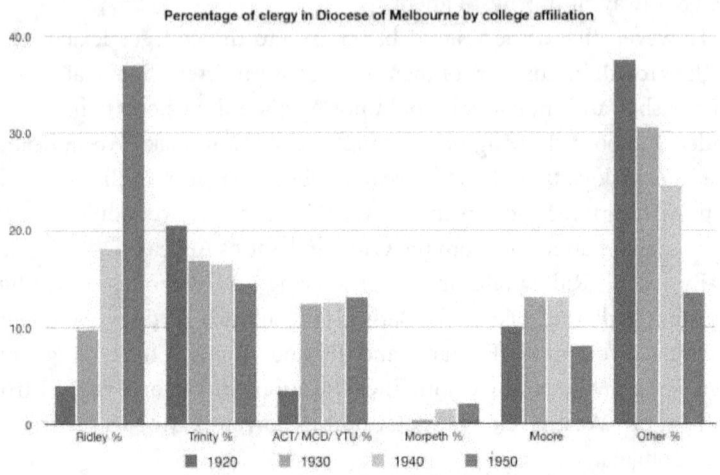

Percentage of Clergy in ADOM by College

In percentage terms, the Ridley figure rose to thirty-seven percent in 1950 and has not dropped below since. Of all colleges and institutions, it has produced by far the largest single share of clergy for the Diocese of Melbourne. By comparison, the next highest figure, that of Trinity College, has never reached above its 1920 level of twenty percent. Writing in 1970, Archbishop Frank Woods said, "Both Diocese and parishes owe more than can ever be told to Ridley-trained clergymen."[197]

Signs of Drift towards Liberal Evangelicalism

After the departure of the antagonistic Clarke in 1920, the new archbishop of Melbourne, the evangelical Harrington Clare Lees, had agreed to become president of the Ridley College Council. His successor, Frederick Head, also came on the council in 1931. Head tried to insist that Ridley become an official provincial training college with closer links to the diocese, but the move

---

196. The percentage of Ridley clergy reached just under 40 percent in 1950 and has tracked just above that level since. The raw number of Ridley clergy in the diocese though has trended upwards in the same period, with the sharpest growth between 1940 and 1980. For analysis up to 2009 see Kuan, "Ridley, Melbourne and Beyond."

197. *Ridley Report*, Special appeal edition, 1970.

was resisted. Ridley may have been "born in distrust," as Clarke declared, but by the 1930s found itself with successive archbishops as council presidents. The loss of two key leaders on the council happened in 1930 when Alfred Kellaway and Bishop Langley of Bendigo both passed away. There was continued growth—forty men in residence, up from thirty-five in 1929, but nineteen of the forty were secular students. Despite Ridley's productivity in terms of numbers of men trained for ministry at home and abroad, signs of insecurity around Ridley's position in Melbourne and Wade's own evangelical convictions began to develop. There was no hiding Wade's more liberal attitude towards the college's ministry. He openly reported in 1930:

> [The college's] evangelical foundation has been interpreted in the most liberal fashion, and students of whatever school of thought have been welcomed, and have been able to pursue their studies without in any way compromising their particular point of view ... Our own position has always been to encourage men to read for their Degree, if it was in any way possible.[198]

This was notably different from the firmly conversionist statements of the founders. But it was not a new development. Ridley's second principal, George Aickin, had earlier already identified with elements of liberal evangelicalism.[199] In an address to leading evangelicals gathered by Canon Sadlier, Aickin asserted, "We are Evangelicals not Low Churchmen." He called for an end to militant low-church antagonism against ritualists, and for a greater unity between evangelicals and those

> ... who are helped, not hindered, by a fuller, and yet a consecrated use of music and art in service and surroundings. Let us trust one another, and, provided there be no symbolism of doctrines which are not of our Church, let us trust those who do things a little differently from ourselves ... (including those) who like a little more ornate service than some Evangelicals.[200]

In the same speech, Aickin asserted that the church in Melbourne should have an "Australian Record" rather than a "Victorian Churchman," indicating the same aversion to conservative evangelical approaches to church polity. The recorder of the speech was L. L. Nash who, unlike his father, was a definite liberal evangelical.[201]

---

198. *Ridley Annual Report*, 1930.

199. See Paproth, "The Principals of Ridley," 70, endnote 2. Paproth noted Aickin's Moorhouse lecture of 1916 and his address in the VC, 23 June 1911.

200. Nash, *Forward Flows the Time*, 190.

201. Liberal evangelicalism persisted at Ridley until the middle of the century, and

Wade repeated the declaration of his liberal interpretation of the evangelical foundations of the college verbatim in the following year's report (1931). He had come to emphasize the ideals of a liberal education instead of the training up of distinctly evangelical men for ministry. It is likely that part of the pressure to move towards a more liberal ethos would have come from an overarching desire to win greater and wider respectability for the still-fledgling college. A similar theme was being played out in the founding of the Baptist Whitley College.[202] The liberal ethos of the age was a powerful factor.

At the turn of the century, there had been enormous confidence placed in the power of education to civilize and improve society. The savagery of WWI put a serious question mark over that assumption—particularly since the main combatants were also the nations most possessed of the same liberal culture. However, the assumptions were hard to resist, and any form of extreme or fundamentalist philosophy—which included for its critics something like decided evangelicalism—was distinctly unfashionable and regarded as outmoded. Evangelicalism, according to this view, would die out as a movement incapable of answering the questions posed by modern human existence. What was required was not the conversionist ethic but the liberalizing effect of education. In theological terms, the doctrine of original sin that required vicarious atonement had been replaced by a doctrine of essential human ability and nobility that required intellectual enlightenment.

The movement's rise in Britain split evangelicals between conservative and liberal groups, expressed in an earlier conflict between the Student Christian Movement and the Cambridge Inter-Collegiate Christian Union and the creation of the Inter-Varsity Fellowship in 1928. Evangelical members of the SCM had formed the CICCU explicitly because of the parent society's refusal to commit to a propitiatory understanding of the atonement. Similar themes were present in the separation of the Bible Churchmen's Missionary Society (BCMS) in 1922 from the CMS. Evangelical members of the CMS had formed the BCMS because they perceived that any denial of

---

although Principals Babbage and Morris were conservative and worked to reverse this ethos, the council remained dominated by liberals and later the powerful masonic figure, George Bearham. The persistence of liberal evangelicalism in the college may be explained by the presence of well-meaning but theologically uncritical laymen who were deferential to the principal. It would be interesting to speculate what ethos Ridley would have had if Neil and the Griffiths brothers had maintained their involvement alongside Hannah, instead of transferring their energies to MBI/ BCV following C. H. Nash.

202. Otzen, *Whitley*. Otzen's history identifies two important themes in the founding of Whitley: the need for quality ministry training, and the desire to gain wider respectability for Baptists.

the doctrine of penal substitution would also mean the loss of any impetus for the work of conversion and evangelism.[203]

The liberal evangelical manifesto had been published in two volumes of essays in the early 1920s.[204] Among contributors were the principals of Wycliffe Hall and St. Aidan's Birkenhead. In Australia, the movement was formed as The Anglican Fellowship by Canon Arthur Garnsey in Sydney in May 1933, partly in protest to the loss of the archbishopric election to conservative evangelicals, who were successful in electing Howard Mowll to the position. Conservative evangelicals in Sydney responded by strengthening their political response through the Australian Church League and were able, through successive conservative evangelical appointments at Moore College, to come to dominate that diocese.[205] In Melbourne, conservatives were less well-organized politically, and most of their energy was poured into the CMS and overseas missions work. In any event, liberal evangelicalism proved infertile; after peaking in the 1920s, the movement died out by the middle of the century.

Despite Wade's open allegiance to liberal evangelicalism, the fiercely conservative and older evangelical foundation members of the council did not press for change. Although Storrs, Hannah, and Lamble were still present, they were aging. Kellaway and Langley had died in 1930. The Great Depression meant that there were few, if any, other ministry positions that Wade could move sideways into; in fact, he retired from Ridley in 1937. The great losses of men and leadership talent during WWI meant that it had been, and continued to be, difficult to find a conservative evangelical scholar of high-enough standing and leadership ability to become principal. Further, despite the difficult conditions, the college had continued to grow in student numbers during Wade's tenure.

Ridley College may have been "founded in distrust" according to Archbishop Clarke, but it had been nurtured through the evangelicals' sacrifice and passion for proclaiming the gospel. It had been founded in a strategic attempt to maintain an evangelical witness in Melbourne and Victoria and, through the CMS, throughout the world. Ridley naturally

---

203. See, for an account of this split and the divergence in British evangelicalism in this period, Bebbington, *Evangelicalism in Modern Britain*. This divergence led those later to be known as conservative evangelicals to found a research library and fellowship to engage with the German scholarship that had given rise to Higher Criticism. See Noble, *Research for the Academy and the Church*.

204. Members of the Church of England, *Liberal Evangelicalism* and *The Inner Life: Essays in Liberal Evangelicalism, Second Series*.

205. Garnsey, *Arthur Garnsey*, 137. Also, Judd and Cable, *Sydney Anglicans*, chapter 14.

struggled against the continued drift towards Anglo-Catholicism—but it also struggled, within evangelicalism itself, against the prevailing general tide of intellectual liberalism. Its second and third principals, Aickin and Wade, spoke publicly using the term "liberal" to describe their theological position. While they subscribed to the doctrine of the inspiration and authority of Scripture, their ministry method was to prioritize the necessity of higher learning and the application of intellectual reason to the Christian life. This effectively reduced the focus on biblical studies and the use of the Scriptures in ministry. Critically, they downplayed the centrality of the substitutionary theory of the atonement and the attendant doctrine of original sin. The threat to the founding vision of Ridley's evangelical forebears was real and great but counterbalanced by the evangelicalism of the missionary societies, in particular, from the 1930s, the CMS League of Youth.

Societies: Taking the Gospel to the Ends of the World

The CMS League of Youth

Part of the reason why change was not more aggressively pushed for at Ridley may have been the growing influence of the CMS League of Youth. At the close of the Wade era, it was the combination of the Ridley alumnus Tom Lawrence, the highly regarded missionary to Uganda,[206] and C. H. Nash that supplied the real leadership and represented hope for the future of Anglican evangelicalism in Melbourne. While convalescing in Melbourne with blackwater fever in 1927, Lawrence observed that, "the heart of CMS is as good as ever but it's growing old."[207] At an annual retreat of evangelical clergy in Olinda that August, the group, which included F. Brammall and Alfred Kellaway, wondered what action could be taken and began planning for a "Picnic For A Purpose" on the banks of the Yarra in Heidelberg for young people. The youth were addressed by Nash, who gave a searching talk, "challenging the youth to service and devotion," and by Lawrence, who issued the call to missionary service.[208]

---

206. Lawrence was appointed a Canon in the Diocese of Lira, Uganda, in 1933. He served in Uganda from 1915 to 1919 then again from 1924 to 1941. See Cable et al., *Index of Australian Clergy*, and the CMS-VIC List of Missionary Personnel in Full Connection 1892–2009. See also CMS, *Lawrence of Lira*.

207. See the official history of the LOY, as well as a subsequent volume of members' memoirs: Cutler, *The Torch*; Cutler, *Bearers of the Torch*. Also, Darling, "Ridley, CMS and Global Mission."

208. Cutler, *The Torch*, 7–8—citing the memory of Christabel Storrs, daughter of W. T. C. Storrs, who was an organizer of the picnic and founding LOY committee member.

Out of the young people who attended, eight were chosen by the CMS Victoria seniors to form a committee. At a subsequent meeting on 7 March 1928, Nash suggested the name "CMS League of Youth" and that it be governed by its own council, backed by the CMS committee. The age of members was to be between fifteen and twenty years. These limits were later revised upward to enable greater continuity and maturing of leadership. Among the founding committee members, and an organizer of the earlier picnic, was Christabel Storrs, daughter of W. T. C. Storrs and subsequent long-term CMS missionary in East Africa with her husband Lionel Bakewell.

The League was to be an organization run for and by young people with a definite commitment to Jesus Christ as Savior and Lord, who were prepared to solemnly pledge that they would serve him at home or abroad as God would direct. Those were the twin requirements for full membership. Associate members pledged commitment to Christ and to take "a definite and prayerful interest" in the work of the CMS. Their motto was John 2:5: "Whatsoever he saith unto you, do it." The constitution was drawn up by the first leaders with this threefold aim:

1. To deepen the spiritual life of the younger members of our Church.

2. To further in every possible way the missionary work of the Church.

3. To keep steadily before young people the claims of Jesus Christ upon their lives of uttermost loyalty and devotion.

The C.M.S. League of Youth.

A Fellowship of Young People (from 15 to 30 years of age) in connection with the Church Missionary Society of Australia and Tasmania, in Victoria.

Motto—"Whatsoever He saith unto you, do it."
John ii. 5.

DECLARATION.—Having accepted the Lord Jesus Christ as my Personal Saviour, I very solemnly before God declare my willingness to give my life entirely to His service, either at home or abroad as He may direct.

PLEDGE.—And I hereby pledge myself, as long as I retain this card of membership

(a) To pray regularly both for God's guidance in my own life and for the missionary undertakings of the Church.

(b) To study diligently the Holy Scriptures and to read missionary literature with a view to knowing more of God's work and will for all mankind.

(c) To help, as opportunity arises, in any missionary work within my power, especially in my own parish and in association with other members of the League of Youth.

(d) To give of my means, as God enables me, for the furtherance of Christ's Kingdom.

UNDERTAKING.—And I undertake annually to renew this pledge very solemnly before God in the presence of other full members of the League of Youth.

Signature

Date:

CMS League of Youth Membership Card

This was the kind of vital piety, utterly responsive to wherever they perceived God was leading them, that characterized the LOY. Activities during the first four years included a quarterly rally, a Christmas camp at Upwey, occasional fellowship meetings, and regular open-air evangelistic work in Port Melbourne and Montague (South Melbourne). At least one drunk was converted through the Port Melbourne work.[209] However, activism was balanced by a concern for serious study of the Scriptures. Here the young people were served by Nash, who for five years ran a central weekly Bible Class for the LOY, first out of St. John's Latrobe Street, then from the crypt of the cathedral, where the CMS had its fellowship rooms. Neil, his sister Jeannie Neil, and Horace Hannah also "brought their culture, scholarship

---

209. Cutler, *The Torch*, 10.

and tested faith to bear upon the movement."[210] Maudie Bennett, another early leader, wrote for the LOY's history, *The Torch*, that:

> We had fantastic opportunities . . . to study fully not only the Bible, but history, archaeology, comparative religions with ready-made inspired leaders and teachers. Some of us absorbed the Bible to such an extent that in after years one found oneself speaking with texts because the words of the Holy Book are relevant to all occasions.[211]

The LOY provided the context in which young people—mainly in Melbourne but eventually also across the country—were infused with the Scriptures and energized for evangelism locally and for missionary service abroad. In the era before parish-based youth groups, it was the LOY that provided the context for youth ministry and inter-parish social activity. It was a remarkable success on both the ministry and marriages fronts, raising up generations of missionaries and home-based workers for the CMS well into the mid-twentieth century. Many of its members also intermarried, thus concentrating the evangelical ethos into particular family units. Many became active clerical and lay leaders in ministry locally, although much of the brightest talent went overseas with the CMS. This diocese-wide evangelical aspect of the LOY was further multiplied when the LOY spread nationally. It provided an effective national network for evangelicals. It gathered missions-focused young people and provided training in the Scriptures, the disciplines of personal holiness, and evangelism. For most, the lessons of their youth persisted for the rest of their lives.[212]

Importantly, the LOY followed Nash's advice and was run by its members, so it gave young evangelicals opportunities for leadership training and experience. Alfred Stanway, for example, was traveling to Adelaide to help plant the LOY in South Australia even before he commenced theological studies at Ridley.[213]

The link between the evangelical CMS LOY and Ridley was inextricable. Almost all male members of the LOY who went on to be ordained or went to the mission field studied at Ridley as part of their training.[214] Examples of LOY members from the late 1920s through the 1930s who did this include Dick Pethybridge, Alf Stanway, Eric Constable, George

210. Cutler, *The Torch*, 12. In later years Leon Morris was a featured Bible Class leader.
211. Cutler, *The Torch*, 15.
212. See testimonies in Cutler, *Bearers of the Torch*.
213. Cutler, *Bearers of the Torch*, 13.
214. Cole, *Sharing in Mission*, 145.

Pearson, Guy Harmer, Wynne Evans, Charles Maling, Wilfred Holt, Frank McGorlick, John Moroney, and Lance and Jack Shilton.[215] Through the middle part of the twentieth century, graduates of the LOY nationally gravitated towards Ridley.[216]

The LOY also gave an outlet for the energies and evangelistic passion of women in this same period. Christabel Storrs (Bakewell), Helen Alder, Madge Dunsford (Prentice), Dorothy Armstrong, Jean Meyer, and Dulcie McLeish were each energized by the LOY and went on to overseas missions service of one form or another.[217]

Ridley's strong connection to the CMS, the common interest in missions work, and the vitality of the LOY meant that Ridley maintained an evangelical witness and identity through the 1930s. Perry's prediction about the importance of overseas missions work in maintaining a vital evangelical spirituality in the home church was proving true. However, it is arguable that evangelicalism in Melbourne was also weakened because significant young evangelical leadership energy and resources was channeled overseas, especially towards East Africa. It remains a moot question as to how evangelicalism might have fared in the diocese if evangelical leaders of the caliber of Lionel and Christabel Bakewell, Alfred and Marjorie Stanway, Wellesley and Phyllis Hannah, George and June Pearson, and Frank and Dorothy McGorlick had served the most energetic years of their ministry lives in Melbourne rather than in East Africa or the Middle East.

Alfred Stanway

Alf Stanway is probably the outstanding example of capable evangelical leadership that was exported for the service of the gospel work overseas.[218]

---

215. See testimonies in Cutler, *Bearers of the Torch*. Also, list of Ridley students in Appendix Nine to Nash, *Forward Flows the Time*. Eric Stockton's testimony dates Frank McGorlick's LOY involvement to the early 1930s; Lance Shilton recalls that in 1939, he was introduced to the LOY by his old Sunday School teacher, Guy Harmer. Shilton remembers "vividly" being converted that year under the ministry of Bob Buchanan at a LOY S1 (South One) regional group meeting at St. Clement's Elsternwick. The *Ridley College Annual Report* 1938 reports that in 1939, Pearson and Holt were both college residents. The list of ordinands and missionaries from LOY who studied at Ridley grows even longer in the following three decades to the end of the 1960s. See Cutler, *The Torch*, 56–57.

216. For example, from the mid-twentieth century David Williams, Ron Pearce, and Peter Corney came from Perth explicitly to study at Ridley.

217. Cutler, *Bearers of the Torch*.

218. See ADEB entry and the personal memoir by his wife, Marjory Stanway, *Alfred Stanway*.

He had been converted under the preaching of C. H. Nash as St. Paul's Fairfield on 29 July 1928. A few months later, the CMS Home Secretary, the Reverend Reginald Long, gave a talk at St. Paul's entitled, "In Darkest Africa: The Challenge of Tanganyika." During the session, Stanway experienced a deeply emotional response. He found a sympathetic ear and blurted out, "God is calling me to Africa!"[219] Long was one of the CMS elders who helped found the LOY, which Stanway promptly joined. He was soon elected chairman. He was twenty years old.

Stanway threw his energies into the LOY, helping organize the movement in its Melbourne base as well as its spread to South Australia and nationally. Stanway was part of the leadership team that saw the growth of LOY rallies and gatherings featuring a Bible talk, open-air evangelism, and lectures on missionary work. In 1936, Stanway helped establish the League camp close to the Upwey Convention site. The LOY purchased property there, aided in large part by the generosity of Geelong member David Lewin. It was to become an important base for camps and house parties.[220] Stanway was already a noted public speaker, with Dick Pethybridge able to recall an occasion in these early years when a visiting missionary guest failed to show up at a meeting at Christ Church Ormond. Stanway was asked to fill in, which he did. Pethybridge recalls: "Off the cuff he delivered an inspiring message which blessed everyone present."[221]

After training at Ridley, ordination, and a curacy at the Mission of St. James and St. John, Stanway sailed to Africa at Kaloleni on the Kenyan coast in 1937. In 1944, he was transferred inland to Maseno as rural dean of Nyanza, where he had oversight of some five hundred churches and the village-based primary school system. His ability in organizing and administering led to his appointment as archdeacon of Kenya in Easter 1949, moving him to Nairobi.[222] As secretary of the African Church Council and the African Education Board, he became responsible for all the African church work in the diocese. Stanway proved to be a missionary statesman *par excellence*, working and negotiating with high-ranking government officials during the transition to postcolonial independence. In 1951, he was consecrated the third bishop of Central Tanganyika, returning to the lands to which he had been called twenty-three years earlier.

219. Stanway, *Alfred Stanway*, 8–9. Stanway kept the flyer advertising that talk for more than 60 years, and it is reproduced on page 9.

220. Cutler, *The Torch*, 11.

221. Cutler, *The Torch*, 11.

222. Audrey Grant notes an error in Stanway, *Alfred Stanway*, which incorrectly dates this to 1948. Stanway's collation in the Cathedral can be accurately dated to 12 July 1949. See also ADEB entry.

Over two decades, Stanway pressed ahead to grow and completely reorganize the diocese: building churches at the rate of two a week; raising funds from Germany and America to build Mackay House, a large and effective central administrative base in Dodoma, and to modernize hospitals at Mvumi and Hombolo; opening Bible schools for evangelists; sending able clergy overseas for further training, including to Ridley; subdividing the over-large diocese into four separate dioceses; and, most significantly, achieving the transition to African leadership. Stanway saw that the future was for able African leadership of the African church, and consecrated the first East African in 1955, his assistant bishop Yohana Omari. He also played a leading role in forming the Province of Tanzania in 1970 with an African metropolitan. At the time of his departure, the geographically smaller Diocese of Central Tanganyika still had more churches and clergy than the original larger diocese at the time of his arrival.

Stanway retired from missionary service to become vice principal of Ridley, but it was a difficult transition into a much more limited role. John Stott, James Packer, and other international Anglican evangelical leaders suggested his name to North American episcopal evangelicals who were looking to found an evangelical school of ministry for their ordinands.[223] Stanway was soon on his way to do a new founding work. It was 1975 and he was sixty-seven years old. He arrived in Sewickly, an outer suburb of Pittsburgh, with a job but no property, no staff, no students, and no funds. Within the year, the Trinity Episcopal School for Ministry was open with three staff and seventeen students. Two years later, at the end of the guaranteed three years of his appointment, TESM was firmly established with support from Episcopal evangelicals from across the country. The council was happy to extend Stanway's principalship, but he was now seventy and sensed that his health was failing.[224] He retired again, to active ministry as a part of St. Andrew's Glen Waverley, leading men's Bible studies and encouraging missionaries.

TESM still remembers Stanway with honor. The school is home to the Stanway Institute for World Mission and Evangelism. TESM's academic dean said in 2008 that Stanway was regarded as a saint by those who knew him and viewed as a fictional hero by later generations, who could hardly believe all he had done in the short time he was in Pittsburgh.[225] At

---

223. See ADEB. Also Leighton, *Lift High the Cross*, 18.

224. Marcus Loane, in his ADEB entry, incorrectly puts Stanway's age at this time as seventy-five.

225. Conversation between Grant LeMarquand, Academic Dean TESM and the author, June 2008.

Ridley College in 2010, the Stanway lecture rooms were the only spaces in the college named for a person other than a past principal.

The Melbourne University Evangelical Union[226]

A second significant evangelical society in this period was the university Christian group, the Melbourne University Evangelical Union. This group became an important network for energetic, missions and evangelism-focused evangelical university students. It also became the main organizer of evangelistic activities on the secular university campus. Through this society, younger leaders were given valuable ministry experience and often went on to overseas missionary work, or, if not, faithful service in local churches. It was interdenominational in character, but many of its key early leaders were Anglicans.

The Evangelical Union's genesis was in a University Men's Camp held in December 1928, organized by Leslie Griffiths, the son of John Griffiths and nephew of James.[227] Leslie had completed an engineering degree in 1923, but after badly injuring his arm in an industrial accident, he was at university again retraining as a doctor. He had married Phyllis Neil, daughter of Edwin Lee Neil, thus cementing an evangelical alliance in a second generation of evangelical lay stalwarts. The camp was held in the grounds of the Griffiths family property in Upwey, "Ferndale," which was a Swiss-style mansion on several acres that the family regularly offered to tired clergy and missionaries on furlough.[228] It was no accident that the Upwey Convention was nearby, as the Griffithses senior were intimately involved in its foundation as well.[229]

That same year, the only Protestant Christian group on campus, the Student's Christian Union,[230] had refused Leslie and its own Medical Branch

---

226. Primary source information by way of testimonies and personal accounts are contained in Angus, *Decisive Years*. The official AFES history up to 1987 is: Prince and Prince, *Out of the Tower*. See also Ting, "'In Utter Dependence'"; Piggin, "Challenging but Glorious Heritage."

227. Angus, *Decisive Years*, 1.

228. See for property history and photographs: Wehner, *Tea and Charity*. "Ferndale" was sold and fell into disrepair before being destroyed in the bushfires of January 1962. Much of the land reverted to government ownership and is now part of the national park.

229. Paproth, "Upwey Convention." Paproth notes accurately that the Keswick movement in both Sydney (Katoomba) and Melbourne (Upwey) was dominated by evangelical Anglicans for most of its early history. In Melbourne virtually the same men founded Upwey and MBI, with C. H. Nash playing a dominant role in both.

230. The nomenclature can be confusing. The Melbourne University Student's

permission to hold an evangelistic mission to the Medical School, with C. H. Nash as the missioner. The SCU leadership were already in disagreement with its Medical Branch over studies in Romans that Nash had been taking over the previous eighteen months. They had ordered that they should cease because "they were not in keeping with the union's search for truth." Harold McCracken recounted that, due to Leslie Griffiths's seniority in age, the small group of evangelical students looked to him for leadership, which he reluctantly provided, initially through the camp at Upwey.[231]

After the camp and convention, the students were energized into prayer, especially for the evangelization of the university campus. Griffiths recruited the law student McCracken to be a co-leader in organizing students into a regular weekly prayer meeting for evangelistic witness in the Medical School and the University as a whole. A peaceful spot on the banks of the Yarra near the Burke Road bridge was chosen. The home of Leslie and Phyllis Griffiths in Kew also became known as a "house of prayer" as male and female undergraduates met frequently in the afternoons and evenings to pray. Prayer and persistent evangelical witness, despite the opposition on the campus, were the features of these students' 1929 academic year.

In March 1930, there was another camp at Upwey. The highly anticipated visiting speaker was Dr. Howard Guinness, who was touring Australia at the invitation of local evangelicals following the founding of Inter-Varsity in Britain in April 1928 and the decisive split from the SCM. Guinness was invited due to reports of remarkable blessing on the student movement in Canada, where he had been conducting a similar tour.[232] The same themes were to be played out in Australia, and the Guinness visit was a catalyst for the formation of both Sydney and Melbourne EUs and the energizing of university student evangelicals. McCracken recounted this memory:

> I still remember the day when Les Griffiths in his old Dodge sedan and I drove into Spencer Street Station with palpitating hearts to meet the one whom we believed God had sent to commence an evangelical witness in the University.[233]

Christian Union was affiliated with the SCM. It later changed its name to the SCM. The Evangelical Union was formed out of this group as "evangelical," which the name made clear. It later changed its name to become the Melbourne University Christian Union, which retains its affiliation with AFES and evangelical identity.

231. Angus, *Decisive Years*, 2.
232. See his autobiography: Guinness, *Journey among Students*.
233. Angus, *Decisive Years*, 3.

Piggin describes the Melbourne EU's birth as "difficult but joyful" in the title of his lecture celebrating its seventy-fifth anniversary.[234] And so it was, amidst opposition from the pre-existing SCU and the charged atmosphere of Guinness's visit. By all accounts, Guinness was as Piggin describes him, a "pioneering, individualistic, maverick. He was striking in appearance, forceful in personality, tireless in energy and adventurous in spirit. Cricket bat readily to hand, he was a magnet for young males."[235]

Guinness's first meeting in Melbourne was in the loungeroom of his hosts, the Griffithses. After recounting the recent story of the formation of Inter-Varsity and similar groups in Canada, he gathered the assembled students in prayer to wait upon the Lord for guidance as to what they should do next. The group prayed for the remainder of the day, which McCracken remembers as "an extraordinary day of prayer."[236] By the end of the month, members of the Medical Branch voted to secede from the SCU and formed their own Evangelical Union with a new constitution and doctrinal basis. Thus, the Melbourne EU was birthed in prayer.

The Griffithses went on to serve as medical missionaries with CMS in the Middle East. Leslie and his son Ian were killed by bandits in Iran in 1942. Phyllis Griffiths returned to Melbourne, where she continued to play a leading role in CMS and at St. Hilary's Kew. McCracken himself emerged as a key leader in the student movement and at least ten other evangelical societies. It was through his organization and chairmanship of the first Australia-wide Inter-Varsity conference at Katoomba in 1936 that the national structure of the Australian Fellowship of Evangelical Students was formed.[237]

The Mission of St. James and St. John

Demographic changes, in particular the decline of inner-city parishes in the early part of the twentieth century, also played their part in releasing evangelical resources for activism in the social justice arena. In 1919, by act of Synod, the Mission of St. James and St. John (MSJSJ) was formed from the evangelical parishes of St. James and St. John's La Trobe Street that had begun to suffer from the movement of residents out of the area. It was initially an evangelistic mission, focused on the few remaining residential areas at the western end of the city proper.

234. Piggin, "Challenging but Glorious Heritage."
235. Piggin, "Challenging but Glorious Heritage," 2.
236. Angus, *Decisive Years*, 3.
237. Angus, *Decisive Years*, 6. See also an autobiography published posthumously from collected materials by McCracken's family: McCracken, *Summing Up:*.

The first missioner was Archdeacon William Hindley, soon followed by the Reverend Ainslie Yeates, who had come from Sydney to take the post. Yeates busied himself with the work of visiting the poor, speaking pastorally and evangelistically in factories and workshops, and running services at St. John's La Trobe Street, such as the Men's Hour series in 1922 where he addressed "Modern Objections to the Bible."[238] By 1923, the *Messenger* was able to report that there were some eighteen to twenty factories in the city where permission for regular addresses had been given to Yeates. The article also reported a particular interest in Christian Healing Missions—a reflection of the social needs of the day.[239]

The evangelical George Lamble was appointed missioner in 1925 and held the post till 1939. Lamble transformed the Mission into an important welfare agency and a kind of society in its own right, expanding its ministry sphere to the entire state. The Mission was recognizably evangelical and supported as such by evangelical parishes, which made up its main base of human resources. Lamble channeled this support into the organizing, founding, and administration of a remarkable number of ministries, including eight children's homes for orphans and other neglected children.

Homes were opened to facilitate ministry to children of all ages: infants went to the Arms of Jesus Babies' Home in East Melbourne (opened 1925 near St. Hilda's Training Home); toddlers went to the Andrew Kerr Memorial Holiday Home for Children at Mornington or to Ramoth at Ferntree Gully (1927) before St. Luke's Toddlers' Home in Bendigo opened in 1932 on the premises of the old Langley Hall theological college; older children went to St. Nicholas' home for boys and St. Agnes' home for girls in Glenroy (1926). Delinquent boys went to St. Paul's Training School for Boys at Newhaven, Philip Island (1926).

In an era when there was little government welfare, the Mission was dynamic and responsive to change. The East Melbourne babies' home was sold and re-established as the larger and more up-to-date St. Gabriel's babies' home in Balwyn (1935). The Kedesh Unmarried Mothers' Home in Carlton was opened in 1926 to address the needs of that group, but itself necessitated the opening of two homes with clinics for women with venereal disease. These were later combined at Fairfield as the Fairhaven VD Clinic in 1927.

Lamble also recruited women workers for the ministry of the Mission, encouraging and utilizing deaconesses and laywomen, most notably

---

238. Cole, *Commissioned to Care*; Monk and O'Donoghue, *Billylids And "Home Kids*," 8.

239. COEM, 26 April 1923. Cited and reproduced as facsimile at ibid.

the able and long-serving Head Deaconess, Minna Johnson.[240] Johnson had been raised in Melbourne but trained in Sydney's Deaconess Institution. She served in the inner-city parish of Ultimo before being recalled by Archbishop Lees to Melbourne to become principal of St. Hilda's Training Home for women missionary candidates. She performed this role in conjunction with her work at the Mission between 1927 and 1933, when she resigned from St. Hilda's. Lamble and Johnson organized the Mission's Leagues of Mission Helpers, which was a society for interested laywomen. Begun in 1926 at Caulfield, it grew to at least 5,000 members by 1934.[241]

From its evangelical parish foundations, the Mission developed into a highly significant welfare agency with substantial resources and expertise. It was easily the largest and most substantial of the three agencies that merged to form Anglicare in 1997. The MSJSJ was recognizably evangelical, well supported by evangelical parishes, and the prime twentieth-century example of evangelical activism expressed in social mission.[242]

In the 1930s, societies like the CMS LOY and MUEU were founded by evangelicals to give outlet to their passion for mission and evangelism. While the MSJSJ provided a focus for evangelicals on the home mission and social welfare front, the LOY and MUEU engaged the younger generation of the day in evangelism and world mission. They also provided the context in which training in evangelism and ministry occurred for younger evangelicals. Critically, they gave younger leaders opportunities to exercise their gifts and grow in confidence. These societies effectively provided a ministry outlet to evangelical youth when the parishes were failing to do so. Although both CMS LOY and MUEU started in a small way, the former quickly became the de facto youth ministry of the diocese and the main channel of evangelical activism. MUEU remained small and under pressure for decades, until late in the twentieth century. Both societies were constitutionally and persistently evangelical and proved able to reinvigorate evangelical passion for proclaiming the gospel. Along with the Upwey Convention, which their members supported with enthusiasm, these societies were the contexts in

---

240. See ADEB entry.

241. Cole, *Commissioned to Care*; Monk and O'Donoghue, *Billylids And "Home Kids,"* 10.

242. See Cole, *Commissioned to Care*; Monk and O'Donoghue, *Billylids And "Home Kids."* The relationship between evangelical social action and evangelical commitment to conversionist ministries is another important theme yet to be adequately investigated. The history of the late twentieth-century demise of the evangelical connection to welfare agencies in the diocese is another important narrative yet to be adequately described and analyzed.

which evangelicalism was nurtured, strengthened, and transmitted to subsequent generations of the movement's leaders.

Ironically, it was the ejection of C. H. Nash from the Anglican ministry that led to his emergence as the pre-eminent evangelical leader in Melbourne for the first half of the twentieth century. Nash later re-entered the Anglican ministry, but it was his influence through the LOY, the Upwey Convention, and the Melbourne Bible Institute that was of greatest effect for evangelicalism's strength and future vitality. In each of these pursuits, he was supported by Anglican laymen—especially Edwin Lee Neil, Horace Hannah, and James Griffiths. Nash was the single most influential clergyman among the younger evangelicals, who looked up to him as a father figure.

Nash's estrangement from the denomination was also mirrored in the experience of those he influenced, so although the LOY was instrumental in the conversion and energizing of the faith of so many young people and leaders, it also influenced them to direct their energies and attention towards the overseas mission field or to the work of interdenominational societies. Few saw engagement with the local church or parish as an inspiring option. Eventually this gradual redirection of leadership talent away from local church ministry to overseas missions led to critical weakness in the parishes and, through the system of synodical representation, in evangelicals' ability to influence the outcome of archiepiscopal elections. This is turn weakened the movement's ability to secure able evangelical clergy for service in its parishes.

Conclusion

This chapter has shown that the period 1901 to 1937 was dominated by evangelicals' growing concern for world mission. This focus was evident in the life of the leading evangelical parishes of the time. The outward focus of world mission led to a decreased emphasis on the parishes' vital contribution to local evangelical continuity within the Diocese of Melbourne. However, the chapter also demonstrates that evangelical leaders of the period were not ignorant of the strategic importance of ensuring a supply of leaders for the next generation. The need to train missionaries for overseas service combined with the need to ensure continuity of evangelical clergy for local ministry, resulting in the founding of Ridley College, which served as an important focus for lay and clerical evangelical energy.

The catalyst for the dramatic step of founding a new and competing theological college in Melbourne was, this chapter has argued, the loss of the vital contribution of a supportive diocesan bishop. Henry Lowther Clarke's policy of centralizing theological formation pleased neither evangelicals nor Trinity College's warden, Alexander Leeper. Clarke's lack of support for evangelicals and perceived persecution of one of their key leaders, C. H. Nash, further cemented the resolve to found an evangelical college. The encouragement of two provincial bishops, Pain and Langley, who were willing to lend their wholehearted support and leadership ability to the project, was critical. This chapter also provides evidence of the lasting influence of Charles Perry, specifically in the constitutional arrangements for the college, in the presence of a strong body of missionary-minded men, and in the desire for a college closely associated with the university.

However, the previous lack of the vital contribution of a firmly evangelical theological college was already being felt in Melbourne. The evangelical character of any given parish was deeply affected by the theology and ministry of its vicar. The chapter has demonstrated that where a subsequent vicar's theology differed, the parish's character changed, removing its vital contribution to the evangelical movement as a whole in the diocese. Even with Ridley's founding, there was a serious deficiency in the supply of theologically able evangelical leaders for the present and future.

The chapter argues that the activity of the evangelical societies—in particular the CMS LOY and the MUEU—in gathering up young energy, enthusiasm, talent, and leadership and directing these towards overseas mission, was a critical development. This meant that the vital contribution of the evangelical societies towards renewing the ranks of leadership for local parishes was relatively diminished, as the most vibrant and able leaders went overseas with CMS. The critical connection between the societies' function of gathering and encouraging young people towards evangelical ministry, and those younger leaders viewing local parishes of the diocese as a good or inspiring option for exercising their life's work, was missing or weakened. Hence, despite the many positive reflex benefits of sending out missionaries that accrued to the home churches, this chapter argues that the long-term impact on the diocese was the loss of potentially excellent vicars for local parishes. All evangelism and mission, all evangelical activism directed towards the purposes of evangelical conversionism, involves a degree of cross-cultural engagement—even when the cultures to be bridged are "non-convert" and "converted to Christ" within the same ethnic, linguistic, and suburban context. To the extent that an ability to engage the unconverted with the claims of the gospel was key to an evangelical parish's long-term success or failure, the loss of its most energetic, able, committed, and evangelistically minded ministry leaders of the future was a serious one.

This chapter reveals that two important themes in Melbourne Anglican evangelicalism emerged during the period 1901 to 1937. First, evangelicals' commitment to overseas mission was a powerful identity marker and focus of activity. The roll call of Ridley's founders reveals a list of men, lay and clerical, with strong links to the CMA and a vital interest in mission. Mission was also the key concern behind two societies founded in this period: the CMS LOY and the MUEU. The vitality of these societies ensured a future supply of able leaders, the great majority of whom went to Ridley for training before deployment to the overseas mission field.

Second, the rise of liberal evangelicalism internationally had a powerful influence on Australian and Melbourne evangelicals. It affected the fledgling Ridley College, which survived and grew initially because of the store of evangelical heritage still within the diocese and province. The support of the bishops of Bendigo and Gippsland was vital in the initial period, before the college became a major supplier of clergy to Melbourne itself. The college's liberal emphasis under Aickin and Wade meant that, although notionally evangelical, its students had a minimal impact on growing evangelical parishes due to the weakening of its emphasis on evangelical biblicism, crucicentrism, and conversionism. The conversionist ministry practitioners, with a clear emphasis on the crucicentrism of classic evangelicalism, were those who had been largely formed by the CMS LOY or MUEU, and who had left for overseas mission work. Although constitutionally evangelical and Reformed, the college's future position as a vital contributor to evangelicalism in the diocese seemed hardly secure until the appointment of the saintly, personally converted, and firmly evangelical Donald Baker in 1937.[243]

---

243. Baker asserted the reality and importance of the conversion experience in a talk given in St. Paul's Cathedral in 1943. It was subsequently published: Baker, *Reality of Conversion*. Two previous editions were published by S. John Bacon.

Conclusion

> Remember your leaders, who spoke the word of God to you
> Consider the outcome of their way of life and imitate their faith.
> Jesus Christ is the same yesterday, today and forever.
>
> HEBREWS 13:7-8

THIS RESEARCH HAS AIMED to describe the history of evangelicalism in the Anglican Diocese of Melbourne for the period 1847 to 1937. It has been primarily interested in the question of evangelical continuity, and in the reasons for evangelical persistence within the diocese. The historical analysis shows that at no point in the period of study have evangelicals in the Church of England in Melbourne enjoyed the presence of all four vital contributors below in support of the movement:

1. vibrant and vital evangelical parishes;
2. vibrant and vital evangelical societies focused on mission and evangelism;
3. a strong Anglican evangelical theological college; and
4. a diocesan bishop willing to promote and support leading evangelicals and their causes.

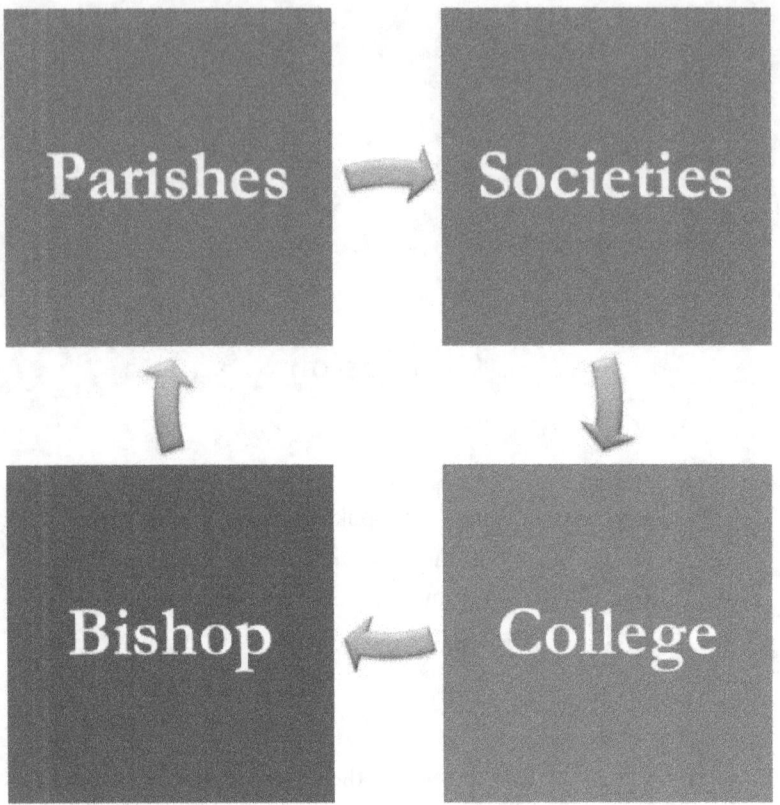

Four Vital Contributors to Growing Evangelicalism in a Diocese

The history of evangelicalism in the Diocese of Melbourne is one that underscores the significance of the four vital contributors outlined above. The history also emphasizes the significance of the circular flow of relationships in the diagram above, for each vital contributor has interrelated with the others in a particular way to strengthen or weaken the evangelical movement within the denomination as a whole.

The literature review in chapter 1 shows that no comprehensive description of Melbourne Anglican evangelicalism has been attempted prior to this research. Existing Australian historiography has either focused specifically on particular individuals, parishes, or agencies, or more broadly on the Anglican denomination as a whole.

Bishop

A main finding of this research is that the founding influence and vital contribution of Charles Perry should not be underestimated. In the founding period, 1847 to 1874, Charles Perry's dominance over the diocese exemplified the action of a diocesan bishop in not only promoting, but personifying, the evangelical cause. Chapters 3 and 4 demonstrate that Perry's achievement was to lay down a deep and firm evangelical foundation in the diocese, which was then coterminous with the present-day province of Victoria. Critically, Perry understood and made the vital contribution by a diocesan bishop of selecting, appointing, and promoting evangelical leaders within his diocese. Perry's firmly evangelical and highly principled views on clergy selection meant that during his episcopate evangelical parishes were able to grow, thrive, and become centers of evangelical activity. However, his commitment to pastoral care of all his clergy, even after their views had changed, meant that seeds for future diversity were planted in his episcopate.

Chapter 4 shows that Perry's administrative leadership, which fostered a degree of lay independence from absolute episcopal control, ensured that evangelicalism could persist in key parishes, so long as their laity were determined to insist on the appointment of a succession of able evangelical vicars. Hence, Perry's vital contribution as a diocesan bishop extended beyond being merely supportive of evangelical ministry. He created structures that made evangelical continuity possible in local parishes even when the later diocesan bishops were unsupportive. His strategic leadership and principled policy decisions still have an impact on the life of the present-day diocese and underscore the significance of robust and effective episcopal leadership.

Robust episcopal leadership of another sort followed in James Moorhouse. Chapter 5 demonstrates that Moorhouse's broad church views and social engagement agenda meant a loss of the vital contribution of a supportive diocesan bishop. Evangelical leaders were no longer supported or advanced through the ranks of the diocese, as Moorhouse focused his ministry energies in areas other than clergy selection, management, and care. His successor, Field Flowers Goe, though personally evangelical, was a weak leader who did not make the vital contribution that evangelicals wished from him. Their support—and angst—was expressed through the *Victorian Churchman*.

Chapter 6 demonstrates that the opposite of a vital contribution was made by Goe's successor, Henry Lowther Clarke. Clarke's centrist agenda and antipathy towards evangelicals, and particularly towards their key leader, Clifford Harris Nash, were the catalysts for a strong response.

Evangelicals, boosted by the support and encouragement of two evangelical diocesan bishops, Arthur Pain in Gippsland and John Douse Langley in Bendigo, acted to establish and ensure the long-missing final vital contribution of a strong evangelical Anglican theological college.

Parishes

This research demonstrates that, critically, except for a period in its earliest history, the diocese between 1847 and 1937 was never without strong evangelical parishes. Parishes, especially those with a sustained period of evangelical leadership from either one or a succession of vicars, have proved to be the main source of evangelicalism's resilience—even as the CMS has proved to be its main source of vitality.

Chapter 4 shows that in the foundation period of the diocese, energetic evangelical leadership focused on building parishes and schools. Church planting following the expanding population was a high priority, as was the kind of social engagement exemplified by Charles Perks of St. Stephen's Richmond. Leading evangelical laity and their families, such as those of Jonathan Binns Were and James Wilberforce Stephens in Brighton, made substantial contributions in this period of growth and establishment.

Chapters 5 and 6 show that much of this resilience emerged out of the context of long-standing partnerships between lay leaders and either a long incumbency, such as W. T. C. Storrs's at St. Matthew's Prahran, or a long succession of evangelical incumbencies, such as at St. Columb's Hawthorn. These lengthy partnerships enabled the formation of a lasting evangelical ethos and ministry able to engage with the local community across the age groups and both genders. Such parishes were centers of evangelistic activity and evangelical activism in their local settings—they were vibrant and vital places. They were also invariably supporters of overseas mission through the CMS, and hence closely linked to another vital contributor to Melbourne evangelicalism. Chapter 6 demonstrates that evangelical parishes rallied around the newly founded Ridley College, providing it with substantial financial and prayer support.

Chapters 5 and 6 also show that parishes were places where young people could be drawn to faith in Christ, converted, and encouraged to offer for future missionary or ordained ministry. Key parishes such as St. Hilary's East Kew, St. Matthew's Prahran, and St. Mary's Caulfield were especially effective in making this vital contribution to evangelical continuity. The ministries of John Christian MacCullagh in the Diocese of Bendigo and of Digby Berry while at Holy Trinity Melbourne, both of whom trained and mentored young clergy and encouraged young men to offer for Christian service, were also highly significant.

Societies

This research demonstrates that the vital contribution of the evangelical societies is complex. On the one hand, societies were important focal points and outlets for evangelical energy and allowed for a degree of evangelical independence from diocesan and ministerial control. Particular aims, such as Bible publication and dissemination, could be focused on, and new and untried methods of ministry and evangelism could be tried. The vital contribution of training future leaders with a sharp focus on evangelism could be made. On the other hand, such training, focus, and freedom meant that evangelicals who were trained and encouraged in the context of societies could find the prospect of parish ministry less appealing than missionary pursuits or more sharply focused evangelistic endeavors.

Chapters 3 and 4 demonstrate the importance of the CMS link to Perry's appointment and the immediate energy for the work of missions and Bible societies among early Melbourne evangelicals. Chapter 6 shows that evangelical societies were an important outlet for evangelicals' missionary enthusiasm. Societies like the CSSM gave rise to new missionary endeavors and new structures for evangelical ministry, such as the Scripture Union, among local children and young people. The CSSM modeled a way of engaging children and youth and encouraging Scripture reading in connection with vital parish life. These ministry skills were funneled back into the parishes and contributed to evangelical continuity in the diocese through children's work. However, few candidates for future ordained ministry emerged from the CSSM work.

Chapter 6 demonstrates the complexity of the relationship between the societies and the parishes. Societies such as the MSJSJ showed that there was still a significant reservoir of evangelical energy in the diocese willing to work to address social needs. The CMS LOY proved to be an effective ministry to young adults, converting and equipping significant numbers of the most enthusiastic believers of successive generations for evangelistic ministry and filling them with a passion for overseas mission work. The continuing link between these young leaders and their home parishes served to keep local evangelicals connected to overseas missions work, highlighting the need to engage in local evangelism and mission. There were many reflex benefits from sending out the "brightest and best" to the overseas mission field. Yet the chapter shows that this dynamic also served to funnel much needed talent and energy away from local parish ministry, especially the increasingly challenging and cross-cultural work of engaging Australians in a rapidly changing social context with the eternal claims of the unchanging gospel. The departure of the most mission-minded and evangelistically effective leaders to overseas fields thus weakened evangelicalism's prospects of continuity and growth within the denomination as a whole. The chapter shows that CMS LOY alumni who went on to Ridley may not have been affected by the increasingly liberal theological trends there, but neither were most of them committed to a Melbourne-based ministry. Instead, their energies went largely to East Africa, constituting a kind of brain and talent drain out of the diocese.

The weakness of the nexus between these two vital contributors, parishes and societies, was a critical one. The characteristic of societies, as parachurch sodalities, of narrow focus on particular activities and demographic groups, meant that they functioned well to energize younger evangelicals, but less well to convince many that leadership of a local church was a good and worthwhile long-term ministry option. The vital contribution of the societies, that of generating numbers of young leaders who would then go on to the college to train for ordained ministry in the diocese, was not sufficiently strong. This was an important impediment to evangelical continuity and substantial future growth.

College

The vital contribution of a firmly evangelical and Anglican theological college, able to train and form men for ordained ministry within the diocese, was recognized from an early stage in the diocese's history. Chapter 4 shows that Perry understood this vital contribution and supported the training provided by Moore College, preferring to rely on an evangelical college rather than prematurely founding a theological college in Melbourne. Chapter 5 shows that the theological school at Trinity College Melbourne, opened by Moorhouse, did not make the vital contribution of a strongly evangelical Anglican theological college. University-level education of a generalized or broad theological kind was insufficient to train and ensure evangelical leadership for the future.

Chapter 6 argues that Ridley College's foundation on firmly evangelical and Anglican principles was an attempt to establish a key plank in the strategy for evangelical continuity and growth in Melbourne. The circumstances and details of its founding indicated that Perry's legacy was still strong in the diocese and its evangelical leaders. The early support it enjoyed from a wide range of parishes indicated that a strong reservoir of evangelical faith was still present in the diocese.

Chapter 6 also shows that, despite growth in student numbers and relatively solid financial support, the appointment of liberal evangelicals as principals matched poorly with the founders' aims and aspirations, threatening the vital contribution that Ridley was founded to make to evangelical continuity in Melbourne. However, the presence of such a college meant that the fourth vital contributor to the movement was at least in notionally place and could be built on by the appointment of a principal who better embodied evangelicalism's biblicism, crucicentrism, conversionism, and activism. Such a principal arrived in 1937 in the person of Donald Baker.

Conclusion

The analysis above goes some way to explaining why Melbourne, unlike the Diocese of Sydney, did not develop from its evangelical foundations to become a firm and perhaps monochromatic evangelical diocese. Without all four vital contributors strongly and simultaneously present for a sustained period, evangelicalism could not establish itself more robustly in Melbourne, and the movement could not gain the necessary intergenerational momentum for growth.

However, the analysis also shows how evangelicalism nevertheless managed to persist and grow because there was sufficient strength in at least two out of the four vital contributors in every period of the history surveyed. Hence, despite weakness in two of the other vital contributors, the movement was able to preserve and generate enough vitality to ensure a degree of continuity. Melbourne, unlike the dioceses of Adelaide or Ballarat or any number of other Australian dioceses, did not move in the opposite theological direction towards a largely high-church, theologically liberal culture. This finding, that two out of the four vital contributors is sufficient to ensure persistence and continuity but not substantial growth, may be applicable to other religious movements in denominational settings. The corollary, that the presence of four out of four vital contributors is the key to sustained long-term growth of a movement, may be equally applicable.

Evangelicalism in the Anglican Diocese of Melbourne between 1847 to 1937 persisted as a result of the presence of two out of four vital contributors throughout the period. Parishes and societies may have represented evangelicalism's resilience and vitality in the period of this study, but the long term continuity and growth of the movement within the diocese was ultimately dependent on two further vital contributions: that of a bishop willing, not just to license and appoint evangelical clergy to parishes, but to make strategic long-term decisions for the advancement of evangelism and overtly evangelical ministries in the diocese, and that of a distinctly evangelical theological college able to produce clergy and workers equipped to translate the claims of the eternal *evangel* for each successive generation and culture through all of the shifts in prevailing philosophy.

Local churches doing local evangelistic ministry, societies able to harness and focus youthful energy and enthusiasm, an evangelical college able to take and train and form leaders for local church ministry in the future, and a bishop or denominational authority willing to support and appoint such leaders into local churches: these are the four vital contributors that explain the long-term persistence, growth, and strengthening of a religious tradition such as evangelicalism within a denominational setting. To the extent that they were present in a period of history of the Anglican Diocese of Melbourne, evangelicalism within it was able to grow in vitality and strength.

Epilogue

> Pay careful attention, then, to how you live
> —not as unwise people but as wise—
> making the most of the time . . .
>
> EPHESIANS 5:15-16A

WHY IS THIS HISTORY and this sort of historical examination of ongoing importance? In the few years since this study was originally completed, two factors have kept highlighting this work's relevance.

Fierce conflict

First, present day evangelicalism—and particularly Anglican evangelicalism—finds itself in fierce conflict with more liberal theological movements within its denominations, to say nothing of conflict with the world. The question of evangelical persistence goes to the question of how evangelicalism might navigate and survive these conflicts.

The numerical rise of the Global South, those Anglican Provinces from the Majority world with largely conservative and evangelical theologies, has created tension within the Anglican Communion which remains dominated, in a structural and political sense, by Minority world dioceses such as those of Canterbury and York, the Episcopal Church of the United States (ECU-SA), Canada and Australia. The theological trajectory of entire dioceses is a matter of passionate interest and debate, as measured in markers such as attitudes to human sexuality and women in ordained leadership.

ECUSA's action in consecrating Gene Robinson in 2003 and the recent Scottish Episcopal Church's (SEC's) endorsement of same-sex marriage in 2017 are but two examples of decisions heightening conflict within Anglicanism. Similar changes are underway in Canada and New Zealand and the Anglican Church of Southern Africa (ACSA), which covers South Africa, Mozambique, Namibia, Lesotho, Swaziland, and Angola. Advocates of the legitimising of same-sex activity and marriage by the Church pursued and are pursuing their cause with vigor. In some North American dioceses, this has included a willingness to eject evangelical congregations that conscientiously object to changes imposed by their canons or synods. The forcing of evangelical congregations through the courts is an indicator of the ferocity of the conflict and a sign that the legitimacy of local parishes within a diocese is viewed as a vital contested space.[1] For, as this study has argued, healthy evangelical local churches are key to evangelical persistence.

Evangelicals and their allies responded by gathering and strengthening behind the Global Anglican Future Conference (GAFCON) movement. Meeting for the first time in 2008, GAFCON issued a Jerusalem Statement and Declaration[2] and founded a global Fellowship of Confessing Anglicans (FCA) of those who would unite around the theological basis outlined in the Declaration. In 2017, in response to actions by the SEC mentioned above, the GAFCON Primates consecrated Canon Andy Lines of Crosslinks (formerly BCMS) a missionary bishop for Europe, including Scotland.[3] Similar responses and actions are likely in other places within the Communion. Episcopal oversight and leadership—including the key function of licencing approved clergy to local parishes—is recognised as a vital contributor to the future of the movement.

The significance of the theological college and theological education has also been a key focus. For example, at GAFCON gatherings in Jerusalem 2008, Nairobi 2013 and Jerusalem 2018 network groups focussed on those involved in theological education were convened. These were partly

---

1. See for example an account of the Diocese of Virginia's action against The Falls Church in J. B. Simmons, *The Awakening of Washington's Church: How a Church Lost Everything and Gained What Matters Most*. Washington: J. B. Simmons, 2016.

2. See http://www.gafcon.org—last accessed 23 July 2017.

3. The Australian Anglican Primate, Archbishop Freier of Melbourne responded with a Primatial letter, http://www.anglicanprimate.org.au/2017/07/03/letter-to-australias-bishops/ which referenced two other letters from the diocesans of Sydney and Tasmania, Archbishop Davies and Bishop Condie, who both participated in Lines' consecration against their Primate's advice. Last accessed Sunday 23 July 2017.

in response to the knowledge that resources from the well-endowed ECUSA network have been flowing into African seminaries, along with their attendant forms of theology. A similar story is being played out in a range of Anglican theological colleges in other parts of the Majority world.

Of the four contributors in this study, only the place and function of evangelical societies is missing or marginalised in the discourse of the present day. The history of the CMS in Victoria has shown that its leaders were key responders to the threats against evangelicalism in Melbourne. Its members were—perhaps appropriately—more focussed on the local and overseas evangelistic mission work they were called to do.

Perhaps what this study indicates is that there needs to be greater attention paid to the creative energy found in evangelical societies, and more reflection on how that energy works with or works apart from the other contributors in the evangelical movement. The aspirations of so many evangelicals—especially the more numerous laity—have been and continue to be better suited to energetic expression within societies rather than parishes. Freedom from ecclesiastical politics, permission to experiment, and a sharp focus on evangelistic ends remain a potent force for evangelical health and persistence.

What this study certainly underscores is the ongoing significance of the health of local congregations for the persistence of evangelicalism as a movement. Where local churches cease engaging in creative and effective evangelism that is borne out of a passionate adherence to biblical teaching, evangelicalism's spiritual energy is diminished and gradually the movement dies.

Institutions matter in the long-term

Second, irrespective of the future of Anglican evangelicalism within any particular diocese, the themes of this study potentially apply more widely to the persistence of evangelicalism within any denominational or institutional setting.

Deep in the heart of the contemporary evangelical believer, is a strong individualistic streak borne of a faith that is deeply personal, whose entry point has typically been a rigorously personal declaration of faith towards Christ as 'personal Lord and Saviour', and rejection of sin, the world and the devil. For such a faith, thinking about the wider institution does not always come naturally. In some more pietistic quarters, all politics and especially church politics are inherently distasteful.

Yet, gospel movements, if successful in winning converts and growing churches, will eventually institutionalize and coalesce into some form of larger organizational form and structure. The tiny corner milk bar or grocery store, if successful, over time may grow into a chain of stores all over a country. Church plants from the many evangelical church planting movements that have sprung up internationally in recent years, if successful, will institutionalize.

Over time, what may have begun as a creative, fleet-footed, responsive-to-context movement inevitably settles into liturgical and operational patterns. Traditions form and processes for the most efficient or consistent way of doing things tend to emerge over the passage of time. At some point in the future—barring the demise or unhealthy stagnation of a movement—the question won't be, 'Will we institutionalize?' but rather, 'What kind of institution are we?' For evangelicals, the question ought to be, 'How will this denomination keep serving gospel ends by using gospel means?'

How will an original evangelical impetus translate into evangelical momentum? How will it be sustained? This study suggests four contributors to keep in mind. It also suggests that inattention to one or more of the four may lead in time to critical weaknesses developing that will spell the end of the movement.

For example, what happens within a denomination when its main training college takes a particular path away from evangelical confidence in the authority of the Scriptures? It will not impact the denomination overnight, but will surely over time as the graduates of the college begin to fill positions of senior leadership.

The corporate world has a leadership maxim: 'The fish rots from the head'. Biologically inaccurate, since fish usually rot from the gut, as any fishmonger will tell you. But metaphorically correct: leadership matters and leaders matter, whether that leader is known as a bishop, moderator or chair. What happens to evangelicalism when a critical leadership position is filled by a person not entirely sympathetic to evangelical priorities? There is a plethora of local churches with stories of disaster experienced in this area.

What critical weaknesses may this study be calling out among present day evangelical denominations and movements? Perhaps, again, it is that lack of attention to the place of evangelical societies within the social, economic and even political fabric of the movement. The problem with societies is that they can be hidden in plain sight from those who are disinterested. Until interrogated, their energy and vital contribution to the whole remains invisible and unaccounted for. If invisible, undervalued and marginalised, evangelical societies' vital contribution may not be missed until it is too late for the movement as a whole.

Would evangelicalism be alive and well today without the powerful influence of the Keswick Convention movement? Without Katoomba in Sydney, Upwey—later Belgrave Heights—in Melbourne, Mount Tamborine in Queensland; and the mirroring of these conventions by the various CMS Summer School conferences? Would Australian evangelicalism have persisted through the twentieth-century without the CSSM or Scripture Union, Crusaders, the CMS League of Youth, and the various AFES university student groups? These are questions worth asking.

Such movements bred networks of evangelicals who learnt to cooperate across denominational lines, focussing on chosen ends—world mission, children's or youth or student ministry, the provision of bibles and literature. The reflex benefits of those relationships and gathered expertise for particular denominations has been significant, but the role of societies in forming these networks, indeed 'societies of men and women', has been undervalued and too little understood.[4] I hope this study has issued a small corrective and a call to arms for further investigations. I sense a rich harvest of encouragement for the willing.

It would of course be a mistake for present generations to lose their focus on the identity of the local church as the basic unit of organisation of the kingdom of God. Every individual who comes to faith in Christ has to belong to a local congregation. Local churches are the basic context in which biblical instruction is delivered, evangelism is organized, disciples are nurtured. Evangelicalism's health is inextricably linked to the health of evangelical local churches, and the movement's persistence in Melbourne has much to do with the unbroken continuity of strongly evangelical congregations throughout the city's history. The faithfulness and creativity in evangelism of the generations of evangelical people that those churches represent is worthy of further careful research.[5] The same priorities are critical in each new generation of evangelical faith. For their persistence, and for each of the vital contributors we have had the privilege of investigating in the course of this study, we are thankful to God.

---

4. A recent major study of the wide and deep impact of evangelicalism and evangelical networks on Australian society is this magnum opus from these two doyens of Australian evangelical historiography: Stuart Piggin and Robert D. Linder's *The Fountain of Public Prosperity: Evangelical Christians in Australian History 1740-1914*. Monash University Publishing, 2018.

5. See for example, Elizabeth Willis, *People of the Risen King: A History of St Jude's Carlton 1866-2016*. St Jude's Anglican Church, 2017. Authored by a professional social historian, it is an exemplary recent history of one of contemporary Melbourne's leading evangelical parishes.

Appendix I

Charles Perry's Letter to the Clergy with Regard to the Use of Music in Services, Reproduced in the *Messenger*, July 1857

This letter is reproduced here as an example of Perry's exercise of episcopal authority and discipline. The controversy over church music has been used to characterize Perry as dour and colorless. However, the text of this circular letter or *ad clerum* reveals clarity of argument and the principled objection that Perry raised. It also reveals his determination to govern as a bishop for all the dioceses, not just for evangelicals who agreed with his views.

> The following Circular Letter has been forwarded, to each Clergyman in the Diocese of Melbourne;—
>
> Bishopscourt, June 23rd, 1857.
>
> Reverend and Dear Sir,
>
> Since my return from England, my attention has been called to some practices, which were introduced during my absence, in the mode of conducting Divine Service in a few of the Churches and licensed Places of Worship in the Diocese. But, although requested to do so, I was reluctant to interfere, except in the way of private advice: first, because I do not regard an absolute uniformity in all particulars as at all essential to the wellbeing of the Church, and some variety (provided the spiritual character of the service is not affected by it,) may be considered as justified by custom; and second, because I am very unwilling to recognise, and thus perhaps promote among the members

of the Church, both clerical and lay, a division of opinion and feeling upon matters of ritual.

The increase, however, of these practices, and the difficulty which some of the Clergy have felt in putting a stop to them, have determined me at length to exercise the authority given to me in the Preface to the Book of Common Prayer, and "take order" concerning them.

There are two to which I particularly allude: viz., the intoning of the service, or parts of the service, such as the responses and particularly the *Amen* at the close of every prayer; and the chaunting of the responses after the Commandments. The use of these practices at Cathedrals and Collegiate Chapels in England has naturally led some of the Clergy, either in compliance with the wish of their choirs, or from their own taste, to adopt them: but they are altogether unauthorised by the Rubric; they give offence to many of our people, and cause them to absent themselves from our services; and they are, in my opinion, wholly unsuitable for ordinary congregational worship.

I would therefore request you, if these, or either of these practices have been adopted in the Church or licensed Place of Worship in your parish, immediately to discontinue them, and to require the choir (for whom, as being under his, control, a minister is responsible,) to discontinue them also.

There is another custom, which, although very common in England, is equally unauthorised by the Rubric, and is, I think, undesirable to be retained here–: viz., the introduction of the words, "Glory be to Thee, O Lord," after the Minister has given out the gospel for the day. The insertion of any words into the service is as much an infringement of the prescribed order, as the alteration or omission of any; and I would, therefore, wish this practice also to be discontinued.

You will understand that I am quite willing to bear the responsibility of exercising the authority, given me as abovementioned in this matter. But, in complying with my directions, you may either refer or not to this letter, as you shall judge to be most expedient for the maintenance of peace and quietness in your parish.

Praying that God will make you approve yourself in all particulars an able minister of the New Testament, and will give you many of your people to be your joy and crown of rejoicing in the presence of the Lord Jesus Christ at His coming.

I remain,
Reverend and Dear Sir,
Your faithful Brother in Christ,

C. MELBOURNE.

Appendix II

Interview Question Guide and Checklist

Personal Questions

Tell me about your conversion experience – did you have one? When were you convinced that you were a Christian believer?

What can you tell me about your devotional life? (Both what you think it should be, and what it actually is.)

Definition and Identity

How was evangelicalism defined in your time? Did this definition change? In what ways?

Who was "in" or "out" and on what basis? Did people transition in and out? Of their own volition, or by others' determination?

General Description

How would you describe the evangelical movement in your time?

What are your reflections on the evangelical movement as you've experienced it through the years?

What kind of involvement, impact, or influence did evangelicals have on the life of the Diocese of Melbourne? . . . of the city of Melbourne? . . . rest of society? How were they regarded?

How did you regard the future of the evangelical movement?

What observations do you have today about evangelicalism in the Diocese of Melbourne?

Leaders and Personalities

Who were some of the significant leaders of evangelical movement (not just Anglican) in your time?

Was the movement clergy or lay driven? Or a combination? Or was this simply not an issue?

Key Issues

What were the key issues facing evangelicals? What were their key concerns?

What preoccupied most of your time in ministry?

What were the key factors affecting the health of evangelical parishes?

What were some successes in evangelical ministry? What were some failures?

Networks

What were the key groupings of evangelicals (not just Anglican evangelicals) in Melbourne?

What were the significant groups or organizations in your time? (SU, League of Youth, Crusaders, Upwey Convention)

What was the significance of EFAC or the Anglican Evangelical Fellowship of Victoria?

What was the connection between evangelicals and other groups or networks? (Freemasons, Evangelical Alliance, Baptists, English evangelicals?)

Special Interest Issues

What was the role of women, indigenous Australians, migrants, non-Anglo-Celtic peoples in the evangelical movement?

What was evangelism like?

Summary Sentence

How would you summarize in a few sentences "the history of evangelicals in Melbourne" as you experienced it?

Other Contacts

Do you know of any other persons I should contact and interview in relation to this project?

Appendix III

Interviews and Conversations

Canon Dr. Peter Adam

Canon Dr. Stuart Barton Babbage

The Reverend Prof. Ian Breward

Canon Dr. Maurice Betteridge

The Reverend Dr. Edmund Keith Cole

The Reverend Prof. Graham Cole

Canon Len Abbott

Lynette Allchin

Donald Boyd

The Reverend Peter Corney

The Reverend Peter Crawford

Faye Curnow

Genevieve Cutler

Gerald Davis

Bishop James Grant

Jean Guy

Bishop John Harrower

Alan Kerr

Archbishop Sir Marcus Loane

Ian Milne

The Reverend Tom Morgan

Archdeacon Emeritus John Moroney

Canon Alan Nichols

John Olsen

The Reverend Dr. Darrell Paproth

The Reverend Mavis Payne

The Reverend Jean Penman

Henry Speagle

Bishop John Stewart

The Reverend Dr. David Williams

Bishop Dr. John Wilson

Bibliography

Primary Sources

Newspapers

Church of England Messenger
The Church Record
The Victorian Churchman
The Argus

Diocesan and Anglican Directory Records

Year Books of the Church of England in Victoria (from 1892)
Year Books of the Anglican Diocese of Melbourne
—Year Books incorporate Synod reports and sermons, and presidential addresses
Australian Anglican Directory

Unpublished MS

Macartney, Hussey Burgh. "Memoirs." 1889.

Parochial and Society Records

The Mollison Library of the Anglican Diocese of Melbourne
Archives of the Anglican Diocese of Melbourne
St. Matthew's Prahran *Church Notes* and other archival records—held in the City of Stonnington Archive Collection

St. Columb's Hawthorn archival records
Archives of the Church Missionary Society (Victoria)
Archives of the Scripture Union (Victoria)
State Library of Victoria Rare Books and Manuscripts Collections—includes Charles and Frances Perry MSS and materials from St. Stephen's Richmond, Holy Trinity Williamstown, and St. Jude's Carlton
Archives of the Evangelical Fellowship in the Anglican Communion (EFAC) Victoria—formerly the Anglican Evangelical Fellowship of Victoria
Minute Books and archival records of the Anglican Evangelical Trust of Victoria—formerly the Church of England of Victoria Evangelical Trust, held by the secretary of the trust, the Revd Neil Bach, St. Mark's Forest Hill

Published Primary Sources

Baker, Donald. *The Reality of Conversion*. Melbourne: Australia Christian Literature Society, 1974.
Correspondence between the Right Reverend the Lord Bishop of Sydney and Metropolitan and the Reverends F. T. C. Russell and P. T. Beamish, Deacons. Sydney: Kemp and Fairfax, 1849.
Head, Frederick Waldegrave. *The Fallen Stuarts*. Cambridge: Cambridge University Press, 1901.
———. *Six Great Anglicans*. 1929.
Lees, Harrington Clare. *The Divine Master in Home Life*. London: Religious Tract Society, 1918.
———. *The Eyes of His Glory*. London: Morgan & Scott, 1916.
———. *The Joy of Bible Study*. London: Longmans Green, 1910.
———. *The Promise of Life, the Life That Is in Jesus Christ*. London: Morgan & Scott, 1919.
———. *St. Paul's Friends*. London: Religious Tract Society, 1918.
———. *The Sunshine of the Good News*. London: R. Scott, 1912.
Perry, Charles. *The Bible: Its Evidences, Characteristics and Effects*. Melbourne: Stillwell and Knight, 1872.
———. *Clerical Education Considered with Especial Reference to the Universities*. Cambridge: T. Stevenson, 1841.
———. *Foundation Truths: Four Sermons Preached before the University of Cambridge*. London: Seeley, Jackson and Halliday, 1864.
———. *The Office and Duty of a Minister of the Gospel*. Melbourne, 1848.
———. "Parents and Children: A Paper Read before the Congress of the Society for the Promotion of Morality." 1870.
———. "The School & the Schoolmaster: Their Religious Character." 1860.
———. "Science and the Bible." Melbourne, 1869.

Ridley College Archives Collection Of Material Up To 1950s

Ridley College Council Minute Books.
Executive of the Ridley College Council Minute Books.

Ridley College Annual Reports.
The Ridley Collegian, 1920–1924, 1931–1932.
Coticula, 1945–1947, 1953, 1954, 1956.
The Ridley College Monthly, published monthly in 1921 only.
The Ridley Quarterly, published in 1922 only.
Labeled and annotated annual student photographs from 1910, 1914, 1916, 1920, 1922, 1928, 1931, 1932, 1935, 1937. The post-1937 collection is largely complete.

Secondary Sources

Adam, Peter. "The Founding of Ridley College." In *Proclaiming Christ: Ridley College Melbourne, 1910–2010*, edited by Peter Adam and Gina Denholm, [13–29]. Melbourne: Ridley Melbourne, 2010.

———. "Theological Education in the Diocese of Melbourne." In *Melbourne Anglicans: The Diocese of Melbourne 1847–1997*, edited by Brian Porter, 159–78. Collingwood: The Joint Board of Christian Education, 1997.

Angus, David E. *Decisive Years: Experiences of Christian University Students*. Delacombe, Vic.: D. Angus, 2005.

The Australian Anglican Directory 2007. Melbourne: Angela Grutzner, 2007.

Bach, Neil. *Leon Morris: One Man's Fight for Love and Truth*. Milton Keynes: Paternoster, 2016.

Balleine, G. R. *A History of the Evangelical Party in the Church of England*. October 1951 ed. London: Church Book Room Press Ltd, 1951.

Barrett, W. R. *History of the Church of England in Tasmania*. 1942.

Batalden, Stephen, Kathleen Cann, and John Dean, eds. *Sowing the Word: The Cultural Impact of the British and Foreign Bible Society, 1804–2004*. Sheffield: Sheffield Phoenix Press, 2006.

Bate, Weston, and Helen Penrose. *Challenging Traditions: A History of Melbourne Grammar*. Melbourne: Australian Scholarly Publishing, 2008.

Bebbington, David. W. *The Dominance of Evangelicalism: The Age of Spurgeon and Moody*, A History of Evangelicalism ; Vol. 3. Downers Grove, Ill.: InterVarsity Press, 2005.

———. *Evangelicalism in Modern Britain: A History from the 1730s to the 1980s*. London: Unwin Hyman, 1989.

———. "The Very Essence of Evangelicalism: The Islington Conference." The *Charles Perry Lecture 2009*. Ridley Melbourne, 2009.

Berry, Digby M. *The Sister Martyrs of Ku Cheng*. Melbourne: Melville, Mullen & Slade, 1895.

Binns, Leonard Elliott. *The Evangelical Movement in the English Church*. London: Methuen & Co. Ltd., 1928.

Boyd, Robin. *The Witness of the Student Christian Movement: Church Ahead of the Church*. Hindmarsh, SA: ATF Press, 2007.

Bradley, Ian. *The Call to Seriousness: The Evangelical Impact on the Victorians*. London: Jonathan Cape, 1976.

Breward, Ian. *A History of the Australian Churches*. Sydney: Allen & Unwin, 1993.

Bride, Graham and Margaret. *Proclaiming the Gospel: Anglicans in Prahran 1854–2004*. Melbourne: St. Matthew's Anglican, Prahran, 2004.

Bullock, Frederick W. B. *The History of Ridley Hall, Cambridge, Vol. 1: To the End of 1907*. 2 vols. Cambridge: Council of Ridley Hall, 1953.
Buntine, Walter Murray. *Caulfield Grammar School Jubilee 1881–1931*. Melbourne, 1931.
Cable, Kenneth, Leonie Cable, and Noel Pollard. *Cable, Cable and Pollard Index of Australian Clergy*.
Cable, Kenneth J. "The Diocese of Newcastle and Sydney." In *Colonial Tractarians: The Oxford Movement in Australia*, edited by Brian Porter and Joint Board of Christian Education, 35–48. Melbourne: Joint Board of Christian Education, 1989.
———. "Good Government in the Church." The Bishop Perry memorial lecture 1983. Melbourne, 1983.
Cameron, Marcia Helen. *An Enigmatic Life: David Broughton Knox: Father of Contemporary Sydney Anglicanism*. Brunswick East, Vic.: Acorn Press, 2006.
———. *Phenomenal Sydney: Anglicans in a Time of Change, 1945–2013*. Eugene, Oregon: Wipf & Stock, 2016.
Cannon, Michael. *The Land Boomers: The Complete Illustrated History*. Carlton: Melbourne University Press, 1995.
Carey, Hilary M., Ian Breward, Nicholas Doumanis, Ruth Frappell, David Hilliard, Katharine Massam, Anne O'Brien, and Roger Thomson. "Australian Religion Review, 1980–2000, Part 2: Christian Denominations." *The Journal of Religious History* 25 (2001) 56–82.
Carolan, Jane. *St. Columb's Hawthorn 1883–1983*. Melbourne: Vestry of St. Columb's Hawthorn, 1983.
Carson, D. A. *The Gagging of God: Christianity Confronts Pluralism*. Grand Rapids, Mich.: Zondervan Pub. House, 1996.
Challen, Michael B. *Sambell: A Man of the Word*. Melbourne: Melbourne University Press, 2008.
Chambers, David. *"Tempest-Tost": The Life and Teaching of the Rev C. H. Nash, M. A.*. Melbourne: Church Press Publications, 1959.
Christ Church Marysville: Seventieth Anniversary Souvenir, 5th January, 1982. Marysville, Vic.: Christ Church (Marysville, Vic.), 1982.
Christ Church, Geelong, Centenary: October 7th, 1843—October 7th, 1943. Geelong: Christ Church, 1943.
Church, All Saints' Anglican. *Green and Growing: 150 Years: Historical Snapshots of All Saints' Anglican Church, Greensborough*. Greensborough, Vic: All Saints' Anglican Church, 2005.
Clack, William S. *We Will Go: The History of 70 Years Training Men and Women for World Missionary Ministry*. Melbourne: Bible College of Victoria, 1990.
Clark, Albert E. *The Church of Our Fathers: Being the History of the Church of England in Gippsland, 1847–1947*. Sale, Vic.: Diocese of Gippsland, 1947.
———. *Supplement to the Church of Our Fathers*: Diocese of Gippsland, 1952.
Clark, Manning. *A History of Australia*. Vol. 4. The earth abideth for ever, 1851–1888. Carlton, Vic.: Melbourne University Press, 1979.
Clyde, Laurel A. *In a Strange Land: A History of the Anglican Diocese of Riverina*. Melbourne: Hawthorn Press, 1979.
CMS. *Lawrence of Lira: A Record of the Missionary Achievement and Joyous Service of the Rev. Canon T. L. Lawrence, ThL: Pioneer, Administrator, Teacher, Translator*. Melbourne: The Church Missionary Society, 1943.

Cole, Edmund Keith. *Commissioned to Care: the Golden Jubilee History of the Mission of St. James and St. John 1919–1969*. North Melbourne: Ruskin Press, 1969.

———. *A History of All Saints' Church, Bendigo: The Rise and Demise of a Cathedral Church*. Bendigo, Vic.: Keith Cole Publications, 1990.

———. *A History of Christ Church, Echuca (1865–1990): Faithful Witness for 125 Years*. Bendigo, Vic.: Keith Cole Publications, 1990.

———. *A History of Holy Trinity, Bendigo: A Spiritual Home*. Bendigo, Vic.: Keith Cole Publications, 1990.

———. *A History of the Church Missionary Society of Australia*. Melbourne: Church Missionary Historical Publications, 1971.

———. *A History of the Diocese of Bendigo, 1902–1976: An Anglican Diocese in Rural Victoria*. Bendigo: Keith Cole Publications, 1991.

———. *A History of the Diocese of Bendigo, 1977–2002*. Bendigo: Bendigo Anglican Diocesan Historical Society Incorporated, 2002.

———. *A History of the Diocese of St. Arnaud, 1926–1976*. Bendigo: Bendigo Anglican Diocesan Historical Society Incorporated, 1998.

———. *Men of Faith and Vision: Archdeacon Archibald Crawford and Dean John Christian Maccullagh*. Bendigo: Keith Cole Publications, 1989.

———. *Oenpelli Pioneer: A Biography of the Reverend Alfred John Dyer, Pioneer Missionary among the Aborigines in Arnhem Land and Founder of the Oenpelli Mission*, Great Australian Missionaries; No. 4. Melbourne: Church Missionary Historical Publications Trust (Victoria), 1972.

———. *Perriman in Arnhem Land: A Biography of Harry Leslie Perriman: Pioneer Missionary among the Aborigines at Roper River, Groote Eylandt and Oenpelli in Arnhem Land*, Great Australian Missionaries; No. 5. Melbourne: Church Missionary Historical Publications, 1973.

———. *Sharing in Mission: The Centenary History of the Victorian Branch of the Church Missionary Society, 1892–1992*. Bendigo, Vic.: Keith Cole Publications, 1992.

———. *A Short History of the C.M.S. Roper River Mission, 1908–1969*. Melbourne: Church Missionary Historical Publications Trust, 1969.

———. *Sincerity My Guide: A Biography of the Right Reverend P.W. Stephenson (1888–1962)*. Melbourne: Church Missionary Historical Publications Trust, 1970.

Cole, Edmund Keith, Bendigo Anglican Diocesan Historical Society, and Taradale Historical Group. *The Church on the Hill: A Short History of Holy Trinity, Taradale, 1859–1999*: Taradale Historical Group and the Bendigo Anglican Diocesan Historical Society, 1999.

Cole, Keith, and Bendigo Anglican Diocesan Historical Society. *A History of St. Paul's Cathedral Church, Bendigo: 125 Years of Worship and Witness 1868–1993*. Bendigo, Vic.: Bendigo Anglican Diocesan Historical Society, 1999.

Cole, Keith, and Church Missionary Society of Australia Victorian Branch. *Servants for Jesus' Sake: Long-Serving Victorian CMS Missionaries*. Bendigo, Vic.: Keith Cole Publications in conjunction with the Victorian Branch of the Church Missionary Society, 1993.

Cole, Keith, and Dick Pethybridge. *Pethy, Lee and Mary, Three CMS Missionaries in East Africa*. Bendigo, Vic.: Keith Cole Publications, 1986.

Cole, Keith, and St. Hilary's Anglican Church (Kew, Vic.). *Letters from China 1893–1895: The Story of the Sister Martyrs of Ku Cheng*. Kew, Vic.: St. Hilary's Anglican Church, 1988.

Covey, Joan. *Our First 100 Years: The Anglican Church of Saint Clement Elsternwick—Victoria*. Melbourne, 1986.

Crombie, Kelvin. *A Jewish Bishop in Jerusalem: The Life Story of Michael Solomon Alexander*. Jerusalem: Nicolayson's Ltd, Christ Church Jerusalem, 2006.

Curry, Norman. "Moorhouse and Melbourne." The *Barry Marshall Lecture 1978*. Melbourne: Trinity College, 1978.

Cutler, Genevieve, ed. *Bearers of the Torch: Testimonies of the Members of the Church Missionary Society League of Youth*, 1993.

———. *The Torch*, 1978.

Danker, Frederick W., and Walter Bauer. *A Greek-English Lexicon of the New Testament and Other Early Christian Literature*. 3rd ed. Chicago: University of Chicago Press, 2000.

Darling, Barbara. "Ridley, CMS and Global Mission." In *Proclaiming Christ: Ridley College Melbourne, 1910–2010*, edited by Peter Adam and Gina Denholm, 89–100. Melbourne: Ridley Melbourne, 2010.

Davis, John C. *Australian Anglicans and Their Constitution*. Canberra: Acorn Press, 1993.

———. "Continuity and Change: Australian Anglicanism and a Constitution, 1920–1987." Melbourne College of Divinity, 1987.

Deasey, Denis Murrell. *The Warrior's Way: Containing Daily (Morning and Evening) Readings from the Psalms (Prayer Book Version) and Other Portions of Scripture and Verses*. Melbourne: League of Soldiers' Friends, 1918.

Dickey, Brian, ed. *The Australian Dictionary of Evangelical Biography*. Sydney: Evangelical History Association, 1994.

———. *Holy Trinity Adelaide, 1836–1988: The History of a City Church*. Adelaide: Trinity Church Trust Inc., 1988.

Doncaster, Ted. *Spinifex Saints: The Diocese of North West Australia, 1910–1985*. Mount Lawley, W.A.: Western Mount Publications, 1985.

Drury, Dianne Reilly. *La Trobe: The Making of a Governor*. Melbourne: Melbourne University Press, 2006.

Durie, Mark. "St. Mary's 150th: 'Naming the Wells.'" 2008.

Edwards, Jonathan. *Select Works Vol. 1*. London, 1965.

Edwards, Rebecca. *New Spirits: Americans in the Gilded Age, 1865–1905*. New York: Oxford University Press, 2006.

Elkin, A. P. *The Diocese of Newcastle: A History of the Diocese of Newcastle, N.S.W., Australia*. Glebe, NSW: Australian Medical Publishing Co., 1955.

Ellis, A. T., ed. *The House of Were: 1839–1954; the History of J. B. Were & Son and Its Founder Jonathan Binns Were*. Melbourne, 1954.

Elwell, Walter A. *Evangelical Dictionary of Theology*. Grand Rapids, Mich.: Baker Book House, 1984.

Erickson, Millard J., Paul Kjoss Helseth, and Justin Taylor, eds. *Reclaiming the Center: Confronting Evangelical Accommodation in Postmodern Times*. Wheaton, Ill: Crossway Books, 2004.

Evans, Robert. *Early Evangelical Revivals in Australia*. Adelaide: Openbook Publishers, 2000.

———. "Evangelicalism in Victoria in 1910—an Overview." *Charles Perry Lecture 2010*. Ridley Melbourne, 2010.

Fletcher, Brian. "The Anglican Ascendancy 1788–1835." In *Anglicanism in Australia: A History*, edited by Bruce Kaye, Tom Frame, Colin Holden and Geoff Treloar, 7–30. Melbourne: Melbourne University Press, 2002.

Frame, Tom. *Anglicans in Australia*. Sydney: UNSW Press, 2007.

———. *A House Divided? The Quest for Unity within Anglicanism*. Brunswick West: Acorn Press, 2010.

Gairdner, W. H. T. *"Edinburgh 1910": An Account & Interpretation of the World Missionary Conference*. Edinburgh & London: Committee of the World Missionary Conference: Oliphant, Anderson & Ferrier, 1910.

Garnsey, David. *Arthur Garnsey: A Man for Truth and Freedom*. Sydney: Kingsdale Press, 1985.

Gibson, Ted, ed. *Great Faithfulness: A Centenary Publication of the Diocese of Gippsland, 1902–2002*. Bairnsdale: Anglican Trusts Corporation of the Diocese of Gippsland, 2002.

González, Justo L. *The Story of Christianity*. 1st ed. 2 vols. San Francisco: Harper & Row, 1984.

Goodman, George. *The Church in Victoria During the Episcopate of the Right Reverend Charles Perry: First Bishop of Melbourne, Prelate of the Order of St. Michael and St. George*. Melbourne: Melville, Mullen and Slade, 1892.

Grant, James. *Episcopally-Led and Synodically Governed: Anglicans in Victoria, 1803–1997*. Melbourne: Australian Scholarly Press, 2010.

———. "Field Flowers Goe: The Bishop: Myths and a Ministry." *Journal of the Royal Historical Society of Victoria* 54, no. 2 (1983).

———. "Overview of the History of the Diocese of Melbourne." In *Melbourne Anglicans: The Diocese of Melbourne 1847–1997*, edited by Brian Porter, 1–26. Collingwood: The Joint Board of Christian Education, 1997.

———. *Perspective of a Century: A Volume for the Centenary of Trinity College Melbourne, 1872–1972*. Melbourne: Council of Trinity College Melbourne, 1972.

———. "The Right Reverend Field Flowers Goe, Bishop of Melbourne 1887–1902." Sydney Herbert Smith Memorial Lecture 1982. Melbourne: Anglican Historical Society, 1982.

Grenz, Stanley. *Renewing the Centre: Evangelical Theology in a Post-Theological Era*. Grand Rapids: Baker Academic, 2000.

Grenz, Stanley, and Roger E. Olson. *20th-Century Theology: God and the World in a Transitional Age*. Downers Grove: IVP, 1992.

Guinness, Howard. *Journey among Students*. Sydney: AIO, 1978.

Hall-Matthews, Anthony F. B. *A Remarkable Venture of Faith: An Examination of the Fiduciary Relationship between the Anglican Church of Australia and the Missionary Diocese of Carpentaria*. Bassendean: Access Press, 2007.

Harley, Ian. *J. C. Ryle, First Bishop of Liverpool: A Study in Mission Amongst the Masses*. Carlisle: Paternoster, 2000.

Harmer, Guy. *A Brief History of St. James Old Cathedral West Melbourne*. 4th ed. Melbourne: St. James Old Cathedral West Melbourne, 1975.

Harris, John. *One Blood: Two Hundred Years of Aboriginal Encounter with Christianity: A Story of Hope*. Sutherland: Albatross, 1994.

———. *We Wish We'd Done More: Ninety Years of CMS and Aboriginal Issues in North Australia*. Adelaide: OpenBook, 1998.

Harris, Khim. *Evangelicals and Education: Evangelical Anglicans and Middle-Class Education in Nineteenth-Century England*, Studies in Evangelical History and Thought. Carlisle: Paternoster, 2004.

Hart, Alison M. "'An Unshakeable Faith': Two Missionaries in China, 1904–1947." 1993.

Hart, Trevor A., ed. *The Dictionary of Historical Theology*. Grand Rapids: Paternoster, 2000.

Hattaway, Paul. *China's Christian Martyrs*. London: Monarch Books, 2007.

Haykin, Michael A. G., and Kenneth J. Stewart, eds. *The Emergence of Evangelicalism*. Nottingham: IVP, 2008.

Head, Edith Mary. *Frederick Waldegrave Head: Archbishop of Melbourne: A Sketch for Those Who Loved Him*. London and Melbourne: SPCK and Diocesan Book Society, 1943.

Henslowe, Dorothy. *Our Heritage of Anglican Churches in Tasmania*. Moonah, Tas: Mercury-Walch, 1978.

Hilliard, David. "The Anglican Schism at Port Lincoln, 1928–1955." *Journal of the Historical Society of South Australia* 23 (1995) 51–69.

———. "The Anglo-Catholic Tradition in Australian Anglicanism." In *Re-Visioning Australian Colonial Christianity: New Essays in the Australian Christian Experience 1788–1900*, edited by Mark Hutchinson and Edmund Campion, 195–215. Sydney: Centre for the Study of Australian Christianity, 1994.

———. "Anglo-Catholicism and the Religious Ecology of Melbourne." In *Anglo-Catholicism in Melbourne: Papers to Mark the 150th Anniversary of St. Peter's Eastern Hill 1846–1996*, edited by Colin Holden, 169–87. Melbourne: The History Department, The University of Melbourne, 1997.

———. "Dioceses, Tribes and Factions: Unity and Disunity in Australian Anglicanism." In *Agendas for Australian Anglicanism: Essays in Honour of Bruce Kaye*, edited by Tom Frame and Geoff Treloar, 57–81. Adelaide: ATF Press, 2006.

———. *Godliness and Good Order: A History of the Anglican Church in South Australia*. Netley: Wakefield Press, 1986.

———. "How Anglican Lay People Saved the Church." *St. Mark's Review* 207 (2009) 49.

———. "Intellectual Life in the Diocese of Melbourne." In *Melbourne Anglicans: The Diocese of Melbourne 1847–1997*, edited by Brian Porter, 27–48. Collingwood: The Joint Board of Christian Education, 1997.

———. "The Ties That Used to Bind: A Fresh Look at the History of Australian Anglicanism." *Pacifica* 11 (1998) 265–80.

———. "The Transformation of South Australian Anglicanism, C. 1880–1930." *Journal of Religious History* 14 (1986) 38–56.

Hilton, Boyd. *The Age of Atonement: The Influence of Evangelicalism on Social and Economic Thought, 1785–1865*. Oxford: Clarendon Press, OUP, 1988.

Holden, Colin, ed. *Anglo-Catholicism in Melbourne: Papers to Mark the 150th Anniversary of St. Peter's Eastern Hill 1846–1996*. Vol. 6, Melbourne University Conference Series (MUCS). Melbourne: The History Department, The University of Melbourne, 1997.

———. *"Awful Happenings on the Hill": E.S. Hughes and Melbourne Anglo-Catholicism before the War: A Series of Lectures Given at St. Peter's Church, Eastern Hill, Melbourne in May 1992*. Melbourne: St. Peter's Church Eastern Hill, 1992.

———. *Church in a Landscape: A History of the Diocese of Wangaratta*. Armadale, Vic.: Circa, 2002.

———. *From Tories at Prayer to Socialists at Mass: St. Peter's, Eastern Hill, Melbourne 1846-1990*. Carlton, Vic.: Melbourne University Press, 1996.

———, ed. *People of the Past? The Culture of Melbourne Anglicanism and Anglicanism in Melbourne's Culture: Papers to Mark the 150th Anniversary of the Anglican Diocese of Melbourne 1847-1997*. Melbourne: The History Department, The University of Melbourne, 2000.

———. "Melbourne Anglicanism: A Distinctive Culture?" web article, http://www.stpeters.org.au/ausanglican/melbourne.shtml, last accessed 26 April 2018.

———. *Saints, Sinners and Goalposts: A History of All Saints, East St. Kilda*. North Melbourne: Australian Scholarly Publishing, 2008.

Holmes, H. R. *The Story of the C. M. A.* 1913.

Hughes, H. J. *Life of Howell Harris, the Welsh Reformer*. London, 1892.

Hutchinson, Mark, and Edmund Campion, eds. *Re-Visioning Australian Colonial Christianity: New Essays in the Australian Christian Experience 1788-1900*, Studies in Australian Christianity. Sydney: Centre for the Study of Australian Christianity, 1994.

Hutchinson, Mark, and Stuart Piggin, eds. *Reviving Australia: Essays on the History and Experience of Revival and Revivalism in Australian Christianity*. Vol. 3, Studies in Australian Christianity. Sydney: Centre for the Study of Australian Christianity, 1994.

Johnstone, S. M. *A History of the Church Missionary Society in Australia and Tasmania*. Sydney, 1925.

Judd, Stephen, and Kenneth Cable. *Sydney Anglicans: A History of the Diocese*. Sydney: Anglican Information Office, 1987.

Kaye, Bruce, ed. *Anglicanism in Australia: A History*. Melbourne: Melbourne University Press, 2002.

———. *A Church without Walls: Being Anglican in Australia*. North Blackburn: Dove, 1995.

———. *Reinventing Anglicanism: A Vision of Confidence, Community and Engagement in Anglican Christianity*. Adelaide: Openbook Publishers, 2003.

Kerr, Alan. *Guided Journey: Some Experiences of a Lifetime*. Gundaroo, NSW: Brolga Press, 1998.

Kiddle, Margaret. *Caroline Chisholm*. Melbourne: Melbourne University Press, 1969.

———. *Men of Yesterday: A Social History of the Western District of Victoria, 1834-1890*. Melbourne: Melbourne University Press, 1961.

Kuan, Wei-Han. "The Perry Heritage." In *Proclaiming Christ: Ridley College Melbourne, 1910-2010*, edited by Peter Adam and Gina Denholm, 159-73. Melbourne: Ridley Melbourne, 2010.

———. "Ridley, Melbourne and Beyond." In *Proclaiming Christ: Ridley College Melbourne, 1910-2010*, edited by Peter Adam and Gina Denholm, 73-88. Melbourne: Ridley Melbourne, 2010.

Kverndal, Roald. "Sowing by Sea: Empowering Seafarers with the Gospel." In *Sowing the Word: The Cultural Impact of the British and Foreign Bible Society, 1804-2004*, edited by Stephen Batalden, Kathleen Cann and John Dean, 327-43. Sheffield: Sheffield Phoenix Press, 2006.

Lake, Andrew. *Changes & Chances: A Personal History of All Saints Jakarta*. Jakarta: All Saints Church, 2004.

Learmonth, Noel F. *The Story of St. Stephens: History of St. Stephens Church of England, Portland, Victoria*. Portland: St. Stephens Vestry, 1956.

Leighton, Janet. *Lift High the Cross: A History of Trinity Episcopal School for Ministry*. Wheaton: Harold Shaw, 1995.

Lewis, Donald M. *The Blackwell Dictionary of Evangelical Biography: 1730-1860*. Oxford; Cambridge, Mass.: Blackwell Publishers, 1995.

Linder, Robert D. *The Long Tragedy: Australian Evangelical Christians and the Great War, 1914-1915*. Adelaide: CSAC, Open Book, 2000.

Lloyd, William V. and Arthur R. Mace. *History of the Parish of St. Hilary's, Kew, 1889-1970*. East Melbourne: Citadel Press, 1970.

Loane, Marcus L. *Archbishop Mowll, the Biography of Howard West Kilvinton Mowll, Archbishop of Sydney and Primate of Australia*. London: Hodder and Stoughton, 1960.

———. *Cambridge and the Evangelical Succession*. London: Lutterworth Press, 1952.

———. *A Centenary History of Moore Theological College*. Sydney: Angus and Robertson, 1955.

———. *Hewn from the Rock: Origins and Traditions of the Church in Sydney*. Sydney: AIO, 1976.

———. *John Charles Ryle, 1816-1900*. London: Hodder and Stoughton, 1983.

———. *John Charles Ryle, 1816-1900: A Short Biography*. London: J. Clarke, 1953.

———. *Mark These Men: A Brief Account of Some Evangelical Clergy in the Diocese of Sydney Who Were Associated with Archbishop Mowll*, Studies in Australian History. Kambah, ACT: Acorn Press, 1985.

———. *Masters of the English Reformation*. Edinburgh, UK; Carlisle, PA: Banner of Truth Trust, 2005.

———. *No Other Name*. Blackwood, S. Aust.: New Creation Publications, 1996.

———. *Oxford and the Evangelical Succession*. London: Lutterworth Press, 1950.

———. *Sons of the Covenant*. Sydney: Angus and Robertson, 1963.

———. "They Shaped My Life—Horace John Hannah." *Southern Cross* November (1981) 26-27.

———. *Three Faithful Servants*. Blackwood, S. Aust.: New Creation Publications, 1991.

Macleod, A. Donald. *C. Stacey Woods and the Evangelical Rediscovery of the University*. Downers Grove: IVP Academic, 2007.

Maddern, I. T. *Light and Life: A History of the Anglican Church in Gippsland, 1845-1977*. Morwell, Vic.: I.T. Maddern, 1977.

Massey, John T. *Sowing and Reaping: A History of the British and Foreign Bible Society in Victoria*. Melbourne: The Victoria Auxiliary of the British and Foreign Bible Society, 1967.

McCracken, John Harold. *Summing Up: John Harold McCracken 1906-1999*. Aranda ACT: Heather and Paul Shelley, 2003.

McCullaugh C. Behan, N. Gwen Rodda. *St. Hilary's Anglican Church Kew, 1888-1988*. Melbourne: St. Hilary's Anglican Church 1988.

McKie, John David. "Four Archbishops of Melbourne: A Lecture." Second Sydney Smith Memorial lecture delivered on 20th of April, 1983, Melbourne.

McPherson, Albert. "Architecture, Music Art and Liturgy in the Diocese of Melbourne." In *Melbourne Anglicans: The Diocese of Melbourne 1847-1997*, edited by Brian Porter, 49-82. Collingwood: The Joint Board of Christian Education, 1997.

Meldrum, Patricia. *Conscience and Compromise: Forgotten Evangelicals of Nineteenth-Century Scotland*, Studies in Evangelical History and Thought. Carlisle: Paternoster, 2006.

Members of the Church of England. *The Inner Life: Essays in Liberal Evangelicalism, Second Series*. London: Hodder and Stoughton, 1925.

———. *Liberal Evangelicalism: An Interpretation*. London: Hodder and Stoughton, 1923.

Monk, Joanne, and Gina O'Donoghue. *Billylids And "Home Kids": The Story of the Mission of St. James and St. John*. West Melbourne: Mission of St. James and St. John, 1994.

Nash, Laurence Langley. *Forward Flows the Time: The Story of Ridley College, Melbourne*. Melbourne: G. B. Publications, 1960.

Nicholls, Paul. *Highs & Lows: The Anglican Parish of Christ Church Brunswick, 1855-2002*. Brunswick: Christ Church Press, 2007.

Nichols, Alan. *David Penman: Bridge-Builder, Peacemaker, Fighter for Social Justice*. Melbourne: Albatross Books, 1991.

Noble, Thomas A. *Research for the Academy and the Church: Tyndale House and Fellowship, the First Sixty Years*. Leicester: Inter-Varsity Press, 2006.

Noll, Mark A. *Princeton and the Republic, 1768-1822*. Princeton: Princeton University Press, 1989.

———. *The Rise of Evangelicalism: The Age of Edwards, Whitefield and the Wesleys*, A History of Evangelicalism. Nottingham: Inter-Varsity, 2004.

Noll, Mark A., D. W. Bebbington, and George A. Rawlyk. *Evangelicalism: Comparative Studies of Popular Protestantism in North America, the British Isles, and Beyond 1700-1900*. New York: Oxford University Press, 1994.

Null, Ashley. *Conversion to Communion: Thomas Cranmer on a Favourite Puritan Theme*. London: St. Antholin's Lectureship Charity, 2000.

Nunn, H. W. *A Short History of the Church of England in Victoria: 1847-1947*. Melbourne: Editorial Committee of the Centenary Celebrations, Melbourne Diocese, 1947.

Okoh, Nicholas, Vinay Samuel, and Chris Sugden, eds. *Being Faithful: The Shape of Historic Anglicanism Today*. London: Latimer Trust, 2009.

Otzen, Roslyn. *Whitley, the Baptist College of Victoria, 1891-1991*. South Yarra: Hyland House, 1991.

Pain, Arthur Franklyn. *In the Master's Service for 52 Years in Australia, Arthur Wellesley Pain, (1841-1920): A Biographical Memoir*. Belrose, N.S.W.: A.F. Pain, 1981.

Paproth, Darrell. "The 1888 Centennial Mission in Victoria." *LUCAS* 1 (2009) 31-65.

———. "The Character of Evangelism in Colonial Melbourne: Activism, Initiative, and Leadership." PhD Diss., Australia Macquarie University, 2012.

———. *Failure Is Not Final: A Life of C. H. Nash*. Edited by Mark Hutchinson and Geoff Treloar. Vol. 1, Library of Australian Christian Biography. Sydney: Centre for the Study of Australian Christianity, 1997.

———. "Hussey Burgh Macartney Jr.: Mission Enthusiast." *LUCAS* 4 (2011-12) 15-44.

———. "The Principals of Ridley." In *Proclaiming Christ: Ridley College Melbourne, 1910-2010*, edited by Peter Adam and Gina Denholm, 57-71. Melbourne: Ridley Melbourne, 2010.

———. "The Upwey Convention and C. H. Nash." *LUCAS* 16 (1993) 26-45.

Patterson, James W. *A Pioneer Church: A History of Sorts of Holy Trinity, Upwey, 1904-2004*. Vestry of Upwey-Belgrave Parish, 2004.

Phillips, Timothy R., Dennis L. Okholm, and Timothy R. Phillips. *A Family of Faith: An Introduction to Evangelical Christianity.* Grand Rapids, Mich.: Baker Academic, 2001.

Piggin, Stuart. "The Challenging but Glorious Heritage, Difficult but Joyful Birth, and Troubled but Triumphant Childhood of the Melbourne University Evangelical Union, 1930 to 1940." Unpublished lecture, Ridley College Library, 2005.

———. *Evangelical Christianity in Australia: Spirit, Word and World.* Melbourne: Oxford University Press, 1996.

———. "Pietism, Pluralism and Provincialism: The Divergent Paths of Melbourne and Sydney Evangelicalism, 1848–1988." The Perry Memorial Lecture, St. James' Old Cathedral, West Melbourne, 19 October 1990.

———. *Spirit of a Nation: The Story of Australia's Christian Heritage.* 2nd edition of *Evangelical Christianity in Australia* (OUP, 1996). Sydney: Strand Publishing, 2004.

Plumb, Eric Uebergang and Mary. *The History of the Parish of Holy Trinity Doncaster, Victoria: "the Church That Stood among the Orchards."* Melbourne: Holy Trinity Anglican Church Doncaster, Victoria, Australia, 1997.

Pollock, J. C. *The Good Seed: The Story of the Children's Special Service Mission and the Scripture Union.* London: Hodder & Stoughton, 1959.

Porter, Brian. *Frank Woods: Archbishop of Melbourne, 1957–77.* Parkville: Trinity College, 2007.

———. "Frank Woods: Archbishop of Melbourne, 1957–77, Primate of the Anglican Church of Australia, 1971–77." Australian College of Theology ThD thesis, 2001.

———, ed. *Melbourne Anglicans: The Diocese of Melbourne 1847–1997.* Collingwood: The Joint Board of Christian Education, 1997.

Porter, Brian, and Joint Board of Christian Education. *Colonial Tractarians: The Oxford Movement in Australia.* Melbourne: Joint Board of Christian Education, 1989.

Poynter, John. *Doubts and Certainties: A Life of Alexander Leeper.* Melbourne: Melbourne University Press, 1997.

Poynter, Marion, ed. *Nobody's Valentine: Letters in the Life of Valentine Alexa Leeper, 1900–2001.* Melbourne: Miegunyah Press, 2008.

Prince, John and Moyra. *Lighting the Lamp: Scripture Union in East Asia and the Pacific 1880–1983.* Hong Kong: Scripture Union ANZEA Regional Council, 1983.

———. *Tuned in to Change: A History of Scripture Union in Australia 1880–1980.* Sydney: Scripture Union of Australia, 1979.

Prince, John, and Moira Prince. *Out of the Tower.* Homebush West, NSW: Anzea, 1987.

Rauschenbusch, Walter. *Theology for the Social Gospel.* New York: Abingdon, 1917.

Rauschenbusch, Walter *Christianity and the Social Crisis.* New York: Macmillan, 1919.

Rawlyk, George A. *The Canada Fire: Radical Evangelicalism in British North America, 1775–1812.* Kingston and Montreal: McGill-Queen's University Press, 1994.

Rawlyk, George A., and Mark A. Noll, eds. *Amazing Grace: Evangelicalism in Australia, Britain, Canada, and the United States:* Baker Books, 1993.

Reed, Colin. "The East African Revival and Australia, 1930–1980." Australian College of Theology ThD thesis, 2003.

———. *Walking in the Light: Reflections on the East African Revival and Its Link to Australia.* Melbourne: Acorn Press, 2007.

Reid, John. *Marcus L. Loane: A Biography.* Canberra: Acorn Press, 2004.

Richmond, St. Stephen's. *A Forty Years' Ministry: St. Stephen's Richmond: 1851-1891, Rev Charles T. Perks, A. K. C. L. Incumbent and Canon of St. Paul's Cathedral Melbourne*. Melbourne: St. Stephen's Richmond, Troedel & Co. Printers, 1893.

Rickards, Edith C. *Bishop Moorhouse*. London: John Murray, 1920.

Riley, Grace. *No Drums at Dawn*, Great Australian Missionaries. Melbourne: Church Missionary Historical Publications, 1972.

Robertson, Paul Struan. *Proclaiming "Unsearchable Riches": Newcastle and the Minority Evangelical Anglicans, 1788-1900*, Monographs in Australian Christianity ; Vol. 1. Sydney, Leominster: Centre for the Study of Australian Christianity; Gracewing, 1996.

Robin, Arthur de Quetteville. *Charles Perry, Bishop of Melbourne*: University of Western Australia Press, 1967.

———. *Making Many Rich: A Memoir of Joseph John Booth, Fourth Archbishop of Melbourne*. Melbourne: Diocese of Melbourne, Church of England in Australia, 1978.

Robson, Leslie Lloyd. *A History of Tasmania. Volume 1. Van Diemen's Land from the Earliest Times to 1855*. 2 vols. Melbourne: Oxford University Press, 1983.

———. *A History of Tasmania. Volume II. Colony and State from 1856 to the 1980s*. 2 vols. Vol. 2. Melbourne: Oxford University Press, 1991.

Rowland, E. C. *A Century of the English Church in New South Wales*. 1948.

———. *The Tropics for Christ: Being a History of the Diocese of North Queensland*. Townsville, Qld.: Diocese of North Queensland, 1960.

Russell, George William Erskine. *A Short History of the Evangelical Movement*. London: Mowbray, 1915.

Russell, Penelope Ann. *"A Wish of Distinction": Colonial Gentility and Femininity*. Melbourne: Melbourne University Press, 1994.

Ryle, John Charles. *Knots Untied: Being Plain Statements on Disputed Points in Religion from the Standpoint of an Evangelical Churchman*. 1964 ed. London: James Clark & Co. Ltd, 1964.

Seiffert, Murray. *Refuge on the Roper: The Origins of the Roper River Mission Ngukurr*. Melbourne: Acorn Press, 2008.

Sharwood, Robin. "Some Aspects of the History of the Faculty of Theology at Trinity College, the University of Melbourne." Fourth Sydney Smith Memorial Lecture. Melbourne, 1985.

Shaw, A. G. L. *A History of the Port Phillip District: Victoria before Separation*. Carlton, Vic.: Melbourne University Press, 1996.

Shaw, George Peter. *Patriarch and Patriot: William Grant Broughton 1788-1853: Colonial Statesman and Ecclesiastic*. Carlton, Vic.: Melbourne University Press, 1978.

Sherlock, Peter. *One Foundation: A Parish Journey in Moreland, 1891-1991*. Brunswick: P. Sherlock, 1991.

———. "Review of Church in a Landscape." *Journal of Religious History* 30 (2006) 380–81.

Shilton, Lance Rupert. *Speaking Out: A Life in Urban Ministry: The Autobiography of Lance Shilton*. Macquarie Centre, N.S.W: Centre for the Study of Australian Christianity, 1997.

Soley, Stuart James. "'The Highest of the High' in 'Marvellous Melbourne': All Saints East St. Kilda as Melbourne's Original High Church, 1858-1908." The University of Melbourne, 1997.

Speagle, Henry L. *A Light in the Hills: A History of St. Michael and All Angels, Mount Dandenong, Victoria*. Mount Dandenong, Vic: Church of St. Michael and All Angels, 1990.

Spooner, John. *The Golden See: Diocese of Ballarat: The Anglican Church in Western Victoria*. Surry Hills, N.S.W: John Ferguson, 1989.

Stanley, Brian. *The Global Diffusion of Evangelicalism: The Age of Billy Graham and John Stott* (Downers Grove: IVP, 2013).

Stanway, Marjory. *Alfred Stanway: The Recollections of A "Little M."* Wanniassa, ACT: Acorn Press, 1991.

Stephens, Geoffrey. *The Anglican Church in Tasmania: A Diocesan History to Mark the Sesquicentenary, 1992*. Hobart, Tas.: Trustees of the Diocese, 1991.

Stock, Eugene. *The History of the Church Missionary Society*. 4 vols. Vol. 1. London: CMS, 1899.

Sturrock, Morna. *Bishop of Magnetic Power: James Moorhouse in Melbourne, 1876–1886*. Melbourne: Australian Scholarly Publishing Pty Ltd, 2005.

———. *Fruitful Mother: St. Stephen's Richmond Parish History, 1851–1991*. Melbourne: St. Stephen's Parish Publishing Committee, 1993.

Sylvester, Nigel. *God's Word in a Young World: The Story of Scripture Union*. London: Scripture Union International Council, 1984.

Thompson, A. T. *Australia and the Bible: A Brief Outline of the Work of the British and Foreign Bible Society in Australia: 1807–1934*. London: The British and Foreign Bible Society, 1935.

Tidball, Derek J. *Who Are the Evangelicals? Tracing the Roots of the Modern Movements*. London: Marshall Pickering, 1994.

Ting, Valerie. "'In Utter Dependence': Melbourne University Christian Union (1930–2005).'" University of Melbourne BA Hons thesis, 2005.

Tout-Smith, Deborah. *Melbourne: A City of Stories*. Melbourne: Museum Victoria, 2008.

Treloar, Geoff. "History as a Vocation: Stuart Piggin as Evangelical Historian and Historian of Evangelicalism." In *Making History for God*, edited by Geoff Treloar and Robert D. Linder, [xx–xx]. Sydney: Robert Menzies College, 2004.

———. *The Disruption of Evangelicalism: The Age of Terry, Mott, McPherson and Hammond* (Downers Grove: IVP, 2017).

"Victoria's Debt to the Irish Church: Sermon and Papers Delivered at the Hussey Burgh Macartney Commemoration, 7–10 October 1994." Melbourne, 1994.

Wehner, Volkhard. *Tea and Charity: The Life and Times of James Griffiths Tea Merchant and Philanthropist*. Melbourne: Volkhard Wehner, 2006.

Welch, Ian. "Pariahs and Outcasts, Christian Missions to the Chinese in Australia." Monash University MA thesis, 1980.

Whitelock, David, and Anthony Baker. *Adelaide: A Sense of Difference*. Melbourne: Australian Scholarly Press, 2000.

Whitington, F. T. *William Grant Broughton, Bishop of Australia: With Some Account of the Earliest Australian Clergy*. Sydney: Angus & Robertson, 1936.

Williams, A. E. *West Anglican Way: The Growth of the Anglican Church in Western Australia from Its Early Beginnings*. Perth: Province of Western Australia of the Anglican Church of Australia, 1989.

Williams, Peter. "'Pragmatic, Comfortable and Unobtrustive': Can the Church of England Ever Learn to Evangelise?" *ANVIL* 26 (2009) 123.

Withycombe, Robert. *Montgomery of Tasmania: Henry and Maud Montgomery in Australasia*. Brunswick East: Acorn Press, 2009.

Wolffe, John. *The Expansion of Evangelicalism: The Age of Wilberforce, More, Chalmers and Finney*. Edited by David W. Bebbington and Mark A. Noll. 5 vols. Vol. 2, A History of Evangelicalism: People, Movements and Ideas in the English-Speaking World. Nottingham, England: Inter-Varsity Press, 2006.

Wyatt, Ransome T. *The History of the Diocese of Goulburn*. Goulburn, N.S.W.: R.T. Wyatt, 1937.

www.ingramcontent.com/pod-product-compliance
Lightning Source LLC
Chambersburg PA
CBHW070235230426

43664CB00014B/2307